SCRIPTURE, LOGIC, LANGUAGE

Essays on Dharmakīrti and his Tibetan Successors

STUDIES IN INDIAN AND TIBETAN BUDDHISM

Scripture, Logic, Language

Essays on Dharmakīrti and his Tibetan Successors

by
Tom J.F. Tillemans

WISDOM PUBLICATIONS • BOSTON

Wisdom Publications
199 Elm Street
Somerville, MA 02144 USA

Library of Congress Cataloging-in-Publication Data
Tillemans, Tom J.F.
Scripture, logic, language : essays on Dharmakīrti and his Tibetan successors / Tom J.F. Tillemans.
p. cm.— (Studies in Indian and Tibetan Buddhism)
Includes bibliographical references and index.
ISBN 0-86171-156-4 (alk. paper)
1. Dharmakīrti, 7th cent. 2. Buddhist logic—History.
3. Buddhism—China—Tibet—Doctrines—History. I. Title.
II. Series.
B133.D484T55 1999
181'.043—dc21 99-36875

ISBN 0-86171-156-4
04 03 02 01 0
06 5 4 3 2

Cover design: Gopa & the Bear
Interior by Gopa Design

Wisdom Publications' books are printed on acid-free paper and meet the guidelines for the permanence and durability of the Committee on Production Guidelines for Book Longevity of the Council on Library Resources.

Printed in the United States of America

For Ken Ray

Publisher's Acknowledgments

The Publisher gratefully acknowledges the generous help of the Hershey Family Foundation in sponsoring the publication of this book.

Table of Contents

Series Editor's Preface

SCRIPTURE, LOGIC, LANGUAGE launches Wisdom's scholarly series, Studies in Indian and Tibetan Buddhism. This series was conceived to provide a forum for publishing outstanding new contributions to scholarship and also to make accessible seminal research not widely known outside a narrow specialist audience. Wisdom also intends to include in the series appropriate monographs and collected articles translated from other languages.

Much of the new scholarly research in Indian and Tibetan Buddhist philosophy and practice is worthy of wider circulation among an intelligent readership. Several outstanding dissertations are produced each year at academic institutions throughout the world. Such significant contributions are normally accessible only through University Microfilms or through research journals that are scattered across the academic landscape.

It is heartening to the editors at Wisdom to see how much of the scholarship being produced today is the result of collaboration with scholars belonging to the indigenous traditions of Tibet and the Indian subcontinent. Wisdom Publications is certain that this approach has the greatest possibilities for enriching both academic scholarship and Buddhist practice. Increasingly, researchers must be able to work in a bewildering variety of languages and disciplines in the humanities and social sciences. What a visionary like the late Richard H. Robinson hoped to produce in his Wisconsin curriculum were scholars able to work with living exponents of the Asian traditions in their own languages. He also dreamt of researchers who would be able to keep abreast of the advances in Western thought. A scholar like Tillemans is a realization of Robinson's dreams.

Tom Tillemans, the author whose work is presented here, is a scholar's scholar. He is able to work in a vast variety of languages: all major Western languages and Sanskrit, Tibetan, Chinese and Japanese. He is trained in modern Western philosophy and can see how the traditions of East and West interact.

The eleven essays presented here were published over the period 1986–1999. They appeared in a number of journals or as contributions to Festschriften. Tillemans has now arranged these essays into a unified and compelling structure. One can now see clearly the underlying structure and understand the significance of Tillemans' contributions to Buddhist logic, language and epistemology.

Tillemans' scholastic ancestry is rooted in the great names of European scholarship, such as F. I. Stcherbatsky, Eugene Obermiller and Erich Frauwallner. Tillemans brings a sophisticated understanding of developments in Western logic and epistemology to the traditional scholarship of Indian and Tibetan thinkers. He presents in these carefully crafted pieces a clear delineation of the varying approaches of the Indic masters and their Tibetan interpreters.

This is a fascinating work with which to begin the new series.

E. Gene Smith
August 1999

Acknowledgments

All of the essays appearing in this volume have been published previously. My thanks go to the various publishers, and to Donald S. Lopez, Jr., the co-author of the final article, for their kind permission to reprint them here. The full bibliographic details for each article are given below. Unless otherwise noted, only minor modifications have been made in the articles, essentially for style and clarity. Some additional annotations appear in the endnotes in square brackets and are marked as author's or editor's notes. My thanks also go to Sara McClintock for her editorial work throughout this project, to John Dunne for translating the article in chapter 9 from the original French, and to Tim McNeill and E. Gene Smith for their willingness to publish this collection as the first volume of Wisdom Publications' new series on Indian and Tibetan Buddhism.

Notes on the Bibliographic Sources

Chapter 1: originally published as "Dharmakīrti, Āryadeva and Dharmapāla on Scriptural Authority." *Tetsugaku* 38, Hiroshima (1986): 31–47. The article is an initial attempt at formulating the broad outlines of Dharmakīrti's position on the authority of scripture and at tracing possible antecedents in Āryadeva and Dharmapāla.

Chapter 2: originally published as "How Much of a Proof is Scripturally Based Inference *(āgamāśritānumāna)*?" in Shōryū Katsura, ed., *Dharmakīrti's Thought and its Impact on Indian and Tibetan Philosophy.* Vienna: Verlag der Österreichischen Akademie der Wissenschaften, 1999: 395–404. The first section of the original article has been omitted, as it recapitulates the essential ideas in chapter 1. The introduction to the present volume develops in more detail the theories of truth and justification briefly sketched out in the article.

Chapter 3: originally published as "Pre-Dharmakīrti Commentators on Dignāga's Definition of a Thesis *(pakṣalakṣaṇa),*" in Tadeusz Skorupski and Ulrich Pagel, eds., *The Buddhist Forum Vol. III.* Papers in Honour and Appreciation of Prof. David Seyfort Ruegg's Contribution to Indological, Buddhist and Tibetan Studies. London: School of Oriental and African Studies, University of London, 1994: 295–305.

Chapter 4: originally published as "More on *Parārthānumāna,* Theses and Syllogisms." *Asiatische Studien/Etudes asiatiques* 45 (1991): 133–48.

Chapter 5: originally published as "On *Sapakṣa.*" *Journal of Indian Philosophy* 18 (1990): 53–79.

Chapter 6: originally published as "Formal and Semantic Aspects of Tibetan Buddhist Debate Logic." *Journal of Indian Philosophy* 17 (1989): 265–97. Some corrections have been made. The account of *vyāpti* has been taken up again and revised in the introduction to the present book.

Chapter 7: originally published as "Dharmakīrti and Tibetans on *Adṛśyānupalabdhihetu.*" *Journal of Indian Philosophy* 23 (1995): 129–49.

Chapter 8: originally published as "A Note on *Pramāṇavārttika, Pramāṇasamuccaya* and *Nyāyamukha.* What is the *Svadharmin* in Buddhist Logic?" *Journal of the International Association of Buddhist Studies* 21/1 (1998): 111–24.

Chapter 9: originally published as "La logique bouddhique est-elle une logique non-classique ou déviante? Remarques sur le tétralemme *(catuṣkoṭi),*" in Jean-Luc Solère, ed., *Les Cahiers de Philosophie* 14. L'Orient de la pensée: philosophies en Inde. Lille, 1992: 183–98. English translation by John D. Dunne. The central argument is, I would maintain, applicable to Indo-Tibetan Buddhist scholasticism, but perhaps less well so to certain paradoxical passages in the *Prajñāpāramitāsūtras*. Cf. the final remarks in the introduction to the present volume.

Chapter 10: originally published as "On the So-called Difficult Point of the *Apoha* Theory." *Asiatische Studien/Etudes asiatiques* 49/4 (1995): 853–89.

Chapter 11: co-authored with Donald S. Lopez, Jr. and originally published as "What Can One Reasonably Say about Nonexistence? A Tibetan Work on the Problem of *Āśrayāsiddha*." *Journal of Indian Philosophy* 26 (1998): 99–129.

Abbreviations

*	indicates a surmised but unattested Sanskrit reading based on Chinese or Tibetan
AS/EA	*Asiatische Studien/Etudes asiatiques*
CS	*Catuḥśataka* of Āryadeva
CSV	*Catuḥśatakavṛtti* = *Catuḥśatakaṭīkā* of Candrakīrti
D.	Derge edition of the Tibetan Tripiṭaka
ed.	edited, edition
Eng.	English
f.	folio
HB	*Hetubindu* of Dharmakīrti
IBK	*Indogaku Bukkyogaku Kenkyū*, *Journal of Indian and Buddhist Studies*
Jap.	Japanese
JIP	*Journal of Indian Philosophy*
k.	*kārikā*, *kārikā*s
MA	*Madhyamakālaṃkāra* of Śāntarakṣita
MĀ	*Madhyamakāloka* of Kamalaśīla
MMK	*Mūlamadhyamakakārikā* of Nāgārjuna
MV	*Madhyāntavibhāga* of Maitreya
NB	*Nyāyabindu* of Dharmakīrti
NBT	*Nyāyabinduṭīkā* of Dharmottara
NM	*Nyāyamukha* of Dignāga
NP	*Nyāyapraveśa* of Śaṅkarasvāmin
NS	*Nyāyasūtra* of Gautama
NV	*Nyāyavārttika* of Uddyotakara
P.	Peking edition of the Tibetan Tripiṭaka
PrP	*Prasannapadā* of Candrakīrti
PS	*Pramāṇasamuccaya* of Dignāga

PST	*Pramāṇasamuccayaṭīkā* of Jinendrabuddhi
PSV	*Pramāṇasamuccayavṛtti* of Dignāga
PSVa	PSV translation by Vasudhararakṣita and Seng rgyal
PSVb	PSV translation by Kanakavarman and Dad pa shes rab
PV	*Pramāṇavārttika* of Dharmakīrti
PV I	*Svārthānumānapariccheda* of PV
PV II	*Pramāṇasiddhipariccheda* of PV
PV III	*Pratyakṣapariccheda* of PV
PV IV	*Parārthānumānapariccheda* of PV
PVBh	*Pramāṇavārttikabhāṣya* of Prajñākaragupta
PVin	*Pramāṇaviniścaya* of Dharmakīrti
PVP	*Pramāṇavārttikapañjikā* of Devendrabuddhi
PVSV	*Pramāṇavārttikasvavṛtti* of Dharmakīrti
PVSVT	*Pramāṇavārttikasvavṛttiṭīkā* of Karṇakagomin
PVT	*Pramāṇavārttikaṭīkā* of Śākyabuddhi
PVV	*Pramāṇavārttikavṛtti* of Manorathanandin
PVV-n	Vibhūticandra's notes to PVV
SKB	*Sa skya pa'i bka' 'bum;* see editor bSod nams rgya mtsho
Skt.	Sanskrit
Svavṛtti	*Pramāṇavārttikasvavṛtti* of Dharmakīrti
T.	Taishō Shinshū Daizōkyō, or the Chinese Tripiṭaka
Tib.	Tibetan
trans.	translated, translation
VP	*Vākyapadīya* of Bhartṛhari
WSTB	Wiener Studien zur Tibetologie und Buddhismuskunde
WZKM	*Wiener Zeitschrift für die Kunde des Morgenlandes*
WZKS	*Wiener Zeitschrift für die Kunde Südasiens*
WZKSO	*Wiener Zeitschrift für die Kunde Süd- und Ostasiens*

Introduction

THE PRESENT COLLECTION of essays spans a number of years of work on various aspects of the philosophy known as "Buddhist logic" or "Buddhist epistemology." This philosophy is generally taken to have begun with Dignāga and Dharmakīrti in the sixth and seventh centuries and to have flourished until the end of Buddhism in India in approximately the thirteenth century. It was taken up with great energy in Tibet, especially from the eleventh century on, the time of the "second propagation" *(phyi dar)* of Buddhism, and has remained an important element of Tibetan Buddhism up to the present day. It is what many people, within or outside the Buddhist community, have considered to be the most philosophical, and even the most critical, form of the Mahāyāna.

Curiously enough, although one speaks of a distinct and influential philosophical school composed of the followers of Dignāga, it was one that remained fundamentally nameless in Sanskrit. In Tibetan traditions, however, the philosophy received the conventional designation, *tshad ma,* the Tibetan equivalent of the Sanskrit term *pramāṇa,* a term which in its more ordinary sense means "measure" and which in its technical use means "a means of valid cognition"/"a means of knowledge." It was in part this Tibetan transformation of the Indian technical term *pramāṇa* into a name for a philosophy and discipline of study that led modern writers to speak of "Buddhist logic" and "Buddhist epistemology" or *pramāṇavāda.* Indeed, the transition from the study of "means of valid cognition" to "epistemology" is relatively natural; "logic," on the other hand, seems to be better based on the term *hetuvidyā/gtan tshigs rig pa,* the "science of reasons," which is one of the important subsidiary domains in *tshad ma* studies. In any case, one should not be misled: these English terms are no more than approximations for a multi-faceted system in which logical theory was a major element, but certainly not the only one. There is no reason to think that this school's elaborate debates on particulars, universals, mind, matter, idealism and realism were somehow more logical or epistemological than metaphysical, or that the arguments concerning the virtues of the Buddha, his omniscience and compassion were any less religious or scholastic than they would seem to be.

If one looks at the present collection of essays, it is quite apparent that "Buddhist logicians" did much more than what we might call "logic" and "epistemology," even in loose uses of those terms. Indeed they very actively pursued the doctrinal and religious aspects of Buddhism, so much so that many Indians and Tibetans, and indeed some modern writers too, would depict the religious as the primary aim of this philosophy. How did these Buddhist philosophers see themselves as doing something unified and coherent? Given that inference and perception (the two "means of valid cognition") would seem to concern rationally decidable matters, how can the apparently non-rational elements belonging to the religious side of Buddhist philosophy be coherently accommodated in this system?

The first section of this collection of essays (i.e., "Scripturally Based Argumentation") consists of three pieces in which I tried to grapple with the Buddhist logicians' stance on religion and rationality. The striking feature of the Dharmakīrtian school is that it holds that religious doctrine *can* be justified and *can* be argued for, and with extremely restricted tools, i.e., perception and inference. Yet if religious matters can be argued for in this way, did the Dharmakīrtian school adopt the conservative view that religious reasoning is just as objective and certain as reasoning about uncontroversial, non-religious matters (like smoky hills having fires)? These are the concerns of the first two essays, i.e., "Dharmakīrti, Āryadeva and Dharmapāla on Scriptural Authority" and "How Much of a Proof is Scripturally Based Inference?" The third essay in this section is somewhat more historical in orientation. Dharmakīrti recognizes that much religious argumentation demands allegiance to a school and to a body of texts, but nonetheless maintains that the ordinary, or unexceptional, uses of logical argumentation should have complete independence from such doctrinal affiliations. This extremely radical view on scripture has as its consequence that when one is arguing about most empirical or even metaphysical matters, conformity with the propositions found in the scriptures of a school is virtually irrelevant. The problem that "Pre-Dharmakīrti Commentators on the Definition of a Thesis" seeks to solve is "Who first came up with this position?" Was it already in Dignāga? If not, how did Dharmakīrti come to hold it?

The second section (i.e., "Logic") is the largest and probably most technical part of this collection, dealing in one way or another with questions of implication, negation, valid reasons and the so-called Buddhist syllogisms—in short, the type of topics that a Westerner would associate, in part at least, with the idea of logic. It should be obvious that no one in the Indian and Tibetan schools could be said to have been doing formal logic. Nevertheless, it is so that these philosophers were aware of questions of logical form, although often inextricably combining questions such as "What is logical implication?" with what might seem to be extra-logical considerations. The first essay in this section, "*Parārthānumāna,* Theses and Syllogisms," looks at the so-called "Buddhist syllogism," and more generally the idea of proof *(sādhana).* The second, "On *Sapakṣa,*" examines the notion of a logical reason and the role of examples in argumentation in Dharmakīrtian and Tibetan logics, focusing on the Buddhist position that certain types of seemingly sound arguments are nevertheless to be rejected because examples cannot be given. The next essay, "Formal and Semantic Aspects of Tibetan Buddhist Debate Logic," investigates the logical structures and semantic notions in Tibetan *bsdus grwa,* a system which is considered by its exponents to be a faithful continuation of Dharmakīrti, and yet which is also, in many ways, quite remarkably original. "Dharmakīrti and Tibetans on *Adṛśyānupalabdhihetu*" then takes up Indian and Tibetan ways to argue for nonexistence, while "What is the *Svadharmin* in Buddhist Logic?" examines the problems that arise when the subject of an argument is itself nonexistent. The section ends with an article translated from French on the general problem as to whether Buddhists somehow reason in a fundamentally different or even incompatible manner from the classical logic that one finds in typical Western works on formal logic.

The third section (i.e., "Philosophy of Language") takes up aspects of the Buddhist semantic theory known as *apoha* ("exclusion"), the fundamental idea being that abstract entities such as universals, concepts and meanings can be analyzed away in terms of double negations (supplemented, at least for Dharmakīrti, by a purely causal account as to how we make judgements of similarity). In its Indian forms, *apoha* yields and reinforces a type of nominalism where the real is the particular.

(Note that "nominalism" is used here in the modern sense as found in Nelson Goodman and W.V. Quine, where the essential requirement is that what exists must be particular; nominalism need not be, and indeed is not for the Buddhists, a philosophy where universals are just mere words alone, or *flatus vocis.*) The peculiarly Buddhist contribution is that abstract entities are not just dismissed, but *accounted for* as mere absences of difference and are hence unreal, just as are all other absences for Buddhists.[1] The first essay in this section, "On the So-called Difficult Point of the *Apoha* Theory," looks at ontological matters and shows that the nominalistic rejection of real universals was considerably modified by certain Tibetan schools who reintroduced a type of realism in the garb of a system as much inspired by *bsdus grwa* as by Dharmakīrti. The second essay, written with Donald S. Lopez, Jr., consists in a translation of a Tibetan text that applies the theory of *apoha* to account for what it is one talks about when discussing nonexistent pseudo-entities. The underlying problem which Indian and Tibetan Buddhists took up is not unlike that which inspired the philosophy of language of Meinong and provoked the reaction that one finds in Bertrand Russell's Theory of Descriptions and later in W.V. Quine's celebrated essay "On What There Is."

The papers presented here are intended to be, broadly speaking, historical, though it is obvious that the conceptual tools employed are often those of contemporary Anglo-American analytic philosophy. It is equally obvious that the history I am pursuing is the history of a philosophy, and as such it should not be surprising that what counts most in this aim are texts and philosophical analyses of them. One of the main reasons why the history of logic in the West has become so well developed and interesting is that historico-philological competence in textual studies has been combined with philosophical sensitivity. There is no reason why such a combined approach should not yield results in an Indo-Tibetan context too. Indeed, in order to disentangle what a Dharmakīrtian or a Tibetan text *could* be saying it is necessary not just to adopt a Principle of Charity, but also to formulate a number of alternatives in terms more precise than the text itself and, if need be, using alien philosophical or logical notions. Being faithful to an historical author does not demand that one keep the possible interpretations couched in the same problematic or obscure language that is the author's. This type of "faithfulness" is the misguided rationale for translations that read like "Buddhist Hybrid English."[2] More generally, such a methodology seems to rest on a fallacy of imitative form,[3] i.e., that talk about something obscure, mysterious, funny, boring, etc., should itself have the same stylistic characteristics as what is being talked about. Using philosophical tools is not, however, an attempt at appropriating Dharmakīrti so that he might somehow become relevant to a contemporary Buddhist philosophy. Perhaps a contemporary "Buddhist theology" using selective doses of Dharmakīrti is possible, but, even if it is not, the absence of blueprints for the present doesn't detract from Dharmakīrti's importance, just as it doesn't detract from that of Plato, Leibniz or Spinoza to whose systems virtually no one subscribes now. Indeed, I would think that Dharmakīrti's system, if better available, would receive a mixed response today; its reductionism, its strict mind-body dualism, and its highly fragmented ontology of partless atoms and instants might well be quite difficult to accept for the many Buddhists who are seeking a more holistic, integrated vision of the world.

A feature of these papers is that they regularly zigzag between Indian and Tibetan contexts. Almost needless to say, this does not mean that we take as given that Tibetan Buddhist traditions are identical with their Indian counterparts. Tibet as being the faithful prolongation or even duplication of India has been a seductive idea, even one which motivated people to do valuable work on Tibet, but it is one whose time is now definitely past. The course that we have taken between Tibet and Dharmakīrti may often be different from that of Tibetans themselves, as is our sense of what is the Indian debate and what is a Tibetan development. But then there is no easy recipe for pursuing an Indo-Tibetan approach, nor are there any shortcuts enabling us to avoid reading both languages and both sets of texts. What makes the effort worthwhile is that history may perhaps be seen in a binocular fashion, in stereo vision, thus lending further depth to our understanding of these texts.

Publishing a collection of this sort allows me to nuance a few things and speculate on some future directions to be pursued. One particularly interesting area for reflection is the question of pragmatism in Dharmakīrti, and more generally the theories of truth and justification implicit in his system. Another is the problem of *vyāpti* (the implication between the reason and what is to be proved), what it is for Indians and what it is for Tibetans. Finally, the question of whether Buddhists ever use a logic different from the usual classical variety is not easily put aside. As it was practically impossible to incorporate these discussions into the articles themselves, let me use the remainder of this introduction to sketch out some of the broad outlines of how these philosophical themes appear to me now.

Pragmatism

First of all, it has sometimes been suggested that Dharmakīrti has some type of a pragmatic theory of truth, especially because the reliability *(avisaṃvādakatva)* of a means of valid cognition *(pramāṇa)* consists in there being "confirmation of practical efficacy" *(arthakriyāsthiti)*.[4] To take one of the most common versions of a pragmatic theory of truth, as found in William James, a belief is true for people if and only if it is in the long run most useful for them to accept it.[5] Now, irrespective of how we translate the term *arthakriyā,* i.e., "efficacious action," "practical efficacy," "goal accomplishment," etc., there is no reason to believe that Jamesian pragmatism or anything much like it is Dharmakīrti's theory of truth, certainly not when it comes to the usual examples of *pramāṇas,* i.e., direct perception *(pratyakṣa)* of things like vases, and inference *(anumāna)* such as that there is fire on a hill because there is smoke. The point for Dharmakīrti, following Devendrabuddhi and Śākyabuddhi, is that an awareness can be asserted to be a *pramāṇa* because of a confirmation—this "confirmation" *(sthiti)* is glossed by Śākyabuddhi as being an "understanding" *(rtogs pa)*—which in typical cases is subsequent to the initial awareness. In other words, we can rationally say that we genuinely saw a vase, and not some vase-like illusion, because after the initial perception we came to perceptually confirm that this seeming vase really does permit us to carry water as we expected and wished. Equally, although initially we might have suspected that what we saw was not actually fire, subsequently we were able to infer that it was indeed fire, because there was smoke. While most initial sights and other sense perceptions are to be confirmed by subsequent perceptions or inferences, an inference itself is something of an exception: it is said to be confirmed simultaneously and needs no subsequent understanding—the point turns on the idea of inference having *svataḥ prāmāṇyam* or "intrinsically being a means of valid cognition." Be that as it may, what is important for us to note in the present discussion is that one understanding is being confirmed by another or in certain special cases by itself. There is nothing at all here in Dharmakīrti, Devendrabuddhi or Śākyabuddhi[6] which suggests a Jamesian account along the lines of "the understanding/belief/statement that there is a vase/fire over there is true for us because it is in the long run most useful for us to believe that there is a vase/fire over there."

Nor for that matter is there very much which would suggest a "pragmaticist" theory like that of C.S. Peirce, who held that "the opinion which is fated to be ultimately agreed to by all who investigate is what we mean by truth."[7] The major similarity between these two philosophers is, as far as I can see, their common commitment to the importance of results and to there being an objectively right version of what there is. However, the idea of truth as an *ideal rational assertibility* is neither asserted nor rejected by Dharmakīrti: what we regularly find for him is that existent things are those that *are* actually established by a means of valid cognition *(pramāṇasiddha)*. Peirce's theory is not that truths consist of opinions that are now established, but that they are the limits to which people's informed opinions will or should converge, i.e., the destined upshot of inquiry.[8] Indeed, his theory defines truth in terms of a consensus which may well never actually be realized (as Peirce himself recognized); this all-important reference to an *ideal* consensus that may even be just a regulative principle is what is absent in Dharmakīrti. In any case, in what follows I will mean by "pragmatism" and "pragmatic theories" essentially the Jamesian version.

In fact we can go further on the question of truth and *arthakriyā*: *arthakriyāsthiti* does not, I think, set forth a theory of truth at all. Let us speak of a *truth theory* as one which gives a definition of truth, i.e., the necessary and sufficient conditions for statements or understandings to be true, while a *justification theory* will provide us with the properties that allow us to reasonably determine that a statement or understanding is true and satisfies the definition. Looked at in that light, *arthakriyāsthiti,* especially as it is explained by Devendrabuddhi and Śākyabuddhi, is best taken as part of Dharmakīrti's justification theory. Dharmakīrti is giving a procedure for truth testing, typically a kind of verification principle along commonsense lines: "Look and see or analyze logically whether the object actually behaves as you think it does, and if it does, you can be confident that you were right in your initial understanding." In short, he is telling us when and how we can be confident that our understandings are true, but not what truth is.

What then is Dharmakīrti's theory of truth and is there any role to be found for pragmatism in his system? It is not clear to me that Dharmakīrti explicitly gives a generalized theory of truth anywhere, although if we cobble one together in keeping with his system it is probably best viewed as turning on stronger and weaker forms of a correspondence theory. To see this better let us briefly look at how Shōryū Katsura depicted truth for Dharmakīrti. Katsura cited what he termed "the time-honored definition of error in India", i.e., "that which grasps *x* as non-*x*," as evidence that Dharmakīrti "believes in some kind of real 'correspondence' between perception and its object, namely, resemblance of the image."[9] He then remarked that this definition of error is used by Dharmakīrti to classify inference as erroneous:

> In other words, inference takes a universal as its immediate object and possesses a partial and generalized picture of the object rather than the true representation of it. There is no real correspondence between inference and its real object [i.e., the real particular in the world], but merely an indirect causal relationship. In short, inference grasps the object through its universal characteristic. Therefore, Dharmakīrti considers inference to be erroneous.[10]

On Katsura's interpretation of Dharmakīrti, while inference is erroneous *(bhrānta)* in that it does not correspond to reality, it is nonetheless true "from a pragmatic point of view," in that it "can lead to the fulfillment of a human purpose."[11]

What Katsura has rightly focussed upon in speaking of perception as being "non-erroneous" *(abhrānta)* and corresponding to its object is the well known principle in Buddhist logic that perception has a certain resemblance with its objects, because it sees only particulars, undifferentiated into substances, qualities, actions, etc., and in reality it is only the undifferentiated particular *(svalakṣaṇa)* entity which exists. The other side of the coin for the Buddhist is that these fundamental distinctions between separate substances, universals, etc., are only invented by the conceptual mind and hence are not mirrored by the facts. There is therefore, in an important sense, no resemblance between how things are *conceived* by inferential cognition and how they are.[12] While it is thus undoubtedly right to say that for Dharmakīrti inference is *bhrānta* in a way in which perception is not, I don't think that it follows that the implicit truth theory in Dharmakīrti's account of inferential understanding must be a type of pragmatism, rather than correspondence. We can untangle this problem by distinguishing two senses of correspondence, and when they are distinguished there will be no need to introduce a pragmatic theory of truth.

A contemporary analytic philosophy textbook surveying truth theories distinguishes between two varieties of correspondence: "correspondence as congruence" and "correspondence as correlation."[13] Both types are correspondence theories in that a certain fact must exist if the relevant proposition, statement or belief is to be true. The first type, congruence, involves an added condition, viz., that there be a structural isomorphism, a type of mirroring relation between the truth-bearer and a fact. (Thus, for example, subject-predicate structures in thought and language might or might not be congruent—depending upon one's metaphysics—with facts composed of real substances and universals.) The second type, i.e., correlation, is a weaker type of correspondence, where there is no such isomorphism, but where it suffices that the fact exist for the statement or understanding to be true. Now, if we accept that for Dharmakīrti there is correspondence involved in perception, as I think we should, then it is the strong kind, congruence, i.e., the undifferentiated perception is congruent with the undifferentiated particulars. For inferences, however, although there is no structural mirroring, there is a causal relation that does link the understanding, or truth-bearer, to a fact, or more exactly to the particular real entities. When we come to understand a subject-attribute proposition like "sound is impermanent," there is, for Dharmakīrti, no separate substance, sound, in which the universal, impermanence, inheres. There are, however, impermanent sounds, which are the real particulars to which the understanding is linked and which must exist if the latter is to be true. Granted, impermanent sounds, hills on which there is smoke, etc., are not in themselves strictly speaking what we might term facts or states of affairs, but the transition to facts like "sound's being impermanent" or the "hill's having smoke" is relatively easily made. For inference and conceptual thought, then, we still have a weak form of a correspondence theory, like in many respects the correspondence theory that was advocated by J.L. Austin in the 1950's or, interestingly enough, like the theory of the great English idealist, J.M.E. McTaggart, who specifically rejected a "copy theory of truth" but nonetheless maintained correspondence.[14]

What is seductive is to take Dharmakīrti's contrast between *bhrānta* and *abhrānta* as also being his explicit formulation of a theory of truth, or his theory of "truth from an epistemological point of view," and to somehow identify this and this alone with correspondence.[15] The problem then arises, however, as to how to classify inferential understanding, which is *bhrānta* and thus would not seem to be true in the sense of correspondence. Hence, we are stuck with an equivocal Dharmakīrtian theory of truth: correspondence for perception and pragmatism for inference. I think that the root of the problem lies in looking for a pan-Indian, and hence Dharmakīrtian, theory of truth in the pair of terms *bhrānta-abhrānta*: for Buddhist logic, at least, we would come up with a more elegant, univocal result by analyzing the notion of truth *implicit* in the concept of *prāmāṇya,* "being a means of valid cognition." In short, we might do better to try to find a *unified* idea of truth which allows Dharmakīrti to say univocally that both inference and perception are *pramāṇa.* That minimalist single notion of truth which Dharmakīrti actually seems to apply in common to both inference and perception is as likely to be correspondence as correlation.[16]

The reason a Jamesian "pragmatic truth" theory should be ruled out as applying to Dharmakīrtian inferences is that it does not require that a certain fact or certain objects must obtain for an understanding/statement in question to be true: on a pragmatic theory, no matter how much we talk about "long term utility," it remains logically possible that a belief be useful, but that there is no such fact. Now contrast this with Dharmakīrti's system. It is a cardinal element in Dharmakīrti's account of how the usual type of smoke-fire inference works that the particular entities to which it is causally related must exist: if there wasn't actually any fire on the hill, the inferential understanding would not make us obtain *(prāpaka)* the object in question and hence could not be a *pramāṇa.* The upshot is that inference does satisfy the condition for the weaker version of the correspondence theory, correlation, because the entities in question must exist for the understanding to be true.

Alas, the terms, *bhrānta* and *abhrānta,* are not naturally translated as "incongruent" and "congruent," but rather as "erroneous" and "nonerroneous." Still, if we are looking for notions close to congruence, these are the likely candidates. In "On the So-called Difficult Point of the *Apoha* Theory," I opted for the usual translation and hence had to put up with the usual infelicities of expression. If we see the *bhrānta-abhrānta* contrast as pertaining to congruence, however, it becomes possible to say, in keeping with Dharmakīrti, that certain understandings, like inferences, are incongruent, i.e., *bhrānta*, but are nonetheless true (because they are *pramāṇas*). The gain in clarity is substantial. I'm afraid that the alternative where one says that inference is *erroneous but also true* is, for the uninitiated at least, bordering on incomprehensibility. At any rate, it makes Dharmakīrti look quite exotic, whereas if the point is one of incongruence being compatible with truth, Dharmakīrti ends up holding a subtle and defendable position.

The last thing to say on this score is that scriptural inference is undeniably something of a special case. In "How Much of a Proof is Scripturally Based Inference?" I argued that this type of (quasi-)inference is the only sort where *some* forms of pragmatism do seem to be involved, precisely because it bears upon facts to which we have no access other than testimony in scripture. (Indeed, because it is not connected with facts for us, Dharmakīrti explicitly denies that it is a real full-fledged inference.) Is this where we would find a pragmatic theory of truth? No, I don't think so. A pragmatic theory of truth is an instrumentalist truth theory, i.e., it allows as possible that statements and beliefs may be true just because they are maximally useful, but without any fact or real entities corresponding to them. There is no evidence to me that Dharmakīrti would want to say that the existence of the supersensible facts spoken about in scripture is somehow not needed, or that it is irrelevant to the truth of the scriptural proposition, or that what constitutes the *truth* of beliefs on such matters is just long term maximal utility. What is more likely is that we have here a pragmatic theory of *justification*, showing how people of limited understanding can and should determine when it is appropriate for them to believe in things like the details of the law of karma, things which they fundamentally cannot understand on their own and without scripture. In other words, if we wish to pursue spiritual "goals of man" *(puruṣārtha),* we have no other criterion for testing scriptural statements on supersensible matters and justifying our belief in them apart from the vital beneficial consequences that believing in such things will have for our spiritual progress. This is part of what is involved in Dharmakīrti's well-known formula that we rely on scripture "because there is no other way" *(agatyā):* our limited understanding cannot have access directly or inferentially to the facts. Nonetheless, nothing in *that* discussion implies that there is no fact to the matter or need not be any fact for scriptural statements to be true. Someone like the Buddha or a yogin with perception of the supersensible would not be in our benighted situation and would not be condemned to the pragmatic justification and the fallible, approximative understanding that is our lot in these matters.

Vyāpti

Turning now to *vyāpti*, the question as to how one formulates this implication between terms has provoked considerable debate in current work on Buddhist logic, as has the question of how we are to understand the so-called "natural relation" *(svabhāvapratibandha)* underlying *vyāpti*. I think that what happened historically in the indigenous Tibetan literature is instructive: that is, the system changes when we make a clear separation between the question of what *vyāpti* is and the question of when we have grounds enabling us to say reasonably that it is present. The two problems, as I tried to show in "Formal and Semantic Aspects of Tibetan Buddhist Debate Logic" are indeed by and large separated by Tibetan writers, who have a consistently applied account as to what *vyāpti* is (i.e., absence of a counterexample or *ma khyab pa'i mu*) and another account as to when we can be confident that *vyāpti* is there (i.e., when we understand, on the basis of an example, that there is a relation between the reason and the property being proved.) This constitutes a significant difference in approach from Dharmakīrti and the post-Dharmakīrti Indian schools in that the purely logical problem of saying what *vyāpti* is is separated from the very difficult epistemological enterprise of providing a procedure to ascertain that there is a relation guaranteeing the absence of a counterexample.[17]

Some writers, such as Bimal Krishna Matilal, have argued that it is a distinctive feature of Indian logic not to separate logical, epistemological and psychological issues.[18] That is, I now think, true. Let us briefly look at some of the details of Matilal's position, in particular the indispensable role of the example. Matilal argues that a multi-faceted approach combining logic with extra-logical matters is evident in the Indian position that *vyāpti* be not just a universally quantified statement but one which is exemplified, as in:

(1) Whatever is produced is impermanent, *like a vase.*

Although the first part of the statement of the *vyāpti* is, according to

Matilal, translatable into first order logic as a statement of the form "For all *x:* if *x* is *F* then *x* is *G*," the example serves to guarantee that we are not arguing about uninstantiated empty statements and that *vyāpti* will always have *existential commitment.* And that is one of the major reasons why, for Matilal, Indian logic is not like a formal logic: a universal premise in a syllogism-like formal structure would have no need for an example at all.[19]

I think that Matilal was indeed onto something here about the Indian context and that it is important to get clear what is right about this characterization to be able to see what happened when we get to Tibet, *where this characterization does not apply.* Now, first of all, it is not fully accurate to say that a genuine example *(dṛṣṭānta)* different from the subject *(dharmin, pakṣa)* is always necessary: as is well known, the "advocates of intrinsic implication" *(antarvyāptivādin)* did not think examples were necessary for "the intelligent," and in fact there is an intriguing passage in Dharmakīrti's *Pramāṇavārttika* which indicates that he himself held a type of proto-Antarvyāptivāda.[20] Nonetheless, even for an Antarvyāptivādin, the *vyāpti* will not be uninstantiated, as it will be instantiated by the subject of the reasoning. More seriously, there are real problems in saying that the first part of the *vyāpti* statement is translatable into a quantified conditional of the usual sort that one finds in first order logic. In first order logic the "for all *x*" will range only over existent things, whereas it can be rather quickly shown that if we are to introduce quantification to account for the *vyāpti* statements in certain Indian Buddhist discussions, the quantifier "for all *x*" must range over both existent and nonexistent things. We see quite clearly in the Buddhist logicians' use of inferences like the so-called *bādhakapramāṇa* (based on Dharmakīrti's *Vādanyāya*) that the example can be a nonexistent thing, like a rabbit's horn or a flower in the sky, and that the scope of the *vyāpti* must therefore range over nonexistents as well as existents. Nor is it particularly infrequent or revolutionary for Buddhists to give such nonexistent items as examples—Bhāvaviveka, who was well before Dharmakīrti, used the example of the sky-flower in *Madhyamakahṛdaya* and *Tarkajvālā* too and even Dignāga used the example "space" *(ākāśa)* in his *Hetucakra*, an example which is not actually existent for a Buddhist.[21] If we wish to formalize *vyāpti* statements into first order logic, we probably need quantifiers which range over actual and non-actual items, such as in the logic developed in Richard Routley's (i.e., Richard Sylvan's) article entitled "Some Things do not Exist."[22] And in that case, it cannot be maintained that the use of the example is to guarantee genuine existential commitment, for in many cases the example itself is not something real at all.

While we cannot maintain that *vyāpti* statements in Indian Buddhist logic must actually have existential import or commitment, we can agree with Matilal in maintaining that the antecedent and consequent terms in *vyāpti*—i.e., the *vyāpya* ("pervaded") and the *vyāpaka* ("pervader")—do have to be instantiated. But this instantiation or exemplification can even be by utterly nonexistent items. Take the so-called *sādhyaviparyaye bādhakānumāna*, or the "inference which invalidates [the presence of the reason] in the opposite of the [property] to be proved" to which we alluded above: "The permanent/non-momentary does not exist, because it does not have any efficacy successively or all at once, like a rabbit's horn or flower in the sky." This inference is usually given in something like the following way:

> (2) Whatever does not have a successive or simultaneous [production of effects], is not capable of effective action [i.e., does not exist], like a rabbit's horn. That which is non-momentary does not have a successive or simultaneous [production of effects].[23]

This *bādhaka*-inference is thus used to establish that existence is absent amongst non-momentary things, or in other words that whatever is non-momentary/permanent does not exist, which is clearly the contraposition of the fundamental principle that whatever exists is momentary. The *vyāpti* statement here is:

> (3) Whatever does not have a successive or simultaneous [production of effects], is not capable of effective action [i.e., does not exist], like a rabbit's horn.

Putting the first part of (3), without the example, into its formal paraphrase yields:

> (4) For all *x*, if *x* does not produce effects successively or simultaneously, then *x* does not exist.

The quantification in this conditional must range over existent as well as nonexistent things. To complete the paraphrase, a statement that the rabbit's horn does not produce effects and does not exist would have to be conjoined to (4). This example statement would then imply:

> (5) For some (existent or nonexistent) *x*, *x* does not produce effects successively or simultaneously and *x* does not exist.

In short, the example statement, "like a rabbit's horn," has the effect of showing that both the antecedent and consequent terms in (4) are not empty. It is not guaranteeing genuine *existential commitment*, but it is guaranteeing that the *vyāpya* and *vyāpaka* must have instances.

Now, what seems to have happened in the case of Tibetan *bsdus grwa* logic is that the Indian requirement that the *vyāpya* and *vyāpaka* be somehow instantiated (either by an example or at least by the subject) was simply dropped. True, the example is cited on occasion, by and large out of deference to the fact that the reasoning in question has been borrowed from an Indian text. Equally, the *theoretical discussion* about examples being needed is there in the Tibetan texts,[24] perhaps essentially because it is there in their Indian ancestors. However, in the vast majority of statements of *vyāpti* in *bsdus grwa* logic texts or in the numerous texts which use *bsdus grwa* logic, no example is given at all. If an example is presented and discussed, it is generally in order to answer the *epistemological question* as to how a particular controversial *vyāpti* is to be established on the basis of an example *(dpe'i steng du grub pa).* That the statement of *vyāpti* itself generally does not include an example suggests fairly clearly that, *de facto* at least, this Tibetan *vyāpti* is different from its Indian homologue, in that it is just a universal implication, and not a universal implication which also has an instance. But one can go further: *bsdus grwa* logicians clearly and explicitly recognize that there are *vyāpti* where in principle no instantiation whatsoever is possible. In these *vyāpti* not just are there no examples of existent or nonexistent things having the property of the *vyāpya*, even the subject doesn't possess the *vyāpya.* In effect, Tibetan *bsdus grwa* logicians recognized the fact that the falsity of the antecedent was a sufficient condition for the truth of the whole conditional—one finds this in the curious statements of *vyāpti* where the antecedent is clearly impossible, as for example when people are arguing about all barren women's children having such and such properties. The principle is known as *gang dran dran yin pas khyab* ("whatever one might think of will be implied") and is similar to the Medievals' *ex falso sequitur quodlibet:* because the antecedent is (necessarily) false, the whole conditional is true, whatever might be given as the consequent.[25] As far as I can see, there is no evidence that Dharmakīrtians in India countenanced any analogue to the idea of *ex falso sequitur quodlibet.* Quite possibly it would have seemed as absurd to them as it has to many in the West, who feel that if *that* is what material implication in formal logic permits, we had better explain our ordinary notions of entailment in some other way, perhaps along the lines of relevance logic or strict implication. In one way or another, people do demand that there be instantiation and a connection between terms for an entailment to hold—falsity or impossibility of the antecedent does not seem enough.

The preceding discussion has some summarizable results. First of all, in "Formal and Semantic Aspects of Tibetan Buddhist Debate Logic" I had thought that "epistemological and logical aspects were perhaps inadequately distinguished" in Dharmakīrti's thought, that "pervasion *itself* in Dharmakīrti translates into the same universally quantified formula as in Tibetan logic," and that "the Tibetans' separation of the formal notion of pervasion from its Dharmakīrtian epistemological baggage does, perhaps, represent a certain progress."[26] It should be clear that I would no longer go to that extreme. Secondly, if we agree with Matilal that one of the main features differentiating Indian logic from Western formal counterparts is the insistence upon the implication being instantiated, then *bsdus grwa* logic's notion of implication is not only rather un-Indian, but it shares the major features of the formal notion. And thirdly, it is clear that there were important formal discoveries in *bsdus grwa,* influenced by the revised understanding of *vyāpti.* As we mentioned, a logical notion of *vyāpti* stripped of requirements about examples and relations between terms led the Tibetans to discover and accept formal principles similar to *ex falso sequitur quodlibet.* Another striking development which this purely logical notion of *vyāpti* permitted was the *bsdus grwa* logicians' discovery that there could be several types of *vyāpti* (i.e., the so-called *khyab pa sgo brgyad* or "eight types of pervasion") by changing the order of the implication and adding negation operators, and that these pervasions would have elaborate formal relations between them. Indeed, 'Jam dbyangs bzhad pa (1648–1721) went very far in this direction, distinguishing twelve pervasions rather than the usual eight; his elaborate calculation of iterated multiples of formal equivalences between these pervasions, abstracted of all content and needing no instances, deserves to be regarded as genuine progress in the formal knowledge of his time.[27]

Deviant Logic

Finally, a word on the perennial question as to whether and to what degree the logic which Buddhists use and advocate is in accord with key theorems of Western logic. Is their logic a more or less classical logic, with perhaps an odd twist or two concerning quantification and existential import, but nothing deviant like a rejection of contradiction or excluded middle? That is essentially what I argued in the essay "Is Buddhist Logic a Non-classical or Deviant Logic?" I would continue to stand by that position in the case of Dharmakīrti and his successors, Indian or Tibetan, and indeed for most of the Indo-Tibetan Madhyamaka too. It can be reiterated that "If there is any deviance, it can only be highly local."[28] I would, however, be prepared to grant that the logic underlying the *Prajñāpāramitāsūtras* and, to a lesser degree, the early Madhyamaka, may after all be something of the exception, more prone to paradox or paraconsistency, indeed that it could perhaps be close to the kind of depiction that scholars like Edward Conze and Jacques May gave it.[29] The result would be that on this scenario Buddhist thought would have a history of going from the very provocative logic of certain Mahāyāna *sūtras*, and perhaps even Nāgārjuna, to the tamer logic of the scholastic. The later Indo-Tibetan scholastic, not surprisingly perhaps, would turn out to have an increasingly conservative reaction to the original writings of their tradition, arguing that the paradoxical or provocative aspects just *cannot* be taken at face value, but must be explained away with qualifiers and hedges. Indeed, interestingly enough, when it comes to logical deviance, a writer like Tsong kha pa would argue very much in the way that people like J.F. Staal have argued: the thought behind the texts *cannot* be like that, if it is not to be irrational.[30] This is undoubtedly a powerful interpretative intuition. But with inconsistent or paraconsistent logics becoming ever more sophisticated and respectable, it becomes increasingly difficult to see that all types of contradictions are equally irrational. Furthermore, notions like the Hegelian *Aufhebung*, which Jacques May relied upon in his interpretations, cannot be dismissed in the cavalier fashion that they were by logical positivists and their successors. I don't now know how to exclude that the *Prajñāpāramitāsūtras* are most simply and naturally read as having more or less the contradictions they appear to have. Indeed that Conze-May scenario fascinates me more and more.

Tom J.F. Tillemans
Lausanne, May 1999

Notes to the Introduction

1 Precisely because *apoha* does try to give an account for the universals to which language is committed, rather than just dismissing them, Hans Herzberger has characterized it as a "resourceful nominalism," as contrasted with the less satisfactory "happy nominalist" variety that he attributes to Jean Buridan and to Nelson Goodman. See Herzberger (1975).

2 The term is that of Paul Griffiths (1981). For more on the necessary intersection between philosophy and philology, see Tillemans (1995c).

3 I don't know who first coined this term. At any rate, compare its use by William Ian Miller in *The Anatomy of Disgust* (1997: ix): "While one need not be boring to describe boredom, nor confusing to describe confusion, it just may be that the so-called fallacy of imitative form is not completely fallacious when it comes to disgust."

4 Cf. the discussions in Dreyfus (1995: 671–91) and in Dreyfus (1997: ch. 17). Although Dreyfus gives a nuanced "No" to the question "Is Dharmakīrti a Pragmatist?" his arguments are rather different from mine and cannot be taken up here. Cf. also R. Jackson (1993: 43–63).

5 Williams James's own formulations of pragmatism are notoriously vague. Here are two samples from James (1907), reprinted in Goodman (1995: 28, 63): (1) "Any idea upon which we can ride, so to speak; any idea that will carry us prosperously from any one part of our experience to any other part, linking things satisfactorily, working securely, simplifying, saving labor; is true for just so much, true in so far forth, true instrumentally." (2) "...an idea is 'true' so long as to believe it is profitable to our lives.... The true is the

name of whatever proves itself to be good in the way of belief." Cf. the reformulation of this position in R. Kirkham (1995: 97): A belief *b* is true for such and such a person *s* when "all things considered and over the long-term, acceptance of *b* helps *s* explain, predict, and manipulate his world and communicate with others better than if *s* did not accept *b*." We could abbreviate this formulation: *b* is true for *s* if and only if it is maximally useful for *s* to accept *b*.

6 See *Pramāṇavārttika* II, k. 1bc: *arthakriyāsthitiḥ / avisaṃvādanaṃ*. Devendrabuddhi comments in the *Pramāṇavārttikapañjikā*, P. 2b2–3:

> *skyes bu ma slus pas ni mi bslu ba ni mngon par 'dod pa'i don dang phrad par byed pa'i mtshan nyid can gyi mngon sum dang / rjes su dpag par khyab par byed pa yin no // de nyid rnam par 'grel pa'i phyir / don byed nus par gnas pa ni / mi bslu ba yin te / zhes bya ba smos te / tshad mas yongs su nges pa'i don gyis (b)sgrub par bya ba'i don byed par rtogs pa'o //* "What is non-belying [i.e., reliable], in that it does not lie to people, encompasses perception and inference, which have the characteristic of making [people] obtain the sought after *(mngon par 'dod pa = abhimata)* object. In order to explain this very fact [Dharmakīrti] states, 'Being non-belying means confirmation of the accomplishing of the [sought after] goal.' I.e., one understands that there is accomplishing of the goal which is to be fulfilled by the object that the means of valid cognition *(pramāṇa)* has determined."

For the rest of the passage, see Dunne (1999: 438–39). As Dunne shows (1999: 286 *et seq.*), Devendrabuddhi and Śākyabuddhi also introduce, into *arthakriyāsthiti*, a distinction between mediated *(vyavahita)* and unmediated *(avyavahita)* effects of a means of valid cognition *(pramāṇaphala)*; the mediated (or "remote") effect is essentially the subsequent understanding of the object's practical efficacy, while the unmediated effect is the understanding, by the cognition itself, of the object's image *(grāhyākāra)* that presents itself as a given. See Dunne (1999: 304): "This [latter] minimal trustworthiness amounts to the claim that, regardless of the determinate interpretation of a cognition's content, one can always reliably know that one is cognizing."

7 C. S. Peirce (1931–1958, vol. 5: 407).

8 See Peirce (1931–1958, vol. 5: 565): "The truth of the proposition that Caesar crossed the Rubicon consists in the fact that the further we push our archaeological and other studies, the more strongly will that conclusion force itself on minds forever—or would do so, if study were to go on forever."

9 See Katsura (1984: 229).

10 Katsura (1984: 229–30).

11 Katsura (1984: 230).

12 Elsewhere I have termed this position the "theory of unconscious error." See the opening section of "On the So-called Difficult Point of the *Apoha* Theory," reprinted as chapter 10 in this volume.

13 Kirkham (1995: 119 *et seq.*).

14 See J.L. Austin (1950); see also Kirkham (1995: 124–30) on Austin. Cf. McTaggart (1921: 12):

> Our theory that truth consists in a certain correspondence with a fact, which correspondence is not further definable, must not be confused with the theory that truth consists in resemblance to a fact—a view which has been sometimes called the 'copy theory' of truth. Resemblance is a correspondence, but all correspondence is not resemblance, and the particular correspondence which constitutes truth is not resemblance.... There is no special resemblance between the belief and the fact.

15 Perhaps one would invoke Aristotle's definition of truth as found in *Metaphysics* 1011b26 ("To say [either] that which is is *not* or that which is not *is*, is a falsehood; and to say that that which is is and that which is not is not, is true") as being essentially the same as the pan-Indian definition of *bhrānti-abhrānti.* The supplementary premise would be to say that Aristotle is defining truth as correspondence, or even correspondence as congruence. This would, however, be a very shaky argument, as it is not at all clear that the supplementary premise is true.

16 In a recent article my colleague J. Bronkhorst quite convincingly showed the importance of a correspondence theory in several Indian philosophies including Madhyamaka, Sāṃkhya and others. This correspondence of which he spoke was correspondence as congruence, involving an isomorphism between the components of the truth bearer (i.e., an understanding or proposition) and the components of reality. Interestingly enough, he recognized that certain Buddhists, such as Vasubandhu, did not seem to accept such a one-to-one correspondence or isomorphism, but that they nonetheless did have important features of a correspondence theory. I would submit that he was

right, not just for Vasubandhu but also, or even especially, for the logicians: if we need a label for the sort of correspondence theory involved in conceptual thought, it is "correspondence as correlation." See Bronkhorst (1996).

Finally, it should also be remarked that the theory of correspondence as congruence and correspondence as correlation applies when Dharmakīrti speaks from a Sautrāntika viewpoint, but also when he adopts the Yogācāra point of view. Notably, from his idealist stance, perception remains *abhrānta* and conceptualization remains *bhrānta*. (The position that the separation between subjects/substances and predicates/universals is only due to conceptualization continues to apply from the Dharmakīrtian Yogācāra perspective.) It might be wondered as to what correspondence could be on the Yogācāra point of view, because there is no external object to correspond to. Nevertheless, there are *pramāṇas* concerning mental particulars, and that would again entail that if a cognition is a *pramāṇa*, and hence true, the relevant particulars (all be they mental) exist. That's *all* we mean by the minimal type of correspondence which every *pramāṇa* has, viz., correspondence as correlation. An understanding is true when the relevant particulars exist, but existence can be *qua* external entity or *qua* mental entity—Dharmakīrti's choice of ontology probably doesn't matter much on that score. Cf. Kirkham (1995: 134–35) on non-realist correspondence theories. J.M.E. McTaggart is, once again, an interesting comparison, as he advocated both idealism and a correpondence theory of truth (i.e., correspondence as correlation). See n. 14. See also McTaggart (1927: 53): "The belief in the non-existence of matter does not compel us to adopt a sceptical attitude towards the vast mass of knowledge, given us by science and in everyday life, which, *prima facie*, relates to matter. For that knowledge holds true of various perceptions which occur to various men, and of the laws according to which these occurrences are connected..."

17 Why am I so pessimistic about the success of Dharmakīrti's program for finding a "natural relation" *(svabhāvapratibandha)*? The problem lies in his establishing causality by induction and claiming that this relation will lead to certainty so that a counterexample is definitively ruled out. No matter how many qualifiers and hedges one adds (and Dharmakīrti adds several of them), it seems highly unlikely that anyone, East or West, is going to solve the problem of induction so that one can say with certainty that one thing is the cause of another, rather than just coincidentally succeeded by that other thing. See B. Gillon (1991) on Dharmakīrti's potential difficulties with induction. Dharmakīrti and his school put forward a threefold and a fivefold method of analysis *(trikapañcakacintā)*. However, in cases where we genuinely do not know what caused what, it is unlikely that this method can come to the rescue. The most we can hope to formulate is a reasonable, but

fallible, hypothesis, and even so, in any difficult case, it will have to be based on many, many more observations than three. Interestingly, Matilal (1998: 111) is about as pessimistic as I am about this doomed quest for certainty; he quotes approvingly the philosopher J.L. Mackie who said, "If anybody claims today to have solved the problem [of induction], we may think of him as being mildly insane."

18 See B.K. Matilal (1998: 14–15). Matilal, like several other scholars, deliberately did not take *vyāpti* and the necessary relation between terms *(sambandha, pratibandha)* as separable concepts. He regularly glossed *vyāpti* as "the inference-warranting relation," as, for example, in the following statement: "This 'inference-warranting' connection was called *vyāpti, pratibandha,* or *niyama...*" (1998: 49).

19 Matilal (1998: 15–16). See P.F. Strawson (1952: 164) on existential commitment:

> Everyone agrees that it would be absurd to claim that the man who says "All the books in his room are by English authors" has made a true statement, if the room referred to has no books in it at all. Here is a case where the use of "all" carries the existential commitment. On the other hand, it is said, we sometimes use "all" without this commitment. To take a classic example: the statement made by "All moving bodies not acted upon by external forces continue in a state of uniform motion in a straight line" may well be true even if there never have been or will be any moving bodies not acted upon by external forces.

20 See n. 33 in our article "On *Sapakṣa*," reprinted as chapter 5 in this volume. See also K. Bhattacharya (1986).

21 See, e.g., *Madhyamakahṛdayakārikā* III, k.140cd: *nāpi cātmāsty ajātānām ajātatvāt khapuṣpavat.* See C. Watanabe (1998: 130).

22 I.e., R. Routley (1966). The first to use these logical tools for Buddhist logic was A. McDermott (1969). See Tillemans (1988: 162–64) for the details of Routley's R*.

23 The reasoning is given in the form of a *parārthānumāna.* See Mimaki (1976: 60 and n. 233); cf. Ratnakīrti's *Kṣaṇabhaṅgasiddhi* (*Ratnakīrtinibandhāvalī,* p. 83): *yasya kramākramau na vidyete na tasyārthakriyāsāmarthyaṃ yathā śaśaviṣāṇasya, na vidyete cākṣaṇikasya*

kramākramau. See Y. Kajiyama (1999: 14).

24 See, e.g., the translation from rGyal tshab rje's *rNam 'grel thar lam gsal byed* in the first appendix (Appendix A) to "On *Sapakṣa,*" pp. 101–2 below.

25 See "Formal and Semantic Aspects of Tibetan Buddhist Debate Logic," pp. 127–28 below.

26 See p. 126 and p. 129 below.

27 See Onoda (1992: 98–106).

28 See p. 194 below.

29 For a short account of Jacques May's use of the Hegelian notion of *Aufhebung* and contradictions, see T. Tillemans, "Note liminaire," in J. Bronkhorst, K. Mimaki and T. Tillemans, eds., *Etudes bouddhiques offertes à Jacques May. Asiatische Studien/Etudes asiatiques* 46/1 (1992): 9–12.

30 See J.F. Staal (1975: chap.1).

SCRIPTURALLY BASED ARGUMENTATION

1: Dharmakīrti, Āryadeva and Dharmapāla on Scriptural Authority

IT IS IMPORTANT TO NOTE that the epistemological school of Dignāga and Dharmakīrti, in spite of its insistence on the two means of valid cognition *(pramāṇa)*, viz., direct perception and inference, did recognize that there was a whole class of propositions which could not be directly justified by means of these two *pramāṇa*s, but demanded recourse to scriptures *(āgama)* or treatises *(śāstra)*.[1] This tension between scripture and reason, which is a recurrent one amongst religious philosophers, was however approached in a novel way by the Buddhists, a way which allowed them to accept certain "propositions of faith" but nonetheless retain a rationalistic orientation and extreme parsimony with regard to acceptable means of knowledge.

The key elements in the epistemologists' position are to be found in *kārikā* 5 of the *Svārthānumāna* chapter in Dignaga's *Pramāṇasamuccaya* (i.e., in PS II, k. 5a) and are developed by Dharmakīrti in the *Svārthānumāna* and *Parārthānumāna* chapters of *Pramāṇavārttika* (i.e., PV I and PV IV, respectively). However, what is remarkable, as we shall see later on, is that Dharmakīrti's presentation also bears important similarities to, and perhaps may have even been influenced by, some passages in chapter 12 of the *Catuḥśataka* (CS) of Āryadeva.

The Epistemological School's Position

Let us begin with some of the relevant passages from Dignāga and Dharmakīrti:

> PS II, k. 5a:[2] Because authoritative words *(āptavāda)* are simi-

lar [to an inference] in not belying, they are [classified as] inference.

PV I, k. 215:[3] A [treatise's[4]] having no *visaṃvāda* ("lies") [means that] there is no invalidation of its two [kinds of] propositions concerning empirical and unempirical things by direct perception or by the two sorts of inference either [viz., inference which functions by the force of [real] entities *(vastubalapravṛtta)* and inference which is based on scripture *(āgamāśrita)*[5]].

PV I, k. 216:[6] As authoritative words are similar [to other inferences] in not belying, the understanding of their imperceptible *(parokṣa)* object is also termed an inference, for [otherwise] there would be no way [to know such objects[7]].

PV I, k. 217:[8] Or, they do not belie with regard to the principal point [viz., the four noble truths[9]], for the nature of what is to be rejected and what is to be realized as well as the method is acknowledged. Therefore [the understanding arising from the Buddha's words can properly] be an inference in the case of the other things [too, i.e., radically inaccessible objects[10]].

Now, first of all, the usual types of inferences which we associate with Dignāga and Dharmakīrti, such as those of sound's impermanence and the like, are said to be *vastubalapravṛttānumāna* in that they derive their truth from the fact that the reason—being a product *(kṛtakatva)*—is in reality, or objectively, related with the property—impermanence—and qualifies the subject, sound. However, an important point which needs to be made clear is that in spite of the numerous passages in which these authors talk about one state of affairs proving another, or about natural connections *(svabhāvapratibandha)* between the terms in an inference, it is not the case that every inference functions by the force of [real] entities *(vastubalapravṛtta)*.[11] (Often, for convenience, we will adopt a less literal translation for this technical term, i.e., "objective inference." The point here, very briefly, is that the usual or paradigmatic type of inference in Dharmakīrti is one which functions objectively, or "by the force of real entities," in that it can and should be evalutated purely on the basis of facts and states of affairs, and not in any way because of belief, acceptance or faith in someone or his words.) *Vastubalapravṛtta* is certainly an unbending requirement for the normal or "straightforward" type of inferences with which we are familiar, but, as we see in PV I, k. 215, there are also inferences based on scripture; that is to say, there exist inferences in which a scriptural passage rather than a state of affairs is given as the reason. The questions then easily arises as to (a) which sorts of scriptural passages can be used in such inferences, and (b) how the admittance of scriptural proofs can be harmonized with the general tenor of Dignāga and Dharmakīrti's thought which is, no doubt, oriented towards *vastubalapravṛttānumāna.*

Let us begin with (b). The epistemological school solves this problem by introducing three sorts of objects: perceptible *(pratyakṣa),* imperceptible *(parokṣa)* and radically inaccessible *(atyantaparokṣa).* The first sort consists of those things such as form *(rūpa),* vases, etc. which are accessible to direct perception, while the second consists of things (such as impermanence, selflessness, etc.) which can be proven through the usual *vastubala* kind of inference. The third kind, however, are objects such as the different heavens *(svarga)* or the details of the operation of the law of karma, which are, of course, inaccessible to direct perception, but which also cannot be proven by citing some other state of affairs as a reason. In short, we might say that these objects are beyond the limits of ordinary rationality.[12] A slight complication which should be cleared up at this point is that Dharmakīrti often uses *parokṣa,* a term which also has an extremely important place in PV III, in the sense of *atyantaparokṣa.* However we see in the commentaries that what is at stake in PV I, k. 216 is indeed *atyantaparokṣa,* and moreover, it is clear from certain passages elsewhere (in PV IV) that Dharmakīrti himself did explicitly accept this threefold division of objects.[13]

So Dharmakīrti limits the scope of scripturally based inferences to cases where the object is radically inaccessible *(atyantaparokṣa),* and hence beyond the range of ordinary ratiocination. By means of this strict delimitation, he can preserve his theory of inferences being objectively grounded, for this will be a requirement of logical reasoning which applies to *pratyakṣa* and *parokṣa* objects. He can also at the same time distance himself from the non-Buddhist schools' use of scripture. In effect the error which a Mīmāṃsaka or Sāṃkhya makes in citing scriptural passages as a means of proof *(sādhana)* is that they apply scriptural arguments to propositions, such as sound's impermanence, etc., which can and should be decided by *vastubalapravṛttānumāna*, and which are not at all outside the bounds of ordinary ratiocination.[14]

As for question (a), viz., the kinds of scriptural passages which can be used, Dharmakīrti introduces what Tibetan scholastics would come to call "the threefold analysis" *(dpyad pa gsum)* for testing as to whether scriptures *(lung = āgama)* are sound bases for inference or not.[15] In particular, as PV I, k. 215 makes clear, such a scripture must be (i) unrefuted by direct perception, (ii) unrefuted by *vastubalapravṛttānumāna*, and (iii) free from contradiction with other propositions whose truth is scripturally inferred. Put in this way it might seem that what is being said is simply that the scripture cannot be refuted by any *pramāṇa*, or that it cannot come into conflict with any of the other three kinds of objects. However, the point at stake, as we find it elaborated in PV I, k. 216, Dharmakīrti's *Svavṛtti* or *Svopajñavṛtti* (PVSV) and Karṇakagomin's *Ṭīkā*, is more subtle, and is essentially an inductive argument: the scripture's assertions concerning *pratyakṣa* and *parokṣa* are seen to be trustworthy, and so, similarly, its assertions about *atyantaparokṣa*, if not internally inconsistent, should also be judged trustworthy. The argument is given an alternative formulation in PV I, k. 217 when Dharmakīrti says that because the (Buddhist) scriptures are trustworthy concerning the principal points, viz., the four noble truths, they should also be trustworthy on radically inaccessible matters. The four noble truths are accessible to proof by *vastubalapravṛttānumāna*—as we see in the second chapter of PV—and thus, as these propositions in the Buddhist scriptures are trustworthy, so the others should be, too.

In short, scriptural argumentation—when applied to *atyantaparokṣa*, which is its only proper domain—*is* an inference: there is no need to postulate an additional *pramāṇa* such as the *śābda* ("testimony") of certain Hindu schools. It is, however, a rather special, indirect case of inference, in that it turns on an inductive generalization which presupposes the use and correctness of direct perception and *vastubalapravṛttānumāna*.

Āryadeva and Dharmapāla

Now, a remarkable point in this connection is that the Tibetan writer Tsong kha pa blo bzang grags pa (1357–1419) in his *Tshad ma'i brjed byang chen mo* noticed that Dharmakīrti's PV I, k. 217cd resembles k. 280 in chapter 12 of Āryadeva's *Catuḥśataka*.[16] Tsong kha pa was followed in this by rGyal tshab dar ma rin chen (1364–1432), who also remarked that CS XII, k.280 was the same reasoning as found in Dignāga and Dharmakīrti *(phyogs glang yab sras).* Subsequently, the Mongolian A lag sha ngag dbang bstan dar (1759–1840), in his *sTon pa tshad ma'i skyes bur sgrub pa'i gtam,* elaborated on the two verses, paraphrasing them into an identical formal argument *(prayoga),* and citing them in his proof that the Buddha is a "person of authority"' *(tshad ma'i skyes bu).*[17] While it seems impossible to definitively establish a direct lineage from Āryadeva to Dharmapāla to Dharmakīrti, the similarities between the verses in question do seem more then coincidental, and it is not at all impossible that Dharmakīrti was aware of Āryadeva's thought, and that he made use of certain elements. Let us look at CS XII, k. 280 with Dharmapāla's commentary.

After Dharmapāla has argued that the doctrines of the non-Buddhist "Outsiders" (*wai dao,* 外道) contain various faults and untruths, his commentary then has the Outsider object:

> In that case, the noble teaching in the Tripiṭaka of the Tathāgata [also] sometimes has statements which are scarcely believable, and so (*shi ze,* 是則 = *evaṃ ca kṛtvā* (?)) all the Insiders' and the Outsiders' texts would be untrustworthy; thus a gross absurdity *(tai guo shi,* 太過失 = *atiprasaṅga)* would ensue. How so? [Because] in the Buddha's *sūtras* are mentioned various miraculous transformations (*shen bian,* 神變 = *vikurvaṇa; ṛddhi*[18]) which are unimaginable. Or [these *sūtras*] speak about objects which have extremely profound (*shen shen,* 甚深) natures; no sentient beings can fathom [these things]. ...[The objector now goes on to describe the miraculous powers and qualities of the Buddha and various other difficult to comprehend facts. He then sums up the objection:] As things such as these are all hardly credible, we harbor deep reservations about them. [Reply:] Phenomena, if they merely existed, could indeed give rise to [such types of] doubts. But phenomena are also void. Hence [Āryadeva] states in the following verse:[19]

> When someone gives rise to doubt concerning
> the inaccessible [things] *(parokṣa)* taught by the
> Buddha, then he should develop conviction in
> these very things on account of voidness.[20]

The point is that correctness of the Buddha's teaching on voidness, which is accessible to ordinary inferential understanding, should lead one to believe that his teachings on matters inaccessible to such inferences are also correct. It is interesting to note that the Sanskrit of Āryadeva's verse employs the term *parokṣa*, which is translated into Chinese as *shen* 深 or "profound" (see n. 20). In Dharmapāla's commentary we see him using the term *shen shen* 甚深 in this context, which would thus very likely be the equivalent of *atyantaparokṣa*, although such an equivalent is not to my knowledge attested elsewhere. (Usually *shen shen* = *gambhīra*.) At any rate, it is clear that the use of *parokṣa/shen* at stake in Āryadeva and Dharmapāla, just as in Dharmakīrti's PV I, k. 216, does refer to propositions inaccessible to direct perception and ordinary inference.

The similarities between Dharmakīrti and Dharmapāla's approaches become even more striking when we look at the argumentation in the subsequent *kārikā* in CS with Dharmapāla's commentary. In this verse, Āryadeva gives a kind of contraposed version of the reasoning found in CS XII, k. 280, arguing that because the Outsiders are mistaken on objects which are accessible to inference, then they must also be mistaken on those which are not. Dharmapāla, at this point, launches into a long refutation of the Vaiśeṣika's metaphysical categories *(padārtha)* and the Sāṃkhya's theory of the primordial nature *(prakṛti)* and the three qualities (*guṇa*) to show that the Outsiders are indeed hopelessly mistaken in their accounts of rationally analyzable objects, and hence cannot be trusted in their accounts of what is unanalyzable and is essentially more difficult to comprehend. Now, not only is this completely consonant with Dharmakīrti's approach in PV I, k. 215–16, but conspicuously, Dharmakīrti in the *Svavṛtti* to k. 215 explicitly mentions the three qualities and the Vaiśeṣika categories of substance, motion, universals. etc. as being prime examples of refutable objects.

I conclude then that the similarities between these authors do seem to represent a common approach, as the Tibetan scholastics maintain. This, of course, may have been because these ideas were more or less commonly familiar to various thinkers of that period of time, rather than due to any more direct relationship. If however we take the hypothesis that Dharmakīrti (ca. 600–660 C.E.) was familiar with, and even influenced by Āryadeva's thought, then it may very well have been via the commentary of Dharmapāla (530–561 C.E.), which is after all the first commentary on the *Catuḥśataka* that we know of. Moreover, we know that Dharmapāla did write a commentary on Dignāga's *Ālambanaparīkṣā*,[21] and as M. Hattori maintains, he may very well have been a "grandpupil of Dignāga"[22]: in other words, on Dharmapāla's side it is clear that he was, in spite of his commentaries on Mādhyamika texts, very close to the epistemological school. It remains to be investigated then as to what other significant points of similarity, or influences, can be found between Dharmapāla and that other illustrious member of Dignāga's lineage, Dharmakīrti.[23]

Notes to Chapter 1

The original publication of this article contains the following dedication: "The present article took shape from work which I did during 1983–85 at Hiroshima University and is offered as a gesture of gratitude to Prof. Atsushi Uno, of whom I retain very fond memories."

1 In what follows the difference between *āgama* and *śāstra* is of no consequence. Also, as Dharmakīrti argues in PV IV, k. 93–107 (Sāṅkṛtyāyana's heading: *āgamasvavacanayos tulyabalatā*), there is no essential difference in the force or trustworthiness of one's own words and those of scripture. The same evaluative procedures apply to both.

2 *āptavādāvisaṃvādasāmānyād anumānatā.* Sanskrit preserved in PVSV: 108.1. For the interpretation of °*sāmānya* as "similarity," cf. PSV: 29b7: *yid ches pa'i tshig nyid gzung nas kyang mi slu bar mtshungs pa'i phyir de yang rjes su dpag pa nyid du brjod do /.*

3 *pratyakṣenānumānena dvividhenāpy abādhanam / dṛṣṭādṛṣṭārthayor asyāvisaṃvādas tad arthayoḥ //.*

4 Cf. PVSVT: 392.15: *asya śāstrasyāvisaṃvādaḥ.*

5 Cf. PVSVT: 392.14–15: ...*anumānena ca dvividhena vastubalapravṛttenāgamāśritena ca /.* Cf. also PVV *ad* PV I, k. 215.

6 *āptavādāvisaṃvādasāmānyād anumānatā / buddher agatyābhihitā parokṣe 'py* asya gocare //* *PVV reads *niṣiddhāpy*. Cf. Tib. *lkog gyur na'ang.*

7 Vibhūticandra comments on PVV's (p.365) phrase *agatyānumānatoktā: ato 'nyathā parokṣe pravṛttyasaṃbhavāt* /.

8 *heyopādeyatattvasya sopāyasya prasiddhitaḥ /pradhānārthāvisaṃvādād anumānaṃ paratra vā* //.

9 Cf. PVSV: 109.15–16: *heyopādeyatadupāyānāṃ tadupadiṣṭānām avaiparītyam avisaṃvādaḥ / yathā catūrṇāṃ āryasatyānāṃ vakṣyamāṇanītyā* /.

10 Cf. PVV *ad* PV I, k. 217: *paratrātyantaparokṣe 'py arthe bhagavadvacanād utpannaṃ jñānam anumānaṃ yuktam iti vā pakṣāntaram* /.

11 Cf. for example PV IV, k. 15: *arthād arthagateḥ*, etc. For *svabhāvapratibandha*, classic sources are to be found in passages such as PVSV *ad* PV I, k. 14. Cf. Steinkellner (1971) and (1984).

12 For the examples of the three kinds of objects, see n.13.

13 In PV I, k. 216, its *Svavṛtti*, and subsequently, Dharmakīrti does not himself use the term *atyantaparokṣa*, but his commentators Manorathanandin and Karṇakagomin do. (Cf. PVV and PVSVT *ad* k. 216.) However, it is clear from passages such as PV IV, k. 51 *(tṛtīyasthānasaṃkrantau nyāyyaḥ śāstraparigrahaḥ)* that Dharmakīrti does accept the threefold classification. *Tṛtīyasthāna* refers to *atyantaparokṣa*. Cf. also PV IV, k. 50 where Dharmakīrti speaks of the first two sorts of objects: *tathā viśuddhe viṣayadvaye śāstraparigraham / cikīrṣo sa hi kālaḥ syāt tadā śāstreṇa bādhanam* //.

> PVV *ad* PV IV, k. 50: *śāstropadarśite viṣayadvaye pratyakṣaparokṣe rūpanairātmyādau tadā pramāṇapravṛttyā viśuddhe nirṇīte sati paścād atyantaparokṣe svargādau śāstreṇa śāstrāśrayaṇenānumānaṃ cikīrṣoḥ sataḥ sa hi kālo 'bhyupagamasya* yadi śāstrabādho na bhavet* / "Suppose that at that time the two [types of] objects taught in a treatise, viz., perceptible and imperceptible [objects], such as form and selflessness, etc., are ascertained by a *pramāṇa* as faultless. Then subsequently, when one wishes to make an inference concerning radically inaccessible [objects] such as heaven, etc. by means of a treatise, i.e., by recourse to a treatise, then if the treatise is not invalidated, this would indeed be the occasion to accept it." *Sāṅkṛtyāyana: *abhyupagamya*. Cf. PVBh: 505.4: *sa hi kālaḥ syād abhyupagamasya* /.

14 Cf., e.g., PV IV, k. 2 and our commentary in Tillemans (1986c).

15 Cf., e.g., rGyal tshab rje's commentary *(rNam 'grel thar lam gsal byed)* to PV I, k. 215, (Sarnath ed., 177–78), where the three criteria in PV I, k. 215 are presented as a formal argument *(sbyor ba = prayoga):*

> *shin tu lkog gyur ston pa'i bcom ldan 'das kyi gsung chos can / rang gi bstan bya la mi slu ba yin te / dpyad pa gsum gyis dag pa'i lung yin pa'i phyir /* "The speech of the Bhagavān which describes radically inaccessible [objects] is non-belying with regard to the [entities] described, because it is a scripture which is [judged] immaculate through the three [kinds of] analyses."

This is more or less a standard version of what in *rtags rigs* literature is categorized as a "reason based on authority" *(yid ches kyi rtags).* Interestingly enough, this literature then goes on to treat such reasons along the same lines as other types of valid reasons, classifying them in terms of effect *(kārya),* essential property *(svabhāva)* and nonperception *(anupalabdhi).* Cf. *Yongs 'dzin rtags rigs,* p.46.

16 See pp. 158–59 where Tsong kha pa cites these two verses together and says that they show the same way *(tshul mtshungs pa)* to prove radically inaccessible propositions.

17 For rGyal tshab, see his *bZhi brgya pa'i rnam bshad,* p.5: *spyi'i rnam gzhag ni phyogs glang yab sras kyis bshad pa dang / shing rta chen po rnams 'dra bar yod do /.* Cf. also *rNam 'grel thar lam gsal byed* (Sarnath ed.: 179). For A lag sha ngag dbang bstan dar, see *sTon pa tshad ma'i skyes bur sgrub pa'i gtam,* pp. 43–44. This author obviously relies on Candrakīrti's commentary to CS XII, k. 280, where the correctness of the Buddha's teaching on voidness is said to be an example *(dṛṣṭānta)* on the basis of which we can infer his correctness in other matters. Finally, for the idea of the *tshad ma'i skyes bu,* see Steinkellner (1983) and the references therein. Cf. also Inami and Tillemans (1986) for the triple division of *tshad ma (= pramāṇa)* into *shes pa* ("consciousness"), *ngag* ("speech") and *skyes bu* ("person"). [Editor's note: this subject is extensively treated in Tillemans (1993a).]

18 *Shen bian* 神變 = *shen tong* 神通 *(ṛddhi).* See H. Nakamura, *Bukkyō-go daijiten.* Tokyo, repr. 1983: 795.

19 T. XXX 1571, 216c. 若爾如來三藏聖教或有所說難可信解是則一切內外經書無可信者成太過失。所以者何。佛經中說種種神變不可思議又說甚深眞實義理諸有情類不能測量。。。如是等事皆難信知故我於此深懷猶豫。事若唯有誠可生疑然事亦空故次頌曰

20 Translated according to the Sanskrit of CS: *buddhokteṣu parokṣeṣu jāyate yasya saṃśayaḥ / ihaiva pratyayas tena kartavyaḥ śūnyatāṃ prati /*. Note that the Tibetan interprets *śūnyatāṃ prati* as "on the basis of voidness" or "relying on voidness": *de yis stong pa nyid brten te // 'di nyid kho nar yid ches bya //*. Cf. the Chinese trans. of CS: 若於佛所說 深事以生疑 可依無相空 而生決定信 "When someone gives rise to doubt concerning the profound things (*shen shi*, 深事) taught by the Buddha, then he can rely on the voidness which is free of all [defining] characters and [can thus] gain sure faith."

21 T. XXI 1625, pp. 889–92.

22 Hattori (1968: 2).

23 I shall further develop some of these points in a translation of CS XII and CS XIII with Dharmapāla's and Candrakīrti's commentaries which I am preparing. [Editor's note: see Tillemans (1990).]

2: How Much of a Proof is Scripturally Based Inference?

IT IS SEDUCTIVE TO THINK that, on a Dharmakīrtian account, *abhyupagama*, acceptance of a scripture's words on radically inaccessible things *(atyantaparokṣa)*, is something which naturally or invariably ensues, or even necessarily follows, from the scripture's satisfying the threefold analysis *(dpyad pa gsum)* and that it is simply an objective matter whether the scripture does or does not pass such tests. This interpretation of Dharmakīrti's account of scripturally based inferences *(āgamāśritānumāna)*,[1] which we shall term for short "inference-like-any-other," is not just a hypothetical possibility. Indeed, with a few minor differences, the idea of scriptural inference as being just one amongst three kinds of inferences, but as full-fledged as the others, is the way Dharmakīrti has been interpreted by many, who have in one way or another taken Dharmakīrti's account of scripture to be a surpisingly rational approach to subjects which, otherwise, would be unknowable to us. Interestingly enough, although it is hard to pin down specific Indian writers on the question of just how rational or probative a Dharmakīrtian scriptural inference is, we do see major Tibetan writers clearly taking scriptural inferences as being as probative as any other inference, just different in subject matter. Nor is this approach restricted to just one Tibetan school.

Consider the following passage from the *dBu ma rgyan gyi zin bris*, where Tsong kha pa is trying to dispel a doubt *(dogs pa gcod pa)* about the possibility of scripturally based argumentation and where he answers with a clear, even very extreme, version of the "inference-like-any-other" interpretation:

> *ston pas gsungs pa'i shin lkog gi blang dor la 'jug pa ni gang zag dbang rnon ni / dpyad pa gsum gyis dag pa'i rtags las shin lkog ston*

pa'i lung rang gi bstan bya la mi bslu bar dpog pa'i yid ches pa'i rtags las 'jug la / de'i tshul gsum dngos stobs kyi rigs pas grub kyang bsgrub bya shin lkog yin pas yid ches kyi rtags su mi 'gal te / rtags kyi rigs 'byed pa ni bsgrub bya'i sgo nas 'byed kyi sgrub byed kyi sgo nas min pa'i phyir te / dper na 'gal dmigs kyi rtags rnams sgrub pa yin yang / dgag rtags su bzhag dgos pa bzhin no //

"As for [practical] engagement with regard to the radically inaccessible things *(shin lkog = atyantaparokṣa)* to be rejected and things to be realized spoken about by the Teacher [Buddha], intelligent people engage themselves by following a logical reason based on authority *(yid ches pa'i rtags),* one where they infer that the scripture teaching radically inaccessible matters is non-belying with regard to what it teaches from the logical reason of its being a scripture [judged] immaculate through the three [kinds of] analyses. Although the three characteristics *(tshul = rūpa)* of that [reason] are established through objective logic *(dngos stobs kyi rigs pa = *vastubalayukti),* still there is no contradiction in [such a reason] being a reason based on authority since what is being proved *(bsgrub bya = sādhya)* is radically inaccessible. For, the classification of types of logical reasons is delineated in terms of what is being proved and not in terms of the means of proof *(sgrub byed = sādhana),* just as, for example, reasons which consist in the apprehension of oppositions *('gal dmigs kyi rtags = viruddhopalabdhihetu)* are [themselves] positive entities *(sgrub pa = vidhi),* but should be classified as negative reasons *(dgag rtags)*."[2]

There is also the following passage from Tsong kha pa's *Tshad ma'i brjed byang chen mo*:

gtan tshigs gsum po bsgrub bya'i ngos nas dbye ba yin gyi tshul gsum nges byed kyi tshad ma'i sgo nas ma yin te / kun kyang mthar dngos stobs kyi tshad mas nges pa la thug dgos pa'i phyir ro // des na shin tu lkog gyur gyi don bsgrub pa'i gtan tshigs la yid ches pa dang / brda' dang 'dod pa tsam gyis bzhag pa'i don bsgrub pa'i gtan tshigs la grags pa dang / dngos stobs kyis zhugs pa'i don bsgrub pa'i gtan tshigs la dngos stobs kyi gtan tshigs zhes bya'o //

> "The three [sorts of] logical reasons are differentiated according to what is being proved *(sādhya)* and not on account of [differing] means of valid cognition *(pramāṇa)* which ascertain the triple characteristic *(tshul gsum)* [needed for valid reasons], because all of them must in the end come down *(thug)* to ascertainments due to objective *pramāṇas (dngos stobs kyi tshad mas nges pa)*. Therefore, we term reasons which prove radically inaccessible matters 'reasons based on authority' *(yid ches pa'i gtan tshigs)*; we term reasons which prove matters established by conventional agreements or by mere intentions 'reasons based on what is commonly recognized' *(grags pa'i gtan tshigs)*; and we term reasons which prove objective matters 'objective reasons' *(dngos stobs kyi gtan tshigs)*."[3]

We see in both these passages a very deliberate attempt to minimize or even virtually eliminate any special status for scripturally based inference. On this scenario, the only relevant feature differentiating a scriptural inference from one of the objective sort is the matter of what one is proving: is it *atyantaparokṣa* or not? All the other considerations are supposedly just as in the case of *vastubalapravṛttānumāna*. To look at some of the details in the Tsong kha pa version of scriptural inferences, the usual criteria for a valid reason, the so-called three characteristics *(tshul = rūpa)*, are said to hold quite unproblematically, even objectively *(dngos stobs kyis = vastubalena)* in the case of scripturally based reasons, i.e., the "reasons based on authority" *(yid ches pa'i rtags)*. In other words, it is objectively so that the reason based on authority is a property of the subject *(pakṣadharma)*, and that it has the two types of pervasion *(vyāpti)*. In the *Tshad ma'i brjed byang chen mo* passage, Tsong kha pa makes the point that all inferences (viz., those concerning objective matters, conventions and those based on scripture/authority) are in fact reliant on the certainty or ascertainments *(nges pa = niścaya; niścita)* due to objective *pramāṇas*; there are no degrees or hierarchies of certainty amongst inferences: all inferences have the same degree of certainty coming from having the same type of *pramāṇas* ascertaining the reasons' characteristics.

To sum up, Tsong kha pa's position, as we see in these two quotations, has the following key features:

(1) Scriptural inference is just to be differentiated from others by its *sādhya*.

(2) Scriptural inference relies on a reason which can be shown objectively *(dngos stobs kyis = vastubalena)* to possesses the three characteristics.

(3) Scriptural inference is a *bona fide*, full-fledged inference leading to certainty *(niścaya)* that the reason proves the *sādhya*.

It should be said that Tsong kha pa is construing the scriptural inference in such a way that it is not actually the words of the scripture which prove anything, but rather the fact that the scripture passes the threefold analysis *(dpyad pa gsum)*. And although Tsong kha pa's views certainly became the majority view in Tibet, there were dissenting writers, such as Tsong kha pa's great critic, the Sa skya pa, gSer mdog paṇ chen śākya mchog ldan, who took the logical reason to be the textual quotation itself.[4] However, although the ensuing debate between the two camps is interesting for other reasons (which we cannot go into now), there are no significant differences between the two camps about points (1) though (3) which I just mentioned. Both camps, *at one stage or another in scriptural argumentation*, rely upon the exact same formal argument *(prayoga)* that such and such a scripture is non-belying with regard to what it teaches because it passes the threefold analysis. Moreover for both Tsong kha pa and Śākya mchog ldan, the characteristics *(rūpa)* of *that* latter logical reason (i.e., passing the threefold test) are objectively proven so that the conclusion ("non-belying") is utterly compelling and certain.[5]

Now, earlier we had said that on the Tsong kha pa version of the "inference-like-any-other" position, all the other considerations, besides the choice of objects for the *sādhya*, are just as in the case of *vastubalapravṛttānumāna*. The same remark will hold for Śākya mchog ldan. But what are these "other considerations" which we were thinking of? Broadly speaking, they are all that pertains to the "probative status" of the inference, i.e., how certain is it and how much can it compel people to believe in the truth of the conclusion, when they do not fully share the same vision of the Buddhist spiritual path as that presented in the scripture, or *a fortiori* when they are not members of the Buddhist community at all. Involved in this same question is the philosophical issue of what kind of theory of truth (or perhaps better, what kind of theory of justification of truth claims[6]) is being advocated, whether scriptural inference is turning on the same type of theory as the usual *vastubala* variety, or whether it leans towards a different type of theory, one which is more along the lines of a form of pragmatism and which might even allow dissent and criticism. In short, the real question at stake is whether Buddhist scriptural statements are true or can justifiably be thought to be true, because belief in their truth is useful, even crucial, to someone who wishes to attain a certain type of spiritual progress and liberation, or whether scriptural statements are true and justified objectively, in virtue of facts, and independently of the utility of believing in them. Saying that scriptural inferences are *vastubala-pravṛtta* is (in a way which we will specify later) to lean towards the latter view and will have predictably conservative consequences.

It is time to turn to Dharmakīrti and some of his Indian commentators. There are, I think, some clear passages which show that scriptural inference is not a full-fledged inference and that, as it functions inductively, it lacks the certainty *(niścaya)* which a real inference should have. In the *Pramāṇavārttika*, at PV I, k. 213–17 and the *Svavṛtti* (PVSV), Dharmakīrti develops the major points of his account of scripturally based inference:

(a) PV I, k. 213: words do not have any necessary connection with entities; they just enable us to infer the intention of the speaker.

(b) PV I, k. 214: scriptures are worth investigating when they are coherent, present appropriate, praticable methods for gaining results, and when they focus on goals which are relevant to the spiritual "goals of man" *(puruṣārtha)*.

(c) PV I, k. 215 presents the threefold analysis (described above) which one applies to scriptures worth investigating.

(d) PV I, k. 216: Dignāga's point in saying that authoritative words are an inference was that when an authority's words (= scripture) have been found to be non-belying on rationally decidable matters, then we are justified to understand radically inaccessible matters based on that scripture. In this particular case, contrary to what was said in k. 213, we *do* infer something more than just the speaker's intention from his words: we also infer that the state of affairs obtains. This one "exception" to k. 213 must be allowed because otherwise there would be no way *(agatyā)* for us to come to know radically inaccessible things.

(e) PV I, k. 217 elaborates upon aspects of k. 216: when the scripture is non-belying on important rationally accessible things it should also be so on the inaccessible things.

The logical status of scriptural inference is then summed up in the *Svavṛtti* to PV I, k. 217: the methods outlined mean that one infers states of affairs from words, with a resultant lack of strict necessity; these are not real inferences.

> PVSV *ad* PV I, k. 217: *tad etad agatyobhayathāpy anumānatvam āgamasyopavarṇitam / varam āgamāt pravṛttāv evaṃ pravṛttir iti / na khalv evam anumānam anapāyam anāntarīyakatvād artheṣu śabdānām iti niveditam etat //* "This fact that scripture is an inference is asserted in both cases [i.e., in PV I, k. 215 and 217] because of the lack of any [other] way. If one engages oneself on the basis of scripture, it is better to engage oneself in this fashion [on the basis of a correct scripture rather than on the basis of one which belies]. But [this understanding] is not at all a flawless inference, for words have no necessary relation to their objects—this has [already] been explained."[7]

In fact, what we see if we also look at later passages in *Pramāṇavārttika* is that there are two reasons as to why scriptural inference fails to have the requisite necessity of a *bona fide* inference. Not only do scriptural words fail to guarantee certainty because of their lack of connection with things, but the inductive procedure whereby one goes from observed correctness on testable things to correctness on otherwise untestable things is also inherently subject to error.

> PVSV *ad* PV I, k. 318: *na kvacid askhalita iti sarvaṃ tathā / vyabhicāradarśanāt / tatpravṛtter avisaṃvādena vyāptyasiddheś ca / agatyā cedam āgamalakṣaṇam iṣṭam / nāto niścayaḥ / tan na pramāṇam āgama ity apy uktam //* "It is not so that because [someone] is unmistaken about some things he will be so in all, for deviance is observed *(vyabhicāradarśanāt)* and it is not established that there is any pervasion *(vyāpti)* between his [verbal] activity and being non-belying. Now, we accept this defining character of scripture for lack of any [other] way. There is no certainty from this [scripture]. Thus it was said that scripture is not a *pramāṇa*."[8]

The connection is explicitly made with PV I, k. 215–17, a link which is expanded upon by Śākyabuddhi and Karṇakagomin, their formulation of the argument being that observation of someone's correctness in one area does not ensure his correctness in all things, including radically inaccessible things, as deviance *(vyabhicāra)* from such a rule is, or could be, observed.[9] It is objected that if this inductive procedure is uncertain, then also in the context of PV I, k. 215's threefold analysis there can be no certainty concerning *atyantaparokṣa.* To this the reply is simply to accept the opponent's objection without reservation. Although the threefold analysis does not yield certainty, one should not and can not require such certainty either. We accept scriptural inference, not because it is a genuine *pramāṇa,* but rather to be able to engage in the spiritual path. As Dharmakīrti had put it, "because there is no other way" *(agatyā).*[10] Karṇakagomin and Śākyabuddhi *ad* PV I, k. 216 are clear on the implications: scriptural inference is an inference because of the thought of people *(puṃso 'bhiprāyavaśāt)* who want to engage themselves *(pravṛttikāma)* on the spiritual path; it is not an inference objectively *(vastutas).*[11]

It looks then that the position of scripture being inference-like-any-other has very little support in Dharmakīrti, or in Indian commentators such as Śākyabuddhi or Karṇakagomin. And it is not surprising to add that for these Indian writers scriptural inference is in no way *vastubala-*

pravṛtta, or objective, either. Scriptural inference, as is amply mentioned in Dharmakīrti and his commentators, depends upon *abhyupagama*, "acceptance," and that in itself is probably sufficient to show that it is not objective. At any rate, as if that were not enough, they explicitly tell us that it is not objective and not certain.[12]

Now, it is true that both Tsong kha pa and Śākya mchog ldan were aware of passages in the *Svavṛtti* which seemed to go against their position on scriptural inference being inference-like-any-other and hence felt obliged to explain why Dharmakīrti in PV I, k. 215–17 spoke of scripture as not being an authentic inference *(rjes dpag mtshan nyid pa ma yin pa)*. The move which we see both these Tibetan authors making is to say that citing the scriptural words lacks certainty and that it was only *that* which Dharmakīrti was talking about, as if PV I, k. 215–17 and k. 318 were not talking about the actual authentic scriptural inferences, but only about quasi-inferences where words are cited to "prove" things. The real inference, not surprisingly, turns out to be the proof that such and such a scripture is non-belying because it passes the threefold analysis. And this inference is supposedly certain and objective. I don't think that this move works at all.

Although the argument that words do not prove things is indeed Dharmakīrtian, I think it is clear that one cannot say that *this* is the only point which Dharmakīrti was making, and arguably it is not even the most telling point against scriptural inference being compelling and certain.

In fact, the threefold analysis constitutes a weak test of scripture, and I think it should be clear that Dharmakīrti and his commentators knew it to be weak, not just because of the lack of necessary connections between words and things, but as we see in the *Svavṛtti* to PV I, k. 318 and the commentaries, because of the inherently inductive nature of the whole procedure. A limited number of observations of correctness does not guarantee that we subsequently won't find errors on testable things (nor I suppose would the fact that we don't see internal contradictions mean that there aren't any). And a limited number of observations on perceptible and inferable matters would not *imply or guarantee* anything about what is radically inaccessible. What emerges from the *Svavṛtti* to k. 318 and from the commentaries is that the first two stages of the threefold analysis, where the scripture is tested for correctness on rationally decidable matters, *guarantee* nothing—they are at most grounds for thinking that such and such a scripture is *as far as we can judge* trustworthy and to be relied upon. The key phrase, oft-repeated, is *varam āgamāt pravṛttāv evaṃ pravṛttir:* "If one engages oneself on the basis of scripture, it is better to engage oneself in this fashion." In short, if we make the move of accepting a scripture's statements on radically inaccessible matters, it is because we are not, as far as we can judge, precluded from doing so and because we want to or need to do so for our spiritual goals. That is all. What is striking in the Dharmakīrtian account, then, is that the threefold analysis does not compel us to accept scripture's accounts of radically inaccessible matters in the way in which a normal *vastubalapravṛtta* kind of inference does compel us to accept the conclusion. Instead of logical compulsion, the Dharmakīrtian is making what could perhaps best be described as an informed, but fallible, choice.

Let us go back to Śākyabuddhi's and Karṇakagomin's idea of scriptural inference being a kind of inference, but one due to *puṃso 'bhiprāyavaśaḥ* ("the force of human thought/intentions"), this being contrasted with full-fledged inference which is objective (*vastutas*). What could this phrase "human thought" or "human intentions" mean? It certainly should not be taken as a trivialization of the role of scripture, for Dharmakīrti is quite clear that in spite of the problematic logical status of scriptural proof, there is no question about scripture's crucial importance to our lives: *nāyaṃ puruṣo anāśrityāgamaprāmāṇyam āsituṃ samartho...* "A man [who wishes to apply himself to spiritual goals] cannot proceed without relying on the validity of scripture..."[13]

Put the problem another way. If we accepted the Tsong kha pa-Śākya mchog ldan position that scriptural inference was inference-like-any-other and was as objective as the smoke-fire variety, the question as to why one would believe in a scripture's propositions would become dead simple. One would perform the requisite threefold analysis and the game would be up: rationally there would be no alternative but to accept the scripture's propositions on *atyantaparokṣa,* just as one has to accept that the hill has fire once one knows how smoke comes about and once one sees that the hill does indeed have smoke. This simplicity is in a sense what some people are attracted to in Dharmakīrti, and not coincidentally they are often conservative Buddhists or even proselytizers: for them, it is Buddhism's force or even superiority that belief in scripture is wholly rational and logical and that acceptance *(abhyupagama)* follows easily and impersonally. But now let us imagine that a Buddhist is not a subscriber to the inference-like-any-other scenario, and that he realizes that the threefold analysis is fallible, that the inference is not a real one, and that it is not objective, not certain, etc., etc. Why and how would such a person, if he is of a Dharmakīrtian bent, nonetheless come to believe in scriptural propositions on radically inaccessible states of affairs? Does *abhiprāyavaśa* mean that after all the Dharmakīrtian account is little more than a type of leap of faith? No. I do think the Dharmakīrtian texts in speaking of *pravṛttikāma* ("desire to engage oneself") and *puruṣārtha* ("goals of man") suggest an account which is more subtle than that of a camouflaged and excessively long path to arrive at a key step that is no more than blind faith. Briefly stated, Dharmakīrti's version as to why one chooses to accept a scripture's propositions, after having done the preliminary three-fold analysis, would seem to be best viewed as a type of pragmatism, one which is not of an objective or person-indifferent variety, but one which would take into account the interests and aims of a specific group of people, those who have an idea of what spiritual goals are and who wish to attain them. To use Nicholas Rescher's term, it would be a subjective pragmatism, in that it would involve a belief being justified because it leads to (and may even be crucial to) the success of such and such a group of people in their specific aims.[14]

Quite a number of years ago, Richard Hayes, in what was for many of us a very thought-provoking article, examined the "question of doctrinalism" amongst Buddhist epistemologists. One way, *inter alia*, in which Hayes formulated this question was "whether the Buddhist epistemologists should be characterized primarily as champions of reason or rather as champions of dogma."[15] Clearly, as Hayes himself recognized, one extremely important element in a response to these types of questions will be our account of how rational or dogmatic is the Buddhist's belief in his own scriptures. Now, if we look at the two types of accounts that we have described so far, the first, i.e., what we have termed inference-like-any-other, makes an obvious attempt at ensuring rationality by stressing the idea of scriptural inference being certain, objective, etc., just as certain and objective as proving fire on the smoky hill. This attitude has a natural tendency toward a certain conservatism, even fundamentalism about scripture, for once the scripture has been determined to pass the three tests then logically any and all of its propositions on *atyantaparokṣa* should be accepted—there is little or no possibility of a half-way house for skeptics who might want to accept some but not other such propositions, for all should be necessary, objective and compelling. It is no coincidence that the Tibetan, and especially dGe lugs pa, use of the ideas of scriptural inference in Dharmakīrti has been in such extremely conservative directions. Equally, it is not surprising that the subjective elements, the pragmatism, the uncertainty, the recognition of the problematic status of scriptural inference have been very much downplayed, in favor of watertight scriptural inferences which rationally must compel conviction. Dharmakīrti was somehow used to build a dogmatic edifice.

What was Dharmakīrti's own degree of dogmatism or doctrinalism? Arguably there could be different and much less conservative *applications* of a Dharmakīrtian methodological position on scripturally based inferences. The uncertainty and inductive character of scriptural reasoning might well allow a Buddhist to maintain that some or even many scriptural passages on karma, cosmology and other subjects *need* not be taken to be true simply because so much else, or so much else which is important, in the scripture seems to be true. There is the possibility that these would be precisely the areas where the inductive character of scriptural reasoning revealed its weaknesses. Someone could go one step further. A left-leaning Buddhist might then come to the additional conclusion that believing in such passages would no longer be of any use in a modern man's spiritual search, and that they could be rationally left to the past. In fact, I don't think that the interpretation of Dharmakīrti's methodology which I am setting forth does invariably place Dharmakīrti, or even Dharmakīrtians, in a left-leaning camp when it comes to applications. I have above all tried to argue against what I take to be an overly facile view of his rationality, one which does, in effect, yield a type of dogmatism in rational garb. What exactly is useful or essential for what kind of spiritual goals remains an open question.

Notes to Chapter 2

1 Several contributions have now appeared on these subjects. See, e.g., Yaita (1987) and Tillemans (1986a). [Editor's note: this latter article is reprinted as chapter 1 in the present volume.]

2 *dBu ma rgyan gyi zin bris,* f.5b. Note that the parallel with reasons which consist in the perception of oppositions *(viruddhopalabdhihetu)* is that when we use a *viruddhopalabdhihetu* to prove that there is no long-lasting sensation of cold in some place because in that place there is a raging fire, the fact that the reason, i.e., "presence of a raging fire," is not an absence *(abhāva)* is irrelevant to its being a genuine negative reason or a reason consisting in a non-perception *(anupalabdhihetu);* what counts is that its *sādhya* is an absence. Equally, reasons in scriptural inferences or "reasons based on authority" *(yid ches pa'i rtags)* are supposedly like any other in satisfying the usual criteria of valid reasons, but just prove a different kind of thing, and that is why and only why they have the classification which they do.

3 *Tshad ma'i brjed byang chen mo* 46b.

4 Thus, on Tsong kha pa's view, the formal argument *(prayoga)* is to be formulated along the lines of:

> *sbyin pas longs spyod khrims kyis bde zhes pa'i lung chos can / rang gi bstan bya'i don la mi bslu ba yin te / dpyad pa gsum gyis dag pa'i lung yin pa'i phyir //* "The scripture which says 'From giving comes wealth, from morality happiness' is non-belying with regard to the proposition which it teaches, because it is a scripture [judged] immaculate through the three [kinds] of analysis."

Śākya mchog ldan's formulation is:

> *sbyin sogs chos can / spyad pa las bde ba 'byung ste / spyad pa las bde ba 'byung bar rin chen 'phreng bar gsung pa'i phyir /* "Take as the subject, giving, etc.; happiness arises from their practice, because it is said in [Nāgārjuna's] *Ratnāvalī* that happiness arises from their practice." See Tillemans (1993a:12–15).

5 See the extensive discussion in Śākya mchog ldan's *Tshad ma rigs gter gyi dgongs rgyan.* In I.229.3–4 (= 115a), Śākya mchog ldan first gives the *prayoga* with the quotation of the scriptural passage figuring as the logical reason; see

n. 4 above. He then on I.230.1 *et sq.* (= 115b) takes up the proofs of the *pakṣadharmatā, anvayavyāpti* and *vyatirekavyāpti:*

> *tshul sgrub pa la / phyogs chos mngon sum gyis 'grub ste / sbyin pas longs spyod khrims kyis bde // zhes gsungs pa mngon sum gyis mthong ba'i phyir rgol zhig la rtags 'di 'god pa yin pa'i phyir / khyab pa sgrub pa la rjes 'gro sgrub pa dang ldog pa sgrub pa'o // dang po ni / rin chen 'phreng ba chos can / rang gi bstan bya'i don la mi bslu ba yin te / dpyad pa gsum gyis dag pa'i lung yin pa'i phyir //* "As for proving the [reason's three] characters, the *pakṣadharma(tā)* is established by perception, for this reason is presented to an opponent who perceptually observes the statement 'From giving comes wealth and from morality, happiness' [i.e., he sees that the statement is indeed present in the text of the *Ratnāvalī*]. As for the proof of the pervasion *(vyāpti),* there are the following two [subsections]: proving *anvaya* and proving *vyatireka.* We now take up the first [i.e., *anvaya*]. Take as the subject the *Ratnāvalī*; it is non-belying with regard to the propositions which it teaches, because it is a scripture [judged] immaculate through the three [kinds] of analysis."

After further discussion on proving *anvaya* and *vyatireka,* Śākya mchog ldan concludes on I.233.3–4 (= 117a):

> *des na khyab pa sgrub byed kyi rigs pa bshad ma thag pa de ni / dngos stobs zhugs kyi rtags yang dag yin te / rin chen 'phreng ba rang gi bstan bya'i don la mi bslu ba de / dngos stobs kyi rtags yang dag gis grub pa'i phyir //* "Therefore, the aforementioned logic proving pervasion is a valid, objective logical reason, for the fact that the *Ratnāvalī* is non-belying with regard to what it teaches is established by means of a valid, objective logical reason."

In short, what Tsong kha pa considered to be the "reason based on authority" *(yid ches pa'i rtags),* Śākya mchog ldan took to be the logic proving pervasion *(khyab pa sgrub byed kyi rigs pa).* But both agreed that the three characters of *that* reason were established objectively so that it was valid and objective *(dngos stobs zhugs kyi rtags yang dag).*

6 The difference between a truth theory (i.e., the necessary and sufficient conditions defining the truth of *P*) and a theory of justification (i.e., the properties which allow us to reasonably determine that *P* is true and satisfies the definition) is not wholly obvious in Dharmakīrti, and will have to be taken up in a later study. On this general difference, see Kirkham (1995: 41 *et sq.*). [Editor's note: see also the introduction to the present volume, pp. 6–12.]

7 PVSV (Gnoli ed.): 109.

8 PVSV (Gnoli ed.): 167.25–168.3.

9 PVT of Śākyabuddhi, P. vol. *nye*, 60a6–60b1; D. 51b7–52a2:

> *mngon sum dang rjes su dpag pas rtogs par bya ba'i don bslu ba med pa'i phyir shin tu lkog tu gyur pa'i don la yang de bzhin du nges pa yin no zhes bya ba yang log pa yin te / gang gi phyir blang bar bya ba dang dor bar bya ba'i don la lar tshad mas mi bslu bas 'khrul ba med par mthong ba'i phyir / des bstan pa gzhan rigs pa ma yin pa thams cad la yang de ltar 'gyur ba ste / bden pa nyid du 'gyur ba ma yin no / ci'i phyir zhe na / yul la lar skyes bu rnams mi bslu bar mthong du zin kyang yul gzhan dag tu yang 'khrul pa mthong ba'i phyir ro //* "Suppose it is said that because [an authority] is non-belying *(avisaṃvāda)* with regard to things which are to be understood by perception and inference, it is certain that he is so [i.e., non-belying] with regard to radically inaccessible things *(atyantaparokṣa)* too. This is wrong for the following reason: Given that one observes that [an authority] is non-erroneous due to [there being a] non-belying *pramāṇa* with regard to some things to be accepted or rejected, then in the case of all the other things which he teaches, [but] which might not be correct, he would also have to be like that [i.e., non-belying]. This [however] would not be true. Why? Because, though we might observe that people are non-belying on certain objects, we also observe deviance [i.e. that they are in error] *(vyabhicāradarśanāt)* concerning other objects." Cf. PVSVT of Karṇakagomin, pp. 592.27–593.12.

The general theme of a finite number of observations not guaranteeing certainty or pervasion concerning other cases is of course a very well-worn argument in Dharmakīrti. Cf. PVSV *ad* PV I, k. 13 (Gnoli: 10):

> *na hi bahulaṃ pakvadarśane 'pi sthālyantargamanamātreṇa pākaḥ sidhyati vyabhicāradarśanāt //* "Although one might see that most [of the rice] is cooked, the fact of [all the rice] being cooked is not established through its merely being in the pot, for one does observe deviance *(vyabhicāradarśanāt)*."

Not surprisingly, Śākyabuddhi and Karṇakagomin take the "code-word" *vyabhicāradarśanāt* in PVSV *ad* PV I, k.318 as also indicating the usual anti-inductive theme.

10 PVT, P. 60b4–7; PVSVT: 593.13–18.

11 PVSVT: 394.20–22: *kiṃ tarhīṣṭasya pratyakṣānumānāgamyasyārtha-syānantaroktena nyāyenāvisaṃvādād anumānam api pravṛttikāmasya puṃso 'bhiprāyavaśāt / vastutas tv ananumānaṃ śabdānām arthais saha sambandhābhāvāt //.*

12 It might well be argued by a contemporary philosopher that it is a *non-sequitur* to say that if certainty, or even full-fledgedness are denied of a type of reasoning, so must be its status as "objective." Indeed it could be said that is quite possible that in a system of inductive logic in some or another philosophy of science, uncertain reasonings would nonetheless give us objective knowledge. Quite true, but that is not Dharmakīrti's understanding of *vastubalapravṛttānumāna*, for semi-certain or uncertain inferences or quasi-inferences nonetheless being objective *(vastubalapravṛtta)* is never entertained as a possibility in his system. Maybe it ought to have been, but it wasn't.

13 PVSV *ad* PV I, k. 213 (Gnoli: 108.2–3).

14 Rescher (1995: 712):

> One overarching fact pervades these divergences in the development of pragmatism: that the doctrine can be seen either as a validation of objectively cogent standards or as a subverter of them. There is a pragmatism of the right, a Peircian or objective pragmatism of 'What works *impersonally*'—through proving efficient and effective for the realization of some appropriate purpose in an altogether person-indifferent way ('successful prediction,' 'control over nature,' 'efficacy in need fulfillment'). And there is a pragmatism of the left, a Jamesian or subjective pragmatism of 'What works for *X*' in proving efficient and effective for the realisation of a particular person's (or group's) wishes and desires.

Note that some type of pragmatism has also often been seen to be behind Dharmakīrti's theory of *vastubalapravṛttānumāna.* In a subsequent article I hope to develop my arguments against this attribution, which is more misleading than clarifying. Suffice it to say here, however, that the subjective form of pragmatism which seems to apply to scriptural inference does *not* convincingly apply to the *vastubala* variety. [Editor's note: for further discussion of pragmatism in Dharmakīrti, see the introduction to the present volume, pp.6–12.]

15 Hayes (1984: 646).

3: Pre-Dharmakīrti Commentators On Dignāga's Definition of a Thesis

A DOMINANT THEME in the writings of Erich Frauwallner and Ernst Steinkellner has been the attempt to trace the philosophical development of the Buddhist logician, Dharmakīrti (6th–7th century C.E.). As their contributions show, in this research it is not only important to trace Dharmakīrti's positions as they evolved throughout his own works on epistemology and logic, but it is equally necessary to gain as much information as possible on the opponents against whom Dharmakīrti argued. And not just the non-Buddhists: we need to collect and analyze the fragmentary presentations of the views of the other Buddhist commentators on Dignāga, positions which Dharmakīrti sought to refute and which often motivated him to formulate his own particular interpretation of Dignāga. In what follows, we shall call these latter commentators "pre-Dharmakīrti" in the sense that their works and ideas were *anterior intellectual influences* on Dharmakīrti—it does, of course, have to be allowed that at least *some* of them might not have been pre-Dharmakīrti in a purely chronological sense and could have been his approximate contemporaries.[1]

Amongst these pre-Dharmakīrti commentators on Dignāga—none of whose actual works survive either in the original or in translation—one stands out fairly clearly: Īśvarasena, Dharmakīrti's probable teacher, who wrote a commentary on Dignāga's *Pramāṇasamuccaya* (PS), one against which Dharmakīrti repeatedly argued.[2] Let us summarize some of the basic elements of recent research on Īśvarasena's philosophical stance. Although Īśvarasena's name is extremely rarely mentioned explicitly in Indian texts, Steinkellner[3] has shown that he was nonetheless spoken of by name by Arcaṭa and Durvekamiśra in connection with a position on nonperception *(anupalabdhi)*. The position was, namely, that nonperception of *x* was just the lack of perception of *x (upalabdhyabhāvamātra),* the mere fact that one does not see *x (adarśanamātra),* and that this constituted a separate means of valid cognition *(pramāṇāntara)* for proving *x*'s nonexistence or absence. This position, which was rejected by Dharmakīrti, was linked with an essentially inductive account of valid reasons, where absence of the reason in dissimilar instances *(vipakṣa)* was to be established by mere lack of perception. In other words, the general principle, or pervasion *(vyāpti),* would be established as not having any counterexamples *merely* because one does not see any. This is the position which Dharmakīrti went to great pains to reject in *Pramāṇavārttika* (PV) I, proposing instead a necessary absence of counterexamples based on a fact in reality, viz., the natural connection *(svabhāvapratibandha)* existing between the terms in the inference.

Subsequently, in his *Hetubindu* (HB), Dharmakīrti would also argue at length against a theory which held that a valid reason needed six characters *(ṣaḍlakṣaṇa),* instead of the usual three. While the attribution of the *ṣaḍlakṣaṇahetu* doctrine to Īśvarasena is still on the level of a reasonable hypothesis, unconfirmed by any specific Indian sources, it is at least corroborated in the indigenous Tibetan commentary on the *Pramāṇaviniścaya* by rGyal tshab dar ma rin chen, where Īśvarasena is named in connection with the *ṣaḍlakṣaṇahetu* doctrine.[4] Īśvarasena, quite possibly in reply to Dharmakīrti's initial critique, seems to have realized that his inductive method of proving the absence of counterexamples was insufficient, and thus proposed three supplementary criteria for validity,[5] all of which were rejected by Dharmakīrti. In short, we can thus reasonably assume with Steinkellner that Īśvarasena was the major catalyst for Dharmakīrti's own interpretation and defense of the triply characterized reason *(trirūpahetu),* his notion of natural connections, and his views on nonperception.[6]

Besides Īśvarasena, there were some other, much more obscure, Buddhist commentators on Dignāga against whom Dharmakīrti consecrated some of his argumentation: in PV IV, k. 27 and 122 Dharmakīrti was apparently refuting "a commentator on Dignāga's *Nyāyamukha*" *(nyāyamukhaṭīkākāra)* whose name is recorded in the Tibetan translation of this portion of Śākyabuddhi's *Pramāṇavārttikaṭīkā* (PVT) as "Mang po len pa'i bu."[7] S. Watanabe, in his article on this subject,[8] has speculated that "Mang po len pa'i bu" might be restored as "Bāhuleya," but this is conjectural and both names are, to our knowledge at least, unfindable in any other works. Compounding the mystery somewhat is that

Śākyabuddhi seems to have alluded to other commentators on the *Nyāyamukha*, that is, he spoke of Mang po len pa'i bu *la sogs pa* (= *ādi* "and others"); and Vibhūticandra's annotations also mention "the commentator on the *Nyāyamukha* and others." Now, there probably *was* at least one other major Indian commentator on the *Nyāyamukha*: Chinese sources tell us that Dharmapāla commented on the *Yin ming lun*, which is the Chinese name for the *Nyāyamukha*.[9] However, this work of Dharmapāla has not survived in the original, in translation or in fragments, and it is thus impossible to know what its specific positions might have been.

Much more significant in the fourth chapter of the *Pramāṇavārttika* is the position of the/a "commentator on the *Pramāṇasamuccaya*." This *pramāṇasamuccayaṭīkākāra*—which, as we shall see below, is the way he is repeatedly identified by Dharmakīrti's own commentators—is one of the opponents in the large section of PV IV which treats Dignāga's definition of the thesis *(pakṣa; pratijñā)* in a logical argument. We can assume that we are dealing, once again, with Īśvarasena:

(a) Īśvarasena is, after all, the only pre-Dharmakīrti commentator on PS that we know of.

(b) Especially if the *ṣaḍlakṣaṇahetu* ascription is correct, Īśvarasena was particularly influential in the development of key aspects in several of Dharmakīrti's works, so that it would be no exaggeration to say that many of the main elements of Dharmakīrti's thought on logical matters developed in a dialectical relationship with Īśvarasena.

(c) Just as Īśvarasena played such an important role in PV I, so too it would be reasonable to assume that he is the one whose ideas recur in PV IV.

Let me briefly give the background from Dignāga and some of the main elements in the section on the thesis in PV IV. A translation and detailed explanation of the relevant verses from PV IV is appearing in an ongoing series of articles, and we shall try to avoid burdening the notes excessively here.[10] As is well known by now, Dignāga gave two definitions of the thesis in NM and PS, definitions whose wording differed but which were essentially the same in meaning (as Dharmakīrti in fact took pains to show in PV IV, k. 86–88). For our purposes it is the definition given in PS III, the chapter on inference-for-others *(parārthānumāna)* which concerns us, for in this chapter Dignāga gave a specification of a number of requirements which a valid thesis should satisfy, each one of which was commented upon *in extenso* by Dharmakīrti in PV IV. The definition is as follows:

> PS III, k. 2: *svarūpeṇaiva nirdeśyaḥ svayam iṣṭo 'nirākṛtaḥ / pratyakṣārthānumānāptaprasiddhena svadharmiṇi //* "[A valid thesis] is one which is intended *(iṣṭa)* by [the proponent] himself *(svayam)* as something to be stated *(nirdeśya)* in its proper form alone *(svarūpeṇaiva)* [i.e., as a *sādhya*]; [and] with regard to [the proponent's] own subject *(svadharmin),* it is not opposed *(anirākṛta)* by perceptible objects *(pratyakṣārtha),* by inference *(anumāna),* by authorities *(āpta)* or by what is commonly recognized *(prasiddha).*"[11]

Dignāga himself, in his *Pramāṇasamuccayavṛtti* (PSV) on PS III, k. 2, commented upon the words *svarūpeṇaiva nirdeśyaḥ* as serving to eliminate unestablished reasons and examples from being theses, thus supposedly insuring that his definition would avoid the faults incurred by rival definitions, such as the *pratijñālakṣaṇa* put forth in Gautama's *Nyāyasūtra* 1.1.33.[12] The phrase *svayam iṣṭa,* however, eliminated theses which were just positions found in a treatise, and which were not those of the proponent himself. We cite the relevant passage as follows:

> PSV *ad* PS III, k.2: *bdag nyid 'dod pa zhes bya ba ni 'dis ni bstan bcos la mi bltos pa'i khas blangs pa bstan pa yin no //* "This [phrase], *svayam iṣṭa,* shows *(darśayati)* an acceptance *(abhyupagama)* which does not rely upon treatises *(śāstrānapekṣa).*"[13]

The section in PV IV commenting upon the word *svayam* (PV IV, k. 42–90) contains the most significant argumentation against what can plausibly be presumed to be Īśvarasena's positions. Dharmakīrti argued there against the view that because the proponent accepted a treatise, all properties ascribed by the treatise to the subject *(dharmin)* must also be part of the thesis for which the proponent is responsible. According to this view, when the proponent seeks to prove that sound is impermanent, the reason, "being produced" *(kṛtakatva),* not only will have to prove impermanence, *but* should also not contradict any of the properties which the proponent's treatise (in particular, the *Vaiśeṣikasūtras*) ascribe to sound, such as that it is a "quality of space" *(ākāśaguṇa).* Now, the argumentation up until PV IV, k. 69 is clearly directed at non-Buddhists. As the repeated advocacy of *ākāśaguṇatva* and other well-known Vaiśeṣika tenets suggests, we are dealing with an adversary who adheres to basic Nyāya-Vaiśeṣika positions. Equally, then, the adversary's view on the thesis, or equivalently on "what is being proven" *(sādhya),* must also be one which was, broadly speaking, ascribable to the Nyāya-Vaiśeṣika.[14] From k. 69 on, however, we see that virtually the same position on the thesis is attributed to a Buddhist, whom Prajñākaragupta terms "a commentator on the *Pramāṇasamuccaya*" *(pramāṇasamuccayasya vyākhyātṛ).* Here, then, is PV IV, k. 69 with the introductory passage from Prajñākaragupta's *Pramāṇavārttikabhāṣya* (PVBh):

> PVBh: 510.8–11: *pramāṇasamuccayasya vyākhyātā prāha / śāstrābhyupagamāt sādhyatā sakalasya śāstradṛṣṭasyānyathā śāstrābhyupagamasya vyarthatā / na hi tadarthāsādhyatāyāṃ śāstropagamaḥ kvacid upayogī / abhyupagamaṃ vārhati / svātantreṇa pramāṇena na kiṃcit / tasmād upagamya śāstraṃ tadarthaḥ sādhanīyaḥ / tatas tadvirodhe doṣa eva //* "A commentator on the *Pramāṇasamuccaya* says [the following]: 'Because one accepts a treatise, all which is found in the treatise is to be proved *(sādhya).* Otherwise, accepting a treatise would be meaningless. Indeed, if its propositions were not the *sādhya,* then accepting the treatise would not be of use for anything, nor would one be entitled to accept [it]. Nothing is [effectuated] by an autonomous *pramāṇa.* Therefore, once one has accepted a treatise, the property [mentioned] in it becomes the *sādhya.* Thus, when there is a contradiction with the [treatise], a fault does indeed occur.' [Dharmakīrti replies:]"[15]

PV IV, k. 69: *śāstrābhyupagamāt sādhyaḥ śāstradṛṣṭo 'khilo yadi / pratijñā 'siddhadṛṣṭāntahetuvādaḥ prasajyate //* "Suppose that because one accepted a treatise, all *[dharmas]* found in the treatise would be being proved *(sādhya).* Then it would follow absurdly that a statement of an unestablished example or reason would have to be a thesis."

The first half of the *kārikā* represents the adversary's view, while the last half is Dharmakīrti drawing the consequence that this adversary would fall into exactly the same trap as one who accepts the definition in *Nyāyasūtra* 1.1.33. What stands out clearly is the fact that the "commentator on the *Pramāṇasamuccaya*" did hold the same view on the thesis, or *sādhya*, as the Nyāya-Vaiśeṣikas against whom Dharmakīrti argued in the *kārikās* preceeding k. 69. Let us from here on, in keeping with the arguments sketched out above, speak of this commentator on PS as being Īśvarasena.

It might be, *prima facie* at least, unclear how Īśvarasena's view on the *sādhya*, as found in PV IV, k. 69 and PVBh *ad cit.*, could have been reconciled with Dignāga's idea in PSV that the proponent's position should not rely on a treatise *(śāstrānapekṣa)*—after all Īśvarasena *does* accept that the thesis, or *sādhya*, includes properties mentioned in treatises, and thus is not independent of treatise-based positions. We might, however, reasonably hypothesize that Īśvarasena took Dignāga's *śāstrānapekṣa* as meaning "no reliance on treatises which are unaccepted by the proponent at the time of the debate." This interpretation is borne out fairly well if we look at the adversary's view discussed in PV IV, k. 72—once again Śākyabuddhi's PVT (322a3) identifies him as being a/the "commentator on the *Pramāṇasamuccaya*" *(tshad ma kun las btus pa'i ṭīkā byed pa = pramāṇasamuccayaṭīkākāra)*—and as before, Īśvarasena seems by far the most reasonable candidate. He proposed the following explanation for *svayam*: the word is needed to show that the treatise in question, whose properties are the *sādhya*, is the very one which the proponent *himself* accepts now, rather than some treatise which he accepted earlier, but now rejects. Here is Devendrabuddhi's explanation of the views which Dharmakīrti is refuting in PV IV, k. 72 *et seq.*:

PVP 338a7–8: *bstan bcos cung zad sngar khas blangs pa de gang yin pa de bor nas / rtsod pa'i dus su bdag nyid kyi 'dod pas bstan bcos gzhan la brten pa'i rgol ba yang 'gal ba yod pa ma yin no zhes //* "Having given up some previously accepted treatise, then it is not contradictory that at the time of the debate the proponent relies on another treatise as he himself wishes."[16]

In short, *svayam* à la Īśvarasena would have served to eliminate doubt about *which* treatise is to be the basis for the *sādhya*.

Let us now try to summarize Īśvarasena's position and contrast it with that of Dharmakīrti:

(a) Īśvarasena seems to have interpreted Dignāga as still allowing that the positions in a treatise would also have to be the proponent's *sādhya* or thesis, *providing the proponent accepted that treatise himself.*

(b) He interpreted *svayam* in a manner which would be consistent with the idea that properties mentioned in an accepted treatise were also the *sādhya.* In particular, *svayam* did not eliminate *all* treatises, but only those which the proponent might have once accepted, but now rejected.

(c) Īśvarasena thus may well have interpreted PSV's phrase *śāstrānapekṣam abhyupagamaṃ darśayati* as meaning that *svayam iṣṭa* shows a position which does not rely upon any treatises which are not accepted by the proponent himself at the time of the debate.

(d) Dharmakīrti took Dignāga's statements in PSV about no reliance upon treatises *(śāstrānapekṣa)* much more radically: at the time the proponent makes an inference concerning rationally accessible matters he does not rely upon, or even accept, any treatises at all; the positions in the treatise do not count as being the *sādhya;* inference which functions by the force of [real] entities *(vastubalapravṛttānumāna)* is completely independent of all scriptures and treatises.[17]

(e) The word *svayam* does not serve to indicate which treatise is to be taken into account to determine the *sādhya.* It shows that only those properties which the proponent intends to prove himself are the *sādhya* (see PV IV, k. 42). Unrelated properties, which happen to be mentioned in a treatise but are unintended by the proponent in the specific debate, are irrelevant (see PV IV, k. 56 and 57).

This, then, is what we can glean about the views of the "commentator on the *Pramāṇasamuccaya*" on the thesis-definition, a commentator whom we have taken to be Īśvarasena.[18] If we are right in our identifications and attributions, then a picture of what must have been a complex dialectic emerges: Īśvarasena seems to have attempted to reconcile Dignāga's views in PS III, k. 2 and PSV with an essentially Naiyāyika position on the *sādhya*—viz., that the *sādhya* is not independent of treatises. This uneasy combination then led him to a very strained interpretation of Dignāga's proviso, *svayam.* Dharmakīrti, by contrast, simplified things and vociferously rejected both those aspects of Īśvarasena's interpretation of Dignāga. In so doing, he reinforced his general position in PV that logical argument on rationally accessible matters stands or falls only on its own merits and not because of any appeals to authority or tradition.

Finally, it is worthwhile to remark that there was probably at least one other commentator whose views on *svayam* seem to have served, in some measure, to stimulate Dharmakīrti's own thought. In PV IV, k. 76 *et seq.* Dharmakīrti argued against an adversary *(anya)* who maintained that *svayam* was destined to eliminate all treatise-based qualities of the subject *(dharmin).* In other words, when we prove sound is impermanent, we are speaking only of sound as it is recognized *(prasiddha)* by common individuals, and not of the theoretical entity, "sound," which is described in the *Vaiśeṣikasūtras* as being a quality of space *(ākāśaguṇa):* according to this adversary, *svayam* insures that the *dharmin* is indeed *prasiddha.* Dharmakīrti's reply in PV IV, k. 77 is that elimination of "theoretical," and hence not commonly recognized, *dharmins* is at any rate already presupposed in any debate on whether a *dharmin* has the property to be proved *(sādhyadharma).* As soon as it is understood that the *dharmin* is not the commonly recognized real entity, the debate will simply cease. Hence, *svayam,* if explained as assuring commonly recognized *dharmins,* would perform no needed function at all.[19]

It is far from clear who *this* adversary was: the commentators say nothing. Vibhūticandra (PVV-n *ad* k. 76, n. 3) does, however, classify him as a *ṭīkākāra* ("commentator"), suggesting that he was not just a hypothetical opponent. However, we have no way of knowing whether he was perhaps the *nyāyamukhaṭīkākāra* spoken of in PV IV, k. 27 and 122 or whether he was someone else. One thing seems likely: he was not the same person as "the commentator on the *Pramāṇasamuccaya*," for his views on *svayam* serving to eliminate all treatise-based qualities of the *dharmin* would run counter to those of the PS-commentator whom we have hypothesized to be Īśvarasena.

Notes to Chapter 3

The original publication of this article is preceeded by the following statement of dedication: "The present article is offered to D. Seyfort Ruegg as a gesture of respect and thanks, and with the wish that Prof. Seyfort Ruegg's exemplary philological skills, erudition and philosophical openness may long continue to inspire those who investigate Indo-Tibetan thought."

1 A difference between chronological and intellectual orders is more than just a theoretical possibility: it may well have occurred in other contexts in Buddhist philosophy, notably the relationship between Jñānaśrīmitra, Ratnakīrti and Ratnākaraśānti, as is argued in Mimaki (1992).

2 See Frauwallner (1961: 862–63).

3 Steinkellner (1966: 78).

4 Steinkellner (1988: n. 47).

5 Viz., (4) *abādhitaviṣayatva* ("[the reason's] not having as its object a [property] which is invalidated [by direct perception]"); (5) *vivakṣitaikasaṃkhyatva* ("that [the reason's] singularity is intended"); (6) *jñātatva* ("that [the reason] is known"). See HB VI in Steinkellner (1967: vol. 2, p. 70f). It is particularly the fourth character which would remedy the inadequacies of the inductive procedure by eliminating the exceptional cases where mere non-observation of counterexamples turned out to be misleading.

6 See Steinkellner (1966; 1967: chap. 5, 6 and notes) and (1988: 1438–1441, n. 47 and 56).

7 PVT 313b2–3: *gang yang ltar snang bcas brjod sogs bkod pa'i zhes bya ba la sogs pa la mang po len pa'i bu la sogs pa rigs pa'i sgo'i ṭīkā byed pa dag gis*...Cf. PVP 326b8 *rigs pa'i sgo 'grel bshad byed pa* and Vibhūticandra's PVV-n *ad* k.

27, n. 4, *nyāyamukhaṭīkākārādi*. On the actual arguments, see Watanabe (1976) and our translation of PV IV, k. 27 and PVV in Tillemans (1987), as well as in Tillemans (1991a).

8 Watanabe (1976: 982, n. 28).

9 See Frauwallner (1961: 861 and n. 44) on the *Yin ming lun*; see also Tillemans (1990:11–13) on Dharmapāla's works.

10 [Editor's note: the PV IV translations were published in a series of articles in WZKS; see Tillemans (1986c, 1987, 1992b, 1993b, and 1995b). These translations have now been compiled and will appear shortly in a book from Vienna.]

11 PS Tib.: *rang gi ngo bo kho nar bstan // bdag 'dod rang gi chos can la // mngon sum don dang rjes dpag dang // yid ches grags pas ma bsal ba'o //*. Skt. of *svarūpeṇaiva... 'nirākṛtaḥ* is found in Dharmakīrti's NB III, 38. The restitution of PS III, k. 2 follows Frauwallner (1957: 885); see also Van Bijlert (1989: 72). Cf. NM, k. 1:

> *svayaṃ sādhyatvenepsitaḥ pakṣo viruddhārthānirākṛtaḥ* // "The thesis is what is intended by [the proponent] himself as the *sādhya* [and] is not opposed by contradicting states of affairs."

See the edition and translation of NM in Katsura (1977:109).

12 On Dharmakīrti and Dignāga's arguments against NS 1.1.33's definition, viz., *sādhyanirdeśaḥ pratijñā* ("a statement of something which is to be established is a thesis"), see Tillemans (1987:152f).

13 PSVb: 125a1, Kitagawa: 471. Cf. also the Skt. fragment of PS found in PVBh 495.2 [Kitagawa (1973: 129, n. 166)]: *svayam iti śāstrānapekṣam abhyupagamaṃ darśayati*. See also the article by M. Ono (1986), which discusses Dharmakīrti's development of Dignāga's definition of the thesis. As Ono points out, while PSV took *svayam iṣṭa* together, Dharmakīrti made a significant split between *svayam* and *iṣṭa*, using the latter to refute sophisms of the Sāṃkhyas and Cārvākas which turned on word-play and equivocation. Following PV IV, k. 28–29, then, the definition in PS III gave specifications of four basic requirements which a valid thesis should satisfy, requirements embodied by *svarūpeṇa*, the particle *eva* ("only"; "alone") in *svarūpeṇaiva*,

iṣṭa ("intended") and *svayam* ("himself")—each one of these four was developed by Dharmakīrti in PV IV.

> PV IV, k. 28–29: *gamyārthatve 'pi sādhyokter asaṃmohāya lakṣaṇam / tac caturlakṣaṇaṃ rūpanipāteṣṭasvayaṃpadaiḥ // asiddhāsādhanārthoktavādyabhyupagatagrahaḥ / anukto 'picchayā vyāptaḥ sādhya ātmārthavan mataḥ //* "Although the statement of what is to be proven *(sādhya = pakṣa)* is something which can be understood [by implication], the [defining] characteristic [of the thesis] was [stated] to dispel confusion. This *[sādhya]* has four characteristics: By means of the words 'proper form' *(rūpa)*, 'alone' *(nipāta*, 'particle' = *eva)*, 'intended' *(iṣṭa)* and 'himself' *(svayam)*, one understands that [the thesis] is unestablished [for the opponent], is not a *sādhana* [i.e., reason or example], is stated according to the [real] sense and is what is accepted by the proponent *(vādin)*. Even though not [explicitly] stated, what is pervaded by the [proponent's] intention is held to be the *sādhya*, as in [the Sāṃkhya's argument that the eyes, etc. are] for the use of the Self *(ātman)*."

Note that we have amended Miyasaka's reading of k. 28 in keeping with Frauwallner (1957:884).

14 Cf. Dharmakīrti's presentation of this view in PVin 291a 5–6:

> *bstan bcos khas blangs pa'i phyir de la mthong ba thams cad bsgrub par bya ba yin no zhes dogs pa srid par 'gyur ro //* "The doubt could arise that because one accepts a treatise, all which is found there [in the treatise] is the *sādhya*."

Although neither Dharmakīrti nor his commentators explicitly identify which Nyāya-Vaiśeṣika(s) held this, it seems clear that Uddyotakara did hold it. This is brought out in the latter philosopher's attack on the specification *śāstrānapekṣa* in the passage from PSV *ad* PS III, k. 2 given above. Uddyotakara argued that if *svayam* showed that the position which the proponent sought to prove was really independent of *śāstra* (*śāstrānapekṣa*), then we should ask what is meant by *śāstra*. If the latter meant what is not contradicted by perception or scripture, then not relying on *śāstra* would be tantamount to holding and proving a false view.

> NV *ad* NS 1.1.33, p. 282, 4–8: *yad api svayaṃśabdena śāstrānapekṣam abhyupagamaṃ darśayatīti atroktam / kim uktam / parāvajñānasyāyuktatvād ity evamādi / kiṃ punaḥ śāstraṃ yad anapekṣam abhyupagamaṃ darśayati / nanu śāstraṃ pratyakṣāgamābhyām aviruddham / āgamas tadanapekṣam abhyupagamaṃ darśayatīti bruvatā*

'pramāṇakam artham abhyupaitīty uktam / yaś cāpramāṇako 'bhyupagamo nāsāv abhyupagantuṃ svasthātmanā yuktaḥ / nāpi pratipādayituṃ yukta iti /.

Note also that Prajñākaragupta (in his introduction to PV IV, k. 53) describes the adversary as holding the view that if one engaged in debate without accepting a treatise, one would simply be a caviller *(vaitaṇḍika)* and a nihilist *(nāstika),* raising objections without having a position of one's own. These are, of course, typically Naiyāyika terms, and the adversary's views would indeed be in keeping with the definition of debate *(vāda)* in NS 1.2.1, which speaks of *vāda* not contradicting the school's philosophical tenets *(siddhāntāviruddha).* For the Naiyāyika, arguing without holding a system of tenets at all would be cavil *(vitaṇḍā)* as defined in NS 1.2.3.

15 Manorathanandin simply speaks of "followers of the Ācarya" *(ācāryīyāḥ).* Cf. PVV: 438.10–11:

> *yad apy āhur ācāryīyāḥ śāstram abhyupagamya yadā vādaḥ kriyate tadā śāstradṛṣṭasya sakalasya dharmasya sādhyatety atrāha //* "But the followers of the Ācarya [Dignāga] argue, 'When a debate is engaged in after one has accepted a treatise, then at that time all the *dharma*s found in the treatise are the *sādhya.*' Here [Dharmakīrti] replies..."

16 Cf. PVV-n. *ad* k. 72, n. 2:

> *svīkṛtaśāstraṃ muktvā vādakāle śāṣtrāntaram icchayā labhyate 'ṅgīkartum //* "Having abandoned a treatise which he had accepted, then at the time of the debate another treatise could be accepted as wished."

17 See e.g., PV IV, k. 48 (additions follow PVV):

> *uktaṃ ca nāgamāpekṣam anumānaṃ svagocare / siddhaṃ tena susiddhaṃ tan na tadā śāstram īkṣyate //* "Now, it has [already] been said that an inference [which functions by the force of entities (*vastubalapravṛttānumāna*)] does not depend upon scripture with regard to its object, [i.e., what is to be proved *(sādhya)*]. What is established by such an [inference], is well established; at the time [of making such an inference], a treatise is not taken into account."

The point applies specifically to *vastubalapravṛttānumāna,* which concerns rationally decidable propositions (like sound being impermanent) whose truth or falsity can be known objectively by logical reasoning alone. Note, however, that Dharmakīrti certainly does allow reliance upon treatises when one is deliberating about rationally inaccessible matters (like the details of karmic retribution), which are radically inaccessible *(atyantaparokṣa)* and cannot be known in any way other than by relying upon scripture. See PV IV, k. 50ff and 94ff. See also the introduction to Tillemans (1993a: 9ff), as well as my translations and explanations of PV IV, k.48 and 50 in Tillemans (1993b).

18 The "commentator on the *Pramāṇasamuccaya*" does reappear in Devendrabuddhi and Śākyabuddhi's elaboration of the discussion of the four types of "opposition" mentioned in the latter half of the thesis-definition. This discussion begins at PV IV, k. 91–92, where Dharmakīrti gives a general explanation of the need to include the provision *anirākṛta* ("not opposed") and presents the four types of possible opposition, viz., by perceptible objects *(pratyakṣārtha)*, inference *(anumāna)*, authorities (*āpta*, i.e., scriptures or the proponent's own words) and what is commonly recognized *(prasiddha)*. Devendrabuddhi (PVP 342b8), commenting on k. 92, spoke of "some people" *('ga' zhig)* who seem to have interpreted the compound *pratyakṣārthānumānāptaprasiddhena* differently—Śākyabuddhi then identifies them as commentators on PS:

> PVT 325a 1: *'dir yang 'ga' zhig ces bya ba ni tshad ma kun las btus pa'i ṭīkā byed pa dag ste / de dag ni tshig gsum zlas dbye ba byas nas rab tu grags pa'i sgra dang / gsum pa'i de'i skyes bur khas len cing grags pa'i sgra yang re re la mngon par sbyor bar byed do //.*

The explanation in PVP and PVT is frustratingly brief and obscure, but it seems that the "commentators on PS" held that *prasiddha* qualified the *dvandva* compound *pratyakṣārtha-anumāna-āpta*, "what is commonly recognized through *pratyakṣārtha*, *anumāna*, and *āpta*." The whole compound becomes an instrumental *tatpuruṣa*. However, while the position may have been that of Īśvarasena, it did not provoke any argumentation in PV itself, but only a short reply by two of Dharmakīrti's commentators. Oddly enough, Śākyabuddhi speaks of "commentarors on the *Pramāṇasamuccaya*," thus using the plural *ṭīkā byed pa dag*—it is not clear to us what we should make of this plural.

19 PV IV, k. 76:

> *samayāhitabhedasya parihāreṇa dharmiṇaḥ / prasiddhasya gṛhītyarthāṃ jagādānyaḥ svayaṃśrutim //* "Another [commentator] has said that by [its] elimination [of any *dharmin*] which has a particularity superimposed by a [philosophical] tradition, the word *svayam* has the purpose of specifying a commonly recognized subject *(dharmin)*."

PV IV, k. 77:

vicāraprastuter eva prasiddhaḥ siddha āśrayaḥ / svecchākalpitabhedeṣu padārtheṣv avivādataḥ // "Since there is actually an undertaking of an investigation [as to whether the property to be proved *(sādhya-dharma)* is present or not in the subject *(dharmin)*], then the locus *(āśraya)* will be established as commonly recognized; for there is no debate about things whose particularities are imagined according to one's own wishes."

LOGIC

4: On *Parārthānumāna,* Theses and Syllogisms

IN 1984 I PUBLISHED AN ARTICLE entitled "Sur le *parārthānumāna* en logique bouddhique,"[1] where I argued, amongst other things, that it is an important logico-philosophical point that an inference-for-others *(parārthānumāna),* taken along Dharmakīrtian lines, cannot state a conclusion or thesis *(pakṣa; pratijñā).*[2] I argued that this point—and others—fundamentally differentiate this version of *parārthānumāna* from Aristotelian syllogisms. Specifically, if we take a typical *parārthānumāna* such as, "Whatever is produced is impermanent, like a vase. Now, sound is produced," the point of this logical form is not to show an actual deduction of the conclusion, "Sound is impermanent," but rather to show only those elements which would prove such a deduction. In short a *parārthānumāna* only presents the "provers" *(sādhana)* of a conclusion or thesis, viz., the triply characterized reason *(trirūpahetu; trirūpaliṅga),* as it is only that which has the "power" to prove.[3] It presents these *sādhana,* however, in a very specific way: to take the above-mentioned case, the *parārthānumāna* shows that the reason "producthood" *(kṛtakatva)* is a valid prover in that the universal implication, or "pervasion" *(vyāpti),* holds, as does the specific case at hand, the so-called *pakṣadharmatva,* or "fact that the reason is a quality of the subject."

In any case—so I argued in 1984 on the basis of Dharmakīrti and his commentators—a thesis will never prove itself or even contribute in the slightest to its own proof and thus is not considered a *sādhana* by Dharmakīrti: it is therefore important for Dharmakīrti that the thesis-statement *(pakṣavacana)* be absent from a well-formed *parārthānumāna.* By contrast, in whichever way we analyse Aristotle's idea of a syllogism in the first book of the *Prior Analytics;* whether we see it as a *rule* along the lines of *"P; Q;* therefore *R"* or as a *proposition* like "If *P* and *Q,* then *R,*" in any case, the syllogism must have a conclusion *(R)*. Such was my argument in 1984 against treating a *parārthānumāna* as a syllogism and so it remains in philosophical and logical discussions on the theme of *parārthānumāna* versus syllogisms. In such discussions, as we shall see below, we make a justifiable gain in simplicity by dealing with the final developed form of the *parārthānumāna*, i.e., the form to which Dignāga's and Dharmakīrti's earlier thought was tending.

The *historical* question as to when exactly the thesis-statement was definitively banned from *parārthānumānas*, however, is more complicated than I had thought in 1984. The present article will provide some evidence to show that the case for Dignāga in the *Pramāṇasamuccaya* (PS) and Dharmakīrti in his early works is probably somewhat different from what I, or the Dharmakīrtian commentators, made it out to be. Dharmakīrti himself seems to have changed his position from that of his earlier works, such as *Pramāṇavārttika* and *Nyāyabindu*, to that of his later *Hetubindu* and *Vādanyāya*. In fact, it is really in the *Vādanyāya* that the prohibition on thesis-statements is at its most clear and absolute—there he stresses that since the statement of a thesis *(pratijñāvacana)* is useless *(vyartha)*, then presenting such a thesis or conclusion in the statement of a *sādhana (sādhanavākya)* is a "point of defeat," or *nigrahasthāna*, for the proponent.[4]

While I'm not a partisan of the current tendency to exaggerate the differences between Dignāga's and Dharmakīrti's philosophies—e.g., I don't believe that Dharmakīrti "washed away Dignāga's philosophical accomplishments"[5]—I do think that here on the question of the members of a *parārthānumāna*, Dharmakīrti inherited an inelegant and overly complicated position from his master, one which did nonetheless contain a number of core ideas that Dharmakīrti, over time, struggled with and tried to unravel and simplify. Unfortunately, some of Dharmakīrti's own commentators, such as Prajñākaragupta and Śāntarakṣita, in true scholastic fashion, attempted to show that Dharmakīrti's (later) view was completely consonant with the textual evidence in Dignāga. In other words, Prajñākaragupta *et al.* wished to show that Dharmakīrti's view was unoriginal and already wholly present in PS. This, I think, was a mistake and blurred a rather complex historical development for Indo-Tibetan writers, and indeed also for the present author when he wrote his article on this subject in 1984.

Dignāga and Dharmakīrti on the absence of a thesis-statement in a parārthānumāna

Dharmakīrti himself finds only one source in Dignāga concerning the role of the thesis-statement. This is PS III, k. 1cd:

> *tatrānumeyanirdeśo hetvarthaviṣayo mataḥ* /. "In this regard, the presentation of the inferendum is held to concern the goal of the reason."

He invokes this passage in PV IV, k. 18ab,[6] and interprets it quite correctly as showing that thesis-statement has no power to prove anything, i.e., that it is not a *sādhana*, an interpretation which, no doubt, fits well with what Dignāga himself says in the *Pramāṇasamuccayavṛtti:*

> PSV *ad* PS III, k. 1cd: *yan lag rnams nas gang rjes su dpag par bya ba bstan pa de ni kho bo cag gi sgrub byed nyid du mi 'dod de / de nyid the tshom skyed par byed pa'i phyir ro //* (Kitagawa: 471.5–7) "Amongst the members, the presentation of the inferendum is not held by us to be a *sādhana*, for it engenders doubt."

Nonetheless, PV IV, k. 18's interpretation of PS III, k.1cd is a far cry from justifying the later Dharmakīrtian view in *Vādanyāya* that the thesis-statement *should not* be in a *parārthānumāna*. In other words, it is clear that in PS Dignāga did not consider the thesis-statement as being a *sādhana*, but nevertheless he most likely allowed its presence in a *parārthānumāna*—we shall see more on this below. Dharmakīrti, in the *Vādanyāya*, seems to have gone one step further on his own in saying that if the thesis-statement is not a *sādhana* it *should not* be in a *parārthānumāna*. How much Dharmakīrti was conscious that this additional step was his own is difficult to say. At any rate, his discussion in PV of Dignāga's actual words can, with little difficulty, be taken as showing that he realized that Dignāga in PS only went so far as to deny that the thesis-statement is a *sādhana*.[7] Indeed, I now think that there are good reasons for thinking that Dharmakīrti in PV held this same position.

In a recent study on the notion of *pakṣābhāsa* ("fallacies of the thesis") in pre-Dignāga logicians, Dignāga and Dharmakīrti, Masahiro Inami has shown that the use of the *pakṣavacana* can be profitably compared with the development of the closely related concept of *pakṣābhāsa*.[8] Inami is of the opinion that Dharmakīrti in PV, the PVin and the NB adhered to the same position as Dignāga in PS III, i.e., he permitted the presence of a thesis, all the while denying that it had any status as a *sādhana*. In this phase Dharmakīrti, like Dignāga before him, also still accepted *pakṣābhāsa*, as we see by the discussions in PV IV, PVin III and NB III. The ban on thesis-statements comes later in the *Hetubindu* (HB) and *Vādanyāya* (VN) and coincides with his rejection of the theory of *pakṣābhāsa*.

Inami's account is, I think, correct, as it seems reasonable to assume that there must be a correlation between the acceptance and rejection of *pakṣābhāsa* and that of the thesis-statement. After all, it is incongruous to give an account of *pakṣābhāsa* in a chapter on *parārthānumāna* and yet maintain that the thesis-statement can under no circumstances be given in such a logical form! I might remark, though, that in practice, when Dharmakīrti gives actual *parārthānumāna* in texts such as PV IV, k. 22; NB III, 8, 21, 23, etc.; and PVin III, he does not give theses, but only presents a two-membered form. The "permissibility" of thesis-statements, then, is at most a theoretical possibility for Dharmakīrti at this stage, but one which he himself did not, to my knowledge, avail himself of in his own argumentation.

Now, Inami's account—to which I am heavily indebted—could be supplemented with one of the motivation behind Dharmakīrti's evolution. There seem to be two basic motivations. One is Dharmakīrti's view (from his early works on) that the thesis is known by *arthāpatti* ("presumption") and is hence unnecessary in the *parārthānumāna*. Whereas Dignāga in PS stresses that the thesis is not a *sādhana*, but that it may be stated to show the "goal of the reason," i.e., the proposition which the argument is about, Dharmakīrti goes one step further in suggesting that this proposition is at any rate indirectly known by means of the statement of the *vyāpti* and *pakṣadharmatva* in a *parārthānumāna*. Progressively he realizes that Dignāga's function for the thesis-statement in terms of *hetvarthaviṣayatva* is usurped by the indirect knowledge stemming from hearing the two other members. In fact, he gives various formulations explaining just how the conclusion can be known from the *parārthānumāna:* in PV IV, k. 22 he uses the term *arthāt* ("by implication"); in NB he speaks of *sāmarthyāt;* and in PVin III[9] we find him using *arthāpattyā* (Tib. *don gyis go bas*). Indeed, what seems to be at stake is "presumption" *(arthāpatti)*—the conclusion is "presumed" from the two statements in the *parārthānumāna* in that these two statements could not both be true unless the conclusion were also.[10] But what is of interest for us here is that it seems that it was the fact that the thesis was known indirectly from the other two statements in a *parārthānumāna* which was one of the driving forces behind Dharmakīrti's own changes of position. In PV IV, PVin, and NB Dharmakīrti probably took the view that the thesis-statement was dispensable because known by implication, but that it could be used and could have *pakṣābhāsa.* Later, from the HB on, it was the same fact of *sāmarthya* which led him to view thesis-statements as completely redundant and to abandon talk of them (and *pakṣābhāsa*) altogether.

> HB 5.23–24: *atra sāmarthyād eva pratijñārthasya pratīter na pratījñāyāḥ prayogaḥ* / "Here, because the thesis is known just simply by implication there is no need for the thesis."

The other driving force for abandoning the thesis-statement completely was the fact, already recognized by Dignāga, that the thesis-statement is not a *sādhana.* This is evident in the progression from the argumentation in PV IV to VN 59, 8–9 where it is argued that the thesis-statement is not a *sādhana* and that its presence is a point of defeat in that it states something useless.[11]

By way of a contrast with this evolutionary view of Dignāga and Dharmakīrti's development let us briefly look at some of Dharmakīrti's commentators. Their view on Dharmakīrti, which would become the received interpretation in later Indo-Tibetan Buddhism, was that Dharmakīrti's position did not evolve from PV to VN: the thesis-statement was completely inadmissable. Not only that, but they maintained that Dignāga in PS had no role at all for the thesis-statement either. Let us for convenience term Prajñākaragupta's and Śāntarakṣita's interpretation of Dignāga, the "Dharmakīrtian commentators' interpretation." This interpretation where one seeks to impose the *Vādanyāya-Hetubindu* position on Dignāga is, I now think, untenable. As it is worth our while to try to see some of its shortcomings in some detail, we shall take up the problems which the Dharmakīrtian commentators had with PS IV, k. 6.

Dharmakīrtian commentators' interpretations

Prajñākaragupta, in his *Pramāṇavārttikabhāṣya*, presents the commentators' problem in his introduction to PV IV, k. 18:

> PVBh 487.30–488.1: *nanv ācāryasya pakṣavacanam abhimatam eva / yad āha / svaniścayavad anyeṣāṃ niścayotpādanecchayā / pakṣadharmatvasambandhasādhyokter anyavarjanam //* "[Objection:] But did not the Master [Dignāga] in fact admit the thesis-statement when he said [in PS IV, k. 6] 'As one wishes to generate certainty for others just like one's own certainty, then anything other than the statements of the *pakṣadharmatva*, necessary connection *(sambandha)* and *sādhya* is excluded.'"

He then argues that in fact when Dignāga spoke of the *sādhya* in this verse, he meant only the *sādhyadharma*, i.e., the property to be proved which occurs in the pervasion *(vyāpti)* of a two-membered *parārthānumāna*—in short, there are not three members, but only the usual two.

> PVBh 488.8–11: *yat kṛtakaṃ tad anityam iti vyāptyantaragatā sādhyoktir na pratijñārūpeṇa / avaśyaṃ hi sādhane vyāpakatvaṃ sādhyasyopadarśanīyam / ato 'vayavadvayam eva darśanīyam / sambandhena rūpadvayākṣepād eva trirūpatā hetoḥ / tasmād anityaḥ śabda iti nādāv ante vā darśanīyam / rūpadvayamātrakād eva sādhyasya siddheḥ //* "The statement of the *sādhya* is included in the *vyāpti*, 'Whatever is produced is impermanent,' but is not in the form of a thesis. For indeed, one does definitely have to show that the *sādhya* is a pervader *(vyapaka)* of the *sādhana*. Hence, one should present only two members [in a *parārthānumāna*]. By means of the necessary connection the [other] two characters [of the reason] are in fact implied, and thus the reason has the three characters. Therefore, neither at the beginning nor at the end should one present [the thesis] 'Sound is impermanent,' for the *sādhya* is established simply by the two characters alone."

Note that Prajñākaragupta's explanation is also what one frequently finds adopted by Tibetan commentators—it figures plainly in rGyal tshab dar ma rin chen's *rNam 'grel thar lam gsal byed.*[12]

Śāntarakṣita, in his *Vādanyāyavṛtti Vipañcitārthā*, also cites PS IV, k. 6 as a potential inconsistency, but seems to "resolve" the problem by saying that the statement of the *sādhya* (i.e., the proposition to be proved) is implied *(ākṣepa)* by the *pakṣadharmatva* and *sambandha*, and that therefore the thesis *(pakṣa)*, application *(upanaya)* and such members of a traditional five-membered reasoning are banished from use.[13]

Now, to get an idea of the fragility of the Dharmakīrtian commentators' interpretation that Dignāga did not allow the thesis-statement at all, consider the following points:

(a) Nowhere does Dignāga say clearly and unambiguously in PS that he rejects the thesis-statement as being a member of a *parārthānumāna.*

(b) In the *Nyāyamukha* (NM) Dignāga definitely did accept the thesis-statement as a member of a *parārthānumāna.*

(c) PS IV, k. 6 and PSV *ad* k. 6 provide good evidence that Dignāga did allow the thesis-statement.

(d) PS IV, k. 6 = NM, k. 13 (ed. Katsura 1981, 5.5; Tucci p. 44) and Dignāga's PSV on PS IV, k. 6 is identical with NM's own explanation of NM, k. 13.

While the Dharmakīrtian commentators' view that the thesis-statement must be excluded finds no hard evidence in Dignāga, there is, by contrast, considerable hard textual evidence to show that Dignāga in the NM and PS did allow a place for the thesis-statement in a *parārthānumāna.* The degree of obligatoriness is, however, different. About the NM, there is no question that at this stage Dignāga held that the thesis should be a member of a *parārthānumāna*, for it was a *sādhana* which, if left out, would bring about the fallacy of the *sādhana* known as "incompleteness" *(nyūnatā).*[14] In PS and PSV it is clear, as we saw above, that Dignāga no longer considers the thesis-statement a *sādhana* and that he has redefined *nyūnatā* to concern only the statement of the characteristics of the reason.[15] The result is that to avoid *nyūnatā*, there is now no obligation to present a thesis. However, while this much is different from NM, there are important passages, such as PS IV, k. 6 and PSV *ad cit.*, which do give evidence that the thesis, while not a *sādhana*, could be present. PS IV, k. 6 has already been given above, but now consider Dignāga's own commentary to this verse in PSVa:

> PSVa *ad* PS IV, k.6: *'di ltar phyogs kyi chos nyid bstan pa'i don du gtan tshigs kyi tshig yin no // de rjes su dpag par bya ba dang med na mi 'byung ba nyid du bstan pa'i don du dpe'i tshig yin no // rjes su dpag par bya ba bstan pa'i don du phyogs kyi tshig brjod do //* "Thus, the statement of the reason is for the purpose of showing the *pakṣadharmatva*. The statement of the example is to show that the [reason] has a necessary connection with the inferendum *(anumeya)*. One states the thesis-statement in order to show the inferendum [itself]."[16]

Dharmakīrti's commentators on his PV IV, k. 18 were obviously troubled by the fact that k. 18 seemed in contradiction with Dignāga's PS IV, k. 6, and they devised various tortuous explanations to resolve the apparent contradiction so that they could continue to maintain that Dignāga completely rejected the thesis-statement. These types of explanations might have been possible for PS IV, k. 6 taken in isolation, but they become extremely problematic in the light of PSV. The *coup de grâce*, however, comes from the fact that PS IV, k. 6, along with the quoted passage (and more) from the PSV, is also found in Dignāga's earlier work, the *Nyāyamukha*,[17] and that in NM's system the thesis-statement *does* indeed figure in a *parārthānumāna*. Now, we cannot reasonably interpret NM k. 13ff. along the lines of Dharmakīrti's commentators, but have to take it as showing that the thesis is stated. Hence, either the same passages would have to mean two radically different things in two different texts of Dignāga—an unlikely prospect—or Prajñākaragupta's and Śāntarakṣita's approaches are impossible.

In short, as typically happens in Indian philosophy, commentators are reluctant to admit that there was an evolution and an historical development of certain notions. If, however, we take a more evolutionary view, we should get the following result: True, Dignāga did make a change in his positions in NM and PS on the questions of the thesis-statement being a *sādhana* and the fallacy of *nyūnatā* being incurred if it is absent, but in PS he still kept some holdovers from his earlier views. Specifically, the lack of a thesis-statement ceases to be a criticizable fallacy in PS, but nonetheless, there is still a theoretical justification for stating a thesis in a *parārthānumāna*. Dharmakīrti initially inherited this view (although in his actual practice of *parārthānumāna* he never actually stated theses), but then moved gradually to simplify Dignāga's inelegant theoretical stance.

Syllogisms

What implications does this revised version of the history of *pakṣavacana* have for our philosophical comparison between *parārthānumāna* and syllogisms? A catalyst for the present reflections is a recent book by V. A. van Bijlert, who makes three basic criticisms of my 1984 article: (a) Dignāga did accord some place for the thesis-statement in a *parārthānumāna*; (b) hence, my anti-syllogism polemic is unfounded or too strong; (c) there are significant similarities between the Buddhist *parārthānumāna* and Aristotelian syllogisms.[18] Van Bijlert's book is a generally valuable contribution and raises some interesting questions concerning the specific problem of *parārthānumāna*. In effect, I think that the above discussion and Inami's paper show that van Bijlert is basically right on the first point.[19] The errors in his second and third points should become clearer below.

To take up (b), the revised historical account of *pakṣavacana* in *parārthānumāna* does not change my earlier point that the thesis-expression, contrary to the conclusion in a syllogism, is fundamentally irrelevant in an inference-for-others. In fact, the basic metalogical views in PS and PV concerning what is and is not a *sādhana* already implied that the thesis-statement was a more or less useless appendage, although it took Dharmakīrti some reflection to actually arrive at the explicit position that it was *thoroughly* useless and should be banned. In making a logical comparison between *parārthānumāna* and syllogisms, then, I would maintain that we can profitably disregard the tortuous historical process that it took for the Buddhist writers to work out the implications of their own key ideas. If we wish to speak of a *parārthānumāna* as a logical form and make philosophical analyses about what is and is not crucial to it, we do better to speak about the fully developed form where the extraneous elements, such as the useless *pakṣavacana*, have been consciously eliminated. In discussions on comparative logic there is a certain justifiable simplicity in relegating the Buddhists' actual discovery of their own implicit notions to the domain of an extremely long footnote.

Let us now look at van Bijlert's remarks on (c), the so-called similarities which make it appropriate for us to use the term "syllogism" for *parārthānumāna.* My critic first gives a paraphrase of Aristotle's definition of the syllogism—"a discourse in which from certain propositions that are laid down something other than what is stated follows of necessity."[20] For the rest of the argument let me cite the relevant passage from van Bijlert (1989: 89–90):

> What is important here [in Aristotle's definition of the syllogism in the *Prior Analytics*] is that from general true propositions another proposition generally follows. If this general notion is kept in mind, we are able to see the correspondence of this with the *parārthānumāna,* for in the latter the *dṛṣṭānta* functions as a proposition enunciating a general *fact* while the *hetu* enunciates a particular *fact.* The thing that was announced for proof follows from both propositions.

Van Bijlert, in brief, is emphasizing that in a *parārthānumāna* too, "the thing that was announced for proof follows from both propositions." Indeed it does. But that is relatively trivial and was certainly not the point I was driving at. What is important for us—as I insisted in 1984—is the way in which syllogisms and *parārthānumāna* are evaluated. Let us take this up again from a slightly different angle.

First of all, most of Aristotle's key discussion of syllogisms in the *Prior Analytics* and in particular that concerning the syllogistic figures is comprehensible only if we include the conclusion with the premises in a syllogism. We get sentences like "If A [is predicated] of no B, and B of all C, it is necessary that A will belong to no C" where syllogism is said to occur and other cases where syllogism is said to fail to occur. We cannot understand these occurrences of syllogisms or non-occurrences, or "syllogistic necessity" (to use Łukasiewicz's gloss on the word ἀνάγκη figuring in syllogisms), without taking into account the conclusion. Take the syllogism's three figures, which William and Martha Kneale simplify as:

(I)	(II)	(III)
$A–B$	$M–N$	$\Pi–\Sigma$
$\underline{B–\Gamma}$	$\underline{M–\Xi}$	$\underline{P–\Sigma}$
$A–\Gamma$	$N–\Xi$	$\Pi–P$

(Here letters show the skeleton of general statements which can be affirmative or negative, universal or particular in accordance with the Square of Opposition. The variables are term variables.[21]) Again it makes no sense to evaluate figures in terms of syllogistic necessity unless we specify which conclusion we are speaking about. Now, I realize that some writers like Łukasiewicz and Bocheński have preferred to take syllogisms as material implications along the lines of "if *P* and *Q* then *R*." In other words, we are not speaking about validity, as in inferences, but rather of the truth or falsity of a sentence. Dr. T.J. Smiley once proposed the interesting solution that the syllogism be seen as a type of formal deduction, viz., a finite series of well-formed formulae satisfying certain specific conditions. Thus the syllogism would have to be the ordered triple <*P*, *Q*, *R*>.[22] At any rate, whatever analysis we adopt, the conclusion is obviously an integral part of the syllogism. This, then, was my point in saying in my 1984 article (87): "un syllogisme, quelle que soit notre manière de l'analyser, doit avoir une conclusion."

I can imagine that at this point someone schooled in traditional logic might argue that all this only serves to show that actually it is the enthymeme (viz., a syllogism-like form where one member is missing) which is a better candidate for a parallel with *parārthānumāna*. Specifically, it might be argued that a *parārthānumāna* is like what older logic text-books[23] would call "an enthymeme of the third order"—those in which the conclusion is the omitted member. This is typically used in cases of innuendo. E.g.,

> Cowardice is always contemptible, and this was clearly a case of cowardice.[24]

Actually shifting to enthymemes changes virtually nothing, for they are simply truncated syllogisms whose necessity is to be judged by that of a corresponding elaborated form. The usual textbook explanation is that we must first determine which member has been omitted, restore it, and then evaluate things in the usual syllogistic fashion: "if the syllogism thereby constructed is formally valid, the original enthymeme is valid, if the syllogism is formally invalid, the original enthymeme is invalid."[25] So, to be blunt, enthymemes are a red herring for this discussion and can best be disregarded.

Now, contrast all this with the Buddhist *parārthānumāna* as we find it already in Dignāga's PS, all of Dharmakīrti and certainly in post-

Dharmakīrti logicians, where the "validity" of the reason and of the *parārthānumāna* which exhibits that reason is not a matter of whether or not the conclusion follows, but whether the *vyāpti* and *pakṣadharmatva* hold. (I am aware that the term "validity" in this Buddhist context is not used in the same way as in formal logic, and indeed that there is no term in Buddhist languages which corresponds fully to the term "validity" in Western writing on logic. When we speak of "valid reasons" in Buddhist logic, we are speaking about *saddhetu, rtags yang dag*, literally "real reasons" or "good reasons." [See chapter 5, n. 40.]) If we want to judge a *parārthānumāna*'s merits, the main question is whether the reason possesses the triple characterization *(trairūpya):* we can and do judge a *parārthānumāna* without even examining the "necessity" of its "conclusion" at all. Granted in PS and the earlier works of Dharmakīrti the thesis may be present, with the result that a *parārthānumāna* can be judged faulty if there are *pakṣābhāsa*. But this was little more than an inessential transitional stage. The gradual elimination of the notion of *pakṣābhāsa* and the growing realization of the redundancy of thesis-statements indicate just how little logical role they played. The streamlined version of the *parārthānumāna* captures all the essential features which Buddhist logic demanded of it. Nor does the *arthāpatti*-version of the way in which a conclusion "follows" from the *parārthānumāna* in any way contradict my fundamental point: we *can* come to know the truth of the conclusion by *arthāpatti*, but in order to evaluate a *parārthānumāna*, the conclusion plays no indispensable logical role.

So, looking deeper at the respective ways to evaluate syllogisms and Dharmakīrtian *parārthānumāna*s we see that the conclusion has a completely different importance in the two sorts of logical forms. This is, in turn, connected with the fact that syllogisms and *parārthānumāna* play very different roles in widely differing accounts of argumentation, the former providing a type of derivation (à la T.J. Smiley), the latter merely giving a perspicuous presentation of the triply characterized reason, nothing more than a preliminary step to inferring a conclusion.

In short, the whole PS, Dharmakīrtian and post-Dharmakīrtian account of *parārthānumāna* is principally governed by their peculiar account of *sādhana*—something totally foreign to Aristotle—and it is in that sense that we could say that the fundamental incommensurability between between syllogisms and *parārthānumāna* stems from two different philosophies of logic, or metalogics. The supposed similarity between Aristotelian syllogisms and the Dharmakīrtian *parārthānumāna* is only correct, then, in a trivial sense. No doubt, conclusions do follow from *parārthānumānas*: they are forbidden in the statement of the *parārthānumāna* itself not because they are *non-sequiturs*, but for metalogical considerations about *sādhana*, i.e., about how logic works.

In my 1984 article I insisted upon this incommensurability between syllogisms and *parārthānumāna* not out of nit-picking compulsion for detail, but rather because if we satisfy ourselves with superficial similarities of the sort which van Bijlert presents we blur the philosophically interesting points where Buddhist logic is *sui generis*. Thus we preclude meaningful, informed attempts at comparative philosophy and content ourselves with a few platitudes. Naturally, if someone wishes to use the word "syllogism" in a new sense and is conscious that the *parārthānumāna* is very different from an Aristotelian syllogism, I'll give him the word. There's clearly no harm here in adhering to Humpty Dumpty's philosophy of language and letting a word mean "just what we choose it to mean—neither more nor less."[26] Far be it from me to prevent writers on Buddhist logic from using "syllogism" in their own way, just as they use "epistemology" to categorize what Dharmakīrti and company did, even though that use of the term bears little resemblance to Western notions of "epistemology" or "Erkenntnistheorie," terms which were developed by neo-Kantians in the nineteenth century.[27] But unfortunately, our secondary literature from Vidyabhusana to Stcherbatsky and onward to van Bijlert is full of evidence that people *did* indeed see *parārthānumāna* as being a kind of quasi-Aristotelian syllogism. And that, I maintain, is a bad misunderstanding.

Notes for Chapter 4

1 Tillemans (1984b).

2 Although the Naiyāyika's five-membered reasoning states the thesis *(pratijñā)* and conclusion *(nigamana)* as two separate members, for our purposes in talking about the Buddhist's two- and three-membered *parārthānumānas* we shall use the English words "thesis" and "conclusion" interchangeably as referring to what is being proven—this allows for an easier comparison with conclusions in Aristotelian syllogisms. So, it should

be stressed that we are not using "conclusion" in the Naiyāyika's particular technical sense of *nigamana*, where it would be something different from *pratijñā*. That said, note, however, that Dharmakīrti's arguments against *pakṣa* / *pratijñā* do apply to the Naiyāyika's *nigamana* too.

3 Cf. Dignāga's definition in PS III, k.1: *parārthānumānaṃ tu svadṛṣṭārtha-prakāśanam* // "An inference-for-others, however, elucidates the state of affairs which [the proponent] has understood himself." The commentators are unanimous in taking *svadṛṣṭārtha* as meaning the triply characterized reason. See Tillemans (1984b: 83ff.). On *artha* in *svadṛṣṭārtha* see PV IV, k. 13–14 trans. in Tillemans (1986c: 159–60). Cf. also NB III,1: *trirūpa-liṅgākhyānaṃ parārthānumānam* // "An inference-for-others is a statement of the triply characterized reason." On the triply characterized reason alone being *sādhana* and having the power to prove the thesis, cf. PV IV, k. 16, 17ab and k. 20 trans. and ed. in Tillemans (1987).

> PV IV, k. 16: *tat pakṣavacanaṃ vaktur abhiprāyanivedane / pramāṇaṃ saṃśayotpattes tataḥ sākṣān na sādhanam* // "So the thesis-statement is a means of valid cognition *(pramāṇa)* for revealing the speaker's intention. [But] as doubt arises from it [as to whether the thesis is true or not], it is not directly *(sākṣāt)* a *sādhana*."
>
> PV IV, k. 17ab: *sādhyasyaivābhidhānena pāraṃparyeṇa nāpy alam* /. "In stating merely the *sādhya*, [the thesis-statement] cannot, even indirectly, [establish it].
>
> PV IV, k. 20: *antaraṅgaṃ tu sāmarthyaṃ triṣu rūpeṣu saṃsthitam / tatra smṛtisamādhānaṃ tadvacasy eva saṃsthitam* // "The intrinsic capability [to prove the thesis], however, is really in the three characteristics *(rūpa)*. Only the statement of the *[trirūpaliṅga]* can really kindle the memory of that [viz., of the *trirūpaliṅga*'s capacity to prove the *sādhya*]."

4 See VN 64, 3–4. *tasmād vyartham eva sādhanavākye pratijñāvacanopādānaṃ vādino nigrahasthānam*. There are two sorts of *nigrahasthāna* spoken about in VN: *asādhanāṅgavacana* and *adoṣodbhāvana* ("not indicating the fault"). As M.T. Much points out in his article on *nigrahasthāna* in Dharmakīrti (1986:135), *asādhanāṅgavacana* is given a double interpretation depending upon where one places the negation, viz., "the non-statement of a member which is a means of proof" or "the statement of a member which is not a means of proof." The statement of a *pratijñā* falls into this latter category. See also n. 11 below.

5 See R. Hayes (1988:310). One finds a similar position throughout the book of R. Herzberger (1986). I argue against both in chapter 1 and Appendix I of Tillemans (1990).

6 *hetvarthaviṣayatvena tadaśaktoktir īritā* // "The statement of that [viz., the *sādhya*] which is powerless is explained as having the goal of the reason as its object."

7 Dharmakīrti argues at length against the view that the thesis-statement provides some sort of indispensable orientation for a *parārthānumāna* (see e.g., PV IV, k. 21–22) and is thus indirectly a *sādhana*. See PV, IV k. 21ab:

> *akhyāpite hi viṣaye hetuvṛtter asaṃbhavāt / viṣayakhyāpanād eva siddhau cet tasya śaktatā* //"[Objection:] If the aim *(viṣaya)* [of the reason] were not stated, then indeed the reason could not occur. Thus, as it does in fact make the aim known, the [thesis-statement] is [indirectly] capable of establishing [the *sādhya*]."

One can read PV IV, k. 21 and the reply *uktam atra* ("This has already been answered") as no more than a restatement of Dignāga's denial of *sādhana*-status to the thesis. The rest of k. 22 would then be Dharmakīrti's additional position that the thesis is understood by *arthāpatti*. Indeed, it is probable that PV IV, k. 21 is an opponent's interpretation of PS III, k. 1cd's phrase *hetvarthaviṣaya*: PVBh 490.17–18, at least, takes it in this way and subsequently shows that what the opponent is saying is that because a statement of a thesis is a necessary condition for stating the reason, this thesis-statement also has probative power and is hence a *sādhana*. The indirect "power" to establish the *sādhya* by showing the aim *(viṣaya)* is rejected as leading to various already explained (see k. 19) absurd consequences, notably, that one would be forced to accept a bloated *parārthānumāna* of ten members, including the proposition which is doubted *(saṃśaya)*, what we wished to know *(jijñāsā)*, etc., etc. If the thesis-statement shows the aim *(viṣaya)* and is thus a *sādhana* for the *parārthānumāna*, the other indispensable conditions should also have membership and be *sādhana*.

8 See Inami (1991).

9 P. 288a.

10 For a definition of *arthāpatti* see Mimaki (1976: 42), "...[L]a présomption est la façon dont le fait 'B' est déduit à partir de l'expérience réelle du fait 'A' et du jugement que le fait 'A' n'est pas possible autrement *(anyathā-*

nupapatti) qu'en présumant un fait tel que 'B'." Compare Dharmottara's gloss on NB's *sāmarthyāt* (NBT 175, 2–3):

> *yadi ca sādhyadharmas tatra sādhyadharmiṇi na bhavet sādhanadharmo na bhavet / sādhyaniyatatvāt tasya sādhanadharmasyeti sāmarthyam //* "If the property to be proved did not exist there in the subject of what is to be proved, then the property which is the prover [i.e., the reason] would not exist [either]. Since this property which is the prover is connected to that which is to be proved, we thus speak of 'implication.'"

The existence of the state of affairs corresponding to the conclusion can be presumed from the fact that the reason exists, i.e., possesses the three characters. For a translation of PV IV, k. 22, see Tillemans (1987).

11 *atha vā tasyaiva sādhanasya yan nāṅgaṃ pratijñopanayanigamanādi tasyāsādhanāṅgasya sādhanavākye upādānaṃ vādino nigrahasthānaṃ vyarthābhidhānāt //.*

12 Sarnath ed., vol. 2, p. 247:

> *slob dpon phyogs tshig sgrub byed du bzhed pa ma yin na / phyogs chos 'brel ba bsgrub bya dag / brjod pa las gzhan spang bar bya / zhes pa ji ltar zhe na / slob dpon phyogs glang phyogs tshig sgrub ngag gi yan lag tu bzhed pa ma yin par thal / rjes dpag bya der bstan pa ni / gtan tshigs don gyi yul du 'dod / ces pa'i tshig de nyid kyis / phyogs tshig des phyogs sgrub pa'i nus pa med pa'i phyogs de ni brjod par bshad pa'i phyir / 'o na tshig snga ma'i don ji lta bu zhe na / de ni bsgrub bya'i chos la / bsgrub bya'i ming gis btags pa yin gyi bsgrub bya mtshan nyid pa min no //* "[Objection:] If the Master [Dignāga] did not accept that the thesis-statement is a *sādhana*, then how could he say [in PS IV, k. 6], 'Anything other than the statements of the *pakṣadharmatva*, necessary connection and *sādhya* is excluded.' [Reply:] It follows that the Master, Dignāga, did not hold that the thesis-statement is a member of a proof [i.e., *parārthānumāna*] because by means of the phrase, *tatrānumeyanirdeśo hetvarthaviṣayo mataḥ*, he asserted that thesis-statement states a thesis which [itself] has no power to prove a thesis. [Objection:] Well then, how [are we to understand] the previous phrase [in PS IV, k. 6]? [Reply:] It [i.e., the *sādhya* spoken about in k. 6] is the *sādhyadharma*. It has been metaphorically termed *sādhya*, but it is not the real *sādhya*."

13 *Vādanyāyavṛtti Vipañcitārthā* (p. 64, 22–24):

kathaṃ tarhy uktaṃ pakṣadharmatvasambandhasādhyokter anyavarjanam iti / nāsti virodhaḥ (/) pakṣadharmatvasambandhābhyāṃ sādhyasyoktiprakāśanākṣepaḥ / tasmād anyeṣāṃ pakṣopanayavacanādīnām upādeyatvena sādhanavākyavarjanam iti vyākhyānāt //.

14 See NM 1 and 1.1 in Katsura 1977:

> 宗等多言說能立 // "The thesis *(pakṣa)* and other terms are called *sādhana.*" 由此應知隨有所闕名能立過 // "Thus it should be understood that lack [of any of these terms] is called a fault of the *sādhana.*" (T. XXI, 1628 i 1a 7 & 10).

Cf. *Nyāyapraveśa* 2 (in Tachikawa ed.): *tatra pakṣādivacanāni sādhanam.*

15 See PSVa (Kitagawa: 470.7–8):

> *'dir yang tshul gang yang rung ba cig ma smras na yang ma tshang ba brjod par 'gyur ro //* "Here [in saying that a statement of a triply characterized reason is an inference-for-others], it was also said [by implication] that incompleteness *(nyūnatā)* occurs when any one of the three characteristics *(rūpa)* is unstated."

Cf. PV IV, k. 23 in Tillemans (1987: 151).

16 PSVa (Kitagawa: 521.18–522.4).

17 This equivalence was already noted by Tucci (1930: n. 79, 80, 81 and pp. 44–45).

18 van Bijlert (1989: 70ff and 88–90, n. 15).

19 Oddly enough, the actual reasons he gives are somewhat inaccurate. He says (1989: 90):

> ...I think he [i.e., Tillemans] is not quite right in saying that the absence of a thesis (on which his interpretation of the *parārthānumāna* as not being a syllogism seems to rest) is a fundamental logical and philosophical characteristic of the *parārthānumāna.* As we will see in my description of the *parārthānumāna* [on van Bijlert's p. 72], Dignāga discusses some sort of enunciation of what is to be proved *(sādhyanirdeśa)* in PS III.1cd–2, although he makes it clear that this is not a separate step in syllogistic reasoning as his predecessors thought.

Now, the unique use, in Kanakavarman's translation of the *Pramāṇasamuccayavṛtti* (see Kitagawa, p. 472.7), of the definition of the thesis *(pratijñā)*, viz., *sādhyanirdeśa*, found in *Nyāyasūtra* 1.1.33 is in itself nothing extraordinary and proves little about Dignāga's view on the thesis. After all, later in PS III, k. 3 Dignāga goes on to discuss this Naiyāyika definition's shortcomings and to reject it in favor of his own definition of the thesis given just previously in PS III, k. 2, viz.:

> *svarūpeṇaiva nirdeśyaḥ svayaṃ iṣṭo 'nirākṛtaḥ / pratyakṣārthānumānāptaprasiddhena svadharmiṇi //* "[A valid thesis] is one which is intended *(iṣṭa)* by [the proponent] himself *(svayam)* as something to be stated *(nirdeśya)* in its proper form alone *(svarūpeṇaiva)* [i.e., as a *sādhya*]; [and] with regard to [the proponent's] own subject *(svadharmin)*, it is not opposed *(anirākṛta)* by perceptible objects *(pratyakṣārtha)*, by inference *(anumāna)*, by authorities *(āpta)* or by what is commonly recognized *(prasiddha)*."

For PS III, k. 3, see PVSa (Kitagawa: 473):

> *bsgrub bya bstan pa zhes bya 'dir // grub pa med la don byas nyid // de lta na yang dpe dang rtags // ma grub brjod pa thal bar 'gyur //* "In this [Naiyāyika definition], *sādhyanirdeśa*, [the word *sādhya*] served the purpose of negating establishment *(siddhyabhāve)*. In that case, it would follow absurdly that statements of unestablished examples and reasons [must be theses]."

The fact that Dignāga cited *sādhyanirdeśa* is thus of no consequence for our purposes. The scholastic problem of the differences between the Naiyāyika definition and Dignāga's own definition of the thesis were also taken up by Dharmakīrti in PV IV, k. 24–26, as well as in PV IV, k. 164–68 and 171–72, but while the argumentation is complex and not without interest, it is not relevant for our purposes of deciding whether or not a thesis is a part of a *parārthānumāna* for Dignāga: the real question is "Why does he speak of theses at all immediately after giving a definition of *parārthānumāna* which supposedly excludes them?"

Finally, concerning Dharmakīrti's account of the reasons for PS III, k. 2, PV IV, k. 28ab states:

> *gamyārthatve 'pi sādhyokter asaṃmohāya lakṣaṇam //* "Although the *sādhya*-statement is to be understood [by implication from a *parārthānumāna*], the definition [of the thesis in PS III, k. 2] is [given] in order to avoid confusion."

In brief, following Dharmakīrti and his commentators, the point of the thesis-definition *(pakṣalakṣaṇa)* in PS III is to refute various wrong views on what theses are, some being the views which the Sāṃkhyas and Cārvākas exploited to prove various sophistical conclusions turning on ambiguity and others being the views on *pratijñā* which Naiyāyikas would use to say that properties of the subject *(dharmin)* which are merely specified in the proponent's treatises also count as part of the thesis. The more than one hundred verses which follow in PV IV treating of PS III, k. 2's *pakṣalakṣaṇa* have to be seen in this light.

20 Aristotle himself defines it as "discourse in which, certain things being stated, something other than what is stated follows of necessity from their being so" (*Prior Analytics,* 24b18).

21 See Kneale and Kneale (1975: 68).

22 See J. Łukasiewicz (1935) and (1957: chap. 1) for a comparison of the Stoic and Aristotelian syllogisms, the former being inference-schemata involving propositional variables, while the latter are logical theses of the form "if... then..." containing term variables. On the notions of "necessity" in Aristotle, see also Günther Patzig (1969: chap. 2). My information on Dr. Smiley's views is based on notes of his lectures of Lent term 1970.

23 See e.g., R.J. McCall (1961: 154–55).

24 Ibid., p. 155.

25 Ibid., p. 151.

26 Lewis Carroll (1974: 274 *et seq.*):

> "When *I* use a word," Humpty Dumpty said in rather a scornful tone, "it means just what I choose it to mean—neither more nor less."
>
> "The question is," said Alice, "whether you *can* make words mean so many different things."
>
> "The question is," said Humpty Dumpty, "which is to be master—that's all."

27 On the development of the Western notion of epistemology, see, e.g., R. Rorty (1980: chap. 3).

5: On *Sapakṣa*

SINCE DHARMAKĪRTI, Buddhist epistemologists have generally held that a reason *(hetu; liṅga)* is valid when it satisfies three characteristics *(rūpa):* (a) the *pakṣadharmatā,* the fact that the reason qualifies the subject *(pakṣa; dharmin);* (b) the *anvayavyāpti,* or the reason's occurring in only "similar instances" *(sapakṣa);* (c) the *vyatirekavyāpti,* or the reason's complete absence from the "dissimilar instances" *(vipakṣa).*[1] Although this much is by now thought to be fairly standard material for us, the second characteristic, or the *anvayavyāpti,* is in fact far from clear in much of our secondary literature, rendering surprisingly complex our general picture of the *trairūpya* theory of valid reasons and that of the fallacy of *asādhāraṇānaikāntikahetu* or "uncertain reasons which are [too] exclusive." The culprit is, as you have no doubt surmised, *sapakṣa.*

It should be of some consolation to us to know that many of the problems with which we are struggling on these questions were also hotly debated among Tibetans, in particular among the epistemologists of the dGe lugs pa and Sa skya pa schools. And indeed, I think that it is fair to say that many authors in the secondary literature, such as Stcherbatsky, Kajiyama, Tachikawa, Gillon and Love, and others, hold a position which, in its essentials, is not far from that of Sa skya paṇḍita (1182–1251) and the followers of the *Tshad ma rigs pa'i gter.* In that sense, one could credibly maintain that the Sa skya pa position embodies quite well what is for us the received view, or the "orthodox scenario" on the matter. The dGe lugs pa position, by contrast, seems startling at first sight, and even among Tibetans, Ngag dbang bstan dar (1759–1840) lamented that it appeared to be rarely understood.[2] It may, then, be useful for someone to play the role of the devil's advocate and explain this heterodox position. That is what I intend to do. But first of all we need to have the background.

The Orthodox Scenario

Here then, in broad outlines, is the Sa skya pa position as it is to be found in the *Rigs gter* literature of Sa paṇ and Go rams pa bsod nams seng ge (1429–1489),[3] and as it is portrayed by the opposition, namely the dGe lugs pa writer Se ra rje btsun chos kyi rgyal mtshan (1478–1546). (The latter author's work, *rNam 'grel spyi don*, is a commentary on the *Svārthānumāna* chapter of the *Pramāṇavārttika*, and in particular on rGyal tshab dar ma rin chen's (1364–1432) commentary, *rNam 'grel thar lam gsal byed*.)

(1) *Sapakṣa* are those items which are similar *(sa = samāna)* to the subject in possessing the property to be proved *(sādhyadharma)*.[4] *Vipakṣa* are all those items which do not possess this latter property.[5]

Corollary: S*apakṣa* cannot be identical with the subject, i.e., they cannot *be* the subject. Thus, sound is not a *sapakṣa* for proving sound's impermanence, but a vase is; *sapakṣa* are all those items which have the *sādhyadharma, except the subject.*[6]

(2) The terms *sapakṣa* and *vipakṣa* also designate respectively the "homologous example" *(sādharmyadṛṣṭānta)* and the "heterologous example" *(vaidharmyadṛṣṭānta)* on the basis of which the *anvaya* and *vyatirekavyāpti* are established.[7]

(3) When a reason is co-extensive with the subject, then it cannot occur in *sapakṣa*, which must by principle (1) be outside the extension of the subject. To take one of the standard cases, audibility (*śrāvaṇatva*), which is co-extensive with sound, cannot occur in *sapakṣa* for proving sound's impermanence; such *sapakṣa* do not exist, as they would have to be both audible and non-sounds. Alternatively, we can say, in keeping with (2), that there is no *sapakṣa qua* example on the basis of which the *vyāpti* could be ascertained. Of course, audibility is also absent from the *vipakṣa*, or the non-impermanent items, with the result that this type of reason will be said to be *asādhāraṇānaikāntika*—a special fallacy which is incurred when a reason is neither present in *sapakṣa* nor in *vipakṣa*.[8]

Now certainly points (1) and (2) are not without support in Indian texts. Dignāga, in the *Pramāṇasamuccaya*, had defined a *trirūpaliṅga* ("triply characterized reason") as a reason which is

> present in the inferendum (*anumeya*) and in what is similar to it, and is absent in what is not [similar to it].[9]

(Note that here *anumeya* designates the subject.[10]) And Mokṣākaragupta in his *Tarkabhāṣā* had explained:

> *Sapakṣa* are instances which are similar *(samāna)*, that is to say, subjects which are examples *(dṛṣṭāntadharmin)* that are similar to the *pakṣa* [i.e., to the subject of the reasoning].[11]

(Note the use of the term *dṛṣṭānta* in this context.) There are also, of course, some important passages from Dharmakīrti's *Nyāyabindu*—but these will be taken up later on.

Although the two quotations given above do not explicitly state the corollary of (1) that *sapakṣa* cannot also be the subject, it can probably be thought of as simply implied by the word *samāna*—a point which Gillon and Love make in their study on the *Nyāyapraveśa*.[12] The Sa skya pas, however, argue for this corollary in a variety of ways. Sa paṇ himself in his *Rigs gter rang 'grel* devotes almost half a dozen folios to arguing against an opposing view which maintained that *sapakṣa* and *vipakṣa* are directly contradictory *(dngos 'gal)*, or in other words, that whatever is a *sapakṣa* is not a *vipakṣa* and vice versa.[13] This position, according to Sa paṇ, held that all knowables *(shes bya)* were determined *(kha tshon chod)* as being in one of the two *pakṣa (phyogs)*, i.e., *sapakṣa* or *vipakṣa*, these being defined respectively as what does or does not possess the *sādhyadharma (bsgrub bya'i chos dang ldan mi ldan)*.[14]

To this, Sa paṇ offers a number of counter-arguments, some of which might seem somewhat arcane, but the main ones for our purposes are as follows:

(a) If the *pakṣa* (i.e., the subject) were also determined, or ascertained *(nges pa)*, as being in the *sapakṣa* or *vipakṣa*, as the opponent's position would imply, then there could be no enquiry *(shes 'dod = jijñāsā)* as to whether it does or does not possess the *sādhyadharma*. In that case, the definition of *pakṣadharmatā*, with its provision that the subject be something about which the opponent enquires, will become problematic. States the *Rigs gter:*

> Because he does not accept something enquired about as being the subject *(phyogs = pakṣa),* the first basis of reliance *(ltos gzhi)* [viz., the *pakṣa* of the *pakṣadharma*] would be nonexistent. For one who does not accept this first basis of reliance, the *pakṣadharmatā*'s definition will be problematic.[15]

(b) The opponent would be unable to term homologous examples *(mthun dpe = sādharmyadṛṣṭānta)* "*sapakṣa,*" because the latter would also include the subject—and the subject is *a fortiori* not a homologous example. (We have here a version of point (2). In fact, Sa paṇ is citing this version of (2) in support of the corollary of (1).) States the *Rigs gter rang 'grel:*

> If the basis of debate *(rtsod gzhi)* [i.e., the subject] is determined as being in [one of] the two *pakṣa,* then one will be unable to call homologous examples *"sapakṣa"; *for the basis of debate will also be a *sapakṣa.*[16]

Sa skya paṇḍita's adherence, then, to the view of a tripartite universe of *pakṣa, sapakṣa* and *vipakṣa* stands out clearly. What is also remarkable is that the opposing view which he describes, and which Go rams pa attributes to "various early scholars" *(sngon gyi mkhas pa rnams),*[17] is in fact very close to the position of the dGe lugs pas. We shall return to this point later on, but for the moment let us without further ado look at some aspects of the dGe lugs view.

Sapakṣa *Taken Etymologically and* Sapakṣa *Properly Speaking*

'Jam dbyangs bzhad pa'i rdo rje ngag dbang brtson 'grus (1648–1721), in his *rtags rigs* textbook, introduces a distinction between *sapakṣa* taken in the etymological sense *(sgra bshad du 'jug gi mthun phyogs)* and *sapakṣa* proper. *Sapakṣa* taken etymologically are those items which are similar to the subject in possessing the *sādhyadharma,* while *vipakṣa* taken etymologically are all those items which are not similar from this point of view.[18] In effect, then, the *sapakṣa* spoken about in the above quotes from the *Pramāṇasamuccaya* and the *Tarkabhāṣā* could—following 'Jam dbyangs bzhad pa's views—be taken as showing *sapakṣa* explained in its etymological sense. For that type of *sapakṣa*, the corollary of (1) might very well follow, although 'Jam dbyangs bzhad pa himself does not say anything either for or against.

At any rate, *sapakṣa* properly speaking, which is what must figure in the definition of the *anvayavyāpti*, is something quite different. Taking the sound-impermanent reasoning as a basis, he defines *sapakṣa* as what is not void *(mi stong)* of the *sādhyadharma*, and *vipakṣa* as what is void. He then goes on to say that *sapakṣa* for proving sound's impermanence is co-extensive *(don gcig)* with impermanence, whereas *vipakṣa* for this proof is co-extensive with non-impermanence *(mi rtag pa ma yin pa)*.[19] Later dGe lugs pa logic manuals, such as that of Yongs 'dzin phur bu lcog byams pa tshul khrims rgya mtsho (1825–1901), have similar definitions. *Yongs 'dzin rtags rigs*, for example, states:

> The definition of *sapakṣa* for proving sound's impermanence is: What, in keeping with the proof mode *(bsgrub tshul)* for establishing sound's impermanence, is not void of impermanence.[20]

"Proof mode" here simply refers to the verbs *yin (yin bsgrub)* or *yod (yod bsgrub)*. Thus, for example, if one is establishing that fire exists *(me yod)*, then the *sapakṣa* will be all those places where fire exists *(yod)* rather than all cases which are *(yin)* fire.[21]

We can, then, summarize 'Jam dbyangs bzhad pa and Yongs 'dzin phur bu lcog's characterization of *sapakṣa* and *vipakṣa* proper as follows:

> For all *x*: *x* is a *sapakṣa* for proving sound's impermanence if and only if *x* is impermanent. For all *x*: *x* is a *vipakṣa* for proving sound's impermanence if and only if *x* is not impermanent.

Now, given this view of *sapakṣa* proper, 'Jam dbyangs bzhad pa clearly does not agree that *sapakṣa* must exclude the subject. And moreover this type of (proper) *sapakṣa* will bear only limited resemblance to the *sapakṣa* of points (1) and (2), viz., *sapakṣa* taken etymologically. In fact, 'Jam dbyangs bzhad pa and Yongs 'dzin phur bu lcog both devote a number of pages in their *rtags rigs* texts to show that the two types of *sapakṣa* stand in a "three point" *(mu gsum)* relationship.[22] What this comes down to is that "*sapakṣa* taken etymologically for proving [some proposition] *P*" *(de sgrub kyi mthun phyogs kyi sgra bshad du 'jug pa)* is a proper subset of *"sapakṣa* for proving *P" (de sgrub kyi mthun phyogs).* (Here it might be useful to remark that Tibetan logic texts have means to express individual and propositional variables: *khyod* ("you") can be used in a manner similar to our individual variables *x, y, z,* etc., whereas *de* ("that") is used as a variable ranging over propositions or states of affairs, much in the same way as *P, Q, R,* etc. are used in formal logic. This is why I have translated *de sgrub kyi* ... as "...for proving *P*," rather than a strictly literal "...for proving that.")

Let us, then, represent the relationship between the two types of *sapakṣa* for proving *P* by means of the following diagram, all the while stressing that *P* can be any proposition one wishes so long as it is the same in both cases.

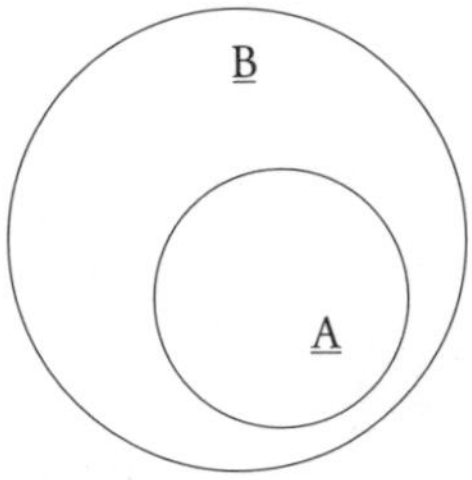

A = the class of *sapakṣa* taken etymologically for proving *P;* B = the class of *sapakṣa* (proper) for proving *P.*

The question naturally arises as to what Indian textual support, if any, can be found for this dGe lugs pa view on *sapakṣa* proper. It is interesting to see that in this context 'Jam dbyangs bzhad pa cites a well-known line from the *Nyāyabindu* (NB II, 7), one which also occurs in the *Nyāyapraveśa.*[23] The Sanskrit and Tibetan are as follows:

> *sādhyadharmasāmānyena samāno 'rthaḥ sapakṣaḥ //*
>
> *mthun phyogs ni bsgrub par bya ba'i chos kyi spyi dang don mthun pa'o //*[24]

The usual interpretation of this verse—as we see, for example, in Stcherbatsky (1930), Tachikawa (1971) and Gillon and Love (1980)—is to read the instrumental *sādhyadharmasāmānyena* as meaning "through..." or "by..." or "insofar..." I might remark in passing that although these authors prefer to take *sāmānya* here in its sense of "sameness," it would seem to me better to take it as meaning "universal," in the technical sense of the noun, all the more so because Dharmottara clearly contrasts it with *viśeṣa:*

> Now, what is to be proved is not a particular *(viśeṣa),* but rather, a universal. Thus, here, he says that it is a universal which is to be proved.[25]

If, following Dharmottara, we take the compound *sādhyadharmasāmānyena* as a *karmadhāraya,* it would then be better translated as something along the lines of "on account of the universal which is the *sādhyadharma,*"[26] and with this amendment the translation of NB II, 7 would become:

> *Sapakṣa* are things which are similar [to the subject, i.e., the *pakṣa*] on account of [possessing] the universal which is the *sādhyadharma.*

So taken, NB II, 7 would seem like a perfect specification of what the dGe lugs pa have been calling "*sapakṣa* taken etymologically"—however, that is not what 'Jam dbyangs bzhad pa seems to take it to mean at all. Here the divergence of interpretations is understandable if we compare the Sanskrit and its Tibetan translation. The Tibetan has (instead of the instrumental) ...*dang don mthun pa,* which can only be translated as "an object similar to ..." Thus, translating the Tibetan of NB II, 7 we get:

> *Sapakṣa* are objects which are similar to the universal which is the *sādhyadharma.*

'Jam dbyangs bzhad pa, using the technical language of debate and *mtshan nyid,* argues that this verse shows that *sapakṣa* (proper) includes both the "exclusion-universal" *(spyi ldog)* of the *sādhyadharma* and all that is similar to it, viz., the "exclusion-bases" *(gzhi ldog).*[27] These are technical terms in dGe lugs pa philosophy, and although a satisfactory explanation would necessitate an excursus into *apoha* theory, for our purposes the point can be expressed in simpler terms: *sapakṣa* includes the *sādhyadharma* universal itself and everything which has this universal. The subject can also be a *sapakṣa.*

But basically, though, to make a long story short, I do not think that we can easily side with 'Jam dbyangs bzhad pa in interpreting NB II, 7. Although there is nothing in Vinītadeva's commentary on the *Nyāyabindu* which would exclude such an interpretation (the Sanskrit is not extant, and the Tibetan naturally speaks of ...*dang don mthun pa*), Dharmottara's commentary does not support it; in fact, Dharmottara clearly justifies a translation such as that of Stcherbatsky, *et al.*, duly amended.[28] In short, although 'Jam dbyangs bzhad pa himself seems to find his textual grounding in NB II, 7, I think that we will have to look elsewhere.[29]

Curiously enough, it is Sa skya paṇḍita who provides the clue as to the Indian precedents for the dGe lugs pa position. (I say "curiously" because the dGe lugs pa are of course post-Sa paṇ.) Recall that earlier on, when we were discussing Sa paṇ's position, we spoke of a view which held that *sapakṣa* and *vipakṣa* are directly contradictory, that all existents are classifiable as either one or the other, and that *sapakṣa* and *vipakṣa* are respectively to be defined as what does or does not posses the *sādhyadharma*. Now, in the *Rigs gter rang 'grel*, Sa skya paṇḍita explicitly states that these definitions of *sapakṣa* and *vipakṣa*—and hence also the other two points, which follow from such definitions—were accepted by "certain people who followed the teacher Śāntipa" (= Ratnākaraśānti, a tenth to eleventh-century thinker who formulated the position of "intrinsic entailment" *(antarvyāpti))*.[30]

Indeed it is true that Ratnākaraśānti himself did put forward these particular definitions; they can be found in his *Antarvyāptisamarthana*.[31] Moreover, it turns out that the dGe lugs pa definitions, along with their consequences, are identical to those of the Antarvyāptivādins. Although 'Jam dbyangs bzhad pa and Yongs 'dzin phur bu lcog had phrased things a little differently, using the terms "non-voidness" and "voidness," it does come down to the same position. And interestingly enough, a few lines further on in the *Rigs gter rang 'grel*, we see that Sa paṇ himself speaks about certain people who took *sapakṣa* as being what is not void of the *sādhyadharma*, and *vipakṣa* as being what is void: he says flatly that this is nothing different from the other formulation *(de nyid las ma 'das so)*.[32]

It can be determined with reasonable certainty that some post-Sa paṇ thinkers, such as Nya dbon kun dga' dpal, did subscribe to Ratnākaraśānti's views on Antarvyāptivāda. Se ra rje btsun chos kyi rgyal mtshan quotes passages from the *Nya ṭīkā*—which is most likely Kun dga' dpal's now lost commentary on the *Pramāṇavārttika*—where the latter author endorses Ratnākaraśānti's views.[33] However, concerning the pre-Sa paṇ Antarvyāptivādins, whom Go rams pa characterizes as "various early scholars," I am unable to ascertain who they were.

What is noteworthy, though, is that while the Antarvyāptivāda definitions of *sapakṣa* and *vipakṣa* seem to have found their way into the dGe lugs pa school, the cardinal tenet of *antarvyāpti* did not.[34] Ratnākaraśānti had argued that for the intelligent examples were not necessary to ascertain the *anvayavyāpti*—it could be ascertained in the subject—and similarly, the fallacy of *asādhāraṇānaikāntikahetu* was only for dullards. Now, the dGe lugs pa do not subscribe to that. In fact, as can be seen from a passage from rGyal tshab rje which I have translated and included as an appendix, the dGe lugs pa came down squarely on the side of the traditional view of "extrinsic entailment" *(bahirvyāpti),* which maintained that examples were necessary and that the fallacy of *asādhāraṇānaikāntikahetu* was inescapable in the case of certain types of reasons. It is probably fair to say that as a unified, coherent system, Antarvyāptivāda caused no more than a few ripples in Tibet. While some thinkers before and after Sa paṇ probably did consider themselves Antarvyāptivādins, they were, it seems, the exception. The Sa skya pa generally did not endorse it, and the dGe lugs pa only subscribed to its views on *sapakṣa* and *vipakṣa,* which, as we shall see, they managed to harmonize with a version of the *asādhāraṇānaikāntikahetu.*

Chos kyi rgyal mtshan on the asādhāraṇānaikāntikahetu

Let us look at a few passages in *rNam 'grel spyi don* where Chos kyi rgyal mtshan debates with the Rigs gter ba, the followers of the *Tshad ma rigs pa'i gter.* First of all, Chos kyi rgyal mtshan presents Sa skya paṇḍita's fourfold classification of the different forms of this *hetu,*[35] the first of the four being the sound-impermanent-audible case, where, in true orthodox fashion, Sa paṇ maintained that the reason was completely absent from both the *sapakṣa* and the *vipakṣa.* Chos kyi rgyal mtshan then argues that such an *asādhāraṇānaikāntikahetu* just does not exist. Why? I quote:

> Because if something is an *asādhāraṇānaikāntikahetu (thun mong ma yin pa'i ma nges pa'i gtan tshig)* for proving sound's impermanence, it must be *present* in only *sapakṣa* for proving sound's impermanence.[36]

With a bit of reflection we can see that this does in fact follow from the dGe lugs pa notion of *sapakṣa* (proper): if something is co-extensive with sound, then it must be exclusively present in impermanent things, i.e., in the *sapakṣa* (taken dGe lugs pa-style).

Next, we get the Rigs gter ba reply:

> To that, the followers of the *Rigs gter* say: "There is a reason for saying that audibility is both completely absent in the *sapakṣa* for proving sound's impermanence and is also completely absent in the *vipakṣa*. For audibility is both completely absent from *sapakṣa* [such as] vases for proving sound's impermanence, and it is also completely absent in *vipakṣa* [such as] space. Therefore, all the preceding consequences [such as, *inter alia*, the nonexistence of such a type of *asādhāraṇānaikāntikahetu*,] do not refute [our position]. For, '*sapakṣa (mthun phyogs)* for proving sound's impermanence' and 'valid homologous example *(mthun dpe yang dag)* for proving sound's impermanence' are co-extensive *(don gcig)*, and 'valid heterologous example *(mi mthun dpe yang dag)*' and '*vipakṣa* for proving sound's impermanence' are also co-extensive. And [furthermore] if [one says that] there does not exist an uncertain reason *(ma nges pa'i gtan tshigs = anaikāntikahetu)* for proving sound's impermanence which is absent in the respective *sapakṣa* and is also absent in the respective *vipakṣa*, then there would be the fault that the text [i.e., the *Pramāṇasamuccaya*] which says, 'the *pakṣadharma* is present or absent in the *sapakṣa*' and so on, could not be accepted literally."[37]

To this Chos kyi rgyal mtshan offers two rejoinders. First, the equation between homologous examples and *sapakṣa* is faulty. If they were the same,

> then it would follow [absurdly] that a rocky mountain, which does not arise from effort, would be a valid homologous example for proving a conch sound's impermanence through the reason, 'arisen from effort', because it is a *sapakṣa* in such a proof.

After all, a rocky mountain is a *sapakṣa*, because it possesses the *sādhyadharma*, impermanence, but it cannot be a homologous example, as it is not an instance of the property which is cited as the reason, viz., "arisen from effort."[38]

Second, when Dignāga in the *Hetucakra* and the *Pramāṇasamuccaya* says that a reason such as "audibility" is completely absent in *sapakṣa* and *vipakṣa*, what he means, according to Chos kyi rgyal mtshan, is that the opponent who ascertains the *pakṣadharmatā* cannot, in this case, *establish* that audibility is present in the *sapakṣa* or *vipakṣa*. The point is that audibility is *in fact* there in exclusively the *sapakṣa*, but the opponent cannot *know* this without an example, and in this case an example is not forthcoming. Thus, we have the fallacy of an uncertain reason *(ma nges pa'i gtan tshigs = anaikāntikahetu)* in that the *anvayavyāpti* cannot be ascertained *(nges pa = niścita)* by one of the parties in the debate.[39]

Accordingly, the key moves in the dGe lugs account of the *asādhāraṇānaikāntikahetu* are that they make a split between their (redefined) notion of *sapakṣa* and that of homologous examples, and then they "psychologize" Dignāga's statements about existence and nonexistence as meaning "...knows that ...exists/does not exist." They can then argue that in certain special cases, such as the sound-impermanent-audible reasoning, where there is no example which differs from the subject, it is impossible (i.e., epistemically impossible) that the opponent ascertains the presence of the reason in the *sapakṣa*. (*A fortiori* he will not ascertain its presence in the *vipakṣa*, because it is in fact not there.) In this context, we should also stress that this interpretation of "existence" /"nonexistence" or "presence"/"absence" is certainly not just an invention on the part of Chos kyi rgyal mtshan, *et al.*, but finds some support in Dharmakīrti's *Svavṛtti* to PV I, k. 28 (the *Svavṛtti* passages are given in bold-face; the rest is Karṇakagomin's commentary as found on p. 84 of Sāṅkṛtyāyana's edition):

> *katham tarhy asādharaṇatvāc chrāvaṇatvaṃ nityānityayor nāstīy ucyata ity āha / **kevalaṃ** tv ityādi / nityānityeṣu śrāvaṇatvasya **bhāvaniścayābhāvāt** / śrāvaṇatvaṃ nityānityayor **nāstīty ucyate** //* "Now then how is it that audibility is said to be absent in both permanent and impermanent [things] because it is an exclusive [attribute]? [Dharmakīrti] answers: But **it is just**... etc. [It is just] **because** audibility **is not ascertained as being** in either permanent or impermanent [things] **that** audibility **is said to be absent** from what is permanent or impermanent."

Finally, as we shall see in the appended passages from rGyal tshab rje, the essential points of the dGe lugs account can be expanded and developed also to refute the Antarvyāptivādin—i.e., even if one dispenses with examples altogether, the opponent will still be incapable of ascertaining both the *pakṣadharmatā* and the *anvayavyāpti*. The basic line, though, remains the same: instead of asking factual questions as to whether or not the reason is present in *sapakṣa*, one inquires about what the opponent can or cannot reasonably know or think—in effect, the *asādhāraṇānaikāntikahetu* has been transformed into a problem of epistemic or belief logic.

Some Brief Remarks on the Formal Issues at Stake

All the preceding may still seem like a series of bizarre moves to one who is accustomed to the received scenario, but it is not, I think, without its merits, especially formal logical merits. (I cannot attempt a very detailed exposition here—only some guidelines—but the main arguments will be fleshed out in formal logic in the notes.)

First, it can be argued, as does S. Katsura (1983), that at an earlier stage in the development of Buddhist logic, *anvaya* and *vyatireka* jointly served as a type of inductive procedure, but that with the addition of the particle *eva* to the formulation of the *trairūpya*—following Katsura this occurs already with Dignāga's *Pramāṇasamuccayavṛtti*—and the requirement that there be a necessary connection *(pratibandha)* between the reason and the *sādhyadharma*, this inductive logic was gradually replaced by notions of entailment which were more rigorous and deductive in character.[40] It seems to me that the orthodox model of *sapakṣa* and *vipakṣa* and the *asādhāraṇānaikāntikahetu* would apply quite well to such an inductive logic; one "observes" that the reason is present in a number of examples/*sapakṣa*, and absent in various counterexamples/*vipakṣa*, and one then induces that a new and different case, viz., the subject, will also have the property in question.

However, applied to a *trairūpya* with *eva*, it can be shown that the orthodox model presents serious formal problems, not the least of which is that the *anvaya* and *vyatireka* are not logically equivalent.[41] Indeed it demands a most acute effort of logical acumen to see how the conclusion could be entailed at all.[42] The main advantage, then, of the dGe lugs pa interpretation of *sapakṣa* and *vipakṣa*—whatever might be its textual and historical grounding—is that it does overcome those formal problems. And moreover, in contradistinction to the Antarvyāptivāda approach—which would also avoid the formal pitfalls, but which would have to sacrifice the role of the example and the fallacy of *asādhāraṇānaikāntikahetu*—the dGe lugs pa can and do still keep these important elements of Dignāga's and Dharmakīrti's logic.

Appendix A: *from rGyal tshab rje's* rNam 'grel thar lam gsal byed

[Opponent:] It does follow that the *vyatirekavyāpti* is established in proving that sound is impermanent by means of [the reason] audibility. For, audibility exists in only impermanent things and never in what is permanent. If it were otherwise, then sound too would not be established as impermanent.

[Reply:] Now then, does a reason make [something] understood like a butter-lamp, i.e., by its mere competence, or does it depend on the ascertainment of a necessary connection *('brel ba = sambandha; pratibandha)* in the example [between it and the *sādhyadharma*]?

Taking the first [hypothesis], it would then follow [absurdly] that one could understand a *sādhya* simply by having a reason such as "producthood" come to be an object of the mind; for, it would make [the *sādhya*] understood in the same manner as a butter-lamp, which, by merely coming to be an object of the mind, clarifies forms. If [the opponent] agrees, then [we reply that] it would follow [absurdly] that no one would be confused about selflessness *(bdag med = nairātmya),* and that [all] would, hence, be effortlessly saved.[43]

But taking the second [hypothesis], then "audibility" could not be established as both the *pakṣadharma* proving sound's impermanence as well as the *vyatirekavyāpti.* This is because it would be impossible to ascertain the necessary connection in the example before establishing the *sādhya.*

[Objection of the Antarvyāptivādin:] To demonstrate the necessary connection to a dullard one does depend on an example. But the intelligent, even without an example, will remember the connection as soon as they see the reason, as they have previously established the entailmen*(khyab pa = vyāpti)* by means of direct perception *(mngon sum = pratyakṣa).* And given this [recollection], they will understand impermanence in [the subject] sound. So although an extrinsic entailment *(phyi'i khyab pa = bahirvyāpti)*, which depends on an example, would not be ascertained, an intrinsic entailment *(nang gi khyab pa = antarvyāpti)* would; hence, audibility will be a valid reason.

[Reply:] This is incoherent. For, if [the opponent] ascertains that things audible are impermanent, then he must also ascertain that sound is impermanent [in which case he could no longer doubt the truth of the *sādhya*, as the criteria for the *pakṣadharmatā* require].[44]

[Objection:] But then it would follow [absurdly] that audibility is not the defining characteristic *(mtshan nyid = lakṣaṇa)* of sound [as it should be possible to ascertain a defining characteristic and not ascertain its *definiendum (mtshon bya)*].[45]

[Reply:] This is not a problem. In general it is so that the two [viz., sound and audibility] have differing degrees of difficulty of ascertainment. But unless one discerns what the subject, sound, is through a means of valid knowledge *(tshad ma = pramāṇa)*, it will be impossible to prove the *pakṣadharma[tā]*, namely, that audibility is established in [sound] in keeping with the mode of presentation *('god tshul)*.[46] So if audibility is not a *pakṣadharma*, then it cannot be a valid reason. But when it is a *pakṣadharma*, then one cannot fail to ascertain sound once one has ascertained audibility. And then, after that, even if audibility might make the *sādhya* understood, it is not possible that one [i.e., the opponent] fails to ascertain that sound entails impermanence when he has ascertained that audibility entails impermanence. [Hence, he cannot have the necessary doubt of the *sādhya*].

Appendix B: Tibetan Text

(From the Sarnath edition [1974] of *rNam 'grel thar lam gsal byed*, vol. 1, pp. 54–55. My paragraphing of the text corresponds to that of my translation.)

mnyan byas sgra mi rtag par bsgrub pa la ldog khyab grub par thal / mnyan bya mi rtag pa kho na la gnas kyi rtag pa la nam yang med pa'i phyir / gzhan du na sgra yang mi rtag par mi 'grub par 'gyur ro zhe na /

'o na gtan tshigs mar me bzhin du rung ba tsam gyis go byed du 'gyur ram / dpe la 'brel ba nges pa la bltos /

dang po ltar na gtan tshigs byas pa sogs blo yul du song ba tsam gyis bsgrub bya go nus par thal / mar me blo yul du song ba tsam gyis gzugs gsal bar byed pa dang / go byed kyi tshul mtshungs pa'i phyir / 'dod na / 'gro ba 'ga' yang bdag med la rmongs pa med pas 'bad pa med par grol bar thal lo //

phyi ma ltar / mnyan bya sgra mi rtag par sgrub pa'i phyogs chos dang / ldog khyab gnyis ka tshogs pa ma grub par thal / bsgrub bya ma grub pa'i sngar 'brel ba dpe la nges pa mi srid pa'i phyir /

gal te rmongs pa la 'brel ba ston pa dpe la bltos pa yin gyi mkhas pas ni dpe med par yang / sngar khyab pa mngon sum gyis grub nas rtags mthong ma thag 'brel ba dran nas de'i rjes su sgra la mi rtag pa go bas dpe la bltos pa'i phyi'i khyab pa ma nges kyang nang gi khyab pa nges pa yod pas mnyan bya rtags yang dag tu 'gyur ro zhe na /

mi rigs te / mnyan bya mi rtag par nges na sgra yang mi rtag par nges dgos pa'i phyir ro //

'o na / mnyan bya sgra'i mtshan nyid ma yin par thal lo zhe na /

skyon med de / spyir de gnyis la nges dka' sla yod kyang / chos can sgra tshad mas gtan la ma phebs par mnyan bya de la 'god tshul ltar grub pa'i phyogs chos grub pa mi srid pas / phyogs chos su ma song na rtags yang dag mi srid la / phyogs chos su song ba'i tshe mnyan bya nges nas sgra ma nges pa mi srid la / de'i rjes su bsgrub bya go bar byed na yang mnyan bya la mi rtag pa'i khyab pa nges nas sgra la mi rtag pa'i khyab pa ma nges pa mi srid pa'i phyir ro //

Appendix C: Author's Remarks Added in June 1989

The present article was written in Hiroshima in 1984 and was destined for the proceedings of the Csoma de Körös congress in Visegrád, Hungary. Unfortunately, however, the Hungarians ran into various financial problems which delayed publication for a number of years, and in the interim—as frequently happens in these situations—I found some other relevant material on the problems at stake. In particular it turned out that Dharmakīrti, in PV IV (*Parārthānumāna*), supported the dGe lugs pa interpretation of *sapakṣa* and *asādhāraṇānaikāntikahetu* much more clearly than I had initially imagined when I wrote "On *Sapakṣa*" in 1984. In an article published in 1988 entitled "Some Reflections on R.S.Y. Chi's *Buddhist Formal Logic*," I discussed Dharmakīrti's position in PV IV, k. 207–59.

Now, "On *Sapakṣa*" has had a certain circulation in *samizdat* form in Japan, and some Japanese colleagues and friends have urged me to publish it as it is. This, then, is what I have done, although I am conscious of the article's inadequacies in treating Dharmakīrti's position. Probably the best and least disruptive way to balance the dossier which I presented in "On *Sapakṣa*" is to quote some passages from pages 160–61 of my 1988 article. The reader will see that when in 1984 I said that "this [dGe lugs pa] interpretation of "existence"/"nonexistence" or "presence"/"absence" is certainly not just an invention on the part of Chos kyi rgyal mtshan *et al.*, but finds some support in Dharmakīrti," I was being overly cautious. Here then are the relevant passages:

[Pages 160–61] "...Dharmakīrti, in *Pramāṇavārttika* IV's long discussion of the *asādhāraṇahetu*, does *not* support the orthodox scenario, but rather comes up with a version (similar to the dGe lugs) which would interpret this fallacy as being essentially a problem of an epistemic and intensional logic in that it involves contexts such as '*X* knows that...'

"*Kārikās* 207–59 of PV IV form part of a larger section loosely treating of Dignāga's *Hetucakra*, and specifically concern the refutation of the Naiyāyika's argument that living bodies have selves *(ātman)* because they have breath and other animal functions *(prāṇādi)*. Although Dharmakīrti does not discuss the sound-(im)permanent-audibility example very much, he does explicitly state in PV IV, k. 218 that the *asādhāraṇānaikāntikahetu*, 'breath, etc.,' is completely logically similar to the example found in the *Hetucakra (śrāvaṇatvena tat tulyaṃ prāṇādi vyabhicārataḥ)*. Here are some of the key verses along with extracts from commentaries.

"Context: In PV IV, k. 205 and 206, Dharmakīrti has been putting forth the recurrent theme that the certainty of the reason's being excluded from the dissimilar instances depends upon there being a necessary connection *(avinābhāva)* between it and the property to be proven. Such a connection will guarantee the pervasion *(vyāpti)*, i.e., the concomitances in similarity *(anvaya)* and in difference *(vyatireka)*. Thus, given such a connection, the reason would be excluded from the dissimilar instances, but in the case of the *asādhāraṇahetu*, such a connection cannot be established; hence there is no such definitive exclusion.

> Devendrabuddhi's introduction to PV IV, k. 207: [Objection:] If in this way the Master [Dignāga] did not exclude *(ldog pa ma yin na)* the special case [i.e., the *asādhāraṇahetu*] [from the dissimilar instances], then why is it said that it is excluded from the similar and dissimilar instances?[47]

> Dharmakīrti's PV IV, k. 207: [Reply:] It is just from the point of view of merely not observing [the reason among the dissimilar instances] that he spoke of it being excluded. Therefore [i.e., since the *vyatireka* is uncertain when it is due to merely not observing the reason], [the Master said that the reason] is uncertain. Otherwise [if there were the certainty that it is excluded from the dissimilar instances], [the reason] would be demonstrative *(gamaka)*.[48]

> PV IV, k. 220: By saying that [the *sādhana*] is excluded just from the contrary of what is to be proven *(asādhya)* [viz., the dissimilar instances], it is asserted [by implication] that it is present in what is to be proven *(sādhya)* [viz., in the similar instances]. Therefore, it was said that by means of one [viz., the *vyatireka* or the *anvaya*], both will be demonstrated by implication.[49]

"The point of PV IV, k. 207, then, is that Dharmakīrti wants to interpret 'absence in the *vipakṣa*' metaphorically: it does not mean that breath, etc. are in fact completely absent from what does not have a self, but rather that the debaters do not observe that breath, etc. occurs in things which have no self. But, although the debater might not see something, that does not necessarily mean that it is not there. In that sense, the debater does not ascertain absence, for indeed, as k. 220 makes clear, if breath, etc. were really absent in the dissimilar instances, then the *vyatirekavyāpti* would hold; hence, the *anvaya* would hold too, and the reason would be valid!

"So in brief, 'exclusion' or 'absence' is to be interpreted metaphorically as meaning 'nonobservation.' And precisely because nonobservation is not probative, the essential point of the *asādhāraṇahetu*, according to Dharmakīrti's interpretation of Dignāga, is that the debaters do not know or ascertain *vyāpti*, be it the reason's absence in *vipakṣa* or its presence in *sapakṣa*."

Note that this interpretation of "absence in the *vipakṣa*" is slightly different from what Dharmakīrti had given in the *Svavṛtti* passage which I had quoted in the body of my article (see p. 99 above). There Dharmakīrti argued that the reason, "audibility," was "not ascertained as being present" *(bhāvaniścayābhāva)* in the *vipakṣa*. (This *Svavṛtti* passage seems to be reflected also in *Yongs 'dzin rtags rigs;* see note 39.) In short, this view apparently construed "absence in *vipakṣa*" as meaning "no ascertained presence." In PV IV, however, Dharmakīrti is explaining the *asādhāraṇānaikāntikahetu*'s "absence in *vipakṣa*" as being an uncertain absence. The two explanations are not completely identical, although undeniably they do complement and reinforce each other.

Finally we might add the following philological observation in connection with PV IV, k. 220 which would seem to support the view that Dharmakīrti is rejecting the "orthodox scenario" in favor of *sapakṣa* and *vipakṣa* along the lines of Antarvyāptivāda. If we examine the Sanskrit of k. 220, we see that Dharmakīrti uses the terms *sādhya* and *asādhya*—Manorathanandin and Devendrabuddhi (cf. PVP 312b6–7) gloss these words as *sapakṣa* and *vipakṣa* respectively. In other words, *sapakṣa* would seem to be *everything* which has the property to be proved and *vipakṣa* would be *everything* which lacks this property.

Notes to Chapter 5

The orginal publication contains the following acknowledgment: "I should like to acknowledge gratefully financial assistance received from the Social Sciences and Humanities Research Council of Canada (program 461) enabling me to present this paper at the Bicentential Csoma de Körös Symposium in Visegrád, Hungary, Sept.13–19, 1984. Thanks are also due to Prof. E. Steinkellner of Vienna who read the paper with a scrutinizing eye and offered a number of useful suggestions."

1 For the different uses of "*pakṣa*" (i.e., thesis, subject, *sapakṣa/vipakṣa*), see Staal (1973). The question if Dignāga also subscribed to this type of formulation of the *trairūpya* with the particle *eva* ("only") is dealt with in Katsura (1983). For an oft-cited formulation from Dharmakīrti, see NB II.5: *trairūpyaṃ punar liṅgasyānumeye sattvam eva sapakṣaiva sattvam apakṣe cāsattvam eva niścitam.*

2 See his commentary on Dignāga's *Hetucakra*, p. 9a (p. 151 in *gSung 'bum* vol. *ka*): *de tsam go mkhan dkon par snang ngo /.*

3 For Go rams pa, I am relying on his two commentaries on Sa paṇ's *Rigs*

gter: the *Rigs gter gyi don gsal bar byed pa = sDe bdun mdo dang bcas pa'i dgongs pa phyin ci ma log par 'grel pa tshad ma rigs pa'i gter gyi don gsal bar byed pa,* and the *Rigs gter gyi dka' gnas = Tshad ma rigs pa 'i gter gyi dka' ba'i gnas rnam par bshad pa sde bdun rab gsal.* Cf. in particular the chapters on *rang don rjes dpag (svārthānumāna),* pp. 91b2–119a5 and pp. 223a3–278b4 respectively.

4 Cf. the quotations from Dignāga PS and Mokṣākaragupta given below. For the substitution of *sa* for *samāna,* see Kajiyama (1966: n. 165) and Durvekamiśra's DP *ad* NB II, 7 (pp. 97–98).

5 Cf. n. 29 below.

6 Cf. e.g., Tachikawa (1971: 135, n. 33): "Both the *sapakṣa* and the *vipakṣa* must be different from the *pakṣa.*" Gillon and Love (1980: 370): "That substratum in which superstratum S is and which is different from *pakṣa* is *sapakṣa.*"

7 Cf. the quotation from *Rigs gter rang 'grel* below (n.16). Note that point (2) is also reflected in modern authors; Mimaki (1976), for example, systematically translates *sapakṣa* by "l'exemple homogène."

8 Kajiyama (1958: 363), writes:

> "If the reason belongs exclusively to the minor term, as in the case of audibility which is supposed to prove momentariness of sound (minor term), no homologous cases which are audible and momentary are available. In this case we cannot ascertain validity of the major premise, 'Whatever is audible is momentary'."

(Kajiyama specifies that he means *sapakṣa* by "homologous cases" and *vipakṣa* by "heterologous cases.") Stcherbatsky (1930: 208, n.1) and Tachikawa (1971: n.33, p. 135) have similar formulations.

9 PS II, k. 5: *anumeye 'tha tattulye sadbhāvo nāstitāsati.* Sanskrit fragment preserved in Uddyotakara's *Nyāyavārttika* 136, 6. See Steinkellner (1973: 131).

10 Cf. PVin II, p. 30, 3–4.

11 *Tarkabhāṣā* (Mysore ed., p. 25): *samānaḥ pakṣaḥ sapakṣaḥ / pakṣeṇa saha sadṛśo dṛṣṭāntadharmīty arthaḥ /.*

12 Gillon and Love (1980: 370): "Also, it is reasonable to assume that the word "*samāna*" ("similar") restricts any two things to be regarded as *samāna* (i.e., similar, as opposed to identical) to non-identical things."

13 *Rigs gter* 18b4–19a4, SKB 5, pp. 163–64. *Rang 'grel* 132b–137b (for the *Rigs gter rang 'grel*, references are to the first set of numbers appearing on the front side of the folios), SKB 5, pp. 233–35.

14 *Rang 'grel* 132b–133a. Cf. n. 30.

15 *Rigs gter* 18b6–19a1, *Rang 'grel* 134b5–6: *shes 'dod phyogs su mi 'dod phyir / ltos gzhi dang po med par 'gyur // ltos gzhi dang po mi 'dod pa // 'di la phyogs chos mtshan nyid dka'//.* For the requirement that the *anumeya (= dharmin)* be enquired about, cf. PVin II, Steinkellner ed., p. 30. Both the Sa skya pa and the dGe lugs pa incorporate this requirement into their definitions of the *pakṣadharma*, by using the term *shes 'dod chos can* ("subject of enquiry") (cf. *Rigs gter gyi don gsal bar byed pa* 96b5–6) or *shes 'dod chos can skyon med* ("faultless subject of enquiry"). This latter dGe lugs pa term is defined in *Yongs 'dzin rtags rigs* (p. 17 ed. S. Onoda) as: *khyod byas pa'i rtags kyis sgra mi rtag par sgrub pa'i rtsod gzhir bzung ba yang yin / khyod byas par tshad mas nges nas / khyod mi rtag pa yin min la shes 'dod zhugs pa 'i gang zag srid pa yang yin pa'i gzhi mthun par dmigs pa /.* The essential point, then, which this definition makes is that it must be possible *(srid pa)* to ascertain that the subject is qualifed by the reason (e.g., that sound is a product) and still doubt or wish to know whether the subject is qualified by the *sādhyadharma* (e.g., whether or not sound is impermanent). Go rams pa and Yongs 'dzin phur bu lcog alike say that for the *pakṣadharmatā* to be satisfied, the reason must qualify such a "subject of enquiry." They both also speak of "bases of reliance" *(ltos gzhi)* of the three characteristics *(tshul = rūpa),* the "subject of enquiry" being the basis for the *pakṣadharma(tā),* and *sapakṣa* and *vipakṣa* being the bases for the *anvaya* and *vyatirekavyāpti* respectively (Cf. Go rams pa, *op. cit.*, 95a6–95b2; *Yongs 'dzin rtags rigs*, p.17 and p.19). Finally, I cannot help remarking that Sa paṇ's argument could probably be answered without too much difficulty by a dGe lugs pa: although it is true, he could answer, that in general *(spyir)* the subject is determined as being in one of the two *pakṣa,* the opponent himself does not determine that fact, and so can preserve his doubt.

16 *Rang 'grel* 135a3–4: *rtsod gzhi phyogs gnyis su kha tshon chod na mthun dpe la mthun phyogs zhes brjod mi nus te / rtsod gzhi'ang mthun phyogs yin pa'i phyir ro //.* Note that *rtsod gzhi* is another term for the subject *(chos can = dharmin).*

17 *Rigs gter gyi dka' gnas* 227b2, SKB 12, p. 114.

18 For the section on *sapakṣa (mthun phyogs)* and *vipakṣa (mi mthun phyogs)*, see 6b–13a (pp. 190–201 in *Collected Works of 'Jam dbyangs bzhad pa*, vol. 15 (*ba*)). Cf. also *Yongs 'dzin rtags rigs*, pp. 19–22. The fact that this question of the two ways of construing *sapakṣa* and *vipakṣa* is usually discussed in *rtags rigs* texts, which are introductions to *pramāṇa* studies for young monks, shows that this was an often debated topic in the dGe lugs curriculum. For *vipakṣa*, cf. also n. 29.

19 F. 8a (*Collected Works*, p. 191). Yongs'dzin phur bu lcog (p. 19) phrases the relationship in terms of *yin khyab mnyam* ("equal entailment"). *Don gcig* and *yin khyab mnyam* are not exactly the same notions—although for our purposes the difference can be overlooked here. For *yin khyab mnyam*, see *Yongs 'dzin bsdus grwa chung*, in particular the third lesson *(rnam bzhag), ldog pa ngos 'dzin. Don gcig* is discussed in Ngag dbang nyi ma's *bsDus grwa brjed tho*, p. 36. At any rate, whether we speak of *F* and *G* being *yin khyab mnyam* or being *don gcig*, it will follow that $(x)\ (Fx \leftrightarrow Gx)$, i.e., for all *x: x* possesses *F* if and only if *x* possesses *G*.

20 *sgra mi rtag par sgrub pa'i bsgrub tshul dang mthun par mi rtag pas mi stong pa / sgra mi rtag par sgrub pa'i mthun phyogs kyi mtshan nyid //* (p. 19).

21 Cf. *'Jam dbyangs bzhad pa'i rtags rigs* 7b. 'Jam dbyangs bzhad pa also uses *'god tshul* ("mode of presentation") and speaks of *yin 'god* and *yod 'god* in the context of *sapakṣa* and *vipakṣa*, which is perhaps slightly unusual, as these terms in other *rtags rigs* texts are more often reserved for the definitions of the three characteristics *(tshul gsum)*. At any rate, the idea is the same: one is explicitly eliminating possible confusions between the Tibetan verbs *yin* and *yod*.

22 *Jam dbyangs bzhad pa 'i rtags rigs* 8b–9a; *Yongs 'dzin rtags rigs*, pp. 20–21. (Yongs 'dzin's heading *(sa bcad) sgra bshad jug gi mu bzhi rtsi ba* must be an error.) Following 'Jam dbyangs bzhad pa's presentation, the three points are: (a) something which is a *sapakṣa* for proving *P* and which is also a *sapakṣa* taken etymologically for proving *P (de sgrub kyi mthun phyogs yin la / de sgrub kyi mthun phyogs kyi sgra bshad du yod pa'i mu /)*. For example, a vase, when one is proving that sound is impermanent. (b) something which is a *sapakṣa* for *P* but is not a *sapakṣa* taken etymologically for *P (de sgrub kyi mthun phyogs yin la / de sgrub kyi mthun phyogs kyi sgra bshad du med pa'i mu /)*. For example, unconditioned space *('dus ma byas kyi nam mkha')* when one is proving that sound is permanent. It is a *sapakṣa* for such a proof, because it is permanent. But it is not a *sapakṣa* taken etymologically because "it and

sound are not both similar in being permanent. Why? Because it is permanent and sound is impermanent " *(khyod dang sgra gnyis rtag par chos mi mthun pa'i phyir te / khyod rtag pa yin pa gang zhig / sgra mi rtag pa yin pa'i phyir /).* (c) something which is neither *(gnyis ka ma yin pa'i mu).* For example, a rabbit's horn. For an explanation of *mu gsum, mu bzhi, don gcig* and such structures in Tibetan debate logic, see Onoda (1979). Finally, it should be noted that both 'Jam dbyangs bzhad pa and Yongs'dzin phur bu lcog also sketch out a three point relationship between *vipakṣa* for *P* and *vipakṣa* taken etymologically for *P*.

23 NP 2.2 in Tachikawa (1971).

24 For the Tibetan, see the edition of de la Vallée Poussin, p. 3.

25 NBT *ad* NB II, 7: *na ca viśeṣaḥ sādhyaḥ, api tu sāmānyam / ata iha sāmānyaṃ sādhyam uktam /.*

26 Cf. NBT *ad* NB 11, 7: *sādhyadharmaś cāsau sāmānyaṃ ceti* ... See also DP. It would seem that Gillon and Love *(et al.)* have taken the compound as an instrumental *tatpuruṣa.* Cf. their denominalization (1980: 370): "*[tasya] sādhya-dharmaḥ [pakṣasya] sādhya-dharmeṇa samānaḥ ity anena [pakṣeṇa] samānaḥ arthaḥ sapakṣaḥ.*" Cf. also Stcherbatsky's translation (p. 59): "A similar case is an object which is similar through the common possession of the inferred property." Vinītadeva can be read as taking the compound as a genitive *tatpuruṣa: ... bsgrub par bya ba'i chos te / de'i spyi ni bsgrub par bya ba'i chos kyi spyi'o /* (p. 57).

27 *rTags rigs* 10b6–11a2. For these terms see the *ldog pa ngos 'dzin* chapter of *Yongs 'dzin bsdus grwa.* Tsong kha pa, in *sDe bdun la 'jug pa'i sgo don gnyer yid kyi mun sel,* p. 40, defines *ldog pa (= vyāvṛtti)* as:

> *rtog pa la rigs mi mthun las log par snang ba'i chos gang zhig / dngos po ma yin pa / rtog pa la gzugs su snang ba lta bu /.* "A *dharma* which appears to conceptual thought as excluded from [all] kinds which are dissimilar to it, and which is not a real entity. For example, what appears as form (= *rūpa*) to conceptual thought."

28 NBT *ad* NB II, 7 (p. 98): *sādhyadharmaś cāsau sāmānyaṃ ceti sādhyadharmasāmānyena samānaḥ pakṣeṇa sapakṣa ity arthaḥ //.* Cf. vol. *she* 59a2–3: *de ni bsgrub par bya ba'i chos kyang yin la / spyi yang yin te / bsgrub par bya ba'i chos kyi spyis phyogs dang mtshungs pa ni mthun pa'i phyogs yin no zhes bya ba'i don to /.* Note that in the Tibetan too, *phyogs dang mtshungs pa (samānaḥ*

pakṣeṇa) renders unambiguous the meaning of NB II, 7. (I should mention that 'Jam dbyangs bzhad pa's *rTags rigs*, in the edition which I have, reads ...*spyi'i don mthun pa* ...for NB II, 7, which must be an error.)

29 Note that in NB II, 8, Dharmakīrti defines *asapakṣa (= vipakṣa)* as what is not *sapakṣa (na sapakṣo 'sapakṣaḥ)*, and here Durvekamiśra glosses on NBT as follows: *sapakṣa yo na bhavatīti sādhyadharmavān yo na bhavatīty arthaḥ* (DP p. 98). Moreover, in NP 2.2 we find *vipakṣo yatra sādhyaṃ nāsti*, which along with Durvekamiśra's comment on NBT, suggests that all and only those things which do not possess the *sādhyadharma* are *vipakṣa*. This seems like what the dGe lugs pa are terming *vipakṣa* (proper). Certainly *vipakṣa* taken etymologically is different from this, as we can see from 'Jam dbyangs bzhad pa's and Yongs 'dzin's arguments that they have a three point relation *(mu gsum)*. Cf. n. 22. (Tachikawa [1971: 117], gives quite the same etymological explanation of *vipakṣa* as the Tibetan authors, saying: "*vipakṣa* means anything dissimilar to the *pakṣa* insofar as it does not possess the *sādhya*.") All this could, then, provide a certain amount of ammunition for a dGe lugs pa argument that there are notions of *sapakṣa* and *vipakṣa* proper in Dharmakīrti.

30 *Rang 'grel* 132b4–5: *kha cig slob dpon śānti pa'i rjes su 'brangs nas bsgrub bya'i chos dang ldan pa mthun phyogs / mi ldan pa mi mthun phyogs zhes zer la /*. For *antarvyāpti*, see Kajiyama (1958), Mimaki (1976).

31 *Antarvyāptisamarthana* (ed. H. Shāstrī p.112, lines 17–18: *sādhyadharma-yuktaḥ sarvaḥ sāmānyena sapakṣaḥ, atadyuktaś cāsapakṣa iti /*. See Kajiyama (1999: 100 and 127).

32 *Rang 'grel* 133a1: *kha cig bsgrub bya'i chos kyis stong mi stong la 'dod na'ang de nyid las ma 'das so /*.

33 *rNam 'grel spyi don* 81b2–4:

> *de ltar yang* nya ṭīkā *las /* chos bram ze *gnyis kyis mnyan bya sgra mi rtag par bsgrub pa'i rtags yang dag ma yin par bshad /* rgyal dbang blo *dang* śānti pas *rtags yang dag tu bshad do // zhes dang / yang* nya ṭīkā *las mkhas grub* śānti pa* *yang rmongs pa la dpe dgos / mkhas pa la mi dgos pas mnyan bya sgra mi rtag par bsgrub pa'i rtags yang dag yin par* ***mkhas pa rnams la ni / gtan tshigs 'ba' zhig brjod par zad*** *ces pas bstan zhes nang gi khyab par*** *bshad de / legs sam snyam mo zhes bshad /*. *Should be śānti pas (?) ** The text has *khyad par*. "In this vein, too, the *Nya Ṭīkā* states: 'Dharmottara and the brahmin

[Śaṅkaranandana] both explained that audibility was not a valid reason for proving that sound is impermanent; Jinendrabuddhi and Śāntipa explained that it was a valid reason.' And the *Nya Ṭīkā* also says: 'The scholar Śāntipa, though, explained *antarvyāpti,* saying that by [*Pramāṇavārttika, Svārthānumāna* chapter, k. 27 which states:] "To the intelligent one should just state the reason alone," it had been taught that since it is dullards who need examples, but not the intelligent, then audibility is a valid reason for proving sound's impermanence. I think that [this view] is correct.'"

The Sanskrit of the portion cited from k.27 is: *viduṣāṃ vācyo hetur eva hi kevalaḥ.* Note that Miyasaka's edition of the Tibetan incorrectly opts for the variant *'ga' zhig* instead of *'ba' zhig (= kevala).* For what little information there is on Nya dbon (i.e., the nephew of a certain Nya dge bshes dar ma rin chen), see van der Kuijp (1983, n.360), who bases his information in part on a mention of this author in A khu shes rab rgya mtsho's *Tho yig,* no. 11851. Nya dbon kun dga' dpal, whom van der Kuijp dates as circa 1300–1380, played an important role in the Sa skya pa lineage of the *Pramāṇavārttika,* and is also mentioned in Tāranātha's lineage of the Profound "Other-voidness" teachings *(zab mo gzhan stong dbu ma'i brgyud 'debs)* (*ibid.*, pp. 41 and 118). Of interest is the fact that Nya dbon mentions Jinendrabuddhi as holding that audibility was a valid reason for proving sound's impermanence. (Chos kyi rgyal mtshan, 81a, seconds this.) In fact, it seems that Nya dbon and Chos kyi rgyal mtshan were probably right on this score. In Jinendrabuddhi's commentary on PS II, k. 5cd (PST re 105b3–5) we find the following suggestive passage:

> *de ltar na yang mnyan par bya ba nyid kyang mi rtag pa'i gtan tshigs la tshul gsum pa nyid du bsgrubs par 'gyur te / rnam pa gzhan du na ma yin te / de la de dang mtshungs pa la yod par gyur pa nyid yod pa ma yin pas so // rjes su 'gro ba ni yod de / rjes su 'gro ba zhes bya ba ni rtags la rtags can yod pa kho na ste / de yang mnyan pa bya ba nyid la yang yod do // de ltar ni gang du mnyan par bya nyid yin pa der mi rtag pa nyid du 'gyur ba kho na ste / rnam pa gzhan du na mnyan par bya ba nyid kho na yang mi 'byung bas so zhes rtogs par byed par 'gyur ro //.*

Thus, it seems that we should also probably consider Jinendrabuddhi as a predecessor of Antarvyāptivāda, or at least as tending in that direction.

34 Cf. the passages from rGyal tshab rje in Appendix A and Appendix B.

35 *Rang 'grel* 154a6–154b2. Sa paṇ characterizes the first sort as: *de la rtags*

gnyis ka la med nas ma mthong ba / dper na sgra mi rtag ste mnyan bya yin pa'i phyir zhes pa lta bu'o / "Here, there are cases where the reason is not seen in either of the two *[pakṣa]* as it is not there, e.g., sound is impermanent because it is audible." Cf. *rNam 'grel spyi don* 45b5–46a3.

36 *Ibid.*, 47a1: *sgra mi rtag par sgrub pa'i thun mong ma yin pa'i ma nges pa'i gtan tshigs yin na / sgra mi rtag par bsgrub pa'i mthun phyogs kho na la yod dgos pa'i phyir /.*

37 *Ibid.*, 47a4–7: *de la rigs gter ba rnams na re / mnyan bya sgra mi rtag par bsgrub pa'i mthun phyogs la yang gtan med / mi mthun phyogs la yang gtan med du bshad pa'i rgyu mtshan yod de / mnyan bya sgra mi rtag par sgrub pa'i mthun phyogs bum pa la yang gtan med / mi mthun phyogs nam mkha' la yang gtan nas med pa'i phyir / des na gong gi thal 'gyur de thams cad gnod byed du mi 'jug ste / sgra mi rtag par bsgrub pa i mthun phyogs dang / sgra mi rtag par sgrub pa'i mthun dpe yang dag don gcig / sgra mi rtag par sgrub pa'i mi mthun dpe yang dag dang / sgra mi rtag par sgrub pa'i mi mthun phyogs don gcig pa'i phyir dang / sgra mi rtag par sgrub pa'i mthun phyogs la yang gtan med / sgra mi rtag par sgrub pa'i mi mthun phyogs la yang gtan med pa'i sgra mi rtag par sgrub pa'i ma nges pa'i gtan tshigs med na phyogs chos mthun phyogs yod med dang zhes sogs kyi gzhung sgra ji bzhin du khas blang du mi rung ba'i skyon yod pa'i phyir /.*

Cf. PS III, 8:

> *phyogs chos mthun phyogs yod med dang // rnam gnyis re re dag la yang // rnam gsum mi mthun phyogs la'ang // yod med rnam pa gnyis phyir ro //* "The *pakṣadharma* is present or absent in the *sapakṣa* or both [present and absent]. To each of these also there are three, as there is also presence, absence and both [presence and absence] in the *vipakṣa*."

Thus, we get the nine reasons of the *Hetucakra.*

38 *rNam 'grel spyi don* 47b4–5: *rtsol* mi byung gi brag ri chos can / rtsol byung gi rtags kyis dung sgra mi rtag par sgrub pa'i mthun dpe yang dag yin par thal / de'i rtags kyis de sgrub kyi mthun phyogs yin pa'i phyir /.* * Text has *rtsol byung gi brag ri,* which is impossible!

39 Cf. the definition of the *asādhāraṇānaikāntikahetu* in *Yongs 'dzin rtags rigs* (pp. 53–54):

> *khyod de sgrub kyi ma nges pa'i gtan tshigs gang zhig / khyod de sgrub pa la phyogs chos can du song ba'i gang zag gis / khyod de sgrub kyi mthun phyogs la yod par ma nges pa yang yin / gang zag des khyod de*

> *sgrub kyi mi mthun phyogs la yod par ma nges pa yang yin pa'i gzhi mthun pa de* // "*x* is an uncertain reason for proving *P*, such that the person for whom the *pakṣadharma* is destined in the proof of *P* both does not ascertain that *x* is present in the *sapakṣa* for such a proof, and does not ascertain that *x* is present in the *vipakṣa* for proving *P*."

I prefer to translate the *mtshan nyid* expression ...*yang yin* ...*yang yin pa'i gzhi mthun pa* non-literally by "both ...and" instead of the cumbersome "common basis" idiom. As the Rigs gter ba had remarked, the dGe lugs pa interpretation of *sapakṣa, vipakṣa,* and the *asādhāraṇānaikāntikahetu* would necessitate a different, and non-literal, interpretation of the *Hetucakra*. And this is forthcoming, as we see in such works as Ngag dbang bstan dar's commentary on the *Hetucakra* (cf. in particular 7a and 7b = pp. 147, 148).

40 Katsura (1983: 541–40). I do not want to lend support to the fairly widespread view that the *trirūpaliṅga* can be assimilated to a Western formal logic structure, in particular, the syllogism. First of all, the *trairūpya* is better seen as a set of second order criteria used to evaluate an informal, ordinary language structure, *A* is *B* because of *C*. Secondly, although the *pakṣadharmatā* and *vyāpti*, when fleshed out as the two members of a *parārthānumāna*, do (formally) entail the proposition to be proved, there is much more at stake in the Buddhist notion of "validity" then just validity in a formal logic sense. Specifically, there is a cognitive element, viz., that both parties in the debate must also ascertain and accept the three characteristics. This provision is implicit in the word *niścita* occuring in the definitions (cf. n. 1). These and other questions of a similar nature are dealt with in Tillemans (1984b).

41 Bearing in mind the cautions of n. 40, it is still true that the provisions of at least the Dharmakīrtian *trairūpya* should imply the (necessary) truth of certain formal logic sentences. Let me adopt the notation of Mates (1972). Also, I would prefer to take the *pakṣa* ("subject") as a general term representable by a predicate letter, rather than by an individual constant. (If the subject is an individual such as Devadatta, this is no problem: proper names can become predicate letters à la Quine.) This accords better with the *ayogavyavaccheda* use of *eva* in the *pakṣadharmatā* definition. Cf. Gillon and Hayes (1982). *Hx* will be interpreted as "*x* has the *hetu* in question," *Sx* will be *x* has the *sādhyadharma*," and *Px*, "*x* has the *pakṣa*." Revising slightly Gillon and Love (1980)'s formulation of the supposed equivalence between *anvaya* and *vyatireka* so that the *pakṣa* becomes a general term, we get:

$$(x)\,(Hx \rightarrow (Sx \mathbin{\&} {\sim} Px)) \leftrightarrow (x)\,({\sim}Sx \rightarrow {\sim} Hx)$$

As Gillon and Love point out, this is not a necessary truth. But the situation is even worse than they depict: it should be apparent that $(x)\ (Hx \rightarrow (Sx\ \&\ {\sim}\ Px))$ is, under our types of interpretation, usually false, with the embarrassing result that on the orthodox scenario the *anvayavyāpti* will rarely hold. This seems to me inescapable on the orthodox scenario if we view *anvayavyāpti* statements as implying universally generalized material implications, as I think we probably must for the "post-inductive" stage of the *trairūpya*, where *eva* occurs.

42 From $(x)\ (Px \rightarrow Hx)$ and $(x)\ (Hx \rightarrow (Sx\ \&\ {\sim}\ Px))$, viz., the *pakṣadharmatā* and *anvaya* on the orthodox view, we could derive the *sādhya* $(x)\ (Px \rightarrow Sx)$. But we could also derive $(x)\ {\sim}\ (Px)$, which would be the absurd statement that nothing is the *pakṣa!* Taking *pakṣa* as a individual constant p, we would fare no better: Hp and $(x)(Hx \rightarrow (Sx\ \&\ x \neq p))$ imply $Sp\ \&\ p \neq p$, hence the unwanted consequence that $p \neq p$, the *pakṣa* is not identical with itself. Katsura *op. cit.*, n.16, has an interesting suggestion as to how to make the *anvaya* and *vyatireka* logically equivalent (on the orthodox scenario): "In my opinion, *pakṣa* should be excluded from the universe of discourse, so that the two *rūpa*s are logically equivalent in the domain consisting of *sapakṣa* and *vipakṣa*." Unfortunately, if "logically equivalent" means that the biconditional must be necessarily true by virtue of its logical form, then this biconditional should be true under all formal semantic interpretations, no matter what the domain. To hold that the equivalence statement between *anvaya* and *vyatireka* is only true on certain appropriately circumscribed interpretations is to credit Dharmakīrti *et al.* with no formal perspective or insight at all concerning this equivalence. Finally, note that all these problems are avoided on the dGe lugs pa and Antarvyāptivāda view of *sapakṣa* and *vipakṣa*. $(x)\ (Hx \rightarrow Sx) \leftrightarrow (x)\ ({\sim}Sx \rightarrow {\sim}\ Hx)$ is necessarily true, and $(x)\ (Px \rightarrow Sx)$ can be derived from $(x)\ (Px \rightarrow Hx)$ and $(x)\ (Hx \rightarrow Sx)$. Representing the *pakṣa* by the constant p, Sp can obviously be derived from Hp and $(x)\ (Hx \rightarrow Sx)$. No logical gymnastics, or even acumen, are required.

[Author's note: this article was written and published well before Oetke (1994), which takes up many of the same issues in considerable detail. It is impossible to discuss Oetke's views in any detail here. Suffice it to say that Oetke gives us a possibility of avoiding the above-mentioned absurdities by placing the exclusion of the *pakṣa* in the antecedent of the conditional rather than in the consequent. One of Oetke's formulations of *anvayavyāpti* is thus $(x)\ ((x \neq p\ \&\ Hx) \rightarrow Sx)$ instead of our $(x)\ (Hx \rightarrow (Sx\ \&\ x \neq p))$. See Oetke (1994: 24).]

43 Simply hearing or reading about a reason for selflessness would immediately bring about an understanding.

44 Cf. n. 15.

45 For some explanation on the Tibetan development of the theory of the defining characteristic *(mtshan nyid),* definiendum *(mtshon bya)* and exemplification *(mtshan gzhi),* see *Yongs 'dzin bsdus grwa bring*'s chapter on *mtshan nyid* and *mtshon bya,* or van der Kuijp *op. cit.*, pp. 65–68. Cf. also my review article on this latter book (Tillemans [1984a: 59–66]).

46 Cf. n. 21.

47 PVP D. 310a3: *gal te 'di ltar slob dpon gyis khyad par ldog pa ma yin na / ji ltar mthun pa'i phyogs dang mi mthun pa'i phyogs las de ldog pa yin no zhes bshad ce na /.*

48 *adṛṣṭimātram ādāya kevalaṃ vyatirekitā / uktā 'naikāntikas tasmād anyathā gamako bhavet //.* My additions in *pāda* c and d have been made on the basis of Manorathanandin's PVV (Sāṅkṛtyāyana ed.): *tasyādarśanamātreṇa vyatirekāniścayād anaikāntika ācāryeṇoktaḥ / anyathā vipakṣād vyatirekaniścaye gamako hetur bhavet //.* Note, however, that with regard to *pāda* a and b, this latter commentator strangely glosses *sapakṣād vyatirekitoktā,* whereas following Devendrabuddhi's line of thought, as well as the general thread of the argumentation, *vipakṣād vyatirekitoktā* would seem more logical. I have essentially followed Devendrabuddhi here. Cf. PVP D. 310a4: *gang gi phyir mi mthun pa'i phyogs la de mthong ba med pa tsam gyis ldog pa yin la / de'i phyir na ma nges pa yin no //.*

49 *asādhyād eva viccheda iti sādhye 'stitocyate / arthāpattyā 'ta evoktam ekena dvayadarśanam //.* For additions, see Manorathanandin, PVV *ad* k. 220.

6: Formal and Semantic Aspects of Tibetan Buddhist Debate Logic

What we shall term here "Tibetan Buddhist debate logic" or "*bsdus grwa* logic," and which Stcherbatsky termed the logic of "sequence and reason" *(thal phyir)*,[1] was something possibly invented by the twelfth-century thinker Phya pa chos kyi seng ge (1109–1169) and his school: one says "possibly" because no logical work of Phya pa survives, and in fact we can only conjecture that it was he who was responsible for its invention in his proto-*bsdus grwa* texts, the so-called "epistemological summaries" *(tshad ma bsdus pa)*.[2] From the fourteenth century on, various schools, such as the Sa skya pa in particular, used debate logic in their texts, but the foremost practitioners of this art were no doubt the followers of Tsong kha pa, the dGe lugs pa tradition.

This debate logic format, which consists largely of series of consequences *(thal 'gyur = prasaṅga)* along the model of "*...chos can ...yin par thal ...yin pa'i phyir*" ("...the topic, it follows that... , because..."), is what one typically associates with the elementary manuals on epistemology and eristics known as "Collected Topics" *(bsdus grwa)*, although it should be stressed that it is far from the exclusive confine of *bsdus grwa* manuals: most of the principal dGe lugs pa authors, such as rGyal tshab rje, mKhas grub rje, Chos kyi rgyal mtshan, *et al.*, regularly alternate between prose and debate logic format in their more extensive commentaries on the meaning of canonical Indian texts.[3] The actual *bsdus grwa* manuals, though, seem to make their first appearance with the fifteenth-century writer 'Jam dbyangs phyogs (mchog?) lha 'od zer (1429–1500), who wrote the *Rwa stod bsdus grwa.* Nonetheless, in terms of the concepts and terminology used, we see that almost all of *bsdus grwa*'s definitions and classifications were already given (in prose) in Tsong kha pa's (1357–1419) *sDe bdun la 'jug pa'i sgo don gnyer yid kyi mun sel* and indeed most of the "lessons" do most likely go back to theories of Phya pa himself.[4] 'Jam dbyangs phyogs lha 'od zer and other *bsdus grwa* writers' contributions, thus, were doctrinally fairly unoriginal, but consisted in recording debates in a more formal, stylized pedagogical manner, one which no doubt was closer to what transpired orally.

Now, the term *"bsdus grwa"* itself admits of a certain ambiguity, frequently being applied in a narrow sense to a group of texts containing in total approximately eighteen lessons *(rnam bzhag),* from an introductory lesson on colors *(kha dog dkar dmar sogs kyi rnam bzhag)* to the presentation of the *apoha* theory of meaning *(sel 'jug sgrub 'jug gi rnam bzhag). "bsDus grwa"* does, however, also have a wider sense, referring to these "lessons" plus a work on the varieties of cognition *(blo rigs)* and one on the logic of valid and invalid reasons *(rtags rigs).*[5] For our purposes, we will speak of "*bsdus grwa* logic" as a type of logical idiom: it is of course typically found in *bsdus grwa* texts, but it is also rigorously used in a genre of texts known as "word commentaries" *(tshig 'grel),* which paraphrase the verses of major Indian texts such as *Pramāṇavārttika* and *Madhyamakāvatāra* into debate logic format. It was, and still is, a commonly accepted medium for monastic students. No doubt at its best it contributed to a certain clarity; at its worst, it seems to have been used to give an appearance of rigor, dressing up dogma in the trappings of logic.

My proposal then is a relatively modest one: to examine basic formal aspects of this logic such as quantification, variables, and entailment and make some remarks concerning certain rather complicated semantical problems which arise in the interpretation of terms. Afterwards I shall bring out the classical character of this logic by examining a dGe lugs pa debate logic treatment of the tetralemma *(catuṣkoṭi),* a part of Buddhist logic which is often taken as a prime candidate for a so-called deviant, or non-classical, logic. The examples and explanations below are based on an examination of a number of elementary texts including *Yongs 'dzin bsdus grwa, Rwa stod bsdus grwa, Yongs 'dzin rtags rigs, bsDus grwa rjes tho* of dGe bshes ngag dbang nyi ma, the *bSe bsdus grwa* of bSe ngag dbang bkra shis,[6] as well as various dGe lugs pa commentaries which are in debate logic format or extensively use these means of expression.[7]

bsDus Grwa Logic as a Real Debate Logic

dGe lugs pa logic has by now received a certain amount of study, notably an early descriptive article by Sierksma, an M.A. and Ph.D. thesis by D. Perdue, the articles in Japanese by S. Onoda and two informative recent articles by M. Goldberg.[8] In Tillemans (1986b), I attempted an analysis of intensional epistemic statements in this system. However, what has yet to adequately emerge from this mass of brute data is the general character of the system: here, modern interpretors have tended to abuse terms, such as "syllogisms" and "sets," borrowed from Aristotelian or modern symbolic logic, as if *bsdus grwa* were somehow a fragment of an odd sort of deductive logic or set theory.[9] In fact, as one immediately sees when one looks at the Tibetan texts, or even at the data which Perdue, Goldberg *et al.* give in a generally accurate way, the logic is through and through a set of rules for conducting a dialogue; this is an obvious fact, but it means that *bsdus grwa* logic is *not* properly speaking a series of "proofs" (to cite Goldberg), "syllogisms" (to cite most writers on Indian or Tibetan logic), enthymemes, or derivations.

Indeed, recently we have seen a growing interest among logicians and philosophers in theories of argumentation and in so-called debate logics *in their own right*, an interest generally founded on the realization that argumentation, while it is to varying degrees translatable into formal logic, is not the same as doing derivations, and indeed that it exhibits fundamentally irreducible elements which deserve to be analysed without the distortions of translation into alien terms. J. Hintikka, E.M. Barth, L. Apostel, P. Lorenzen and numerous other philosophers writing in a wide range of languages have attempted to provide analyses of rational argumentation which offer alternatives to translations into elementary first-order predicate logic, and indeed some writers, such as Lorenzen, have even reinterpreted this elementary logic in terms of a formalized dialogue logic.[10] It is not my intention to try to present the various currents in this new domain of "argumentology," but to stress that the key steps which such theoreticians share is to conceive of argumentation and dialectics in terms of games, strategies, rights and obligations for the participants and finally, winning and losing. In short, to use Eric C. W. Krabbe's (1982) terms: If we present a logic in a "derivational garb," the "validity" of arguments will be defined as derivability in some system; if we use a "dialectical garb," "validity" becomes the existence of a winning strategy in a dialogue-game.[11]

It should be clear to anyone familiar with *bsdus grwa* logic, that the key terms such as *'dod* ("I agree"), *rtags ma grub* ("the reason is unestablished"), *khyab pa ma byung* ("there is no pervasion"), *ci'i phyir* ("why?") and so forth embody a system of moves, responses, rights and obligations in a rigidly structured game, a game in which certain strategies will lead to subvictories punctuated by the exclamation *tsha!* and, eventually, to a final victory marked by *rtsa ba'i dam bca' tsha*, "*tsha!* to [your] fundamental thesis."

It is unnecessary to restate all the rules and procedures of this game—others have already done that. To make my point about the particularities of a debate logic, suffice it to cite here the rules, rights and obligations governing "pervasion" *(khyab pa = vyāpti),* i.e., the entailment between the reason *(rtags = liṅga)* and the property to be proved *(bsgrub bya'i chos = sādhyadharma).* If a proponent presents a statement of the form *a* has property *F* because *a* has property *G*, his opponent is faced with three possiblities of which he must choose one: (i) he may say that he agrees that *a* has *F;* (ii) he may assert that *a* does not have *G;* (iii) he may assert that not everything which has *G* has *F*, or in other words: For not all *x:* if *x* has *G* then *x* has *F*. Should he choose the third option, the opponent will then be summoned to show a counterexample *(ma khyab pa'i mu),* viz., something which has *G* but does not have *F;* if the opponent fails to give anything at all within a "reasonable" time period, or if the example turns out to be bogus, the proponent will have the right to assert that the pervasion does indeed hold.

While we obviously can translate debates about pervasion into a natural deduction system, where we speak of premises, universal instantiation, etc., and where truth is defined in the usual way relative to a domain of objects, this loses sight of the fundamental fact that debate is an *activity*, where the ontological question as to whether there *is* a counterexample or not is replaced by the *practical activity* of seeking and finding one.[12] In short, a universally generalized conditional, "For all *x*: if *x* has *G* then *x* has *F*," is true in normal first order predicate calculus if there is no member of the domain which *in fact* has the property assigned to *"G"* but lacks the property assigned to *"F."* In a debate logic, one is *allowed* to assert the generalization if the opponent cannot follow a certain set of procedures and then find a counterexample. We shall look at the details and consequences of this type of view of pervasion, below, but first of all, by way of a preliminary, let us take up the problem of quantification and variables.

Formal Structures

Quantification and variables

First, it should be pointed out that language used in debate is a rather technical, artificial form of Tibetan, and in this idiom we find an extensive technical use of pronouns in a manner which is analogous to the use of variables. Indeed, it has been often said that variables are artificial languages' analogue to the ordinary pronouns in daily discourse. In the case of Tibetan debate logic, however, this parallel between pronouns and variables is even more marked, for the Tibetan idiom is itself artificial and the pronoun *khyod* which is used as a variable-analogue does not have its ordinary sense of "you," the second person pronoun standing for people whom one addresses, but instead usually stands for inanimate things and notions. So without any more ado let us speak of *khyod* and its cousin *chos de* in such contexts as being, for our purposes, the variables in debate logic: *khyod* is used when one variable is all that is necessary, and *chos de* (lit., "that *dharma*," "that element") when a second variable is called for. Propositions are represented by *de* (lit., "that") as in *de sgrub kyi rtags yang dag*, "a valid reason for proving *P*." In most cases when a predicate is monadic, the variable *khyod* will be dropped as unnecessary and cumbersome: *khyod* can however always be explicitly added, if one wishes to do so, and the reasoning functions as if it were implicitly present. For example,

(1) *sgra chos can mi rtag ste* (lit., "sound, the subject, is impermanent...")

could be phrased as:

(2) *sgra chos can khyod mi rtag pa yin ste* (lit., "sound, the subject, you are impermanent...").

In a dyadic predicate such as "*x* is the cause of *y*" *(khyod chos de'i rgyu yin)* or "*x* is identical with *x*" *(khyod khyod dang gcig yin)*, the variables must be used. (For more on the use of *khyod*, see Onoda [1979b].)

Now the obvious question to ask is: What is the purpose of continually saying "the subject" *(chos can = dharmin)* when stating propositions? In fact, it plays a very necessary role, but let me bring this out in two steps.

First of all, *chos can* is not really a subject marker, but rather a marker of the topic under discussion. (Readers of Japanese when confronted with *bsdus grwa* logic for the first time, invariably think of the Japanese topic-marker *wa*, and the analogy is apt.) In the usual sound-impermanent reasonings, "sound" is actually the subject, but if we take the Tibetan renditions of the classic Indian smoke-fire reasoning, viz., *parvato vahnimān dhūmāt* = *du ldan la la chos can me yod de du ba yod pa'i phyir*, we see immediately that in Tibetan the word "hill" is not a simple nominative as in Sanskrit, but rather has the *la* particle (viz., *du ldan la* ***la***). To translate the Tibetan literally we would have: "On the smoky hill, the topic, there is fire, because there is smoke." It is apparent then that *chos can* is indeed more like a topic-marker, rather than a marker of the grammatical subject.

This however is at most the beginning of an explanation. More interesting is to see the use of the marker *chos can* as indicating a special type of quantification. To see this more clearly, let us take a sample reasoning with *khyod* being used as a variable:

(3) *bum pa chos can khyod khyod dang gcig yin te khyod yod pa'i phyir* (lit., "the vase, the topic, you are identical to yourself because you exist").[13]

This then is a statement of the form, *F* because *G*, and naturally the proponent can ask whether the corresponding generalization or pervasion holds. We shall represent this pervasion as a universal generalization, viz., a statement of the form (*x*)(if *Gx* then *Fx*) which one should read as: For all *x*: if *x* has *G* then *x* has *F*. (I should mention that quantification must range over existent and nonexistent items—everything from vases to rabbit's horns. In another article I discuss the problems which this poses in the context of Indian Buddhist logic. I refer the reader to the discussion there for precisions on this problem; for our purposes it is not necessary to enter into details again.[14])

In Tibetan the pervasion of (3) becomes:

(4) *khyod yod na khyod khyod dang gcig yin pas khyab* (lit., "if you exist then you are pervaded by being identical with yourself").

Formalizing things, we could represent the predicate "exists" by "E!"

and thus come up with:

(5) (x)(if E!x then $x = x$).[15]

Now it should be clear that the variable *khyod* used in (4) also figures in the original reasoning (3). How then could we formalize (3) all the while showing *khyod* as being a variable? How, in effect, are to make the phrase "the vase, the topic," *(bum pa chos can)* be anything more than a useless appendage followed by an unbound variable x? The answer is to treat it as being a quantifier which binds variables in the usual way; however, instead of the usual existential and universal quantifiers, what is at stake here is what J.A. Faris (1968) terms "singular quantification." Consider the following:

(6) Ollie loves Nicaragua.

(7) Ollie is such that he loves Nicaragua.

(8) Ollie, he is such that he loves Nicaragua.

If we treat the pronoun "he" in (8) as a variable then we can see that "Ollie," in indicating the pronoun's antecedent, is in effect binding the variable. Following Faris, sentence (8) could be formalized as:

(9) (Ollie x)(x loves Nicaragua). Read: "Of Ollie as x, it is so that x loves Nicaragua."[16]

As Faris shows, this type of quantifier-matrix form for singular statements can be integrated into the fabric of first order logic without any special problems; in fact the main reason which one can see for not doing it in modern logic is that it is horribly cumbersome and does not really do anything that individual constants don't already do. But in *bsdus grwa* logic it does have explanatory power. Sentence (3) becomes

(10) (the vase x)($x = x$ because E!x), or equivalently,

(11) (the vase x)(if E!x then $x = x$)

From (11) we only need to change the quantifier to universal quantification to get (5). In short, *khyod* functions as a bound variable in both sorts of statements, the singular statements (3)/(10) and the universal statements (4)/(5): what changes is the type of quantifier which binds it. In the first case singular quantification is conveyed by the topic-marker, *chos can*; in the second case, universal quantification is conveyed by the idiom of "pervasion" *(khyab pa).*

A curiosity in Tibetan debate, which is worth mentioning as it brings out further the likeness between topic-markers and quantification, is the possibility of redundant quantifiers, that is to say, in this logic we can and frequently do find quantifiers which prefix formulae which have *no* variables whatsoever. The result is that the quantifier becomes redundant—just as can occur in modern predicate logic—because it fails to bind any variables.

In modern logic redundant quantification is a possibility, of course, but one of little practical importance. Not so for the Tibetans. To bring this out more clearly, let us look at the following examples:

(12) (*x*)(if Robert Johnson sang "Crossroads" then Son House sang "Death Letter Blues").

(13) (*x*)(if sound is impermanent then vases are products).

(14) ([the] knowable thing *x*)(sound is impermanent and vases are not products).

Obviously, for (12) to be true it is sufficient that either the antecedent (Robert Johnson sang "Crossroads") be false or the consequent (Son House sang "Death Letter Blues") be true. Similarly for the Tibetan-style example (13). It is interesting, however, to look at the manner in which this basically banal logical phenomenon presents itself in debate logic. Should an opponent assert the contrary of (13), the proponent will naturally say "Show me a counterexample," and here he will be asking for a statement prefixed by a topic-marker such as in (14). It should be apparent that whatever topic the opponent might choose as a candidate for a counterexample, it will be ineffectual, for the statements "sound is impermanent" and "vases are products" will remain true. Failing to show a counterexample, the opponent has to accept the pervasion.

In cases such as (14) Tibetan debaters regularly *say* that the *chos can* is *nus med* ("powerless"), although I have never seen this particular term used in a text. At any rate, it is quite an apt description and brings out the element of redundancy in that the *chos can* is not the antecedent of any pronoun in the subsequent proposition: in our terms it is redundant because the proposition contains no variables for it to bind.

Finally, note that in (14) the topic given was "the knowable thing" *(shes bya)* but in fact it could have been anything whatsoever, all be there a type of practical convention among debaters which leads one to use "knowable thing" as a virtual powerless topic of choice which is immediately recognized as such by competent debaters familiar with the "code." This redundant quantification, I may add, is what is frequently chosen to dress up doctrinal propositions in the trappings of logical rigor, as we see in dGe 'dun grub pa's commentary, the *dBu ma 'jug pa gsal ba'i me long*, where there are elaborate debate logic paraphrases of the verses in the first five chapters of the *Madhyamakāvatāra*, chapters which concern essentially dogmatic subjects having little or nothing to do with logical argumentation. Typically the powerless topic of such reasonings is represented by "the knowable thing," which is followed by two complete sentences with no pronouns or variables, the second sentence ending in *phyir* and showing the reason for the first.[17]

Pervasion for Tibetan logicians and pervasion for Dharmakīrti

At the risk of saying a few things which are becoming fairly well known by now, let us briefly look at the Indian Buddhist account of *vyāpti* as represented by Dharmakīrti; this provides a significant point of contrast to pervasion in Tibetan debate logic.[18] Specifically, two questions need to be examined: (i) What is pervasion in the two logics? (ii) How is it established?

Now, for Dharmakīrti, the key point is that the implication between a reason *(hetu)* and a property to be proved *(sādhyadharma)* must be founded on a necessary connection *(sambandha; pratibandha)* between the terms, be this a causal connection *(tadutpatti)* or one of essential identity *(tādātmya)*.[19] If there is such a connection, then it is certain that the former term entails the latter and it is *impossible* that there be a counterexample.

One might want to take "certain" and "impossible" in a suitably modal sense, one which is construed in terms of causal necessity or the necessity between two conceptually-fabricated distinctions (i.e., *sāmānyalakṣaṇa*) of the same real particulars *(svalakṣaṇa)*. Following this line, the temptation would be to say that for Dharmakīrti the terms *G* and *F* are in a relation of pervasion if and only if

(15) N (*x*)(if *Gx* then *Fx*)

where "N" is a necessity operator. In fact, though, it is not clear as to whether Dharmakīrti means *that*, or whether his point is more of an epistemological one, i.e., that one cannot know or be sure about the truth of (*x*)(if *Gx* then *Fx*) *unless one knows that there is a connection between G and F*. I am of the opinion that the epistemological version is a more accurate account of Dharmakīrti's thought, although in the final analysis one probably has to say that epistemological and logical aspects were perhaps inadequately distinguished. At any rate, the key position which he is opposing is primarily a certain epistemological stance, viz., Īśvarasena's view that pervasion is based on "mere nonobservation" *(adaraśanamātra)* of a counterexample. More exactly, what this means is that one could assert (*x*)(if *Gx* then *Fx*) with no *grounds* other than not seeing something which had *G* but did not have *F*. So, to simplify things a bit, let us provisionally say that pervasion *itself* in Dharmakīrti translates into the same universally quantified formula as in Tibetan debate logic: the important difference, as we shall see, is in their respective justifications for asserting that there is pervasion.

In point of fact, in Dharmakīrti's epistemology it is quite complicated to establish the necessary connection justifying the assertion that there is pervasion. How is one to know that such a connection exists and hence that there can *never* be a counterexample? In *Pramāṇavārttika* IV, k. 245–57 Dharmakīrti explains what later became a standard account of the method to establish causal connections: causality between *A* and its effect *B* is established when observations of previously nonexistent *B*'s are preceded by those of *A*'s, and nonobservations of *A*'s are followed by nonobservations of *B*'s.[20] As for *tādātmya*, identity, he argues in PV IV, k. 258 that this sort of necessary connection is to be established by analyzing whether the real nature to which the concepts correspond is the same or not. Subsequently, in the *Vādanyāya*, Dharmakīrti will use a different method.[21] But here in PV he relied upon a type of conceptual analysis. Here is k. 258 with Devendrabuddhi's introduction:

> Devendrabuddhi: "So indeed, the necessary connection between cause and effect is like this. The essential property *(rang bzhin = svabhāva),* i.e., the reason which is an essential property is as follows:"[22]

> PV IV, k. 258: "The necessary connection of the essential property is to be understood by considering the reason according to its [real] nature *(yathāsvam),* just like [the proof of identity *(tādātmyasādhana)*[23]] between perishability and producthood which was previously explained."[24]

So much for Dharmakīrti's stance. Of course, this view about necessary connections, and in fact all the basic features of Dharmakīrti's logic, were known to the Tibetans and were held in reverential awe as *the* guidelines on how to do logic. But while that may be so, the logic which they actually used, viz., the debate logic, was probably something which would have made Dharmakīrti wince a bit, particularly as it comes very close to the accursed *adarśanamātra* method of establishing pervasion. If we refer to the rules and obligations of this debate logic, we see that if an opponent challenges a pervasion (i.e., asserts the contrary), the proponent will say "Show me a counterexample!" In other words, in an actual debate, necessary connections and that sort of thing play very little role: a pervasion is accepted when one cannot find a counterexample.[25] No doubt the mixture of Dharmakīrtian theory and actual Tibetan debate is slightly schizophrenic, but it is probably true that the simplified approach to establishing universal generalizations is indeed what one finds most of the time in real arguments, be they among Buddhist logicians, members of Oxford debating unions or lawyers in an Assize court. Alas, nobody caught in the rough-and-tumble of debate can take much time out to do conceptual analysis of necessary relations between terms.

Ex falso sequitur quodlibet

Surprisingly enough, not only is it so that *in practice* Tibetan debaters did not need to ascertain a necessary connection between terms in order to establish pervasion, but this necessary connection is not even a strict *theoretical* requirement. Let us suppose that we have a statement of a pervasion where we are sure that the antecedent is false, e.g., the antecedent could involve an item universally recognized as being nonexistent, such as the barren woman's son, a rabbit's horn and the like. In that case it will be impossible to show a counterexample, not because of the barren woman's son's necessary connection with the term in the consequent (the barren woman's son isn't connected with anything at all!), but rather because there are no instances of such "sons." Once again, failing to show a counterexample, one must then accept the pervasion.

Consider the following formulae, the first representing a pervasion, the second showing the dGe lugs pa view that nothing, existent or nonexistent, is a rabbit's horn:

(16) (x)(if x is a rabbit's horn then x is impermanent).

(17) $\sim(Ex)$(x is a rabbit's horn).

It should be clear that (16) follows from (17).[26] Indeed, given (17), the consequent of (16) could have been anything at all: so long as the antecedent remains "x is a rabbit's horn," the whole conditional will be true. This is in fact a version of the medieval logician's principle of *ex falso sequitur quodlibet*,[27] a principle which has its correspondent in Tibetan debate logic:

(18) *ri bong rwa yin na gang dran dran yin pas khyab* ("if something is a rabbit's horn then it is pervaded by being whatever one can think of").[28]

The Medievals generally made a distinction between *consequentiae* whose antecedents were necessarily false (i.e., contradictory) or contingently false, a distinction which is not explicitly formulated in Tibetan debate logic, but the logical insight at stake here, while somewhat less elaborated in the case of the Tibetans, is turning on the same point.

Naturally, if a Tibetan has such a view on pervasion, exegetical problems will arise as to how he is to interpret Dharmakīrti's strictures concerning necessary connections. Their solution is to make a split between pervasion *simpliciter*, such as one might find in "consequences" *(prasaṅga)* used in a debate, and pervasion as the *anvayavyāpti* and *vyatirekavyāpti* in the context of the theory of the triple characterization *(trairūpya)* of valid reasons; it is only in the latter case that a necessary connection is required.[29] Frankly, I do not know how a consistent Dharmakīrtian would have to react to such a split, but I would go so far as to say that the Tibetans' separation of the formal notion of pervasion from its Dharmakīrtian epistemological baggage does, perhaps, represent a certain progress, in that they explicitly developed precisely those cases which show that the logical problem of formulating what we mean by saying that a pervasion holds is different from the epistemological problem as to how we we can know or come to be sure that it holds.[30]

Semantic Aspects

While the formal aspects of *bsdus grwa* logic, such as those which I have discussed above, can be explained with a relative degree of clarity and rigour, the semantic problems of interpreting what the individual terms refer to in Tibetan arguments are often nightmarishly complex. Margaret Goldberg, in two recently published papers, had the courage and patience to try to disentangle and classify some of these problems. She noticed that there are a number of rules where one can predict certain results providing the case is a "normal" one, or in her terms, "providing no contradictory condition is present."[31] *Prima facie* this might seem to boil down to the simple tautology that cases are normal providing they are not odd and seemingly inexplicable exceptions, but in fact there is more to it—she tried to give some rules which would explain when some of these "exceptions" occur. Unfortunately, much of her exposition is either an intrasystemic mass of data—largely correct, valuable, but as complex as the *bsdus grwa* arguments themselves—or involves an attribution of some alien and ill-fitting concepts. I think that we can and should simplify things a bit by diagnosing a few ambiguities and equivocations.

The basic problem in *bsdus grwa* logic which guarantees "exceptional cases" is the ambiguity of the terms used as topics. Thus, e.g., almost all young Tibetan debaters end up scratching their heads in puzzlement at the following pair of statements:

(19) *shes bya chos can rtag pa yin* (lit., "knowable thing, the topic, is permanent").

(20) *shes bya yin na rtag pa yin pas ma khyab, dper na gser bum chos can* (lit., "if something is a knowable thing then it is not pervaded by being permanent, for exam-

ple, the topic, golden vase").[32]

The oddity is that (19) is saying that "knowable thing," taken as the topic, is permanent, while (20) means that not every knowable thing is permanent—vases are knowable but are not permanent.

Goldberg tried to explain cases such as (19) by "the rule that says that any entity which includes a mixture of permanent and impermanent instances is permanent."[33] This is true, although it does not get us much further than merely repeating the intrasystemic reason which Tibetans themselves invariably give and usually do not understand either. Let us take up two more notions which she discusses.

(21) *mtshan nyid chos can mtshan nyid ma yin te mtshon bya yin pa'i phyir* (lit., "defining property, the topic, is not a defining property, because it is the object of a defining property").

(22) *mtshan nyid yin na mtshan nyid yin pas khyab* (lit., "if something is a defining property, it is pervaded by being a defining property").[34]

So, finally, what is going on here? First and foremost, we have the purely linguistic fact that Tibetan does not have a definite article and rarely uses the indefinite article or abstraction-designators such as the *-tva* or *-tā* which we find in Sanskrit. It might be objected straightaway that *tva*/*tā* do have their equivalent in Tibetan, viz., *nyid*, but while that is so for Tibetan translations of Indian texts, in indigenous Tibetan logic or in literary Tibetan which is not translationese, *nyid* is almost never used in this role. Nobody would say *shes bya nyid chos can* or *bum pa nyid chos can*.

If we do not use articles, it is of course difficult to know whether we should understand *shes bya* as meaning "the knowable thing [over there]" or "a knowable thing" or even "all knowable things" or "some knowable things." Lacking a distinction such as that between *jñeya* and *jñeyatva* we do not know whether *shes bya* means "a/the/some/all knowable thing(s)" or "knowableness." This, then, is the first element in disentangling the "exceptions" in *bsdus grwa* logic: in cases such as (19) the Tibetans are *not* meaning "an/the/some/all *A*(s)," but rather may be taking the term more in the sense of the property *A*-ness. More exactly speaking, it is *we* who have to take the term as meaning *A*-ness: they fail to make the distinction. At any rate, once we make such a distinction, the paradoxical quality of asserting both (19) and (20) vanishes, for the paradox arises if we take *shes bya* as implicitly meaning "all knowable things" rather than knowableness. Certainly, in Tibetan logic substantives must often be understood as meaning "all ...", but there are many cases where we have to take the Tibetan term as implicitly meaning the abstract property in question.[35]

Now, it should be of some interest to know that this sort of ambiguity is by no means restricted to Tibetan logic: the Medievals had a similar problem in their theory of supposition *(suppositio)*, a theory which I. Bocheński has termed "one of the most original creations of Scholasticism, unknown to ancient and modern logic."[36] For us it is impossible and unnecessary to enter into the details of the complete theory, a well-developed doctrine on which most every post-twelfth century logician had something to say. What is relevant to us, however, is the medieval logicians' attempt to explain the varieties of attribution and designation which one and the same substantive could have, and here a root cause of these logicians' problems seems also to have been that Latin too has no articles.

If we take the theory as formulated by the thirteenth-century writer, William of Shyreswood, the same term *homo* can be used to mean "a/some/all men," or "man" in the sense of the property or species, i.e., one can say *homo currit, [omnis] homo est animal,* or *homo est species.* The case which is of interest to us is the third one, where, according to William, the term *homo* "simply stands for what is signified without referring to the things."[37] This latter *suppositio simplex pro significato sine comparatione ad res* seems to have been somewhat controversial among the medieval logicians, but at any rate it was recognized that a term such as *homo* could in certain contexts refer to the property, or "variety" rather than any or all individual men: another term for this *suppositio* is *manerialis, quia supponit pro ipsa manerie speciei* ("manerial supposition because it stands for the very manner [i.e., specific character] of the species").[38]

Let us now return to the pair of statements, (21) and (22). If we take the term *mtshan nyid* as referring to the various entities which are themselves defining properties, then (21) will lead to the paradox that a/some /the/all things which are defining properties are not defining properties. However, taking (21) as a kind of *suppositio simplex sine comparatione ad res*, it asserts that being a defining property, or defining-propertyness, is not itself a defining property. To Sanskritize things, the point at stake may be taken to be that *lakṣaṇatva* ("defining-propertyness") is something which can itself be defined, therefore, it is the object of a defining property *(mtshon bya = lakṣya)* and is not itself a defining property.[39]

Curiously enough, although the Tibetans never developed a theory approaching the complexity of the Medievals' theory of *suppositio*, they do seem to be aware that a special type of reference is occurring when one uses terms as in (19) and (21). They will insist that what is meant is just "its own exclusion" *(rang ldog)* rather than the "exclusions of its bases" *(gzhi ldog)*, thus making use of Tibetan (?) adaptations of the terminology in the Indian Buddhist theory of *apoha*, a theory which holds that the referent of any word is always some sort of exclusion *(ldog pa = vyāvṛtti)* of what is contrary.

Nonetheless, the use of the term "exclusions" is not of crucial importance for us: the real point at stake is whether a word is referring *only* to the general notion or property (i.e., *rang ldog*) or whether it is also in some way referring to the things which have that property (i.e., *gzhi ldog*), in other words what the Medievals termed respectively *suppositio simplex pro significato sine comparatione ad res* and *suppositio simplex pro significato comparato ad res.*[40] While Tibetans will draw upon the terms *rang ldog* and *gzhi ldog* in an *ad hoc* fashion to explain away paradoxical cases (in that sense one could say that they potentially have the conceptual machinery necessary to construct a theory of different sorts of *suppositio*),[41] there is no clear attempt to systematically explain and generalize upon the fundamental logical differences between such statements as *bum pa lto ldir zhabs zhum chos skyor gyi don byed nus pa yin* ("vase[s] are bulbous, splay-bottomed [and] able to perform the function of carrying water"[42]) and *byas pa sgra mi rtag par sgrub pa'i rtags yang dag yin* ("product[hood] is a valid reason for proving that sound is impermanent").[43] And yet, obviously, in the first case there *must* be references to actual vases in addition to the reference to the *rang ldog*, whereas in the latter it would be incoherent for the term *byas pa* to refer to actual products of causality such as seeds, sprouts and pillars—nobody would want to pretend that a pillar is a valid reason for proving that sound is impermanent.

Ultimately we have have no choice but to diagnose ambiguities and equivocations, for if we remain rigourously faithful to what is written in the texts, the result will certainly be that we end up with a more or less incomprehensible logic of the sort which Goldberg, alas, accurately describes in her list of "puzzles." At any rate, we do not get far in our understanding by saying things like "the dGe lugs pas assume that there is an almost consistent universe," or by exaggerating the importance of a few *bsdus grwa* brain-teasers so that we end up with a "unique non-Western formulation of topics related to set theory including logical antinomies similar to Russell's paradox."[44] In fact, it is probably fairer to say that the dGe lugs pa generally were hardly confronted with the problem of inconsistency in a logic, largely because their debate logic was not sufficiently formalized so that this problem would arise clearly. What they were doing was nothing so elevated as the postulation of a "semi-consistent" universe: it was very often a matter of simply patching things up. In short, while it is not necessary to go so far as to say (as does Quine) that there can be no logics which really do deviate from the classical logical laws of contradiction and excluded middle, it is better to explain away the anomalous phenomena in *bsdus grwa* as resting on misunderstandings, equivocations, translational problems and the like.[45]

So much for the comparative philosophy approach to solving logical anomalies which arise in articleless languages.[46] There are other conundrums which arise because of the *apoha*-based view that entities such as *byas pa* "(product[hood]") and *mi rtag pa* ("impermanent"/"impermanence") cannot be identical *(gcig)* in some very strong sense of the term "identity." But I have developed these points elsewhere and will not again enter into the details of the Tibetan notions of identity.[47] What is perhaps of interest as a final section to this article, is to look at how the Tibetans used debate logic in their interpretations of a key Indian Buddhist doctrine, the *catuṣkoṭi* ("tetralemma"; Tib. *mu bzhi*). For the sake of brevity, let me presuppose a certain familiarity with the broad outlines of the Indian Madhyamaka and restrict myself to the position of the dGe lugs pas without making comparisons with other Tibetan schools, who, it should be remembered, did have very different positions.

The Catuṣkoṭi *as Seen via the Perspective of dGe lugs pa Debate Logic*

A classic Indian statement of the *catuṣkoṭi* occurs in k. 21 of chapter 12 of Āryadeva's *Catuḥśataka:*

> Existent, nonexistent, both existent and nonexistent, neither existent nor nonexistent, that is the method which the learned should always use with regard to oneness and other such [theses].[48]

As phrased in this way, we have denials that anything exists, is nonexistent, is both or neither. The commentary of Candrakīrti makes it clear, however, that this tetralemma also applies to other dichotomies, such as one/many, and so forth—in other words, it can be generalized to apply to any proposition *P*, and not just to the usual context of "...exists," "...is nonexistent," etc.[49] Ruegg (1977: 9) sums up the Mādhyamika use of this schema:

> This type of analysis of a problem thus constitutes one of the basic methods used by the Mādhyamikas to establish the inapplicability of any imaginable conceptual position—positive, negative or some combination of these—that might be taken as the subject of an existential proposition and become one of a set of binary doctrinal extemes *(antadvaya)*.

While one might somehow find a way to rationalize this fourfold negation, *prima facie*, it looks as if it would lead to a deviant logic, a fact which, of course, has not gone unnoticed by Western interpreters. If we take the negations of the four lemmas as being $\sim P$, $\sim\sim P$, $\sim(P \,\&\, \sim P)$, $\sim(\sim P \,\&\, \sim\sim P)$, then these four cannot be maintained together unless we grant that the negation operator is not that of classical logic: in other words, inter alia, $\sim\sim P$ cannot imply *P*, and other such classical laws cannot hold either. In point of fact, many Western interpreters are quick to say that the negation operator is not classical, that it is *prasajyapratiṣedha*, a type of negation which would not be bound by the law of double negation.

Now, indeed, in spite of Ruegg's excellent paper, the Indian *catuṣkoṭi* and *prasajyapratiṣedha* is, no doubt, a subject on which many writers will continue to seek interpretations, especially those who are philosophically cautious about embracing non-classical logics and negations. Fortunately, *that* problem need not be solved here; what is of interest to us now is the fact that the dGe lugs clearly felt the same sort of qualms about a literal interpretation of the tetralemma, an interpretation which would necessitate a non-classical view of negation. They avoid these unpalatable consequences by adding the qualification *bden par grub pa* ("truly established")—or equivalently, *rang bzhin gyis grub pa* ("established by own-nature") or *don dam par* ("ultimately")—wherever necessary to avoid paradox.[50] This is in keeping with the fundamental view of Tsong kha pa that statements in Madhyamaka arguments, in general, cannot be taken literally, but must be prefixed by a qualification which specifies exactly what it is that is being refuted *(dgag bya)*. Failure to qualify *yod pa* ("existence"/"existent") as *bden par yod pa* ("truly existent") would, besides engendering paradoxes in *catuṣkoṭi*-style arguments, also lead to a complete denial of conventional truth.

Consider the following passage from Se ra rje btsun chos kyi rgyal mtshan's *sKabs dang po'i spyi don* where the author first presents a literal version of the *catuṣkoṭi*, which he considers untenable. He then gives a duly qualified version:

> An opponent might say: "The ultimate mode of being is that all *dharmas* are not existent, nor nonexistent, nor both, nor neither, for in the *sūtra* it is said that all *dharmas* are not existent, nonexistent, both or neither, and the *Ratnakūṭa [sūtra]* states: 'Kāśyapa, saying that [a thing] exists is one extreme, saying that it does not exist is the other extreme. Abandoning these two extremes is the Middle Path.'" [Reply:] This is incorrect for the following reasons: the meaning of the first scriptural citation is the point that all *dharmas* are not ultimately existent, [and thus] are not truly established, nor are they conventionally nonexistent, [and thus] established as being that [i.e., nonexistent], nor are they truly established as being both ultimately existent and conventionally nonexistent, nor are they truly established as being neither [ultimately existent nor conventionally nonexistent]; the meaning of the second [citation] is to show that the view [that things are] truly existent is the view of permanence and that the view that they are conventionally nonexistent is the view of annihilation. If it were not like this, then it would follow that all *dharmas*, the topic, are existent, because they are not nonexistent. ...Or, what is more, it would follow that all *dharmas*, the topic, are existent and are also nonexistent, both and neither, because all *dharmas* are not existent, not nonexistent, not both nor neither—the reason is what you hold.[51]

In fact, Chos kyi rgyal mtshan's qualified version is somewhat complicated to interpret. We might take "truly established" *(bden par grub pa)* or "truly" *(bden par),* "ultimately" *(don dam par)* as a kind of modal operator which we could symbolize by "$\Box$". Thus $\sim\Box P$ means "it is not truly so that P." In that case, Chos kyi rgyal mtshan's version asserts: $\sim\Box P; \sim\sim P; \sim\Box(\Box P \,\&\, \sim P), \sim\Box(\sim\Box P \,\&\, \sim\sim P)$. First of all, note that the third lemma, in particular, seems unnecessarily circumscribed, i.e., he could have simply said $\sim(\Box P \,\&\, \sim P)$: on either solution though, we see that the third lemma would not be a simple restatement of the law of contradiction, as it is in the literalist version. At any rate what concerns us most in Chos kyi rgyal mtshan's version is that no contradiction is derivable from the conjunction of the four negated lemmas. In simpler terms, to take his version of the *Ratnakūṭa*'s famous pronouncement, the "Middle Path" would be an assertion of an unqualified statement P; the "extremes" would be $\Box P$ and $\sim P$; there is no contradiction in a formula which denies the "extremes" and asserts P, viz., $((\sim\Box P \,\&\, \sim\sim P) \,\&\, P)$.

At this point, though, I should make an exegetical aside with regard to the interpretation of the negation of the second lemma, which, in Chos kyi rgyal mtshan, is to be taken as denying that things are completely nonexistent. In other words, for Chos kyi rgyal mtshan, this comes down to the statement which we sometimes see in other dGe lugs pa texts that phenomena are *gtan nas med pa ma yin pa* ("not completely nonexistent").[52] Such a version of the second lemma seems to correspond with his interpretation of the "extremes" *(mtha' = anta)* which are to be avoided and indeed one finds no shortage of allusions to this idea in dGe lugs pa commentaries.

Be all this as it may, the dGe lugs pa do in fact recognize two versions of the extreme of nonexistence *(med mtha'):* (a) "one which denies something legitimate" *(skur 'debs kyi med mtha')*—this is what Chos kyi rgyal mtshan is talking about; (b) "one which involves reification [of the negation]" *(sgro 'dogs kyi med mtha').*[53] The latter type of *med mtha'* would be something like saying, "it is truly so that things do not truly exist," and its denial would therefore be, "it is not truly so that things do not truly exist," or in symbols, $\sim\Box\sim\Box P$.[54] Note that here too, there is nothing contradictory about asserting $(\sim\Box P \,\&\, \sim\Box\sim\Box P)$. What is significantly different from the denial of the *skur 'debs kyi med mtha'*, however, is that $\sim\Box\sim\Box P$ does not in any way imply or contradict P; $\sim\Box\sim\Box P$ is compatible with P and also with $\sim P$.

Now, turning to the absurd consequences which Chos kyi rgyal mtshan maintains follow from the literalist position, we see further evidence that the debate logic which he is using gives results analogous to what one would expect from a classical propositional calculus. In other words, to use propositional calculus with the normal negation operator, we can tautologically derive *P* from ~~*P*, and that is just what Chos kyi rgyal mtshan does. Indeed, debate logic analogues to the laws of double negation in classical logic are nicely described in *Yongs 'dzin bsdus grwa*'s treatment of negation:

> The negation-of-not-being [an *A*] *(ma yin pa las log pa)* is equivalent to being [an *A*] *(yin pa);* the negation-of-being [an *A*] *(yin pa las log pa)* is equivalent to not being [an *A*] *(ma yin pa);* however many times one accumulates [occurrences of] negation-of-not-being, it is equivalent to one [occurrence of] negation-of-not-being; an even number of [occurrences of] negation-of-being [an *A*] is equivalent to negation-of-not-being; if a [term] has an odd number of [occurrences of] negation-of-being, it is equivalent to [the term with] one negation-of-being.[55]

Not surprisingly then, *prasajyapratiṣedha*, as explained in *bsdus grwa* texts and in Tsong kha pa,[56] turns out to be unexceptional and conforms to classical negation. In sum, one occurrence of a negation operator such as *ma yin pa* or the negative particle *ma, mi,* etc. in terms such as *bum pa ma yin pa* ("not being a vase"; "non-vase") or ...*bden par ma grub pa* ("not being truly established") will be counted as a *prasajyapratiṣedha*, because no positive assertion about a phenomenon is implied.[57] Two occurrences of *ma yin pa* or an occurrence of *ma yin pa las log pa* will be an implicative negation *(paryudāsapratiṣedha).*

If we look at Chos kyi rgyal mtshan's rendering of the *catuṣkoṭi*, he has clearly taken pains to add *bden par ma grub* ("not truly established"), which is a *prasajyapratiṣedha* and implies no positive assertion at all. His exegetical weak point, however, is his denial of the second lemma, for he must accept such a denial will imply the positive statement (i.e., ~~*P* implies *P*): in that sense it is difficult for him to maintain that *all* the negations in the *catuṣkoṭi* are *prasajyapratiṣedha.*[58] Furthermore, on Chos kyi rgyal mtshan's version of the *catuṣkoṭi* involving the *skur 'debs kyi med mtha'*, there will be conventionally false existential propositions (e.g., "The creator of the world exists") for which it will be impossible to negate all the lemmas: a dGe lugs pa could not say that the creator of the world is not conventionally nonexistent, because the creator would then have to exist. Thus, we have another exegetical problem in that we will not be able to apply the *catuṣkoṭi* to any proposition we like. A little reflection, however, shows that if we take the second lemma as being the *sgro 'dogs kyi med mtha'*, the negation operator will still behave classically, but neither of these two exegetical problems will arise.

Notes to Chapter 6

1 Stcherbatsky (1932: vol. 1, 38).

2 On Phya pa and his oeuvre, see van der Kuijp (1978), (1983: chap. 2).

3 Indeed, after Tsong kha pa, we see dGe lugs authors regularly alternating between prose and debate logic format in their more extensive commentaries on the meaning of canonical Indian texts. Tsong kha pa may also have used it in his lectures, although in works written directly by him (i.e., not the lecture notes of rGyal tshab and mKhas grub), he does not seem to use it. Cf., e.g., *mNgon sum le'u'i ṭīkā rje'i gsung bzhin mkhas grub chos rjes mdzad pa*, p. 529: *rjes dpag tshad ma chos can / snang tshul phyin ci log gi blo ma yin par thal / yul gi gtso bo la snang tshul phyin ci log gi blo ma yin pa'i phyir / 'khor gsum ga khas blangs tshul snga ma ltar ro //*. Admittedly, it might very well be mKhas grub who put Tsong kha pa's thought into this form.

4 Theories which specifically seem to be Phya pa's inventions, not based on Indian *pramāṇa* texts, are the *rdzas chos ldog chos rnam bzhag*, viz., the lesson on substantial *dharma*s and excluding *dharma*s (see Onoda [1980 : 385]), and the lesson on *rjes 'gro ldog khyab*, a systematization of the possible sorts of pervasions, which in spite of its name has little to do with the *anvayavyāpti* and *vyatirekavyāpti* of the Indian Buddhist logicians (see Onoda [1983 : 437]). Cf. also Ngag dbang nyi ma's remarks (p. 20) stating that Phya pa (= Cha pa) was responsible for *rdzas chos ldog chos* as found in *bsdus grwa: de dag la cha pa'i lugs kyi rdzas ldog zer / spyir rdzas chos dang ldog chos kyi don 'jog lugs dang mi 'dra // yin na'ang / cha pa chos kyi seng ges rdzas ldog gi rnam bzhag de dag rgyas par mdzad la / 'jam dbyangs bla ma phyogs lha'i 'od zer gyis / de dag ni gzhung gi go ba la dgag gzhi drug sgra thal 'gyur sogs dang*

'dra ba'i phan che / zhes gsungs so //.

5 Cf., e.g., the full title of *Yongs 'dzin rtags rigs: Tshad ma'i gzhung don 'byed pa'i bsdus grwa'i rnam par bshad pa rigs lam 'phrul gyi lde'u mig las rigs lam che ba rtags rigs kyi skor.*

6 Cf. dMu dge bsam gtan's brief biography of this author in *Tshad ma'i dgongs don rtsa 'grel mkhas pa'i mgul rgyan = Yinmingxue gaiyao ji qi zhushi,* pp. 373–74. bSe ngag dbang bkra shis (1678–1738) was a disciple of 'Jam dbyangs bzhad pa ngag dbang brtson 'grus (1648–1722) and was an abbot of Bla brang bkra shis 'khyil. Note that 'Jam dbyangs bzhad pa himself wrote a *bsdus grwa* in verse form, the *bsDus sbyor gyi snying po kun bsdus rig pa'i mdzod.*

7 The examples which I give from *bsdus grwa* texts are not generally direct quotations, but are simplified versions of passages to be found in such texts and are completely typical of what transpires in actual debates. In controversial cases, I give passages on which my examples can be based.

8 See Sierksma (1964); Perdue (1976); Onoda (1979a; 1979b; 1980; 1982a; 1982b; 1982c; 1983); and Goldberg (1985a; 1985b). Onoda (1992) is an English work based on his Japanese articles.

9 While predicate calculus, set theory, etc., can be profitably used on occasion in explaining structures in *bsdus grwa,* we must bear in mind that these modern logic structures are at most approximate analogues of the structures in *bsdus grwa* itself: in effect, we make a trade-off between the precision and facility gained in our explanations versus the fidelity lost with regard to the actual *bsdus grwa* argumentation. Goldberg, however, systematically blurs the distinction between a description of the debate logic and its possible analogues or translations into Aristotelian or formal logic. Cf. Goldberg (1985a):

> 157: "The theory of logic which I encountered deals with inferences as single syllogistic units.... The rules of inference of Detachment (Modus Ponens), its contrapositive (Modus Tollens), and Substitution are *known and used* [my italics].... Negation of implications, conjunctions, and disjunctions (including DeMorgan's Laws) are also *known*...The Aristotelian techniques of direct proof, reductio ad absurdum (including reductio ad impossibile and consequentia mirabilis) and ecthesis are used routinely." *Ibid,* 156: "The dGe lugs pa theories of formal logic are theories of predicate

logic." *Ibid*, 158: "dGe lugs pa logic presents a calculus of arbitrary sets, properties and extensions...."

What does Goldberg mean by saying that all these things "are known and used"? They are never explicitly formulated nor, with perhaps the exception of contraposition, are they even discussed clearly. Of course, *we* can, if we wish, use this Aristotelian terminology for comparative purposes, or we can even try to transpose/translate *bsdus grwa* into such a logic. We could, with limited utility, do the same thing with regard to the arguments that occur between lawyers, but it would be somewhat silly to say that debaters in courts of law *know and use* Aristotelian logic. As for the "dGe lugs pa theories of formal logic" and the "calculus" of sets, etc., this falsifies the character of dGe lugs pa argumentation: there are no "theories of formal logic" or calculi, if she is using these terms in anything other than a very loose or solecistic manner. A few debate rules and obligations are informally presented in the third book of *Yongs 'dzin bsdus grwa*, but many are not explained at all—the student has to "pick them up" as best he can. For the problems in using the terminology of sets, see n. 44.

10 See the extensive chronological bibliography of research in this area in Barth and Martens (1982).

11 See Krabbe (1982: 126–27).

12 The essential change of perspective which this way of doing logic brings out has been interestingly described by Barth in her introduction to Barth and Martens (1982: 6) as follows: "...the habit of logicians, old and new, of basing logic as well as their philosophy of language on some kind of "ontology"—that is to say, on things, properties and values that "are there," potentially or actually, in some "domain" or other—this habit should give place to a semantics in terms of the *human activities* of seeking and finding."

13 Cf. *Rwa stod bsdus grwa* 4a1 (= p. 7): *de chos can / khyod khyod dang gcig yin par thal / khyod tshad ma'i gzhal bya yin pa'i phyir. yod pa* ("existence") and *tshad ma'i gzhal bya* ("what is to be discriminated by a *pramāṇa*") are equivalent or co-extensive *(don gcig).*

14 See Tillemans (1988).

15 Note that I am fully aware of the fact that *gcig* is a much stronger sort of identity than what we represent by "=" (See Tillemans [1986a]), but for the moment nothing depends upon that fact: purists can, if they wish,

understand "=" in a suitably Buddhist sense.

16 Cf. Faris (1968: 4–9). Faris gives two possible translations of "(Claudius *x*) *Fx*": "Claudius *x* is such that *x* has *F*"; "Of Claudius as *x* it is true that *x* has *F*." I would prefer not to introduce the potentially complicating phrase "it is true" and say "it is so" instead.

17 See for example *dBu ma 'jug pa gsal ba'i me long*'s explanation (10a5–6) of the name of the fifth chapter in the *Madhyamakāvatāra*: *shes bya chos can / sa de la sbyang dka' ba zhes bya ste / sa lnga pa la gnas pa'i byang sems bdag nyid chen po de lha'i bu'i bdud rnams kun gyis kyang sbyang dka'i sa las pham par nus pa ma yin pa'i phyir /*. The verse on which he is commenting, viz., chap. 5, 1a–b, reads: *bdag nyid che de bdud rnams kun gyis kyang // sbyang dka'i sa la pham par nus ma yin //*. Trans. by de la Vallée Poussin (p. 512): "Dans la terre Sudurjayā, ce magnanime ne peut être vaincu même par tous les Māras." See also dGe 'dun grub pa's commentary (p. 2b3–4) to the opening verses of *Pramāṇavārttika*'s *Svārthānumāna* chapter, where Dharmakīrti explains his own motivation in writing the work: *shes bya chos can / dpal ldan chos grags bdag la rnam 'grel 'di ni gtso cher gzhan la phan pa yin zhes bsam pa'ang med de / skye bo phal cher phal pa'i bstan bcos la chags shing / legs nyes 'byed pa'i shes rab kyi rtsal med pas na legs bshad rnams don du mi gnyer la / de kho nar ma zad legs bshad la phrag dog dri ma dag gis yongs su sdang bar gyur ba des na'o.*

18 For the history of *vyāpti* in Indian logic up to Dharmakīrti, see Katsura (1986a) and an English summary in Katsura (1986c).

19 On these terms see Steinkellner (1971: 201–4). Stcherbatsky (1932: vol. 1, p. 554) characterized *tādātmya* as follows: "the Buddhist law means reference of two different concepts to one and the same point of reality; the concepts are identical in that sense that one is included in the other."

20 The Buddhist theory of causality *(kāryakāraṇabhāva)*, involving observation and nonobservation, was elaborated according to a fivefold set of cognitions by Dharmottara and according to a threefold set by Jñānaśrimitra. Cf. Y. Kajiyama (1966: 113 and n. 305) and (1963).

21 [Author's note: for this *bādhakapramāṇa*, see the introduction to the present volume, p. 14.]

22 PVP 321a4: *de ltar re zhig rgyu dang 'bras bu'i med na mi 'byung ba nyid yin no // rang bzhin te / rang bzhin gyi gtan tshigs ni //*.

23 See Manorathanandin's PVV *ad* PV IV, k. 258.

24 My translation follows the Sanskrit. PV IV, k. 258: *nāntarīyakatā jñeyā yathāsvaṃ* hetvapekṣayā / svabhāvasya yathoktaṃ prāk vināśakṛtakatvayoḥ //*. *Read *yathāsvaṃ* instead of Miyasaka's *yathā svaṃ*.

25 From my observations and personal experience, I can affirm that the opponent in a Tibetan debate will have about fifteen seconds to come up with something or another, otherwise his audience will begin to clap their hands and jeer quite loudly and he will be forced to accept the pervasion in question.

26 To put things in the usual, but long-winded, fashion of predicate calculus: given the truth of (17), the conditional (16) must also be true because no matter which individual constant ß we substitute for the variable *x* occuring in (16), the formula "rabbit's horn *x*/ß" will be false and the falsity of the antecedent is a sufficient condition for the truth of the whole conditional. See Mates (1972) for explanations, including the notation $\Phi\ \alpha/$ß. A debate logic explanation is shorter: Given an acceptance of (17), one will invariably fail to show a counterexample for (16).

27 Pseudo-Scotus' formulation was: *ad quamlibet propositionem falsam sequitur quaelibet alia propositio in bona consequentia materiali ut nunc.* See Kneale and Kneale (1962: 281). "From any false proposition there follows every other proposition in a material consequence which is good as things are now." "Good as things are now" is very roughly speaking the same as "contingently true," although cf. the Kneales' caution on p. 280.

28 Sometimes one finds *gang dran te yin pas khyab* or *gang dran dran.* E.g., *Yongs 'dzin bsdus grwa chung* 20a6: *dngos po'i spyir gyur pa'i dngos po yin na / gang dran dran yin pas khyab pa'i phyir /* "...because if something is a real entity which is a universal of real entities, it is pervaded by being whatever one can think of."

29 Cf. the definitions of the *anvayavyāpti (rjes khyab)* and *vyatirekavyāpti (ldog khyab)* for proving sound's impermanence in *Yongs 'dzin rtags rigs* (5b; p. 24 ed. Onoda): in both cases, the definitions specify *khyod mi rtag pa la 'brel.*

30 We see that Dharmakīrti, when speaking about pervasions in consequences *(prasaṅga)*, still insisted on there being a necessary connection. See PV IV, k. 12 and especially Manorathanandin's *vṛtti*, translated in

Tillemans (1986c).

31 Goldberg (1985a: 172) *et passim.*

32 Cf. *Rwa stod bsdus grwa* 4a2 (= p. 7): *shes bya chos can / dngos po ma yin par thal / dngos med yin pa'i phyir / ma grub na / de chos can / der thal / rtag pa yin pa'i phyir.* Ibid., 4a3: *gzhi grub na rtag pa yin pas khyab zer na / gser bum chos can / der thal / de'i phyir.* Note that *gzhi grub* ("established basis") is co-extensive with *shes bya.*

33 Goldberg (1985a: 178). This is the principle which Tibetans routinely express by the formula ...*khyod rtag pa yin te khyod rtag pa dang gzhi mthun yod pa'i phyir.*

34 Cf. *Yongs 'dzin bsdus grwa 'bring,* 11a1–2: *kho na re shes bya'i mtshan nyid de mtshan nyid yin par thal / shes bya'i mtshan nyid yin na mtshan nyid yin pas khyab pa'i phyir zer na ma khyab.* Ibid. 11b1–2: *mtshan nyid chos can / mtshan nyid ma yin par thal / mtshon bya yin pa'i phyir /.*

35 A good example: in *rtags rigs* one typically says *byas pa chos can sgra mi rtag par sgrub pa'i rtags yang dag yin* ("product, the topic, is a valid reason for proving that sound is impermanent"). In Sanskrit one would not say that *kṛta* or *kṛtaka* ("a/the/all product[s]") is the reason: rather the reason is *kṛtakatva* ("producedness"; "producthood"). But in Tibetan it would be silly to say *byas pa nyid chos can,* although that is the point at stake. [Author's note: this explanation in terms of an implicit *tva/ tā* is now unsatisfyingly simplistic to me. Cf. n. 18 in "On the So-called Difficult Point of the *Apoha* Theory," reprinted as chapter 10 of the present volume.]

36 Bocheński (1956: 162).

37 *Suppositio simplex pro significato sine comparatione ad res.* Kneale and Kneale (1962: 252).

38 Translation is that of the Kneales, (1962: 756), except that I would prefer "stands for" for *supponit* instead of their "suppones."

39 Interestingly enough, there is a passage in Red mda' ba's commentary on the *Catuḥśataka,* chapter 15 where the three defining characteristics *(mtshan nyid)* of conditioned phenomena are being refuted. In the course of the argument against *lakṣaṇa* and *lakṣya* being one, Red mda' ba gives the absurd consequence that *mtshan nyid mtshan nyid du mi 'gyur* (p. 192), "defining

character would not be a defining character." In fact, the sense is clearly that it would absurdly follow that things which are defining characters would not be defining characters. A good illustration of the ambiguity of terms in Tibetan.

40 An example of the latter is *piper venditur hic et Romae* ("Pepper is sold here and in Rome"), where there is not just a reference to the variety or type of thing, but also to the concrete peppercorns which are actually sold.

41 For *rang ldog* and *gzhi ldog*, see the third chapter of *Yongs 'dzin bsdus grwa chung* on *ldog pa ngos 'dzin*. A good example of the use which the dGe lugs make of these terms is in the theory of *apoha*, where they want to say that the likeness of the object which appears to the conceptual mind and is the meaning of a word is a conceptually created fiction, a *sāmānyalakṣaṇa*. However, that which has that likeness, viz., the *svalakṣaṇa* (i.e., the real particulars in the world), is not conceptually created. We find *bsdus grwa* arguments on *apoha* such as the following:

> *bum 'dzin rtog pa la bum pa ma yin pa las log par snang ba chos can spyi mtshan yin.* "Appear[ance] as non-non-vase to the conceptual mind thinking about vase[s], the topic, is a *sāmānyalakṣaṇa*."
>
> *khyod bum 'dzin rtog pa la bum pa ma yin pa las log par snang na khyod spyi mtshan yin pas ma khyab, dper na bum pa bzhin.* "If *x* is something which appears as non-non-vase to the conceptual mind thinking about vase[s], then *x* is not pervaded by being a *sāmānyalakṣaṇa*, for example, as in the case of a vase."

Cf. *Yongs 'dzin bsdus grwa che ba*, the chapter on *apoha (gzhan sel)*. Note that *bum pa'i don spyi*, the "object-universal of a vase", or the mentally-created likeness which is the basis for words and concepts, is explained in *bsDus grwa chung* and *che ba* as *bum 'dzin rtog pa la bum pa ma yin pa las log par snang ba*. lCang skya rol pa'i rdo rje in effect explains the point brought out in the above two statements by using the terminology of *rang ldog* and *gzhi ldog*—the "appearance" itself *(rang ldog)* is the conceptually fabricated basis for applying mental and verbal conventions such as "ox," but the individual oxen which appear as non-non-ox are the *gzhi ldog* of this appearance and are *svalakṣaṇa*. Cf. *lCang skya grub mtha'* p. 104 for a classic explanation of *apoha* à la dGe lugs pa: *de ltar na 'di ba lang ngo / snyam pa'i blo'i tha snyad dang de ltar brjod pa'i sgra'i tha snyad 'jug pa'i gzhi'i rang ldog ni rtog pas btags pa tsam dang spyi mtshan yin la / de dag gi gzhi ldog tu gyur pa'i ba lang sogs ni rang mtshan yin pas …*

Finally, it should be understood that lCang skya's explanation of *apoha* is largely based on Tsong kha pa's *Tshad ma'i brjed byang chen mo*, many passages of which he uses almost verbatim. Cf. A lag sha ngag dbang bstan dar's *Rang mtshan spyi msthan rnam bzhag* for a similar explanation, one which is more or less standard textbook fare. [Editor's note: see also Tillemans (1995a), reprinted as chapter 10 in the present volume.]

42 Cf. *Yongs 'dzin bsdus grwa chung* 6a where *lto ldir zhabs zhum chos skyor gyi don byed nus pa* is also given as the defining property of vases *(bum pa)*.

43 Cf. *rTags rigs*, 8b6 (= p. 31, ed. Onoda): *byas pa sgra mi rtag par sgrub pa'i gnyis pa* [i.e., *sgra mi rtag par sgrub kyi khyad par ltos pa pa'i rang bzhin gyi rtags yang dag*].

44 For the first quotation, see Goldberg (1985a: 177); for the second, see ibid. p. 153. The usual version of Russell's paradox arises in the context of a nineteenth-century set theory. Now *bsdus grwa* is far from being a *theory* of sets, nor is it even likely that topic terms regularly refer to anything even similar to sets. This is easily seen by the following typical example: *bum pa chos can bum pa yin te lto ldir zhabs zhum chos skyor gyi don byed nus pa yin pa'i phyir* (lit., "vase, the topic, is a vase because it is bulbous, splay-bottomed and can perform the function of carrying water.") But the *set* of vases is not a vase, nor can it carry water.

Goldberg (1985b: 295) says: "This entity [viz., *rang ma yin pa*] was not mentioned in my studies of dGe lugs pa logic but its existence is obvious from the postulates." Disregarding the hyperbole and inexactitude of talking about "postulates" in dGe lugs pa logic, it is worth mentioning that it is really Goldberg who came up with this paradox of *rang ma yin pa* ("not being itself"), a paradox which is hardly clearly extractable from the *bsdus grwa* arguments on *rang ma yin pa'i ldog chos*, etc. Granted, there seems to be something like a paradox in the latter arguments, but it is arrived at in an extremely roundabout and woolly way. Secondly, the terms *rang ma yin pa* and *rang ma yin pa'i ldog chos* suffer from a similar type of ambiguity as the cases which we saw above. If one felt less charitable one could, it seems to me, justifiably say that one does not understand what the terms mean and that the whole thing is a type of pseudo-paradox. But taking a more charitable point of view, we could understand *rang ma yin pa* in the sense of the "property of not qualifying itself" or the "property of not being predicable of itself"—this, given what we saw previously about the ambiguities of terms in Tibetan, is probably a much more legitimate possibility than something about sets. If we take that course, however, then *rang ma yin pa* looks like Russell's property of "impredicability": a property f that is not predicable of itself will be termed "impredicable", i.e., $Impr(f)$ if and only if $\sim f(f)$.

Let the property "impredicable" be *f*. Then *Impr (Impr)* if and only if *~Impr (Impr)*. See Copi (1971: 9). In other words, if there is a parallel with Russell, it is better understood as *not* being a version of Russell's set theoretical paradox, but as a paradox turning on properties. The inescapable impression which one gets from *bsdus grwa* and Goldberg, however, is that the Tibetans did not have a clear awareness of such paradoxes, nor of their consequences; they stumbled onto something and then adopted a patchwork solution with the notion of *rjes mthun pa* ("semblant entities"). Coming up with explicitly formulated logical paradoxes is quite a different thing.

45 Cf. Quine (1970: 80–87), or (1960a: 387) where he gives the simplistic view that apparent logical conflicts are always results of mistranslation: "prelogicality is a myth invented by bad translators." Actually as Susan Haack (1974) shows, Quine's position is not wholly consistent. If we adopt his views in "Two Dogmas of Empiricism" that there is no fundamental difference between so-called "necessary" logical truths and factual truths, then it is theoretically possible that some circumstances would lead us to revise logical laws. This theoretical possiblity is to be governed by his "maxim of minimum mutilation," which reminds us of the awesome consequences. See Haack (1974, ch.2) for a discussion of the question, "Could there be good reason[s] for a change of logic?"

46 Note that one could reproduce similar ambiguities in Chinese, and it would be interesting to see whether the Mohist logicians did have similar logical problems and how they solved them.

47 See Tillemans (1986b).

48 *sad asat sadasac ceti sadasan neti ca kramaḥ / eṣa prayojyo vidvadbhir ekatvādiṣu nityaśaḥ //.*

49 See CSV *ad* CS XIV, k. 21:

> *ekatvam anyatvam ubhayaṃ nobhayam ity ekatvādayaḥ / eteṣv ekatvādiṣu pakṣeṣu vādinā vyavasthiteṣu sadasattvādyupalakṣito dūṣaṇakramaḥ sudhiyā* yathākramam avatāryaḥ //.* * Better to read *sudhiyā* (= Tib. *blo bzang pos*) than *svadhiyā*, which is the reading found in Haraprasād Shāstrī and V. Bhattacharya. "Oneness, otherness, both, neither—that is what is meant by 'oneness and other such [theses]'. The person of excellent intelligence should systematically apply the method of refutation which was shown—i.e., existence, nonexistence, etc.—to these theses concerning oneness, etc.

which were established by the proponent."

See Ruegg (1977) for examples from early Buddhism such as the finitude/infinitude of the world, its eternity/non-eternity, the soul's being different or identical with the body, etc.

50 rGyal tshab in *bZhi rgya pa'i rnam bshad* to CS XIV, k. 21 (ch. 14, p. 12) adds the qualification *bden par grub pa : mkhas pas bden par grub pa'i gcig nyid dang / gzhan nyid dang / gnyi ga dang / gnyi ga min pa sogs 'gog pa dag la rtag tu sbyar bar bya'i /*... Note that Candrakīrti does not use this qualification here; nor does Dharmapāla in his 大乘廣百論釋論 *Guang bai lun shi lun*. T. XXX 1571.

51 *sKabs dang po'i spyi don* 104a5–104b2 and 104b7–105a1: *kha cig chos thams cad yod pa yang ma yin / med pa yang ma yin / gnyis ka yang ma yin / gnyis ka ma yin pa yang ma yin pa gnas lugs mthar thug yin te / mdo las / chos thams cad yod pa yang ma yin / med pa yang ma yin / gnyis ka yang ma yin / gnyis ka ma yin pa yang ma yin / zhes gsungs pa'i phyir dang / dkon mchog brtsegs par / 'od srung yod ces bya ba ni mtha' gcig go / med ces bya ba ni mtha' gnyis so // mtha' de gnyis spangs pa ni dbu ma'i lam mo // zhes gsungs pa'i phyir / zer ba mi 'thad de / lung dang po'i don ni / chos thams cad don dam par yod pa ma yin pa bden par ma grub / tha snyad du med pa ma yin pa yang der ma grub / don dam par yod pa dang tha snyad du med pa gnyis ka yin pa yang bden par ma grub / de gnyis ka ma yin pa yang bden par ma grub ces pa'i don dang / gnyis pa'i don ni bden par yod par lta ba rtag lta dang / tha snyad du med par lta ba chad lta yin par bstan pa'i phyir / de ltar ma yin na / chos thams cad chos can / yod pa yin par thal / med pa ma yin pa'i phyir /... gzhan yang / chos thams cad yod pa yang yin / med pa yang yin / gnyis ka yang yin / gnyis ka ma yin pa yang yin par thal / chos thams cad yod pa yang ma yin / med pa yang ma yin / gnyis ka yang ma yin / gnyis ka ma yin pa yang ma yin pa'i phyir / rtags khas /*. The same passage in the copy of the *sKabs dang po'i spyi don* in the Tibetan collection of the Faculty of Letters of Tokyo University (89a6–89b3 and 90a1–2) shows no variants. For the quote from the *Ratnakūṭa*, see *Kāśyapaparivartta* 60, ed., Staël-Holstein: *astīti kāśyapa ayam eko 'ntaḥ nāstīty ayaṃ dvitīyo 'ntaḥ (/) yad etayor dvayor antayor madhyam iyam ucyate kāśyapa madhyamā pratipad.*

52 See e.g., Kalff (1983).

53 See Tsong kha pa's *rTsa she ṭīk chen*, p. 15.

54 Cf. *rTsa she ṭīk chen* (Sarnath ed., p.15; *Collected Works*, vol. *ba* 10a2–3 = p. 19):

> *de la yang dag par yod pa tha snyad du yang mi srid pas yang dag par med pa tha snyad du yod pa'i phyir don dam par med ces pa med pa'i mthar 'dzin dang de ltar ma yin zhes 'gog pa med mtha' 'gog pa min kyang / dgag bya bkag pa'i med pa yang dag par yod do zhes 'dzin na dngos po med pa'i mthar ltung bas de 'gog pa yang med mtha' 'gog pa yin no //* "Here, since true existence is impossible even conventionally, not being truly existent does exist conventionally. Thus it is not the case that [thinking] 'it is not ultimately existent' is grasping at the extreme of nonexistence and that the negation 'it is not like that' is a negation of the extreme of nonexistence. But if one thinks that the nonexistence of the negandum which has been negated does [itself] truly exist, then one has fallen into the extreme of entities being nonexistent, and thus the negation of that is the negation of the extreme of nonexistence."

For this "negation of a truly existent negation" in the context of the fourfold discussion of causality, see ibid p. 47 (ed. Sarnath) *et seq.* which has the heading *(sa bcad): rang bzhin med pa rigs shes kyis grub na bden par grub pa'i rtsod pa spang ba,* "Rebutting the argument that if one establishes that there is no *svabhāva,* then [this absence of *svabhāva*] is truly established." See also Ruegg (1983: 226)'s summary of the *sKal bzang mid 'byed*:

> Accordingly, when it is known that what is to be established in MMK I,1 has the form of *prasajya*-negation (cf. 109a2), one understands that there is established the pure negative determination of production in ultimate reality *(don dam par skye ba rnam par bcad tsam sgrub kyi)* without there being an additional establishment of the existence of some (putative) ultimately real non-production *(de min pa'i don dam pa'i skye med yod par mi sgrub pa)* (111b2).

55 *bsDus grwa chung* 14a: *ma yin pa las log pa dang / yin pa gnyis don gcig / yin pa las log pa dang / ma yin pa gnyis don gcig / ma yin pa las log pa du [ma] brtsegs kyang / ma yin pa las log pa gcig pu dang don gcig / yin pa las log pa cha dang / ma yin pa las log pa don gcig / yin pa las log pa ya dang bcas na / yin pa las log pa gcig pu dang don gcig yin pa'i phyir ro //.*

56 See e.g., *rTsa she ṭīk chen,* (Sarnath ed., pp. 39–41) and *Yongs 'dzin bsdus grwa che ba: gzhan sel dgag sgrub kyi rnam bzhag.* For a general explanation of the notions at stake see Kajiyama (1973). Lately we have seen many modern writers explaining *prasajya/paryudāsa* in terms of "verbally-bound" or "nominally-bound" negations. Interestingly enough, this account fits badly with the dGe lugs explanations on the subject.

57 I deform things a bit here in speaking about "positive assertions"—more precisely, it is (psychologically) positive phenomena *(sgrub pa = vidhi).*

58 My thanks to Georges Dreyfus for confirming that the Tibetan debaters also felt that this potential exegetical problem would arise if one denied the *skur 'debs kyi med mtha'.* A solution seems to have been to take the denial as *rang bzhin gyis med na med mi dgos pa* ("it is not necessary that *x* is nonexistent if *x* does not exist by its own-nature") instead of simply *tha snyad du med pa ma yin pa.*

7: Dharmakīrti and Tibetans on *Adṛśyānupalabdhihetu*

THE PROJECT TO STUDY Buddhist epistemology by using indigenous Tibetan sources seems to have two major orientations nowadays. The first, broadly speaking, seeks to describe the long and tortuous process by which the Tibetans themselves assimilated the philosophy of Dharmakīrti. Here there is a constellation of questions, ranging from purely factual matters like the history of transmissions of the *Pramāṇavārttika, Pramāṇaviniścaya,* etc., to philological and philosophical points, such as the history of certain intra-Tibetan debates on key Dharmakīrtian notions. So long as one does not attempt to *evaluate* these Tibetan debates as to their accuracy or fruitfulness in elucidating Dharmakīrti's thought, one can treat them as purely Tibetan events, and indeed one can even quite justifiably go a long way in investigating this part of Tibetan philosophical history without preoccupying oneself very much with Dharmakīrti's actual works. The result is what one could term a purely Tibetological approach.

The second orientation is evaluative in nature and does therefore presuppose an understanding of Dharmakīrti's own system: one shuttles back and forth between the indigenous Tibetan commentaries and the original Indian texts (in Sanskrit where available), seeking to use Tibetan materials to gain a deeper understanding of Dharmakīrti's own thought. The question then inevitably arises as to what kind of understanding of Dharmakīrti we can get in this manner. Here there is no one simple answer. Sometimes Tibetans do give us valuable pieces of specific historical information on the Indian debates figuring in Dharmakīrti's works, such as identifying Īśvarasena as being the proponent of the *ṣaḍlakṣaṇahetu* doctrine against which Dharmakīrti repeatedly argued.[1] More frequently, however, the Tibetan contribution to our understanding of Dharmakīrti does not concern specific historical figures, facts, or events, but rather what I have termed elsewhere "internal history," and where the essential procedure is not unlike what David Seyfort Ruegg, if I understand him correctly, would explain as systematical hermeneutics.[2] In short, the Tibetan commentators often attribute ideas to Dharmakīrti which are implied or presupposed by the whole system of his thought, although Dharmakīrti himself may never have subjectively entertained such ideas, or if he did, it was in a highly condensed, or even perhaps sometimes a dimly understood fashion.

Let us very briefly mention a few of the important Tibetan contributions to understanding Dharmakīrti, contributions where the Tibetans are largely proceeding by systematical hermeneutics, rather than by rigid adherence to Dharmakīrti's words:

(1) The notion of *tshad ma'i skyes bu* ("person of authority") which figures in the exegesis of PV II.[3]

(2) The differentiation between the various types of universals *(sāmānya)*, some of which should be acceptable to a Dharmakīrtian, and others which should be totally unacceptable.[4]

(3) The formulation of the so-called "reasons/inferences from authority" *(yid ches pa'i rtags; yid ches pa'i rjes dpag)*. Dharmakīrti in PV I and PV IV, in keeping with Dignāga, had explained that citations from scriptures could be used for certain sorts of inferences. Tibetan commentators then speculated on just what the formal reasonings *(prayoga)* in such inferences should look like, and what degree of probative status scriptural inferences had vis-à-vis other types of inferences, a problem which led to the infamous *lung gnod byed/lung gegs byed* debate between Sa skya pas and dGe lugs pas over the question of whether a scripture *(lung = āgama)* could really serve to invalidate *(gnod byed = bādhaka)* a thesis, or whether it could at most conflict with the thesis, or more literally speaking, "impede it" *(gegs byed = pratibandhaka)*. Some Tibetan commentators (such as dGe 'dun grub pa [1391–1474] in his *Tshad ma rigs pa'i rgyan*), maintained that the debate had historical Indian proponents (viz., "disciples of Dignāga"), but they never actually identified these "Indian thinkers," and it seems more likely that the debate is better viewed as an important contribution to systematical

hermeneutics, albeit one which was dressed up as an historical pseudo-event.[5]

In what follows we shall take up another Tibetan contribution to understanding Dharmakīrti, namely, the development of two significantly different types of reasoning consisting in the non-apprehension of putative states of affairs, in other words, two different types of *anupalabdhihetu (ma dmigs pa'i gtan tshigs).* As is well known by now, the standard account of *anupalabdhihetu* which we find in Dharmakīrti's works and those of later logicians is that the absence of a perceptible type of entity *(dṛśya)* is proven when that entity is not apprehended: it would be apprehended if it were present in a certain spot, but in fact it is not apprehended, and thus it is absent. It is repeatedly stressed, however, that if the entity is not perceptible *(adṛśya),* that is, if it is the type of thing, like a spirit *(piśāca),* which is not empirically accessible to ordinary beings, then merely not apprehending it does not prove its absence at all. This type of argument from non-apprehension is thus fallacious.

This much should be relatively ho-hum for any Dharmakīrtian scholar. What is not obvious at all for someone relying on only the Indian texts is that, following Tibetan exegesis on Dharmakīrti, there was a use of *adṛśyānupalabdhi* which *was* fully probative. In other words, Tibetans recognized two equally valid, but different types of *anupalabdhihetu,* viz., the familiar *dṛśyānupalabdhi (snang rung ma dmigs pa),* non-apprehension of a perceptible thing, and a specific, well-circumscribed use of *adṛśyānupalabdhi (mi snang ba ma dmigs pa),* non-apprehension of an imperceptible thing. Dharmakīrti thus supposedly recognized a type of *adṛśyānupalabdhihetu* which could not be assimilated to the frequently criticized fallacious use, but which actually was a valid reason for proving a certain type of negative proposition. As we shall see below, at least one modern writer, Ernst Steinkellner, recognized that Dharmakīrti sometimes spoke of inferences based on *adṛśyānupalabdhihetu* as being means of valid cognition *(pramāṇa),* but for Steinkellner (or rather, to be fair, for Steinkellner in 1967 when he published his translation of the *Hetubindu*[6]), a negation of the *adṛśyānupalabdhi* sort was only hypothetical *(hypothetisch)* and not as real *(echt)* as the usual *dṛśya* sort. Significantly, the Tibetans made no such distinction, and I believe they were probably better off in not doing so. At any rate, following the Tibetan scholastic, both sorts of valid *anupalabdhihetu* were of *equal status,* and led to negations and hence to inferential *pramāṇas* which were equally full-fledged and equally authoritative.

Let us now look at typical Tibetan examples of the valid sort of *adṛśyānupalabdhihetu.* We first take up the version of Tsong kha pa (1357–1419) as found in his short work on logic, *sDe bdun la 'jug pa'i sgo don gnyer yid kyi mun sel,* p. 48:

> *mdun gyi gzhi 'dir sha za bskal don du song ba'i skyes bus sha za yod nges kyi tha snyad don mthun mi 'jug par sgrub pa la sha za bskal don du song ba'i gang zag gis sha za ma dmigs pa bkod pa lta bu //* "It is like stating [the reason] that someone for whom spirits *(sha za = piśāca)* are inaccessible entities *(bskal don = viprakṛṣṭārtha)* does not apprehend a spirit, in order to prove that a person for whom a spirit is an inaccessible entity will not apply a correct *vyavahāra (= tha snyad don mthun)* that a spirit is certain *(nges = niścaya)* to be present in the place in front."

This basic idea is given in the form of various *prayogas* ("formal argument") in dGe lugs pa *rtags rigs* texts; *prayogas* and definitions are also given, with various modifications, by Sa skya pa writers such as Go rams pa bsod nams seng ge (1429–1489), Glo bo mkhan chen bsod nams lhun grub (1456–1532) and gSer mdog paṇ chen śākya mchog ldan (1428–1507). To avoid overly burdening the text here we shall present these variants in our notes (see n. 7). To begin our discussion, then, here is the formal argument given by a later scholar, Yongs 'dzin phur bu lcog (1825–1901), who, in his monastic textbook on *rtags rigs,* presents an elaborate dGe lugs pa version of the *prayoga:*

> *mdun gyi gzhi 'dir chos can / sha za bskal don du song ba'i gang zag gi rgyud la sha za nges pa'i dpyad shes don mthun med de / sha za bskal don du song ba'i gang zag gi rgyud la sha za dmigs byed kyi tshad ma med pa'i phyir /* "The topic [is] 'with regard to the place in front.' In the [mind]-stream of someone for whom a spirit is an inaccessible entity, there is no correct subsequent cognition *(dpyad shes don mthun)* ascertaining a spirit there [in front], because in the [mind-]stream of someone for

whom a spirit is an inaccessible entity there is no means of valid cognition *(tshad ma = pramāṇa)* which apprehends a spirit there."[7]

This type of reasoning is classified by Yongs 'dzin phur bu lcog and others as a *mi snang ba'i rgyu ma dmigs pa,* "non-apprehension of the cause with regard to something imperceptible." In effect, the later Tibetan schoolmen have transposed some categories which we find in the usual Dharmakīrtian classifications of *dṛśyānupalabdhihetu* onto the rather special case of *adṛśyānupalabdhihetu.* Thus the logical structure of the above reasoning is very similar to what *Pramāṇavārttika* I, k. 4 termed *hetvasiddhi* and what the *Vādanyāya* termed *kāraṇānupalabdhi*—in the usual example of this sort of reason one proves that there is no smoke in such and such a place because its cause, viz., fire, is not there. The point in the Tibetan example of the *adṛśyānupalabdhihetu* is that the cause of a correct subsequent cognition *(dpyad shes)* must be a *pramāṇa,* and in the case of cognizing inaccessible entities like spirits, ordinary beings simply do not have such *pramāṇas.*

Now, the initial temptation might well be to object that anyone, Tibetan or not, who speaks positively of an *adṛśyānupalabdhihetu* as being a valid reason like *dṛśyānupalabdhihetu* has, *ipso facto,* understood nothing about Dharmakīrti's system. After all, didn't Dharmakīrti explicitly say in PVin II, k. 32cd and NB II, 27 that "in the case of inaccessible things *(bskal pa = viprakṛṣṭa)* absence is not certain *(bskal pa rnams la ni / med par nges pa yod ma yin = viprakṛṣṭeṣu...abhāvaniścayābhāvaḥ)*"? Here, so it would be argued, what was meant was that various existent things could be inaccessible to our perception, i.e., literally "remote" *(viprakṛṣṭa),* because of their subtle natures, or their distance from us in time or space. Such inaccessible entities would be *adṛśya,* and indeed simply not seeing them would not give any certainty that they were nonexistent. Thus, tolerating or advocating an *adṛśyānupalabdhihetu* would run completely counter to Dharmakīrti.

I have in fact heard this objection voiced, and indeed not so long ago. But is it cogent? I don't think so. What the Tibetans are advocating as being a valid *adṛśyānupalabdhihetu* is not at all like this fallacious use. The Tibetans in the above type of example are not seeking to establish the certainty that a thing which does not lend itself to being perceived is absent, rather they are establishing the simple absence of any certainty, or of any cognition which is certain about presence or absence of *viprakṛṣṭārtha.* In short, they accept the *Pramāṇaviniścaya's* idea of absence being uncertain in the case of *viprakṛṣṭārtha,* and then they go one step further: they give valid reasons to prove that there is no certainty with regard to the presences or absences of *viprakṛṣṭārtha.* It is, thus, this type of reason which is the acceptable sort of *adṛśyānupalabdhi:* an *anupalabdhihetu* which, like all such reasons, proves a negative proposition, but in this case what is being negated is the existence of an ascertaining cognition.

In fact, there are some difficult passages in Dharmakīrti's PVin II and in the PVSV which are probably best interpreted as supporting the Tibetans on this matter. We shall first translate these passages and then attempt to superimpose upon them the idea of an acceptable *adṛśyānupalabdhihetu,* one which is as valid—no more, no less—as a *dṛśyānupalabdhihetu.*

> PVin II, 23.24–23.27 (ed. Steinkellner): *bskal pa'i yul la mngon sum dang rjes su dpag pa med pa de ni yod pa'i shes pa dang sgra dang tha snyad 'gog pa'i 'bras bu can yin te / de dag ni dmigs pa sngon du 'gro ba can yin pa'i phyir ro /* "The fact of there being no perception or inference with regard to inaccessible objects *(bskal pa'i yul = viprakṛṣṭaviṣaya)* results in negating cognition of, speech about and action directed towards present things, for these [three] are preceded by apprehension *(dmigs pa = upalabdhi).*"

Much of the rest of the PVin passage also figures in the *Svavṛtti* (PVSV) *ad* PV I, k. 3—the relevant Sanskrit text will be given below. First of all, however, let us cite PV I, k. 3. This is the verse which Tibetan writers themselves, be they dGe lugs pa or later Sa skya pa, will take to be the main Indian source for a twofold classification of valid *anupalabdhihetu* into *adṛśyānupalabdhi (mi snang ba ma dmigs pa)* and *dṛśyānupalabdhi (snang rung ma dmigs pa):*

> PV I, k.3: *apravṛttiḥ pramāṇānām apravṛttiphalā 'sati / asajjñānaphalā kācid dhetubhedavyapekṣayā //*[8] "Non-activation of *pramāṇa*s results in [one's] not acting towards that which is not present. Some [non-activation], by relying on specific features of the reason, results in cognition of an absence."

We now can present PVSV *ad* PV I, k. 3 (the words of the *kārikā* are indicated in bold script):

> ***apravṛttiḥ pramāṇānām*** *anupalabdhiḥ* ***apravṛttiphalā 'sati*** */ sajjñānaśabdavyavahārapratiṣedhaphalā / upalabdhipūrvakatvāt teṣām iti / ...* ***asajjñānaphalā kācid dhetubhedavyapekṣayā*** */ hetur anupalabdhiḥ / bhedo 'syā viśeṣaṇam upalabdhilakṣaṇaprāptasattvam / ...evam anayor anupalabdhyoḥ svaviparyayahetvabhāvabhāvābhyāṃ sadvyavahārapratiṣedhaphalatvaṃ tulyam / ekatra saṃśayād anyatra viparyayāt / tatrādyā sadvyavahāraniṣedhopayogāt pramāṇam uktā / na tu vyatirekadarśanādāv upayujyate / saṃśayāt / dvitīyā tv atra pramāṇaṃ niścayaphalatvāt //* "Non-activation of *pramāṇas*, i.e., *anupalabdhi*, results in [one's] not acting towards that which is not present. That is to say, it results in negating cognition of, speech about and action directed towards something present, for these are preceded by apprehension *(upalabdhi)*. ...Some [non-activation], by relying on specific features of the reason, results in cognition of an absence. *Anupalabdhi* is a logical reason *(hetu)*. Its specific feature is the qualifier that presence meet the conditions of [amenability to] apprehension. ...Thus both these [types of] *anupalabdhi* are the same in their resulting in negating action *(vyavahāra)* directed towards something present, either through a lack of [valid] logical reasons for [affirming] a thing itself or through the existence of [valid] logical reasons for negating [it]. For, in the first case, there is doubt, while in the second, there is negation. The first of them is said to be a *pramāṇa* in that one uses it to negate action directed towards something present. But it does not serve to prove exclusion, etc., for doubt remains. The second, however, is a *pramāṇa* for this [proof of exclusion], for it results in certainty."[9]

Some remarks on the salient points of Dharmakīrti's thought as reflected in the above passage:

A. The first half of PV I, k. 3 speaks of both *adṛśya* and *dṛśyānupalabdhihetu*, but the emphasis is on the former. Thus, an *adṛśyānupalabdhi* results in no cognition of presence of certain types of entities, nor can we legitimately speak of them or act on the knowledge that they are there. Both PVin and PVSV speak of the nonexistence, or non-activation *(apravṛtti)*, of *pramāṇas* "resulting" in a negation of cognition, etc. This idiom "resulting" is not to be taken in a purely causal way, but rather in a logical sense, meaning "establishing" or "proving." In other words, the nonexistence of *pramāṇas* is a reason which establishes the conclusion that there is no cognition, etc. of presence. Indeed, Śākyabuddhi, in commenting on the *Svavṛtti* to k. 3, makes it clear that we are dealing with a process of reasoning, i.e., two types of *anupalabdhihetu* which have different conclusions.[10]

> PVT D. 13a7: *yod pa dgag pa'i gtan tshigs ni bltar mi rung ba mi dmigs pa'o (/) med pa sgrub pa'i gtan tshigs ni dmigs pa'i mtshan nyid kyi gyur ba mi dmigs pa'o* / "The logical reason which negates presence is [one by] *adṛśyānupalabdhi (bltar mi rung ba mi dmigs pa)*. The logical reason proving absence is that of *anupalabdhi* of what has the character of being apprehendable *(dmigs pa'i mtshan nyid kyi gyur ba = upalabdhilakṣaṇa)*."

B. Only some kinds of *anupalabdhi*, namely *dṛśyānupalabdhi*, lead to a certainty that an object is absent, but nonetheless, both *adṛśya-* and *dṛśyānupalabdhi* are to be classified as *pramāṇas*. This fact that both are *pramāṇas* is clearly brought out in the latter part of the *Svavṛtti* passage, and I think that we have to take the passage as meaning that both *are equally full-fledged pramāṇas*. Let me take this up by examining a modern *pūrvapakṣa* in some detail.

Ernst Steinkellner, in a long note to his 1967 translation of the *Hetubindu*, had discussed the passage in the *Svavṛtti* and had concluded that the negation spoken about in connection with *adṛśyānupalabdhi* was only "hypothetical" *(hypothetisch)*, and that it was *dṛśyānupalabdhi* which would have the status of a full-fledged and real *(echt)* negation.[11] The result, according to Professor Steinkellner, was as follows: "Since by means of this non-apprehension one does not obtain any certain knowledge, Dharmakīrti also concedes that we should not regard it to be a *pramāṇa*."[12] According to Steinkellner's reading of Dharmakīrti, it was supposedly only *dṛśyānupalabdhi* which would elicit certainty *(niścaya)* and which would definitively prove of some putative entity that "it is not there," or in other words, "it is not present" *(Es ist nicht; Es ist nicht vorhanden)*. The former type, viz., *adṛśyānupalabdhi*, would lead to doubt about some entity's absence and could only prove at most that "it is not so that it is there" *(Es ist nicht, dass es ist)*. I think that the point is best interpreted somewhat differently. In what follows I will try to present my reasons.

First of all, a "hypothetical" negation, or what is worse, a "hypothetical" or somehow inferior type of *pramāṇa,* is an extremely puzzling notion, and we would be better off if we could avoid burdening Dharmakīrti's system with something that we can hardly understand. Thus, our interpretation obviously would make considerable gains in simplicity and elegance if we could do as the Tibetans and speak of both the *adṛśyānupalabdhi* and the *dṛśyānupalabdhi* mentioned in k. 3 as being equally full-fledged inferential *pramāṇas* involving equally full-fledged real negations.

Second, from a logical point of view, can we, or could Dharmakīrti, reasonably make a difference between "It is not there" and "It is not so that it is there"? Perhaps a difference could be discerned by a sophisticated modern logician, but one would have to have a rather acute concentration for any such supposed difference to become apparent. Do we really want to impose on Dharmakīrti some complicated logical structures which would make a distinction between *Es is nicht* and *Es ist nicht, dass es ist?* I think the answer is that if we can avoid it, we had better not complicate an otherwise formally simple seventh-century logic.

Third, there seems to be Indian evidence in support of the Tibetan interpretation. Karṇakagomin, who essentially follows Śākyabuddhi, may well give us a clearer idea of how to take the occurrences of the terms "doubt" and "certainty" in the *Svavṛtti* passage. These commentators even anticipate the objection that the "doubt" spoken about in the *Svavṛtti* would make it impossible for *adṛśyānupalabdhi* to be a real *pramāṇa,* and then they go on to explain, in reply, that *adṛśyānupalabdhi* is a *pramāṇa* in one respect and not in the other: in particular, it is a *pramāṇa* for denying cognition of, speech about, and action directed towards presences *(sajjñānaśabdavyavahārapratiṣedha),* but it is not a *pramāṇa* with regard to absences or exclusion *(vyatireka),* for *in this respect* (and I would stress *only in this respect*) doubt persists.[13] In short, instead of speaking about *adṛśyānupalabdhi* in a general way as something lesser or "hypothetical" leading to doubt, the commentators seem to support the view that we need to make precise distinctions specifying the exact propositions for which it is a *pramāṇa* and those for which it is not. This is certainly in keeping with the Tibetan approach which distinguishes where *adṛśyānupalabdhi* is a *pramāṇa* and where it is not.

Fourth, according to indigenous Tibetan texts, the proposition which is being proven is that for such and such a person, there is no correct subsequent cognition or no *pramāṇa* of an imperceptible thing in front of him *(...nges byed kyi dpyad shes don mthun med pa; ...nges byed kyi tshad ma med pa)*, or that this person cannot reasonably maintain or act upon the proposition that such a thing exists in a specific place *(yod ces dam bca' mi rigs pa; yod nges tha snyad mi 'jug pa)*. This is a credible interpretation of *sajjñānaśabdavyavahārapratiṣedhaphalā*. Instead of taking Dharmakīrti to mean that *adṛśyānupalabdhi* serves to establish a proposition like "It is not so that it is there," the Tibetan scholastics argue that this type of *anupalabdhi* is proving that we ordinary beings cannot *know* or *say* that an imperceptible thing is present. And that is something quite different. After all, proving "We do not know whether *x* is there" is definitely not the same thing as proving "It is not so that *x* is there."

Last, I can imagine the following doubt à la Steinkellner: If you say Dharmakīrti and his commentators maintain that *adṛśyānupalabdhi* is a real *pramāṇa*, there must then actually be some proposition with regard to which it is in fact certain. Which one? Given our Tibetan-style interpretation of Dharmkīrti's words *sajjñānaśabdavyavahārapratiṣedhaphalā* and *sadvyavahāraniṣedhopayogāt*, the doubt is, fortunately, quite easily resolved. *Adṛśyānupalabdhi* would be a perfectly good negation and a perfectly good *pramāṇa*, as good as *dṛśyānupalabdhi*, and would even yield a type of certainty, although, of course, not one concerning absences of putative objects. The specific proposition that is being proven by an *adṛśyānupalabdhihetu*, namely the denial that there is cognition, etc. of presence, would be just as certain as the *sādhya* of the usual *anupalabdhihetu* where one proves absence of smoke when there is no fire.

C. Are there any other passages in Dharmakīrti's works, or in the works of other Indian authors, which clearly show an acceptance of a *fully probative adṛśyānupalabdhihetu*? Probably not. Or at least, very few. Apart from the discussion in the *Svavṛtti* concerning PV I, k. 3, the similar passages concerning PV I, k. 198–202 and the borrowings from the *Svavṛtti* in PVin II, there are not many other sources, at least as far as I can tell. There is, however, one passage in PV IV, k. 276–277, which deserves mention and which is interpreted by some Tibetans, such as rGyal tshab rje and dGe 'dun grub pa, as speaking about the two types of *anupalabdhi*.[14] But the grounds provided by PV IV, k. 276–277 for imputing recognition of a fully probative *adṛśyānupalabdhihetu* are quite slim, and one would only take these verses in that sense if one had already been convinced by the discussion concerning PV I, k. 3. As for other Indian authors, it is, of course, impossible for us to check everywhere, but certainly this second type of *anupalabdhihetu* is not nearly as developed or as clear as it is in the Tibetan literature. There is of course always the possibility that the term, or even an example of the *prayoga*, might crop up now and again in other Indian authors' works, but, provisionally at least, it seems to me unlikely that there are other very important Indian sources. It is interesting to note that 'Jam dbyangs bzhad pa'i rdo rje ngag dbang brtson 'grus (1648–1721), who in his *rTags rigs* almost invariably cites numerous Indian textual sources for the various logical notions which he discusses, in this case only seems to cite PV I, k. 3 and 200, the *Svavṛtti* passage to PV I, k. 3 and a small passage from the PVin.[15] These sources have either already been discussed by us or are very similar to the passages which we have taken up. 'Jam dbyangs bzhad pa gives nothing other than that. One can probably conclude that other Indian sources, if there were any, were either unknown to this great Tibetan scholar, or seemed to him so brief, obscure or inconclusive as to be not worth mentioning.

Let us now sum up our discussion of the Tibetan contribution to understanding Dharmakīrti's use of *adṛśyānupalabdhi*. Although Indians like Śākyabuddhi and Karṇakagomin did shed some light on the otherwise obscure passages of the PVSV and the PVin, Tibetans scholars undoubtedly went much further, their major contribution being that they gave definitions of this type of *hetu* and explicitly formulated the *prayogas* at stake, and thus showed clearly the exact procedure for arriving at an inferential *pramāṇa* based on an *adṛśyānupalabdhihetu*. It is especially this explicit formulation of the *sādhya*, *hetu*, etc. which is lacking in Śākyabuddhi and Karṇakagomin, and which gives us so much trouble if we base ourselves only on the Indian sources.

Finally, what information can be gleaned about the indigenous Tibetan developments concerning *adṛśyānupalabdhihetu?* Sa skya paṇḍita kun dga' rgyal mtshan (1182–1251), in the section of his *Rigs gter rang 'grel* (p. 240.1.4ff.; f. 146bff.) concerning *anupalabdhi,* conspicuously did not even speak of a valid *adṛśyānupalabdhihetu.* gTsang nag pa brtson 'grus seng ge (twelfth century)[16] and Bu ston rin chen grub (1290–1364) in their commentaries on the PVin passage which we cited above (and which largely resembles the key passage from the PVSV) did speak of an *adṛśyānupalabdhihetu,* but they gave explanations which did not go much further than the *Svavṛtti* and Śākyabuddhi's *Ṭīkā* on PV. Significantly, they did not give the *prayogas*, and their explanations are little more than paraphrases of Dharmakīrti.[17] The same holds for the commentary on PV by 'U yug pa rigs pa'i seng ge (thirteenth century).[18]

By the fourteenth and fifteenth centuries, however, texts of the dGe lugs pa school gave detailed interpretations of PV I, k. 3, definitions of the *adṛśyānupalabdhihetu* as well as illustrative *prayogas*, often with an elaborate discussion of the fine points of the wording of these reasonings.[19] Equally, the Sa skya pa *Rigs gter* tradition by this time must have had their own definitions and *prayogas,* although their general treatment was certainly different from that of the dGe lugs and even seems comparatively simpler and less sophisticated. An idea of the Sa skya pa/Rigs gter ba position can be gained from the *rTags rigs* of Glo bo mkhan chen (1456–1532), which is the earliest Sa skya pa text in this genre of literature which we possess. (It is true that other sources inform us of the existence of fourteenth-century Sa skya pa *rtags rigs* texts—such as that of gYag ston sangs rgyas dpal [1348–1414]—but these are, at present at least, unavailable.) By comparing Glo bo mkhan chen's *rTags rigs* and passages in rGyal tshab rje's *rNam 'grel thar lam gsal byed* (see our n. 7), it is clear that Glo bo mkhan chen's position on *adṛśyānupalabdhihetu* reflects an earlier Rigs gter ba view, one which was already known to rGyal tshab (1364–1432) and which the dGe lugs pa scholar had attempted to refute in his *rNam 'grel thar lam gsal byed.* Other Sa skya pas—notably, Śākya mchog ldan (1428–1507)[20]—also adopted the same formulations which had earlier been the target for rGyal tshab rje's refutations, so that it seems that by the time of Śākya mchog ldan and Glo bo mkhan chen, a distinctive Sa skya pa/Rigs gter ba view on the definitions and *prayogas* of *adṛśyānupalabdhihetu* had been relatively well established for some time. It also seems likely that this Rigs gter ba position constituted a significant addition or modification to the system of Sa skya paṇḍita. As we saw above, Sa paṇ did not speak about *adṛśya* in his discussion on *anupalabdhihetu,* confining himself to the *dṛśya* variety, all of which would suggest that although he probably knew about the existence of such a type of reasoning from Indian commentaries, he attached little philosophical significance to *adṛśyānupalabdhihetu.* It is interesting to note that both Glo bo mkhan chen and Śākya mchog ldan cited a key passage from *Rigs gter rang 'grel* which spoke *only* of *dṛśyānupalabdhi;* they then argued that Sa paṇ, in this passage, *must* also have intended to include the *adṛśya* variety. It is clear that for these authors, too, Sa skya paṇḍita's omission was problematic, and it is difficult to resist the impression that they sought to incorporate a later philosophical debate into Sa paṇ's *Rigs gter.*[21] We might well hypothesize then that the major Tibetan developments on *adṛśyānupalabdhi* took place in the context of the dGe lugs pa-Sa skya pa dialectic, around the fourteenth century. And if we can offer hypotheses about when things happened, we might go one step further and speculate as to where. It would not be at all surprising if it turned out that these developments in logic centered around the celebrated monastery of gSang phu (s)ne'u thog, which had both dGe lugs pa and Sa skya pa colleges and which was a decisive influence in the development of these respective logical traditions.[22]

Notes to Chapter 7

1 The attribution to Īśvarasena of the doctrine of the "logical reason possessing six characters" *(ṣaḍlakṣaṇahetu),* albeit a very reasonable hypothesis, seems to be unconfirmed by any specific Indian sources. It is, however, corroborated in the indigenous Tibetan commentary on the PVin by rGyal tshab dar ma rin chen, where Īśvarasena is explicitly named in connection with the *ṣaḍlakṣaṇahetu* doctrine. See Steinkellner (1988: n. 47). [Editor's note: see also Tillemans (1994), reprinted as chapter 3 in the present volume.]

2 See Ruegg (1985). See also Tillemans (1990, vol.1: 16ff).

3 The matter has been explored by Steinkellner and others. See Steinkellner (1983) and the introduction to Tillemans (1993a).

4 The unacceptable, or completely nonexistent, type of universal which Dharmakīrti is supposedly refuting, is one which is substantially existent *(rdzas yod)* and is a different object from its particulars *(spyi don gzhan).* Tibetan commentators stress, however, that there are universals which are simple mental constructs and have at least conventional existence. In other words, it is argued that Dharmakīrti recognized the mental *apoha (blo'i gzhan sel),* or more exactly speaking, the *don spyi,* "object-universal," which

figures so prominently in dGe lugs and Sa skya exegesis. This notion of a *don spyi* is used to great advantage in explaining Dharmakīrti's thought, although it is not clear that the term *don spyi (=*arthasāmānya)* itself ever explicitly figured in this exact use in Dharmakīrti's or even in other Indian logician's works. Cf. the use of the term *don spyi/don gyi spyi* in Vinītadeva's *Nyāyabinduṭīkā ad* NB I.5. See, e.g., the characterization in the context of the definition of *kalpanā* (p. 41.9–11 ed. L. de la Vallée Poussin): *shes pa gang la rjod pa dang 'drer rung ba snang ba yin te / don gyi spyi'i ni don gyi rnam pa shes bya ba'i tha tshig go /.* [Editor's note: see n. 15 in Tillemans (1995a), reprinted as chapter 10 in the present volume.]

Undoubtedly what is much more speculative is the dGe lugs pa idea that Dharmakīrti accepted a fully real universal which was in essence identical with its particulars *(rang gi gsal ba dang ngo bo gcig)*. The justification for attributing this type of universal (i.e., *spyi dngos po ba*, "real universal") to Dharmakīrti's system is much less clear than the case of the *don spyi*, and it certainly solicited long and intricate debates amongst Tibetans themselves, so much so that it would be presumptuous for us to take sides in the context of this mini-résumé. For a fuller development, see Dreyfus (1991: 237–328) and Dreyfus (1992). Suffice it to say here that this dGe lugs pa version of *sāmānya* may well give us a highly fertile and radically different way of reading Dharmakīrti's statements on *apoha*. [Editors note: see chapter 10 in the present volume.]

5 See Dreyfus (1991: 773ff.); Tillemans (1990: 27, n. 75); Tillemans (1993a: 12–15). The debate turns on the interpretation of PV IV, k. 95ff. Here is k. 95:

> *tatprastāvāśrayatve hi śāstraṃ bādhakam ity amum / vaktum arthaṃ svavācāsya sahoktiḥ sāmyadṛṣṭaye //* "Indeed, in order to state this point that a treatise can invalidate *(bādhaka)* when it is the basis for the discussion, [Dignāga] spoke of these [authoritative words] together with one's own words so as to show similarity [between the two]."

6 I should remark that Steinkellner, during the discussion following the presentation of this paper in Oslo in August 1992, made it quite clear that he no longer holds this view of the matter.

7 *Yongs 'dzin rtags rigs*, pp. 33–34. Cf. also the usual textbook definition of *adṛśyānupalabdhihetu* which we find in dGe lugs pa logic manuals. *Yongs 'dzin rtags rigs* p. 33:

> *de sgrub kyi ma dmigs pa'i rtags yang dag kyang yin / rang nyid kyi rtags*

> *kyis de sgrub kyi dgag bya'i chos su brtags pa'i don de spyir yod kyang / rang nyid de sgrub kyi phyogs chos can du song ba'i gang zag gi tshad ma la mi snang ba de / khyod de sgrub kyi mi snang ba ma dmigs pa'i rtags yang dag gi mtshan nyid //* "The defining characteristic of *x* being a valid *adṛśyānupalabdhihetu* for proving [a proposition] *P* is as follows: *x* is a valid *anupalabdhihetu* for proving *P;* and although the entity which is imagined as the property to be negated when proving *P* by this reason does in general exist, it does not appear to the *pramāṇa* of the person for whom there would be a *pakṣadharma* for proving *P*."

It is interesting to note that the Sa skya pa *rtags rigs* (stemming from the *Rigs gter* tradition) seems to have adopted a more rudimentary definition, one which lacks the numerous sophisticated provisos which are to be found in the dGe lugs pa versions and which were obviously designed to eliminate the absurdities which would be raised in debates. The *rtags rigs* of Glo bo mkhan chen gives the following definition and *prayoga* (ed. Onoda [1992: 204]):

> *bsgrub chos yod nges 'gog pa la tshul gsum tshang ba de mi snang ba ma dmigs pa'i mtshan nyid yin / dper na / mdun gyi gzhi 'dir sha za yod nges ma yin te / de ltar tshad mas ma dmigs pa'i phyir zhes pa lta bu'o //* "The defining characteristic of an *adṛśyānupalabdhihetu* is 'that which satisfies the three characters for refuting that the *sādhyadharma* is certain to exist.' For example, it is like saying: 'It is not certain that a spirit exists/is present here in front, because it is not so apprehended by a *pramāṇa*.'"

The dGe lugs pa writer, rGyal tshab rje (1364–1432), was clearly aware of this version and rejected it as inadequate. See *rNam 'grel thar lam gsal byed*, vol. 1, p. 20:

> *mdun gyi gzhir sha za yod pa ma yin pa dang / yang yod nges ma yin pa dang / yod nges kyi bcas shes don mthun mi 'jug ste sha za tshad mas ma dmigs pa'i phyir zhes pa mi snang ba ma dmigs par 'dod pa mi rigs te / de lta na der sha za med nges su thal / de yod na dmigs su rung ba la de ma dmigs pa'i phyir //* "It is not correct to accept as *adṛśyānupalabdhi* that a spirit in front does not exist, or is not certain to exist, or that a correct subsequent cognition ascertaining existence does not occur, because the spirit is not apprehended by a *pramāṇa*. In such a case, it would follow absurdly that the spirit here is certain to be nonexistent, for if it existed it would be apprehendable, but it is not apprehended."

rGyal tshab's objection thus turned on the need to include the phrase *sha za bskal don du song ba'i gang zag gi ngor / rgyud la* ("For someone for whom a spirit is an inaccessible entity") in the *prayoga.* He rejected the version without this phrase as leading to the absurd consequence that the spirit would be absent/nonexistent. The point, as developed further on by rGyal tshab rje, was that if the spirit existed, at least the Buddha would have a *pramāṇa* apprehending it, and would be certain of its existence. Therefore if we say that there is absolutely no *pramāṇa* apprehending a spirit in front of us, this is tantamount to saying that the spirit is nonexistent. In short, rGyal tshab rje was aware of a tendency to omit the proviso *sha za ... gang zag gi ngor* and to understand the *prayoga* as something like "It is not certain that a spirit is present/existent here in front, because there is no *pramāṇa* apprehending such a spirit." For our purposes, it is important to point out that this version which rGyal tshab had rejected was precisely the one which was later adopted in Glo bo mkhan chen's *rTags rigs*, and probably represents the basic Sa skya pa/Rigs gter ba view.

The Sa skya pa Śākya mchog ldan (1428–1507) also omits the specification concerning *sha za bskal don du song ba'i gang zag gi ngor.* See his *Kun bzang chos kyi rol mtsho* f.5b1–3 (p. 198). Go rams pa, curiously enough, seems to have had a somewhat vacillating position. He put forth two quite different, and virtually incompatible, versions of the *prayoga* in his PV commentaries. In his *Kun tu bzang po'i nyi ma* 3b 4–5 (= p. 197), composed in 1474, he gives a version which resembles that of the dGe lugs pa: *sha za skal don du song ba'i gang zag gi ngor / mdun gyi gzhi 'di(r) chos can / sha za yod nges min te / sha za tshad mas ma dmigs pa'i phyir / zhes bkod pa'i tshe / sha za tshad mas ma dmigs pa de chos can / de ltar sgrub pa'i gtan tshigs yang dag yin te / de sgrub kyi tshul gsum tshang ba'i gtan tshigs yin pa'i phyir //.* His other version, in the *Kun tu bzang po'i 'od zer*, follows more strictly the wording of PV I, k. 3. The result, however, looks quite similar to the type of "misconception" which rGyal tshab rje had earlier attacked. *Kun tu bzang po'i 'od zer* 64b2–3 (= p. 32): *skal don sha za'i bum pa lta bu la bstan bcos la sogs pa'i tshad ma rnams ni mi 'jug pa de chos can / gzhi 'ga' tu med pa ste / skal don de la yod nges kyi tha snyad mi 'jug par go bar byed pa'i 'bras bu can yin te / gzhi 'gar skal don yod nges ma yin par sgrub pa'i tshul gsum tshang ba'i phyir /.* In his commentary on *Rigs gter*, however, he clearly sides with rGyal tshab's version. He first of all states that "most Tibetans" *(bod phal cher)* formulate the *prayoga* as simply *mdun gyi gzhi 'dir chos can / sha za yod nges kyi dpyad shes don mthun mi 'jug* (i.e., the version which rGyal tshab criticizes), and then he argues that the provision *sha za bskal don du song ba'i gang zag gi ngor* must be added. See his *Tshad ma rigs gter gyi don gsal byed* 101a–b.

8 Cf. PV Tib.: *tshad ma rnams ni mi 'jug pa // med la mi 'jug 'bras bu can // gtan tshigs bye brag la ltos nas // 'ga' zhig med shes 'bras bu can //*. Cf. the commentary on the first half of this verse in dGe 'dun grub pa's *Tshad ma rnam 'grel legs par bshad pa* p. 6:

> *gsum pa la gnyis / mi snang ba ma dmigs pa / snang rung ma dmigs pa'i rtags so // dang po ni / sha za bskal don du song ba'i gang zag gis sha za dmigs pa'i tshad ma rnams ni mi 'jug pa chos can / mdun gyi gzhi 'dir sha za bskal don du song ba'i gang zag gi ngor sha za yod nges kyi bcad shes mi 'jug par sgrub pa'i 'bras bu can te rtags yang dag yin te / de sgrub kyi tshul gsum yin pa'i phyir //* "To the third [i.e., *anupalabdhi*] there are the following two [divisions]: *adṛśyānupalabdhi-* and *dṛśyānupalabdhiliṅga*. As for the first: Take as the topic the non-activation [or non-occurrence] *(mi 'jug pa = apravṛtti)* of *pramāṇas* which apprehend spirits by people for whom spirits are inaccessible entities; this results in *('bras bu can = phalā)*, or in other words, is a valid logical reason for establishing that for a person for whom a spirit is an inaccessible entity, there will not occur *(mi 'jug pa = apravṛtti)* a subsequent cognition ascertaining that there is a spirit there in front; this is because the [reason] is a triply characterized one for establishing that [proposition]."

9 See Karṇakagomin's PVSVT: 34.18–27 on the above-cited passage from PVSV (words and phrases from the *Svavṛtti* text are highlighted in bold print): ***ekatrety*** *adṛśyaviṣayāyām anupalabdhau sattvasya* ***saṃśayāt*** *tato niścayātmakaḥ sattvavyavahāro nivartata eva / saṃdigdhas tu sattvavyavahāro na nivartate /* ***anyatra*** *tu dṛśyānupalabdhau* ***viparyayād*** *iti saṃśayaviparyayo niścayas tasmāt / asattvasya niścayād ity arthaḥ / yady adṛśyānupalabdhau saṃśayaḥ katham sā pramāṇam ity āha /* ***tatrādye****tyādi / tatra dvayor anupalabdhyor madhye* ***ādyā*** *'dṛśyānupalabdhiḥ* ***pramāṇam uktā sadvyavahāraniṣedhe upayogāt*** *vyāpārāt / kva tarhi tasyā aprāmāṇyam ity āha /* ***na tv*** *ityādi* ***vyatirekasyābhāvasya darśananiścayaḥ*** */* ***ādi****grahaṇāc chabdo vyavahāraś ca gṛhyate /* ***saṃśayād*** *yato nābhāvaniścaya utpadyate / tasmān na pramāṇam /* ***dvitīyā tv*** *iti / dṛśyaviṣayā 'nupalabdhiḥ /* ***atreti*** *vyatirekadarśanādau* ***niścayaphalatvān*** *niścaya eva phalam asyā iti kṛtvā /*. Cf. also the translation and explanation of the passages from the *Svavṛtti* in Gillon and Hayes (1991), who do not, as far as I can tell, accept the possibility of a valid *adṛśyānupalabdhihetu.*

10 For arguments in favour of the name "Śākyabuddhi" rather than "Śākyamati," see Inami, *et al.* (1992: v).

11 Steinkellner (1967: 157, notes): "'Hypothetisch' in dem Sinne, dass die

Negation hypothetisch ist, weil ihr ein Objekt nicht gesichert werden kann." See also ibid. (p. 158, notes): "'Echt' in dem Sinne, dass Dharmakīrti nur dieser Nichtbeobachtung Massgeblichkeit bei der Erkenntnis des Nichtvorhandenseins zuspricht."

12 Steinkellner (1967: 158, notes): "Da mit dieser Nichtbeobachtung keine sichere Erkenntnis zu erhalten ist, räumt Dharmakīrti auch ein, dass man sie nicht als Erkenntnismittel ansehen muss."

13 Here is the relevant passage from Karṇakagomin with the words of the *Svavṛtti* reproduced in bold print:

> *yady adṛśyānupalabdhau saṃśayaḥ kathaṃ sā pramāṇam ity āha /* ***tatrādyetyādi*** */ tatra dvayor anupalabdhyor madhye* ***ādyādṛśyānupalabdhiḥ pramāṇam uktā sadvyavahāraniṣedhe upayogāt*** *vyāpārāt / kva tarhi tasyā aprāmāṇyam ity āha /* ***na tv*** *ityādi* ***vyatirekasyābhāvasya*** ***darśananiścayaḥ*** */ ...* ***saṃśayād*** *yato nābhāvaniścaya utpadyate / tasmān na pramāṇam //* "[Objection:] If there is doubt in the case of *adṛśyānupalabdhi*, then how can this [type of non-apprehension] be a *pramāṇa*? [Dharmakīrti] replies: 'The first of them' etc. Of them, in other words of the two *anupalabdhi*, the first, or *adṛśyānupalabdhi*, is said to be a *pramāṇa* in that one uses it *(upayoga = vyāpāra)* to negate action directed towards something present. [Objection:] In what respect is it then not a *pramāṇa*? [Dharmakīrti] answers: 'But it does not' etc. It does not serve to prove, or ascertain, exclusion, i.e., absence. ... This is because doubt remains, i.e., it is because no certainty of absence is produced. And thus it is not a *pramāṇa*."

14 See *rNam 'grel thar lam gsal byed,* vol. 2, p. 377.

15 In his discussion on *adṛśyānupalabdhihetu* (*rTags rigs*, pp. 270–80), 'Jam dbyangs bzhad pa briefly quotes PVin (*rTags rigs,* p. 273, 277), PV I, k. 3 (p. 270, 277), PV I, 200 (p. 279) and parts of the *Svavṛtti* passage which we cited (p. 278, 279–80).

16 On gTsang nag pa's dates, see van der Kuijp (1989), p. 2.

17 See Bu ston's *rNam nges ṭīkā* 121b1ff. (= p. 252).

18 See 'U yug pa's *Tshad ma rnam 'grel gyi 'grel pa rigs pa'i mdzod* 103–5.

19 For Tsong kha pa, see *sDe bdun la 'jug pa'i sgo don gnyer yid kyi mun sel*, pp. 47–48. See rGyal tshab rje's *rNam 'grel thar lam gsal byed*, vol. 1 p. 20ff.; mKhas grub rje's *rNam 'grel ṭīk chen* 37b (= p. 690). For some idea of the debates on the wording of the *prayoga*, see n. 7.

20 See n. 7.

21 Cf. *rTags rigs* of Glo bo mkhan chen (ed. Onoda [1992] p. 201):

> *de yi don* rigs pa'i gter *las / chos kyi grags pas sbyor ba yi // sgo nas gsum du nges par mdzad // ces dang / dgag rtags mtha' dag snang rung ma dmigs par 'du ba'i phyir / dpe gcig gi steng du gtan la dbab tu rung bas gcig tu 'dus la / sgrub rtags kyi sbyor ba dpe gcig la sbyor du mi rung ba'i phyir gnyis su phye bas sbyor ba'i sgo nas gsum du grangs nges pa yin no //* zhes gsungs so // 'di ltar na / mi snang ba ma dmigs pa yang 'dir bsdus pa yin no //* Rigs gter rang 'grel* 146b 3–4.

Śākya mchog ldan also attempts to add *adṛśyānupalabdhi en filigrane* in the above-mentioned passage of Sa skya paṇḍita. See *Tshad ma rigs gter gyi rnam bshad*, pp. 665–66: *'dir mi snang ba ma dmigs pa'i gtan tshigs ma bshad pa dang / gong du sgrub byed kyi dbye bar yid ches pa'i gtan tshigs ma bshad pa gnyis kyi dgongs pa brtag par bya dgos la /.*

22 This monastery, founded in ca. 1073, was located not far from Lhasa in the gSang phu valley on the eastern bank of the sKyid chu River. For its history and importance, see van der Kuijp (1987) and Onoda (1992: 13–22).

8: What is the *Svadharmin* In Buddhist Logic?

THE LOGICAL FALLACY of *āśrayāsiddha,* or "unestablished basis," occurs when the "basis" *(āśraya),* or subject *(dharmin),* of an argument is nonexistent—for our purposes, we shall call such a situation, "subject failure." Now, clearly it is more or less East-West common sense that, in usual cases at least, subject failure implies that one will not succeed in demonstrating the whole proposition in which that subject figures. To take the well-worn Western example, a proposition like "The present king of France is bald" is either false or neither true nor false, depending upon one's philosophical analysis, *because* there is no such king to whom we can ascribe baldness. The logical dependence of the truth of the proposition upon the subject's existence is agreed upon, even though the question whether subject failure implies falsity or presuppositional failure is not. Equally, a similar basic logical insight that the proposition's truth is dependent upon the subject is to be found amongst Buddhist logicians, who hold that a thesis *(pakṣa)* cannot be established when the subject fails, because debate about its properties will naturally cease.[1] That said, there are problematic cases where a philosopher, Buddhist or otherwise, would certainly wish to maintain that subject failure, or *āśrayāsiddha,* does *not* occur, even though the subject is nonexistent. For the Buddhist logician, this philosophical problem—i.e., when *āśrayāsiddha* genuinely occurs and when the accusation is simply misplaced—typically comes up in connection with such arguments as proofs of momentariness *(kṣaṇabhaṅgasiddhi),* refutations of pseudo-entities accepted by non-Buddhists, and in the later Madhyamaka proofs of the absence of intrinsic nature *(niḥsvabhāvatā).* Thus, for example, to take an argument which figures in Dharmakīrti's *Pramāṇavārttikasvavṛtti* and in the third chapter of his *Pramāṇaviniścaya,* if someone manages to show that the Primordial

Matter *(pradhāna)* accepted in Sāṃkhya philosophy does not in fact exist, then the Sāṃkhya proponent's thesis that *pradhāna* has such and such properties will thereby be invalidated. This much is fairly obvious (and little different from the case of the French king's baldness). The potential problem arises, however, when the Buddhist himself actually wants to show that a pseudo-entity like *pradhāna* does not exist, or when the Buddhist wants to simply deny that *pradhāna* has the essential properties which the Sāṃkhyas attribute to it. We can readily understand that for the Buddhist, in *this* type of context, where he is proving a simple denial of existence, a charge of *āśrayāsiddha* must somehow be ruled out, on pain of an absurd self-refutation.

The point of departure in many later Indian or Tibetan discussions on *āśrayāsiddha* is very often Dignāga's definition of the thesis *(pakṣalakṣaṇa)* in *Pramāṇasamuccaya* III, k. 2, in particular, the specification that the thesis should not be opposed *(anirākṛta)* by perception and other means of valid cognition *with regard to the proponent's own intended subject* (*svadharmiṇi* "with regard to his own subject").

> PS III, k. 2: *svarūpeṇaiva nirdeśyaḥ svayam iṣṭo 'nirākṛtaḥ / pratyakṣārthānumānāptaprasiddhena svadharmiṇi //* [A valid thesis] is one which is intended *(iṣṭa)* by [the proponent] himself *(svayam)* as something to be stated *(nirdeśya)* in its proper form alone *(svarūpeṇaiva)* [i.e., as a *sādhya*]; [and] with regard to [the proponent's] own subject *(svadharmin),* it is not opposed *(anirākṛta)* by perceptible objects *(pratyakṣārtha),* by inference *(anumāna),* by authorities *(āpta)* or by what is commonly recognized *(prasiddha).*

By saying that the thesis or "what is being proven" *(sādhya)* should not be opposed *(anirākṛta)* "with regard to [the proponent's] own [intended] subject *(svadharmiṇi),*"[2] Dignāga supposedly recognized that not only the property to be proved *(sādhyadharma)* should be unopposed by any means of valid cognition *(pramāṇa),* but also that the proponent's subject must be existent, for if the subject were not existent it could not have the property, and hence the thesis would be invalidated.[3]

Now, the term *svadharmin,* which figures briefly in Dignāga's *Pramāṇasamuccaya* (but not in his earlier *Nyāyamukha*), will be commented upon *in extenso* in Dharmakīrti's PV IV, k. 136–48 as meaning that one has to make a distinction between the subject actually intended by the proponent himself *(svadharmin)* and one which is just unrelated, "isolated" *(kevala),* or (to adopt a frequent Tibetan gloss on *kevala*) is simply "nominal" in the sense that it is spoken about but is not the actual subject at stake.[4] It is only when the proponent's actual intended subject fails to exist that the fallacy of *āśrayāsiddha* will occur. The necessity to make a separation between the two especially arises in the cases where one wishes to prove that a certain pseudo-entity is in fact nonexistent or does not have such and such an essential property, for, as we saw earlier, it is especially in this type of case that *āśrayāsiddha* would be an absurd self-refutation. What is it in nonexistence proofs that makes them of different logical structure from other proofs, so that differences of *svadharmin* and *kevaladharmin* can (and indeed must) be made? What is the *svadharmin* and what is the *kevaladharmin* in *such* proofs?[5]

What we find in the Indian Buddhist literature is that Dharmakīrtian commentators, like Devendrabuddhi and Śākyabuddhi, in their explanations of PV IV, k. 136–48, emphasize the idea that subjects, like space, taken as real *(dngos por gyur pa = vastubhūta)* by the opponents, are *kevala* in proofs where the property to be proved and the reason are "mere exclusions" *(rnam par gcod pa tsam = vyavacchedamātra);* in these special cases, the subjects can be negated with impunity. Although Devendrabuddhi himself does not gloss these "mere exclusions" by the notion of non-implicative negations *(prasajyapratiṣedha)* so often invoked in Buddhist philosophy, the transition is very natural and is, indeed, explicitly made by Śākyabuddhi: mere exclusion means that no entity or positive property is stated, implied or presupposed.[6] The idea then is that so long as we are merely denying that such and such a pseudo-entity has a property *P* (e.g., existence, permanence, etc.), no positive assertion of any other property is implied at all, and *hence* a charge of *āśrayāsiddha* would be misplaced. Such a position was adopted by writers such as Prajñākaragupta, Kamalaśīla and by Tibetan writers such as Tsong kha pa, lCang skya rol pa'i rdo rje, A lag sha ngag dbang bstan dar and the Sa skya pa, Śākya mchog ldan *et al.,* with the *further development* that when a Buddhist logician is proving a mere exclusion, or non-implicative negation, such as that the Vaiśeṣika's space *(ākāśa)* is not a permanent unity or that the Sāṃkhya's Primordial Matter *(pradhāna)* does not exist, the *kevaladharmin* is just the space or Primordial Matter which the adversary takes to be real, whereas the Buddhist proponent's intended subject, the *svadharmin,* is the conceptual image of these pseudo-entities. In that case, the proponent's own intended subject, i.e., the *svadharmin,* will be unreal externally *(avastubhūta),* but will nonetheless exist *qua* conceptual representation; the fallacy of *āśrayāsiddhahetu* will thus be avoided.

This is, in its essentials, the approach which was advocated by later Indian writers as well as by Tibetans, although with a number of innovations and refinements centering on the theory of *apoha* and on the nature of the conceptual representations, as well as some interesting discussions in the Tibetan literature on subtleties such as whether *prasajyapratiṣedha* would *always* allow us to avoid *āśrayāsiddha* or whether a conceptual subject could *only* legitimately have *prasajyapratiṣedha* as its properties.[7]

In fact, as we shall show, there are competing scenarios as to what the *svadharmin* was for Dharmakīrti and Dignāga when they dealt with Buddhist refutations of the pseudo-entities accepted by their adversaries.

> ***First scenario:*** The proponent's own intended subject *(svadharmin)* in nonexistence proofs and proofs of simple negations is taken to be just a *conceptual representation* of the entity in question and not the entity itself.
>
> ***Second scenario:*** The reasoning in question should be *paraphrased* so that the *svadharmin* and the property to be proved are to be understood in ways acceptable to the Buddhist proponent himself.

Now, the first way to take the *svadharmin,* which we shall designate as being the "Principle of Conceptual Subjects," turns on a deliberate rapprochement with Dignāga's discussion, in his *Nyāyamukha,* of the argument against the existence of Primordial Matter *(pradhāna = prakṛti)* and hence with the corresponding discussions in Dharmakīrti's PVSV and PVin III.[8] The second approach (i.e., the "Method of Paraphrase") is probably what figures in the discussion on *svadharmin* in *Pramāṇasamuccaya(vṛtti)* III and *Pramāṇavārttika* IV. It is, broadly speaking, close to the Method of Paraphrase which was used in *Nyāyamukha* to analyse the Sāṃkhya's supposed proof for *pradhāna* existing because of the individual things all bearing the same general characteristic.

Let us first look at the *Nyāyamukha* and *Pramāṇasamuccaya* in a bit more detail.[9] In the *Nyāyamukha,* Dignāga had discussed different arguments in connection with the Sāṃkhya school, the first argument being a supposed Sāṃkhya proof of the existence of *pradhāna* due to the various individual things possessing the same general characteristic, the second being a Buddhist argument to show *pradhāna*'s nonexistence. In both cases, given that the subject of the argument was *pradhāna,* a pseudo-entity, there was a potential charge of *āśrayāsiddha.* Dignāga, in the first case, had avoided this charge by giving what he took to be a more rigorous philosophical *paraphrase* of the opponent's argument:

> "For them, [as for the first syllogism,] they should formulate the thesis as 'The various individuals certainly possess one and the same cause [i.e., *pradhāna*],' in which case they do not prove [directly the existence of] the Primordial Matter [i.e., *dharmin*]."

Dignāga then took up the second reasoning, "Primordial Matter *(pradhāna)* and so forth are nonexistent because they are not perceived" *(na santi pradhānādayo 'nupalabdheḥ),*[10] and avoided the fault of *āśrayāsiddha* by invoking the idea of the subject being merely conceptual:

> "When they [i.e., the Buddhists] argue that [Primordial Matter] does not exist [because of nonperception], 'nonperception' is a property of the imagined object [i.e., *pradhāna*] *(kalpitasyānupalabdhir dharmaḥ).*"

It is noteworthy that later, in the subsequent parallel discussion in PS III, Dignāga prudently avoided even mentioning the problematical second reasoning and that elsewhere, taking up *pradhāna,* he seems to have advocated more rigid strictures, excluding as illegimate all arguments which had such unacknowledged pseudo-entities as subjects. Primordial Matter was not to be a subject of inference. As Katsura has pointed out recently, what may be the case is that Dignāga had little place in *Pramāṇasamuccaya* for such proofs at all, and that Dignāga, in his later writings, tended towards a logic in which unreal or conceptual subjects could have no role.[11]

Be that as it may, Dharmakīrti used the argument in Dignāga's *Nyāyamukha* proving the nonexistence of *pradhāna* as well as the *Nyāyamukha*'s phrase *kalpitasyānupalabdhir dharmaḥ*[12] to come up with a general principle in PV I, k. 205–12, the *Svavṛtti* and PVin III that the directly signified objects of words were always conceptual representations *(kalpanā);* he then maintained that although *pradhāna* did not exist as something real and external, its conceptual representation, or in other words, the object of the word *(śabdārtha)* existed, so that the charge of *āśrayāsiddha* did not apply. The argument relies on ideas from the theory of *apoha,* but is situated in the context of the general discussion of nonperception *(anupalabdhi).* To take PV I, k. 205–6 (= PVin III, k. 53–54):

> *anādivāsanodbhūtavikalpapariniṣṭhitaḥ / śabdārthas trividho dharmo bhāvābhāvobhayāśrayaḥ // tasmin bhāvānupādāne sādhye 'syānupalambhanam / tathā hetur na tasyaivābhāvaḥ śabdaprayogataḥ //* "The verbal object *(śabdārtha),* which is completely derived from conceptualization proceeding from beginningless tendencies, is a *dharma* of three kinds: based on something existent, something nonexistent or both.[13] When this [verbal object, such as *pradhāna,* etc.], which is without any existent substratum, is being proven, then the nonperception of this as being in such a way [i.e., as existing externally] is the logical reason. The nonexistence of this very *[śabdārtha]* itself is not, for we do use words [like '*pradhāna,*' etc.]."[14]

Commentators, on the other hand, use the passages in the *Svavṛtti* and in the PVin III, in which there is no talk of *svadharmin* but only of conceptual representations, as their textual justification for *also* taking the *svadharmin* spoken of in PV IV as being a conceptual representation when the Buddhist is arguing against pseudo-entities accepted by other schools. Significantly enough, though, the actual passages in *Pramāṇavārttika* IV (and in *Pramāṇasamuccaya* III) which discuss *svadharmin* do not mention or even allude to this idea of the subject in such proofs being a conceptual representation at all. The application of the general idea of *apoha* and *śabdārtha* found in PV I, k. 205–6 to the *svadharmin-kevaladharmin* context figures only in the commentators.

We seem to have commentators taking notions from one context, i.e., the anti-Sāṃkhya discussion in the *Nyāyamukha, Svavṛtti* and *Pramāṇaviniścaya* and the theory of *anupalabdhi* and *apoha,* and imposing them on another, namely, the discussion about *svadharmin* in *Pramāṇasamuccaya(vṛtti)* III and *Pramāṇavārttika* IV. How well does this stratagem work? It may work as a creative synthesis, but not, I think, as a faithful textual account.

Significant here are Prajñākaragupta's explanations of *Pramāṇavārttika* IV, k. 141–42 in that we find this eighth-century commentator *ex-*

plicitly stating that there were the two scenarios (which we spoke about above) when interpreting Dharmakīrti's refutation of the Vaiśeṣika notion of really existent and permanent space (i.e., a pseudo-entity which no Buddhist will accept). In particular, Prajñākaragupta makes it clear that one interpretation of these *kārikās* was to invoke what we have termed the "the Principle of Conceptual Subjects": the actual intended subject is not the space which the Vaiśeṣika takes to be a real external entity *(vastubhūta)*—that is only the nominal subject, the one which is spoken about, but is not what possesses the properties to be proved or the reason—the *svadharmin* is the conceptual representation of space. Thus, according to Prajñākaragupta, on this first scenario the *svadharmin,* on the basis of which the proponent proves that space does not have "a novel nature unproduced [by causal conditions]" *(na...anutpādyāpūrvarūpa),*[15] is unreal *(avastubhūta)* and is completely derived from conceptualisation.

The other interpretation of *Pramāṇavārttika* IV, k. 141–42 mentioned by Prajñākaragupta—an interpretation which clearly turns on the Method of Paraphrase—is that the *svadharmin* is not the Vaiśeṣika's permanent unitary space, nor the conceptual representation, but rather the impermanent space which the Buddhist himself accepts. The argument in k. 141–42 thus has to be paraphrased and actually means that space is impermanent because it produces effects sequentially. We quote k. 141–42 along with Prajñākaragupta's *Pramāṇavārttikabhāṣya:*

> PV IV, k. 141–42: *yathā parair anutpādyāpūrvarūpaṃ*[16] *na khādikam / sakṛc chabdādyahetutvād ity ukte prāha dūṣakaḥ // tadvad vastusvabhāvo 'san dharmī vyomādir ity api / naivam iṣṭasya sādhyasya bādhā kācana*[17] *vidyate //* "For example, when [the Buddhist] states that space, etc. do not have a novel nature unproduced by other [conditions] because they are not causes for [producing their qualities such as] sound, etc. all at once, then the [Vaiśeṣika] adversary might say that like that the subject, space, etc., would also not have the nature of a real entity. [Dharmakīrti's position:] In this fashion [even though the subject is invalidated[18]], there is in fact no invalidation of the intended [proposition] to be proved *(sādhya)* at all."

PVBh *ad* PV IV, k. 141–42: "Here an opponent might say: 'But this proves that space and the like are not novel natures unproduced [by causal conditions]. In that way, it proves that a subject such as space is not real *(vastutvābhāva)*.' [Reply:] An unrelated invalidation of the subject is not faulty. Indeed, the proponent commits no fault like this. For, precisely what he intends to prove is that space and so forth are not real. Consequently, there is no fault in saying with reference to a subject, unreal space *(avastubhūtākāśadharmiṇi)*, that space does not have a novel nature unproduced [by other causal conditions], because it is not a cause [for producing its effects such as sound] all at once. This is because [he] establishes the [property] to be proved on the basis of a subject which is completely derived from conceptualization *(vikalpapariniṣṭhite dharmiṇi sādhyasādhanād)*. But a real thing is not the subject of that [property]. Therefore, although there is invalidation of this unrelated *(kevala)* [subject], there is [in fact] no fault. This is what is meant by the word *svadharmin* [in *Pramāṇasamuccaya*]. Indeed, when the opponent's subject is invalidated it is not so that this property [i.e., nonexistence] will be unestablished. So, as there is nothing annuling the establishment of the property to be proved *(sādhyadharma)*, there is no fault.

Alternatively, this [reasoning that space] does not have a novel unproduced nature because it is not the cause [for its effects] all at once, has the following meaning: space is impermanent. To this an adversary might say that the subject, permanent space, has been invalidated. But let it be invalidated. Even so the subject will be impermanent space. For, the contrary of the [property] to be proved will definitely be invalidated by the logical reason. And indeed a permanent subject is not the locus for the property to be proved under discussion, so when it is invalidated how could there be any fault at all!"[19]

The question immediately arises: Which of the two interpretations, or two scenarios, best fits *Pramāṇavārttika* IV? Or, in other words: How exactly did Dharmakīrti make the distinction between the proponent's own intended subject *(svadharmin)* and unrelated *(kevala)* subjects in PV IV, k. 136–48? Did Dharmakīrti opt for an approach which relied upon the Principle of Conceptual Subjects or did he use the Method of Paraphrase? In our opinion, there can be little doubt: Dharmakīrti's position in PV IV was the Method of Paraphrase. The commentators' attempts to read a Principle of Conceptual Subjects into k. 136–48 are an attempt to read the *Svavṛtti-Pramāṇaviniścaya* discussion of *apoha, śabdārtha* and *anupalabdhi* into a context where it does not easily belong. That said, most, if not all, of the later Indo-Tibetan tradition has understood the relevant *kārikās* in Dharmakīrti's *Pramāṇavārttika* IV according to the first scenario!

If we look at the rest of the discussion in this section of *Pramāṇavārttika* IV, it is clear that k. 144–45 is a complete parallel to k. 141–42: what holds for the latter should hold for the former. In k. 144–45, Dharmakīrti is confronted by the objection that if his refutation of the Vaiśeṣika's permanent space is correct, then a certain Buddhist argument against the Sāṃkhya will fail, for the Buddhist will have to face the charge that refuting the subject would lead to invalidation of the whole thesis and hence *viruddhahetu*. Briefly said, the negative existential proof would turn out to be self-refuting. The stated subject of the anti-Sāṃkhya argument is "pleasure, etc." *(sukhādi),* that is to say, "pleasure, pain and bewilderment," each of these terms being understood in the light of Sāṃkhya philosophy where each feeling is correlated with one of the three *guṇas* ("qualities"), these *guṇas* in turn being of the essence of Primordial Matter. The Buddhist then argues that pleasure, etc., i.e., *pradhāna,* is not the permanent nature of the various effects or transformations *(vikṛti)* making up the world, because if it were, then all its effects such as sound and the like would have to be produced simultaneously, and such is not in fact the case. Here the Sāṃkhya supposedly retorts that refuting the permanence of pleasure, etc., i.e., *pradhāna,* is tantamount to refuting the subject itself. Dharmakīrti then uses the Method of Paraphrase, to maintain that what the proponent is actually proving is that ordinary (and real) pleasure, etc., which are acknowledged by all, are impermanent, because they produce their effects sequentially *(kramakriyā)*—thus one does not refute the proponent's actual subject, which is pleasure, etc. taken as the ordinary, impermanent and fully real entity *(vastubhūta)* accepted by Buddhists and others alike, and not the theoretical pseudo-entity "pleasure, etc." as accepted by only Sāṃkhya philosophers.

The parallel with k. 141–42 is striking and deliberate: the arguments have the exact same reasons and virtually the same *sādhyadharma,* differing only in their choice of subjects, i.e., space, etc. or pleasure, etc. If

Dharmakīrti's whole argument is to work, then the *svadharmin* in k. 141–42 cannot be the conceptual representation, it must be the Buddhist's own accepted notion of impermanent space; just as in k. 144–45 the *svadharmin* is *not* an unreal conceptual representation, but is just the ordinary accepted entities. Not only that, but if we look at the terms used in Prajñākaragupta's description of the first approach (i.e., relying on the Principle of Conceptual Subjects), when Prajñākaragupta speaks of *vikalpapariniṣṭhite dharmiṇi sādhyasādhanād* the choice of words deliberately mirror k. 205's *anādivāsanodbhūtavikalpapariniṣṭhitaḥ*. The matter is thus probably as follows: the first approach, where one takes *Pramāṇavārttika* IV's discussion of *svadharmin* versus *kevaladharmin* along the lines of the first scenario is a commentator's strategy consisting in a transposition into *Pramāṇavārttika* IV of a discussion elsewhere in Dharmakīrti, but it is a transposition which probably does not fit the actual context of Dharmakīrti's argumentation of *svadharmin* and *kevaladharmin*.

I would not want to suggest that this "transposition" grossly falsifies the notion of *svadharmin*—that type of conclusion would not only look somewhat arrogant on our part but would denigrate the creative syntheses that commentators typically make in juxtaposing a doctrine in one part of a work with one in another. Nonetheless, I think it is important to see this later synthesis for what it is and that it probably did not *already* figure in Dignāga and Dharmakīrti's own thought. The question of conceptual representations being the subject in negative proofs was most likely not at stake in *Pramāṇavārttika* IV, k. 136–48, this in spite of the fact that so many authors from Prajñākaragupta and Kamalaśīla to Tsong kha pa and Ngag dbang bstan dar cite these *kārikās* as the source for the idea that the *svadharmin* is a conceptual representation.

A final remark. It is probably fair to say that the history of Buddhist thought about *āśrayāsiddha* and *svadharmin* would have been quite different if the Method of Paraphrase had been emphasized and further developed by later writers. Was it a good thing that the solution by conceptual representation became predominant in Buddhist logic? A type of Method of Paraphrase can be used very well to deal with the problem of talk about non-being, as we see in certain contemporary applications of Russell's Theory of Descriptions. We can, for example, paraphrase "Pegasus does not exist," or "Pegasus does not fly" as repectively: "There is no *x* which is Pegasus" or "There is no *x*, such that *x* is Pegasus and *x* flies, etc."; these approaches avoid the problem of a pseudo-entity nonetheless existing somehow as a concept. Paraphrase starts with the assumption that what is literally said is often not what is actually meant, and this assumption yields an extremely effective approach for avoiding commitment to needless conceptual entities. Thus a sentence like "I did it for Peter's sake" bears only an apparent similarity to "I did it for Peter's brother." Although we are committed to the existence of brothers, we are not actually obliged to accept that there are odd metaphysical or purely conceptual entities known as "sakes": "sakes" can be paraphrased away when we reformulate what we really mean. However, the Buddhists did not go that route; arguably they took a less promising path, fraught with avoidable problems. Indeed, the later Tibetan writings on the problem show just how complicating a development it was to mix *apoha* with the *svadharmin-kevaladharmin* problem. It is curious that most elements for a satisfactory theory of talk about non-being were already present to varying degrees in Dharmakīrti and some of the earlier commentators: a developed use of philosophical paraphrase and a theory of negation without presupposition of existence. The problem of *āśrayāsiddha* could have been treated purely as one concerning the *logical form* of statements and negations, but the temptation to turn to the all-purpose and ever-present semantic theory of *apoha* seems to have been irresistable. In the hands of commentators less taken with *apoha,* things could perhaps have turned out to be much simpler, but they did not.

Notes to Chapter 8

1 Cf. PV IV, k. 76–79, translated in Tillemans (1995b). Several studies have dealt with the Indian debates on *āśrayāsiddha,* one of the best still being Matilal (1970).

2 Cf. Vibhūticandra's gloss on *svadharmiṇi,* PVV: 459, n. 5: *vādineṣṭasya svasya dharmī svadharmī tatra.*

3 See PV IV, k. 137–39.

4 The term *kevala[dharmin]* = *chos can 'ba' zhig pa* does not seem to figure in Dignāga, but is introduced first in PV IV, k. 140:

> *nanv etad apy arthasiddhaṃ satyaṃ kecit tu dharmiṇaḥ / kevala-syoparodhe 'pi doṣavattam upāgatāḥ //* "[Objection:] But surely this too is established by implication. [Reply:] That is true. But some hold that [the thesis] is faulty even when an unrelated *(kevala)* subject is negated."

Devendrabuddhi is sparing in his gloss on *kevala,* describing it as *yan gar ba* ("isolated, alone, separate"); see PVP D. 297b2. PVBh *ad* k. 143 speaks of this "unrelated/nominal" *dharmin* as *tadasambaddhaparaparikalpitadharmin* ("a subject imagined by the opponent and unrelated to that [property to be proved]"). The term *yan gar ba* will be taken up again by Tsong kha pa, in his *dBu ma rgyan gyi zin bris:*

> *chos can 'ba' zhig pa ni / chos can du smras kyang skabs de'i bsgrub bya'i chos kyi rten min pas / chos can yan gar bar song ba'i don no /* "*kevala-dharmin* means that although it is stated as the subject it is not the basis of the property to be proved in that context [of the discussion] and is thus an isolated subject"; see Tillemans (1984c: 366–67).

Cf. Ngag dbang bstan dar's explanation (in his *gCig du bral gyi rnam bzhag,* p. 455.3) of *chos can 'ba' zhig pa* as *smras pa'i chos can* "the stated subject"; the section on *āśrayāsiddha* in this work has been translated in Tillemans and Lopez (1998). [Editor's note: this article has been reprinted as chapter 11 in the present volume.]

Finally, note that the Sa skya pa *Rigs gter* tradition as explained by Śākya mchog ldan speaks of the two types of subjects in terms of a somewhat different opposition, that of *song tshod kyi chos can* versus *rlom tshod kyi chos can,* "the subject as it [actually] is" versus "the subject as it is taken by inflated misconception." Cf. *Tshad ma rigs gter gyi dgongs rgyan smad cha* f. 76a2–4:

> *de lta na yang skabs 'dir dpyad pa 'di 'jug dgos te / gtso bo chos can / yod pa ma yin te ma dmigs pa'i phyir / zhes pa lta bu / med par dgag pa gtan tshigs su bkod pa rnams la rlom tshod kyi chos can med kyang / chos can gyi ngo bo ma grub par mi 'gyur la / yang gtso bo yod te / khyad par rnams rjes su 'gro ba'i phyir / zhes pa lta bu sgrub pa'i gtan tshigs su bkod pa rnams la song tshod kyi chos can yod kyang / rlom tshod med na chos can gyi ngo bo ma grub par 'jog dgos pa yin te / de lta bu'i tshul gnyis ka sde bdun mdzad pa'i gzhung las gsal bar gsungs pa'i phyir //.*

On the *song tshod* vs. *rlom tshod* opposition, see Dreyfus (1997: 161, 168); see also Tillemans (1995a: 869–70, n. 19). [Editor's note: this latter article has been reprinted as chapter 10 in the present volume.]

5 Note that Tibetan writers coined and widely used the term *rang rten chos can,* "the subject which is his own basis," and used this term instead of the term *svadharmin* [= *rang gi chos can*]. It can be shown that this was an error which came from relying on the wrong translation of the PSV. However, the idea is the same as *svadharmin.* The translation of the PSV by Vasudhara-rakṣita is extremely bad here. The text in Kitagawa (1973: 472) reads: ...*ma bsal ba'o // mngon sum don dang rjes dpag dang yid ches grags pas rang rten la'o.* This passage is what was cited by numerous authors, including Tsong kha pa, lCang skya and also Sa skya pas like Go rams pa bsod nams seng ge, but only as *mngon sum don dang rjes dpag dang yid ches grags pas rang rten la'o,* which, without *ma bsal ba,* is little better than gibberish. The problem is that the phrase *ma bsal ba'o = anirākṛta,* having a final particle *('o)* was probably not understood to go together with *mngon sum ... rang rten la'o,* and as a result it was not cited at all. The translation of Kanakavarman correctly has *rang gi chos can la mngon sum ... grags pas ma bsal ba'o (= 'nirākṛtaḥ / pratyakṣārthānumānāptaprasiddhena svadharmiṇi //);* see Tillemans (1984c: n. 42). The phrase *rang rten la'o* is also sometimes cited in earlier works, such as on p. 438 of the thirteenth-century work, *rNam 'grel gyi rnam bshad gangs can gyi rgyan* of bTsun pa ston gzhon, who followed the *Rigs gter* of Sa skya Paṇḍita; however *rang rten chos can* may be a later invention. At any rate, it is found in Tsong kha pa's *dBu ma rgyan gyi zin bris* and in the numerous dGe lugs explanations of *āśrayāsiddha* based on this *zin bris.*

6 PVP D. 296b4 *et seq.;* PVT D. 269a4–5: *gtan tshigs rnam par gcod pa'i ngo bo ma grub pa nyid ma yin no zhes bya ba ni / cig car sgra sogs rgyu min phyir / zhes bya ba'i gtan tshigs rnam par gcod pa tsam gyi ngo bo* med par dgag pa *tsam gyi mtshan nyid ma grub pa nyid ma yin te / dngos por gyur pa'i chos can med na yang tha snyad pa'i chos can rnam par gcod pa tsam la gnod pa med pa'i phyir ro //.* On *prasajyapratiṣedha* versus *paryudāsapratiṣedha* ("implicative negation"), see Kajiyama (1973) and the references in its n. 1.

7 These are developed in Ngag dbang bstan dar's *gCig du bral gyi rnam bzhag.* See Tillemans and Lopez (1998: 101–2). [Editor's note: see pp. 250–51 in the present volume.]

8 PVin P. 306a–307a; PVin III, k. 53–57 = PV I, k. 205–8 and 210.

9 For the *Nyāyamukha,* see Katsura (1992: 230–31), Katsura (1978: 110–11), and Tucci (1930: 16–17); the parallel passage in PSV is P. 128b6–8. The translations from the *Nyāyamukha,* in what follows, are those in Katsura (1992: 230).

10 See PVSV (Gnoli: 105): *atha yad idaṃ na santi pradhānādayo 'nupalabdher iti /...*

11 See Katsura (1992: 231).

12 PVSV (Gnoli: 107): *yat punar etad uktaṃ kalpitasyānupalabdhir dharma iti ...*

13 The point in k. 205's specifying three kinds of *śabdārtha* is that the conceptual representation which is the direct object of words can have as its substratum an existent thing like a cloth, or a nonexistent thing like a rabbit's horn, or something which is "both existent and nonexistent"—in this latter case, pseudo-entities like *pradhāna* or *īśvara* ("God") are existent *qua* concepts, but nonexistent *qua* external entities. Cf. PVV *ad* k. 204: *katham ity āha / bhāvābhāvobhayāśrayaḥ / sadasadubhayavikalpavāsanāprabhavatvāt / tadadhyavasāyena tadviṣayatvāt / tatra bhāvopādāno vikalpaḥ paṭādir abhāvopādānaḥ śaśaviṣāṇādiḥ / ubhayopādānaḥ pradhāneśvarādiḥ /.*

14 Additions based on PVV.

15 This is the same as proving that space is not a permanent unity.

16 The reading in Miyasaka's edition, i.e., *anutpādyā pūrvarūpan,* is wrong.

17 Miyasaka, *kvacana;* cf. Tib. *'ga' yang.*

18 PVV *ad* k. 142: *evaṃ dharmibādhane 'pi.*

19 *atra prativādy āha / athaivāyam anutpādyāpūrvarūpatābhāvaṃ sādhayati vyomādīnām (/) tathā vyomādidharmiṇo 'pi vastutvābhāvaṃ sādhayati / na dharmibādhanaṃ kevalaṃ doṣavat / na hy evaṃ vādino doṣaḥ / tena hi vastubhūtam ākāśādikaṃ na bhavatīty etad eva sādhayitum iṣṭam / tato 'vastubhūtākāśadharmiṇy anutpādyāpūrvarūpam ākāśādikaṃ na bhavati sakṛd ahetutvād iti na doṣaḥ / vikalpapariniṣṭhite dharmiṇi sādhyasādhanād vastubhūtas tu dharmī na tasya / tena tasya kevalasya bādhāyām api na doṣa iti svadharmivacanam / na hi paradharmiṇi bādhyamāne sa dharmo na sidhyati / tataḥ sādhyadharmasiddher* avyāghātād adoṣaḥ //*
*atha vānutpādyāpūrvarūpaṃ na bhavati sakṛd ahetutvāt / asyāyam arthaḥ / anityam ākāśam (/) tatra paraḥ / nityam ākāśaṃ dharmibādhitaṃ bhavati / bādhyatāṃ tathāpy anityam ākāśaṃ dharmī bhaviṣyati / avaśyaṃ hi hetunā sādhyaviparyayo bādhitavyaḥ / nityo hi dharmī na prakṛtasādhyadharmādhāras** tatas tadbādhane ka iva doṣaḥ /.* *R. Sāṅkṛtyāyana reads: *sādhyadharmisiddher;*

but see Tib. P. 234a5: *des na* bsgrub bya'i chos *'grub pa la gnod pa med pa'i phyir nyes pa ma yin no* // **Read *prakṛtasādhyadharmādhāras* following B (= Dānaśīla's ms) instead of *prakṛtasādhyadharmākāras.*

9: Is Buddhist Logic Non-Classical or Deviant?

FOR SOME YEARS we have witnessed among philosophers a growing interest in the epistemological and logical systems of Asian cultures. One of the pioneers in this regard was undoubtedly the Polish philosopher Innocentius Bocheński, whose *History of Formal Logic* contains an entire chapter devoted to Indian logic—a chapter that is not only still useful, but that also bears witness to this celebrated logician's open-mindedness. Likewise, the Dutch logician Evert Willem Beth emphasized on numerous occasions[1] the importance of the study of Indian logic for the general philosophy of logic. It was, however, Beth's compatriot, J.F. Staal, who actually undertook concrete research on the subject. Staal treated the topic in several articles, including one on the Nyāya-Vaiśeṣika theory of definition, another on negation according to the Mīmāṃsakas, and a third concerning the use of contraposition in various Indian schools. In this regard, we should also mention the works of the late Bimal Krishna Matilal of Oxford University. This remarkable philosopher, trained in both the traditional logic of Nyāya-Vaiśeṣika and analytical philosophy, has left us numerous studies on the logical and epistemological problems within the Indian philosophical schools. In 1970, he founded the *Journal of Indian Philosophy,* a journal whose aim is to apply the methods of analytical philosophy to the problems of Indian philosophy.

To demonstrate the importance of such studies, we could, of course, cite the names of many other scholars who work on the border between Asian studies and philosophy. We must recognize, however, that this approach bears considerable difficulties and that it can currently be practiced by only those who have sound training in Asian languages. The present state of research is such that translations and editions of numerous principal texts are far from completion, and among those that are available, a good number are mediocre. It is thus understandable that some scholars maintain that it would be premature to attempt serious work on comparative logic or epistemology—an opinion one often hears among both Asianists and philosophers. In part, this objection is justified, since at this point, a philosopher who is not competent in Asian languages runs the risk of basing his analyses or theories on incomplete or erroneous data.

There is another objection against a philosophical approach to Asian studies—an objection that even now has numerous advocates, at least among Anglo-American philosophers. Allow me to cite a particularly revealing passage from Anthony Flew's work, *An Introduction to Western Philosophy,* published in 1971:

> ...philosophy, as the word is understood here, is concerned first, last and all the time with argument. It is, incidentally, because most of what is labeled *Eastern Philosophy* is not so concerned—rather than any reason of European parochialism—that this book draws no materials from any source east of Suez.[2]

The objection amounts to two points: (a) philosophy should devote itself primarily to rational argumentation; (b) Asian philosophers do not exercise any—or, at least, very little—rational argumentation. Most probably, the second point stems from the opinion that Asian philosophers are primarily mystics, and that *hence,* they are irrational and bereft of argumentation. Professor Matilal devoted a large part of his academic career to the refutation of this received idea, and it is not necessary to replicate that discussion here. Let us simply note that in the philosophies of India, Tibet and China, there is an imposing number of philosophical and rational works that are not mystical at all. And in any case, when a religious goal—or even a mystical one—figures explicitly or implicitly in a text, the argumentation is often so autonomous that it is of considerable philosophical interest even for one who does not share the author's religious goals.

The idea, moreover, that Indian philosophy is essentially mystical and that *hence* it is bereft of rational argumentation is a *non-sequitur.* Let us suppose that a good part of these traditions are influenced by some type of mysticism: it does not *thereby* follow that rational argumentation stemming from or leading to those mystical ideas will be absent or insignificant. To take a similar case in Western philosophy, would we dare to be so severe with the mystical philosophy of the *Tractatus,* where Wittgenstein sought the limits of language so as to transcend those limits? No one would claim that Wittgenstein had renounced rational argumentation. In the Buddhism of the Madhyamaka school—of which we will often speak in this article—the philosopher also uses logic to arrive at an understanding beyond all argumentation and discursive thought. But as with the *Tractatus,* the majority of Madhyamaka writings are devoted to rational argumentation.

If Anthony Flew's ideas are typical of an approach where one tends to underestimate the role of argumentation in Asian thought, there is another widespread belief regarding Asian thought. On this view, one admits that these philosophies employ arguments, but one maintains that their ways of reasoning diverge substantially from our own, or even that their forms of rationality are incommensurable with occidental thought. Indeed, there are Indian texts containing arguments that may seem difficult to reconcile with the most fundamental laws of Western logic. We are thinking primarily of problematic passages found in Buddhist texts such as the *Sūtra on the Perfection of Wisdom (Prajñāpāramitāsūtra),* the famed *Stanzas on the Middle Way (Madhyamakakārikā)* composed by Nāgārjuna (third century C.E.), or the *Four Hundreds (Catuḥśataka)* of his disciple Āryadeva. Within Buddhist thought, the structure of argumentation that seems the most resistant to our attempts at formalization is undoubtedly the tetralemma or *catuṣkoṭi.* This structure appears scattered throughout the canonical Mahāyāna literature, but it is above all found in the works of Nāgārjuna and Āryadeva, where it becomes the method *par excellence* used by the Madhyamaka to refute all philosophical theses.

The *Catuḥśataka* speaks of the tetralemma in the following manner:

> *sad asat sadasac ceti sadasan neti ca kramaḥ / eṣa prayojyo vidvadbhir ekatvādiṣu nityaśaḥ //* "Being, non-being, [both] being and non-being, neither being [nor] non-being: such is the method that the wise should always use with regard to identity and all other [theses].[3]

We have here the four alternatives at their most abstract level: being, non-being, both at the same time, and neither one nor the other. The Madhyamaka method for arriving at absolute truth is to refute all four alternatives, regardless of the proposition to which they apply.

Clearly, the conjunction of these four negations would make a Western logician dizzy, since, at first glance, the Madhyamaka offers us the following four statements:[4]

[1] $\sim P$
[2] $\sim\sim P$
[3] $\sim(P \,\&\, \sim P)$
[4] $\sim(\sim P \,\&\, \sim\sim P)$

Since (1) and (2) would imply $\sim(P \vee \sim P)$, the law of the excluded middle falls by the wayside, but what is worse, we would likewise encounter various contradictions: $\sim P \,\&\, \sim\sim P$ from [1] and [2]; $(\sim P \,\&\, \sim\sim P) \,\&\, \sim(\sim P \,\&\, \sim\sim P)$ from [1], [2], and [4]; or again simply $P \,\&\, \sim P$ from [1] and [2] by the law of double negation.

A logically trivial interpretation of the tetralemma would be to consider it to be a uniquely "therapeutic" use of language and hence close to what the positivists of the Vienna Circle called "non-cognitive statements." The four negations would therefore be pseudo-propositions devoid of any truth-value: they would just be one of the many Buddhist techniques designed to halt ordinary thought—as with the riddles *(koan),* the blows from the teacher's staff, or the sudden shouts that fulfill the same function in the Zen schools. The great Asianist Louis de la Vallée Poussin thought that the tetralemma could be understood only in this manner, that is, as a psychological technique designed to induce a certain meditative state: "Nāgārjunism [i.e., Madhyamaka] is without philosophical significance…[it] contains nothing but a method for purifying the mind."[5]

Louis de la Vallée Poussin's notion has appeared with numerous permutations in the works of diverse authors. We cannot address all of these permutations here, but they nearly always have as their consequence the denial of any propositional content or truth value as applicable to any of the tetralemma's four negations. And it is precisely in this regard that this interpretation is insufficient, for it minimizes the role and the seriousness of argumentation in the Madhyamaka system. True, the contemplation of the four negations is indeed a method, an *upāya,* for halting discursive thought. Nevertheless, to say that the tetralemma is nothing but a psychological technique amounts to neglecting—or trivializing—the numerous rigorous arguments advanced by the Madhyamaka in support of each negation. Typically, the Madhyamaka uses this structure to argue in detail against opposing positions that, according to him, adopt one or another of the alternatives. He thus employs premises that are acceptable to the adversary so as to show him that his position is absurd, and that it actually implies its own contrary. But if Nāgārjuna uses the logic and metaphysics of his adversaries to refute their positions, one must nevertheless suppose that he believed his own reasoning by *reductio ad absurdum* to be not a mere ruse or sophism, but rather an argument that was valid and that resulted in a true conclusion, albeit negative.

We find among Asianists a long debate on the question of whether the tetralemma—as well as other, similar forms of reasoning rooted in the canonical texts of the Mahāyāna—stands as an example of a radical divergence between Asian logics and the classical logic of the West. Professor D. Seyfort Ruegg, in his excellent article on the use of the tetralemma,[6] has summarized the numerous attempts at translating this structure of Buddhist thought into the terminology of classical Western logic. He has likewise summarized the analyses that rely on alternative logic, including, for example, L. Mäll's semiotic analysis and the treatment by J.F. Staal based upon intuitionist logic.[7]

Undoubtedly, we must admit that the initial attempts at applying classical logic to the most recalcitrant structures of Mahāyāna Buddhist thought—most notably the tetralemma—have been failures. But what conclusion should we draw from these repeated setbacks? The stakes are high, for numerous philosophers currently apply themselves to the problem of knowing whether the formal calculi of alternative logics really have a field of application. It is thus of some importance to determine whether Buddhist texts provide examples of discourse that obey logical laws other than those of classical Western logic. In short, our problem is essentially located within the scope of a philosophical debate, initiated by W.V. Quine,[8] on the question of knowing whether alternative logics are possible and whether they have, in fact, a field of application.

At this point, our terminology requires some clarification. First of all, we must alert the reader that our term "Buddhist logic" does not translate any Sanskrit term. Generally, the term is used as a conventional designation for a certain school of Buddhist philosophy or a type of thought identified particularly with the school of Dignāga and Dharmakīrti—that is also how we have used the term in other publications.[9] Here, however, what we shall call "Buddhist logic" is a translation—as faithful as possible—into modern logic of the formal structures of thought found in Buddhist texts. Our project requires such a translation, since one obviously cannot ask about the possible deviance of a system that has not been sufficiently formalized. Hence, in the following pages, our arguments will essentially concern the adequacy of certain formal translations of the structures of Buddhist thought and the formal properties of the calculi employed in such translations.

By the term "classical logic," we understand the first order propositional and predicate calculus that one generally finds in a work on elementary logic.[10] What then would be the difference between a *non-classical* logic and a *deviant* one? Since the beginning of this century, various types of logics have proliferated: sometimes they are studied for their possible philosophical contributions, at other times, for their formal character. Among these logics, several types, such as modal or epistemic logic, are not true *rivals* of classical logic; rather, they are *supplements*—to employ the distinction presented by Susan Haack in the first chapter of her *Deviant Logic.*[11] According to Haack, a logic L_1 is a supplement for logic L_2 when:

(a) the sets of formulae and theorems of L_2 are included in the respective sets of L_1

(b) all of the surplus theorems of L_1 contain vocabulary that is supplementary to that of L_2.

If L_2 is classical logic, the supplementary logic L_1 described by (a) and (b) will be considered a non-classical logic, but not a deviant one. In contrast, an L_1 will be deviant relative to L_2 if L_1 has the same formulae and logical vocabulary as L_2, but nevertheless does not have the same set of theorems as L_2. Thus, a logic can have the same set of formulae as classical logic and use its vocabulary, while still rejecting some of the most important classical theorems. This is precisely the case for J. Łukasiewicz's multi-valued logic—as it is the case for intuitionist logic—that does not accept as theorems the laws of the excluded middle and double negation. These logics are not supplements but rather rivals to classical logic.

Another distinction proposed by Haack will prove useful: this is the one between *global deviance* and *local deviance.* The first type of deviance applies to all subjects of discourse, while the second is restricted to a limited domain of discourse. It is thus possible to use a deviant logic for mathematics or quantum physics while still retaining the use of classical logic in other domains of discourse—this would be a case of local deviance. In contrast, some neo-intuitionists such as M. Dummett apply their logic to all cases and would thus recommend a global deviance.

Let us return now to Buddhist logic, or more precisely, to our attempts at translating the statements of Buddhist philosophers into a formal logic. We should begin by noting that any potential deviance in Buddhist logic would be, at most, *local.* The structures of argumentation most frequently employed by Buddhists—including the Madhyamakas —do not present any violation of our classical logical laws. Here, we are thinking, for example, of the so-called "Buddhist syllogism," or more precisely, what the Buddhists themselves call an "inference-for-others" *(parārthānumāna).* Consider this example:

> All that which is conditioned is impermanent, like a vase.
> Now, sound is conditioned.

In fact, this form of argumentation is not a syllogism in the Aristotelian sense. The *parārthānumāna*—at least the version unanimously accepted after Dharmakīrti (sixth to seventh century C.E.)—only has two members and cannot itself state a conclusion. Indeed, from the seventh century onward, the addition of a conclusion, such as "therefore, sound is impermanent," is considered a "point of defeat" *(nigrahasthāna).*[12] Clearly, though, there is no question as to whether the logic involved here is deviant or not. Although the metalogical explanations for the functioning of inference diverge from our own, we are not confronted with a reasoning that would necessitate a translation into a logic that rejects or violates the most fundamental laws of logic, such as contradiction, double negation and the excluded middle.

We should likewise note that no surprises arise from formalization of other Buddhist notions, such as those analogous to material implication, conjunction, disjunction and other logical constants. Nor does the famous theory of *vyāpti* or "pervasion" provoke any formal surprises. For example, when Buddhist authors say that the property "is conditioned" *(kṛtakatva)* is pervaded by the property "impermanence" *(anityatā),* they mean that all conditioned things are impermanent. In other words, in our terminology, *vyāpti* is translatable, in part at least, as a universal statement: for all *x,* if *x* is conditioned, then *x* is impermanent.[13] Interestingly, the quantification expressed by "for all *x*" is certainly not limited to existent things, because the variable *x* also represents fictive entities. Nevertheless, while this reinterpretation of quantification differs from the usual interpretation in predicate calculus, it does not entail any deviance at all. In short, in many cases Buddhist argumentation might possibly require the introduction of some operators and terms that would be *supplementary* with regard to those of first order predicate logic. We would thus be obliged to employ a non-classical logic (in the sense of the term that we have specified), but the vast majority of arguments found in Buddhist texts do not require translation into a deviant logic. *If there is any deviance, it can only be highly local.*

Before continuing our analysis, we should respond to a possible objection. Is it possible that the tetralemma—which appears to violate the law of contradiction—might constitute a case of *local* deviance? One can easily show that any contradictory statement whatsoever entails all other statements, even those that are in violation of the most fundamental laws of logic. As a result, a single inconsistency appears to lead inexorably to the most global deviance imaginable.[14] An intuitionist logic, such as that of L. Brouwer and A. Heyting, only rejects the laws of double negation and the excluded middle, and this rejection does not entail uncontrollable implications. It is, however, far more difficult to envisage a calculus that does not admit the inviolability of the law of contradiction. It is hence imperative to know whether one can limit a logic's deviance while at the same time admitting exceptions to the law of contradiction.

Clearly, until recently the law of contradiction has been considered as an inviolable principle almost unanimously among logicians. Nevertheless, the old menace of uncontrolled implications has now been called into question by some of our more illustrious logicians, and inconsistent logics have thus become an acknowledged field of research. We can distinguish two strands within modern research on such logics: (a) formal calculi which contain several truth-values, such as the calculi of G. Priest,[15] and which admit contradictions but preclude unlimited implications; and (b) the semantics of N. Rescher and R. Brandom,[16] which admits an uncontrolled implication only in the case of a strong inconsistency (for Rescher and Brandom, it is possible, for example, to affirm that *P* is true and to affirm that non-*P* is true without, however, admitting the truth of the statement, *P* and non-*P*—this latter would in effect be a strong contradiction). The lesson that we can draw from these modern developments in logic is at once radical and surprising: *there is no formal requirement that* a priori *prevents us from adopting a literal reading of the paradoxical passages in the Madhyamakakārikā, the Catuḥśataka, and the Prajñāpāramitāsūtra. From the perspective of formal logic, these texts can include inconsistencies without becoming irrational discourses.*[17] In other words, nothing in formal logic stops us from saying that, in the vast majority of cases, the Buddhist uses a consistent logic but that, in certain contexts, he clearly accepts paradoxes. Of course, a paradoxical interpretation of Buddhist discourse is nothing new. Some of the early great Buddhologists, such as E. Conze and D. Suzuki, were convinced that "the logic of the *prajñāpāramitā*" is indeed paradoxical. This position may currently have few adherents, but it is nevertheless important to emphasize that one cannot exclude it without systematic, textual arguments: one cannot *a priori* sweep this opinion under the carpet by saying that the acceptance of contradictions amounts to irrationality.

This is not the place to examine passage after passage of the works of Nāgārjuna and Āryadeva. The reader can profitably consult the publications of scholars such as D. Seyfort Ruegg, J. May, G. Bugault, P. Williams and others. Elsewhere, we have already discussed the logic of the Madhyamaka and its interpretation in recent publications.[18] We will content ourselves here with raising three systemic points that militate against the attribution of a paradoxical logic to Buddhists:

(a) The prohibition against "contradiction" *(virodha)* is accepted by all schools of Indian philosophy, including the Buddhist schools. It would thus be surprising if a treatise by a great Buddhist philosopher were to go against such a key principle.[19]

(b) Buddhists themselves invoke a schema of two truths—the absolute truth and the superficial—so as to explain how one can affirm a proposition from one point of view and yet negate it from another. And since the time of Aristotle, we have considered a real contradiction to be the affirmation and negation of the same proposition *from the same point of view.*[20]

(c) A number of Indian authors exhibit the stylistic tendency to choose condensed, enigmatic, and provocative modes of expression. These statements inevitably assume a non-paradoxical meaning when they are explained by the authors themselves or by their commentators.

Let us take two particularly revealing examples of this stylistic tendency to deliberately employ paradoxical turns of phrase. The first example occurs in the *Madhyāntavibhāga,* a Mahāyānist text attributed to Maitreya:

> *sattvād asattvāt sattvāc ca madhyamā pratipac ca sā //* "Due to existence, due to nonexistence, and due to existence, this is the middle way." [21]

At first glance, at least, this passage may seem contradictory, but Vasubandhu (fourth century) clearly tells us that Maitreya is speaking of the existence of unreal conceptual constructions *(abhūtaparikalpa),* the nonexistence of all duality, and the existence of the emptiness of the unreal conceptual constructions. One can only agree with Ruegg, who concludes his discussion of this passage with this remark: "there seems therefore to be no question here of attributing to one and the same entity opposed properties on the same level of reference and from the same point of view."[22]

Let us now turn to an example of this same stylistic tendency in the *Vākyapadīya,* a work of the non-Buddhist author Bhartṛhari:

> *tan nāsti vidyate tac ca tad ekaṃ tat pṛthak pṛthak /saṃsṛṣṭaṃ ca vibhaktaṃ ca vikṛtaṃ tat tad anyathā //* "It [i.e., substance] does not exist, and it exists; it is one and it is divided; it is conjoined and it is separate; it is modified and it is other [than modified]."[23]

As J. Bronkhorst points out, in the context of Bhartṛhari's system this stanza must be understood as a description of substance from two different points of view—namely, as an absolute and indivisible reality, and as the phenomenal diversity of the world. Bronkhorst explains: "The indivisible totality is real, one and without modifications; its division—that is, the phenomenal world—is unreal, variegated, separate and modified."[24] As with Vasubandhu and Maitreya, here too the paradoxes disappear.

How then are we to dissipate the seeming paradoxes of the tetralemma's four negations within an adequate translation of that structure into modern logic? First of all, the Madhyamaka, in using the tetralemma, appears to wish to refute above all the attribution of properties (whether affirmative or negative) to real entities *(bhāva)*.[25] Such a project involves negations that concern things' absolute status—it does not seem to easily involve four unqualified negations in a simple propositional calculus, as we have presented them in [1]–[4]. Some commentators—such as Bhāvaviveka, but especially some Tibetans—have tried to add qualifications such as "truly established" (Tib. *bden par grub pa*) or "established from an absolute perspective" (Tib. *don dam par grub pa*)" so as to indicate clearly the level of discourse implicit in the use of the negation operators. This technique was used with great mastery by Tsong kha pa blo bzang grags pa, the great Tibetan commentator of the fourteenth century; he managed to transform the tetralemma into a sort of modal logic where the laws of double negation, excluded middle, and contradiction function in a classical manner.[26] Let us just consider here his version of the first two negations; they respectively become: "*P* is not established from an absolute perspective" and "non-*P* is not established from an absolute perspective." It is evident that these two propositions can both be true without imperiling the laws of contradiction and excluded middle. The result is that the negations of the tetralemma would be translated into structures that are at most supplementary with regard to classical logic.

Indisputably, Tsong kha pa's interpretation offers advantages in terms of its logical clarity, but as an exegesis of Madhyamaka, his approach may seem somewhat inelegant, since it obliges us to add words almost everywhere in the Madhyamaka texts. Remarkably, Tsong kha pa himself actually accomplished this project down to its most minute details in his commentary on the *Madhyamakakārikās*—perhaps at the price of sacrificing the simplicity of Nāgārjuna's language.[27] Hence, is there a simpler and more elegant interpretation of the tetralemma that also takes account of the negation of *bhāvas*, this denial of all ontology that lies at the heart of Madhyamaka philosophy? In the final portion of this article, we will sketch out a solution by proposing two ways of understanding the quantification implicit in the Buddhist's statements.

A logic without ontological commitment is possible. For some years, scholars such as R.B. Marcus, N. Belnap, R. Routley and others have regularly reinterpreted quantification in such a manner that the variables do not refer to objects in a domain but rather to terms that form a *substitution* class.[28] This tactic consists in proposing a substitutional semantics in lieu of the usual referential semantics, and it has been profitably employed within modal and epistemic contexts, as well as in fictional contexts, where one reasons about "things" that are devoid of any reality. In short, when interpreted in an substitutional manner, (*Ex*) *Fx* ("there is an *x* such that *Fx*") does not mean that there actually exists a real entity that has the quality *F*, but rather that there is a name *a* such that the substitution of *a* for the variable *x* in *Fx* yields a true sentence. Thus, if we wish, we can avoid all ontological commitment. In fact, most Western logicians who use a substitutional interpretation believe that reference to things is essential to any veritable language, and that as a result, one must introduce a referential relation that ties at least *some* names to objects. Nevertheless, a purely substitutional interpretation devoid of any such reference to real things remains feasible. D. Vernant describes such a semantics:

> ...the truth of the atomic sentences [of the language] L_0 is defined, *ab initio,* in a purely conventional fashion, abstracting from all actual reference. This is what occurs, for example, in *mythological* discourse, which defines as true the sentence "Pegasus is a winged horse," without inquiring into reference. In more general terms, such is the case for all *fictional discourse.* Without asking oneself about the actual reality of the objects arising from the creative imagination of an author, we can nevertheless assign a truth value to assertions about those objects. In this manner, we know full well that it is false to say that Hamlet is Ophelia's brother.[29]

A possibility that, to our knowledge, has not been seriously considered in Western logic would be to *universalize* this ontologically neutral use of a substitutional interpretation. Ruth Barcan Marcus had argued in her 1978 article, "Nominalism and the Substitutional Quantifier," that the substitutional interpretation would offer a nominalistic way out of commitment to higher-order objects like kinds, universals, propositions, etc. It would only be concerning the lowest order of the things, i.e., nominalistically acceptable particular objects, that the interpretation would remain referential. She concluded: "it is not at all clear that such a program is wholly feasible, but it is surely a nominalistic program."[30]

Now, it is conceivable that a philosopher might, for some metaphysical reasons, go even further beyond this rigorous nominalism and simply reject *all* reference to real entities, and that he therefore would accept only a logic interpreted in the ontologically neutral substitutional fashion. This is, arguably, the case for the Madhyamaka when he accepts the superficial truths of the world. In effect, the Buddhist's two truths, i.e., the conventional and the absolute, can be understood as two different ways of interpreting language: without reference to real entities and with such reference, respectively. For the superficial truth, or the conventions generally recognized by the world, it is the substitutional interpretation which applies. Thus, under such an interpretation, it could be said that there are tables, chairs, buddhas and atoms (but no rabbits' horns!)—the Madhyamaka too would accept those conventional statements because for him they only involve language without any corresponding entities. In contrast,when the question as to whether there are or not such actual *entities* is being posed, the debate has shifted to the absolute level of truth, and the interpretation must be referential. For a metaphysician who does not accept any real entities, then the conventional affirmations accepted earlier will no longer be maintained: there are no tables, chairs nor buddhas when "there are" means that there actually are such kinds of real objects in a set of entities to which we refer. It is in this manner that it would be possible to affirm, on the one hand, that conventionally there are forms *(rūpa),* sounds *(śabda),* odors *(gandha),* and so on, while on the other hand saying that there really are none. Interestingly, the Madhyamaka also appears to accept some of the most important elements of a substitutional interpretation. In fact, there is a cliché—one found in other schools as well, including the Chinese traditions—that maintains that nothing exists substantially *(dravyasat),* but rather that things exist merely as designations *(prajñaptimātrasat)* or in a purely nominal fashion *(nāmamātra).* This applies to all superficial reality, even to buddhas and *nirvāṇa:* these are but designations without any corresponding, real entity.[31]

We are now in a position to give a translation of the tetralemma into formal logic: the four alternatives will be statements preceded by existential quantification. Here we will just give the first two, namely: "There is an x such that x has property F" and "There is an x such that x does not have F." In symbols, these would be rendered: $(Ex)Fx$ and $(Ex)\sim Fx$. Since we are dealing with a tendency to attribute properties to entities, the semantics here must be referential; in other words, the opponent maintains that there really is some thing that has, or does not have, property F. It is precisely this attribution of properties to *entities* that the Buddhist wishes to oppose. As a result, the four negations that the Buddhist maintains are:

For any predicate F:

[1'] $\sim(Ex)Fx$
[2'] $\sim(Ex)\sim Fx$
[3'] $\sim(Ex)(Fx \,\&\, \sim Fx)$
[4'] $\sim(Ex)(\sim Fx \,\&\, \sim\sim Fx)$

If we interpret the quantification in a referential manner—as we must do in this context—all four alternatives can be denied without the least logical deviance. The statements $(Ex)Fx$ and $(Ex)\sim Fx$ are false for the Madhyamaka philosopher who does not accept the existence of entities; the statements are false because, for him, the domain cannot contain any objects. In fact, we are dealing here with a banal principal of modern logic: *any statement having the form* $(E\alpha)\ \Phi$ is false in an empty domain.[32] [1']–[4'] would thus reflect the Buddhist's rejection of all ontology: no attribution of properties to objects can be accepted.

In conclusion, the response to our initial question—to know whether Buddhist logic was deviant or not—comes almost as a corollary to the preceding discussion. When we translate the Madhyamaka's statements into a logic with two types of interpretations, we will not encounter any violation of the laws of contradiction, excluded middle or double negation, or of any other fundamental theorems of classical logic. There thus will not be any significant deviation.[33] In sum, looked at in this way, Buddhist logic appears to be at most a non-classical logic, in the sense that its operators and its vocabulary are somewhat peculiar, but it is not a rival of classical logic.

Notes to Chapter 9

The original publication contains the following note: "This article is a reworked version of a lecture I delivered in February 1990 at the Séminaire de Philosophie of the University of Neuchâtel. The principal ideas were initially developed in Appendix II of Tillemans (1990)."

1 See, for example, Beth (1970: 131–33).

2 Flew (1971: 36). See also the critique of Flew by Matilal (1986: 4ff).

3 CS XIV, k. 22.

4 Concerning logical notation, the following conventions have been followed: *~P* signifies the negation of the proposition *P*, in the sense of "It is not the case that *P*." The symbol & stands for "and," while the symbol ∨ means "or." The formula *(Ex)Fx* means: "there is an *x* such that *x* has property *F*." Thus, *~(Ex)Fx* means: "there is no *x* such that *x* has property *F*."

5 "Le Nāgārjunisme est sans portée philosophique ... [il] ne contient qu'une méthode de purification de l'esprit." L. de la Vallée Poussin (1933: 59).

6 Ruegg (1977).

7 See Staal (1975: chap. 1). It is not clear to me how an intuitionist logic would avoid the contradictions in the tetralemma. Let us consider, for example, the thirteen axioms of intuitionist logic as they are presented by Grzegorczyk (1975: 97–98). The conjunction of our statements [1] and [2] gives us *~P* & *~~P*. However, *~(P* & *~P)* is a theorem (see Grzegorczyk: 115, theorem #68) and consequently, *~(~P* & *~~P)* likewise becomes a theorem by substitution. We would thus arrive at the contradiction:
(~P & *~~P)* & *~(~P* & *~~P)*.

8 See Quine (1970: chap. 4).

9 [Author's note: see the introduction to the present volume, pp. 1–2, 3.]

10 See, for example, sections 1.3 and 1.5 in Grzegorczyk (1975).

11 Haack (1974).

12 See Tillemans (1984b) and Tillemans (1991b). The latter article is reprinted as chapter 4 in the present volume.

13 [Author's note: see the introduction to the present volume (pp. 12–17) where it is argued that statements of *vyāpti* for Indian logicians generally include an example. At least *vyāpti* for them is always instantiated by some item. The indigenous Tibetan Buddhist logic does not require examples, nor even any instantiation at all.]

14 In the classical calculus, the derivation of an arbitrary statement Q from the contradiction $P \& \sim P$ is simple:

(1)	$P \& \sim P$	Premise.
(2)	P	From (1).
(3)	$P \vee Q$	From (2).
(4)	$\sim P$	From (1).
(5)	Q	From (3) and (4).

15 See Priest (1979).

16 See Rescher and Brandon (1980).

17 Cf. the opinion of Staal (1975: chap. 1), who suggests that the rejection of logical contradictions is a necessary condition for rationality.

18 See Tillemans (1990: Appendix II). See also above, chapter 6: 133–38.

19 What are the principal examples of the term *virodha/viruddha* in Nāgārjuna's works? In this context, some scholars have cited MMK VII, k. 30:

> *sataś ca tāvad bhāvasya nirodho nopapadyate / ekatve na hi bhāvaś ca nābhāvaś copapadyate //* "First of all, a real entity *(bhāva)* cannot have any cessation because if [entities and non-entities *(abhāva)*] are identical, then neither an entity *(bhāva)* nor a non-entity *(abhāva)* is possible" (see PrP 170.7: *tasmād ekatve sati bhāvābhāvayoḥ*).

R. Robinson (1976: 50), for example, thought that this stanza does demonstrate Nāgārjuna's acceptance of the law of contradiction. But it seems to us that this opinion is probably based upon a dubious translation of the second half of the stanza: "Existent and inexistent in a unity is not true to fact." This stanza does not say that *bhāva* and *abhāva* are not found in the same thing. Rather, it says that, if *bhāva*s could cease, then *bhāva*s and *abhāva*s would become identical, and that in that case, neither would be possible. In fact, it is Candrakīrti's commentary on MMK VII, k. 30 (PrP: 170.7–9) that gives us a version of the law of contradiction by way of the term *parasparavirudddha* ("mutually contradictory"):

> *atha vā parasparaviruddhatvād ālokāndhakāravad ekatve sati na hi bhāvaś ca nābhāvaś copapadyate //* "Or again if they are identical, then neither a *bhāva* nor an *abhāva* are possible, since they are mutually contradictory, as is the case with light and darkness."

That much said, it is nonetheless true that Nāgārjuna himself uses the term *parasparaviruddha* in MMK VIII, k. 7:

> *kārakaḥ sadasadbhūtaḥ sadasat kurute na tat / parasparaviruddhaṃ hi sac cāsac caikataḥ kutaḥ //* "An agent that is real and unreal does not accomplish this [action] that is real and unreal because how can the real and unreal, which are mutually contradictory *(paraspara-viruddha),* be unified?"

20 Cf. the formulation in the *Metaphysics,* Γ3, 1005b19–23.

21 MV I.3cd.

22 Ruegg (1977: 26).

23 VP III.123.

24 See Bronkhorst (1992: 64). [Passage translated by J. Dunne.]

25 D. Seyfort Ruegg (1986: 233) also emphasizes the importance of *bhāva* for the Madhyamaka in the rejection of all philosophical theses *(pratijñā, pakṣa):*

> In sum, the Mādhyamika's approach to the question of the *pratijñā* and *pakṣa* stems from his rejection of epistemic commitment to any proposition—positive or negative—that presupposes the existence of a *bhāva* or *dharma* possessing a *svabhāva* and posits such an entity in terms of the binary structure of *vikalpa* and the quaternary structure of the *catuṣkoṭi.*

See also G. Bugault (1983 and 1989). Bugault highlights the importance of the rejection of *bhāva* and *svabhāva* ("own nature") in Nāgārjuna's arguments, but he maintains that the principle of contradiction *must* be tied to a belief in entities:

> Or, comme Aristote lui-même en est parfaitement conscient, le principe logique de contradiction suppose, au moins implicitement, une métaphysique de la quiddité: il faut croire aux choses.

It follows that the Buddhist himself, who does not believe in real entities, cannot be constrained by this law in his own thought. In fact, this type of Aristotelian point of view—which demands that logic be tied to an ontology—currently seems far less defensible. As we will see, a substitutional semantics allows us to accept the law of contradiction without any ontological commitments whatsoever.

26 See the last section of Tillemans (1989), reprinted as chapter 6 in the present volume.

27 To gain some notion of how complex and weighty the dGe lugs pa's modal interpretation of the tetralemma becomes, see the passage from Se ra rje btsun chos kyi rgyal mtshan (1469–1546), translated and discussed above (chap. 6: 135–38). Finally, note also that in a recent article, C. Oetke (1991) also offers us a modal interpretation of the tetralemma. He remarks (318):

> It is of greatest importance to become clear about the logical structure of this proposition [viz. the central tenet that on the highest level of truth there is nothing of any kind]. It contains as ingredients something like a sentential operator "on the level of highest truth (it is the case that)" and a negated existential proposition, which could be represented by an expression of the form "~(*Ex*) ... *x*..." (...). The feature of the central tenet that it has a negative general existential proposition as its component necessitates the rejection of all statements in which something is attributed to something (at the highest level of truth).

28 See Marcus (1962 and 1972); Belnap and Dunn (1968); and Vernant (1986).

29 Vernant (1986: 291):

> ...la vérité des phrases atomiques [du langage] L_0 est définie, *ab initio,* de façon purement conventionnelle, abstraction faite de toute référence effective. C'est ce qui se produit, par exemple, dans le discours *mythologique* qui, sans poser la question de la référence, définit comme vraie la phrase 'Pégase est un cheval ailé.' Plus généralement, c'est le cas de tous les *discours de fiction.* Sans devoir s'interroger sur la réalité effective des objets issus de l'imagination créatrice d'un auteur, on pourra toutefois assigner une valeur de vérité aux assertions portant sur eux. Ainsi sait-on pertinemment qu'il est faux que Hamlet soit le frère d'Ophélie.

30 Marcus (1978: 124).

31 This idea plays an important role in the major currents of Buddhist philosophy since Nāgārjuna and Candrakīrti, among Indian Madhyamakas, and on up to Lin Ji, the Chan master of the Tang dynasty. Cf. Candrakīrti's *Catuḥśatakavṛtti* (P. 173b4):

yang rang gi sde pa 'dus ma byas ming tsam nyid du mi rtogs shing mya ngan las 'das pa rdzas su yod pa rtag pa nyid du rtog par 'gyur ba kha cig dag ... /"Some of our co-religionists who do not understand that [even] unconditioned [things] exist only as names, and imagine that *nirvāṇa* exists substantially and is permanent ...."

Cf. also the *Lin Ji Lu (Rinzai Roku)* in Yanagida (1959: 148):

世與出世無佛無法亦不現前亦不會失設有者皆是名言章句。//"In this world or in the beyond, there is neither Buddha nor Law; they did not previously appear, nor will they disappear; if they exist, they are only names and phrases."

32 See, for example, Grzegorczyk (1985: 184): "...every sentence beginning with an existential quantifier is false in the empty domain." See also Quine (1954).

33 A logic with substitutional quantification is not entirely devoid of deviance because there are well known divergences in the case of the class of theorems that concern non-denumerable sets, such as the irrational numbers.

PHILOSOPHY OF LANGUAGE

10: On The So-Called Difficult Point of the *Apoha* Theory

A BUDDHIST LOGICIAN, when he wishes to develop his theory about universals, concepts, identities, negations and the like being mind-created and hence fictional, is soon faced with the problem as to how these fictional pseudo-entities can nonetheless lead us to knowledge about the real world. If, for example, all logical reasons *(hetu)*, properties to be proven *(sādhya; sādhyadharma)*, means of proof *(sādhana)* and other such terms in reasoning are mind-created universals, then how can an inference, which depends upon these terms, give us any true information about the real world of particular entities *(svalakṣaṇa)*, and how can we be induced to act correctly in a world which is not just itself a fiction? Dharmakīrti and his school had a complex solution to this conundrum, a solution which for want of a better designation might be called the "theory of unconscious error," one whose essential points can, for our purposes, be characterized along the following lines:

(a) What appears to conceptual thought *(vikalpa)*, or is apprehended *(grāhya)* by conceptual thought, is always a fiction and a universal, one which is created by a process of exclusion *(apoha)*.

(b) A type of error *(bhrānti)* is always present in conceptual thought. Specifically, an essential feature of such thought is that it involves a determination *(adhyavasāya)* of the apprehended fiction as being a real particular, and thus, by an unconscious error, this thought can make us reach *(prāpaka)* a particular in the world.

These two points are brought out clearly in sources such as Dharmakīrti's *Pramāṇaviniścaya* (PVin) II and Dharmottara's commentary (NBT) on Dharmakīrti's *Nyāyabindu* (NB) I.12.

PVin II.2,8–10 (ed. Steinkellner): *svapratibhāse 'narthe 'rthādhyavasāyena pravartanād bhrāntir apy arthasambandhena tadavyabhicārāt pramāṇam //* "There is error *(bhrānti)* in that [conceptual thought] practically applies by determining *(adhyavasāya)* its own representation *(svapratibhāsa),* which is not the [actual] object, to be the object. Nonetheless, it is a *pramāṇa,* in that, by having a necessary connection *(sambandha)* with the object, it is non-deviant with regard to that [object]."[1]

NBT 71.5–72.2 (ed. Malvania) *ad* NB I.12: *tathānumānam api svapratibhāse 'narthe arthādhyavasāyena pravṛtter anarthagrāhi / sa punar āropito 'rtho gṛhyamāṇaḥ svalakṣaṇatvenāvasīyate yataḥ, tataḥ svalakṣaṇam avasitaṃ pravṛttiviṣayo anumānasya / anarthas tu grāhyaḥ / ...* "Similarly, inference does not apprehend the [actual] object either *(anarthagrāhin),* in that it practically applies by determining its own representation, which is not the [actual] object, to be the object. Still, because the imagined object which is being apprehended is determined to be a particular, the determined particular *(svalakṣaṇam avasitam)* is therefore the object of practical application *(pravṛttiviṣaya)* of inference, but what is apprehended [by conceptual thought] is not the [actual] object."

Now, what we find discussed regularly and in detail in Tibetan logic texts are the exact ways in which the error and the process of *adhyavasāya* inherent to conceptual thought occur. (In what follows, for the sake of a considerable economy of expression, I'll just use "thought" for *vikalpa.* It should however be understood that we will always mean thought which proceeds invariably by concepts, and not just any and every type of mental activity, or just "what is in one's mind.") Of course, for a Dharmakīrtian logician, while all such thought proceeds along the lines of points *a* and *b,* some does lead to knowledge of particulars, via *adhyavasāya,* and some does not—inferring fire on a smoky hill does, while thinking about nonexistent things like barren women's children does not, and the criterion here is whether the putative object possesses *arthakriyāsāmarthya* ("ability to accomplish an aim"). Equally, there is, in Dharmakīrti, a very important causal account which complements the *arthakriyā* criterion: particulars cause perceptions, which leave imprints on one's mind, and these imprints in turn condition subsequent thought. Thus there can be a necessary connection *(sambandha; pratibandha)* of causality between particulars and thought, albeit indirect, which explains why *adhyavasāya* can work so well as to "make us reach" or "make us obtain" *(prāpaka)* the real world, and also why we can continue to say justifiably that in certain cases a conceptually created fiction, i.e., a universal, is a property of real things and in other cases that it is not.[2] Certain Tibetan schools, however, developed other aspects of the process of unconscious error, supplementary and even alternative accounts, which tried to explain the fine points and sometimes the step-by-step details of the internal mechanisms of the thought process. And indeed, whatever be the merits of their answers, the interest of the questions "Just how do thought and determination actually work to reach reality?" and "What are the necessary ontological conditions for them to be able to work in this way?" was by no means exhausted by the Dharmakīrtian account.

dGa' ldan pa and later dGe lugs pa writers developed a very complex answer to these two questions, devoting a strikingly minimal amount of energy or ingenuity to elaborating upon the Dharmakīrtian causal account, the account of *prāpakatva* or even that of *arthakriyā*. Rather, they pursued an approach which was depicted by Tsong kha pa and rGyal tshab rje as depending, above all, upon properly seeing through a so-called obstacle *(gegs)* or difficult point *(dka' gnas/gnad)* which people have when tackling issues connected with *apoha*.[3] In what follows, we shall look at this dGa' ldan-dGe lugs approach, trying to see why it came about, and contrasting it with certain Indian and Indian-like positions, such as those of Sa skya paṇḍita and certain Rigs gter bas, who, as was so frequently the case in Tibetan epistemology, had complex debates on this matter with Tsong kha pa, his predecessors and his successors. (In what follows, I will, for the sake of simplicity, drop the difference between "dGa' ldan pa" and "dGe lugs pa," and speak only of "dGe lugs pa," with the caveat that this is something of a distortion which attaches Tsong kha pa and his two main disciples to a rigidified version of their thought developed by later interpreters.[4])

To begin with, Tsong kha pa *et al.* felt that in order for thought and inference to be able to bear upon or "contact" *(reg pa)* the real world, it was necessary that at least some universals, some *sādhya,* some *dharmin,* some reasons, some examples, some identities, some differences, etc., etc. should actually be fully real entities *(dngos po)* and particulars *(rang mtshan).* Georges Dreyfus, in important studies on the dGe lugs theory of universals, has termed their theory a type of "moderate realism"—viz., the position that real universals exist, but only "in" the particular entities *(don la gnas pa),* or in other words, that universals are substantially/essentially identical *(rdzas gcig/bdag nyid gcig)* with the particulars they qualify.[5] Now, this realism does, of course, seem to fly in the face of well-known principles of the *apoha* theory found in Dignāga, Dharmakīrti, and most later logicians, about universals being unreal, and not surprisingly, it was vociferously rejected by anti-realist exponents of the Sa skya pa Rigs gter ba tradition.[6] Go rams pa bsod nams seng ge and gSer mdog paṇ chen śākya mchog ldan, for example, dismiss it as a Tibetan invention, in other words, as being completely without basis in Indian texts. Indeed, Sa skya paṇḍita himself was very aware of various Buddhist realist positions—he attributes them, contemptuously, to "Tibetans" *(bod rnams),* the term by which he generally refers to the rNgog and Phya pa traditions developed in gSang phu sne'u thog monastery. We can be confident that much of the dGe lugs pa's tradition of realism was nothing fundamentally original on their part, but was inspired largely by the gSang phu positions, especially based upon the *Tshad ma'i bsdus pa* of the early twelfth-century thinker, Phya pa chos kyi seng ge.[7]

All that said, Go rams pa and other Sa skya pas may well have been a bit too harsh in accusing "Tibetans" and their "later followers" of *completely* inventing things, for there probably was also a weakening in later Indian Buddhist logic of the stricture that all universals must be unreal. As I showed briefly in an article some years ago, Śaṅkaranandana seems to be one plausible candidate for being an Indian Buddhist realist, and indeed the dGe lugs pa frequently cite a passage from his commentary on *Pramāṇavārttika* (PV) I, k. 40 (= PVin II, k. 29) as their prime Indian source on the question.[8] Dreyfus (1992) has looked at other potential Indian sources in much more detail, examining *inter alia* some aspects of Dharmottara's writings. We also need to take very seriously the possibility of realism or realistic trends being present in Kashmir and being communicated to Tibet by rNgog lo tsā ba, as seems to be indicated by passages in Go rams pa's *Tshad ma rigs gter dka' gnas,* which describe Bhavyarāja, the Kashmiri paṇḍit and co-translator of *Pramāṇavārttika* and numerous other *pramāṇa* texts with rNgog, as promoting the position of *spyi dngos po ba* ("real universals").[9] The history of the often roundabout ways in which Indian currents influenced the formation of Tibetan theories of universals is complex and murky, and still needs much investigation. Suffice it to say here that the dGe lugs pa probably did have some Indian antecedents for a *general* view of realism. Nonetheless, the details of their own position and their actual arguments or the route which they took to "resolve" prima facie contradictions with Dignāga and Dharmakīrti and arrive at their own version of moderate realism, turn on a curious ensemble of ideas which has no parallel that I know of in Indian thought. This is what is involved in the so-called difficult point.

The basic source for the dGe lugs pa position on the "obstacle"/"difficult point" and many other aspects of *apoha* seems to have been Tsong kha pa's *Tshad ma'i brjed byang chen mo,* a work which is described as being rGyal tshab's recording of Tsong kha pa's lectures on *pramāṇa (rGyal tshab chos rjes rje'i drung du gsan pa).* The key passages from this work are taken almost verbatim by such authors as dGe 'dun grub pa and lCang skya rol pa'i rdo rje, while rGyal tshab rje and mKhas grub rje's philosophical debts to the position laid out in the *Tshad ma'i brjed byang* are also clear, even if the textual passages are not borrowed word by word. On the other hand, a proviso is in order to avoid giving the mistaken impression that all dGe lugs pas routinely use the term "difficult point"/"obstacle" in this connection. It is just Tsong kha pa who speaks of the "obstacle," and it is rGyal tshab rje in *rNam 'grel thar lam gsal byed* who speaks somewhat bombastically of "the supreme main point of our difficulties of understanding in this tradition" *(gzhung lugs 'di'i rtogs dka' ba'i gnas [or gnad] kyi gtso bo dam pa).* True, besides rGyal tshab, textbook *(yig cha)* writers such as Paṇ chen bsod nams grags pa and Se ra rje btsun chos kyi rgyal mtshan do also use the term *dka' gnas/gnad* (with interchangeable spellings) in this connection, but this is nothing very remarkable because they are simply directly commenting on rGyal tshab's *rNam 'grel thar lam gsal byed.*[10] In short, the terms *gegs,* and *dka' gnas/gnad* are not actually themselves all that frequent in discussions on these matters, but, as will become clear, the doctrine is almost omnipresent in the dGe lugs pa's *apoha*-based philosophy of language and logic and in their *apoha*-dependent ontological positions.

We begin with some passages from *Tshad ma'i brjed byang chen mo.* The parallel passages from rGyal tshab rje will be given in the notes. Tsong kha pa, first of all, speaks of a "point of doubt which arises amongst the knowledgable" *(rtogs ldan la skye ba'i dogs pa'i gnas):*

> *Tshad ma'i brjed byang chen mo* (f. 16b–17a; pp. 183–84): *dang po [rtogs ldan la skye ba'i dogs pa'i gnas 'god pa] ni / spyi dang bye brag dang rtags dang bsgrub bya dang dpe dang / dgag pa dang / sgrub pa dang gcig dang tha dad la sogs pa rnams rtog pas sgro btags su bshad pa'ang mthong zhing / spyi yin na sgro btags yin pas khyab pa dang de bzhin du rtags sogs la'ang khyab na / 'bras bu don gnyer la nye bar mkho ba'i don byed nus pa phal pa rnams dang / mngon par 'dod pa'i don gyi gtso bo kun mkhyen la sogs pa'i rnam gzhag bya sa med par 'gyur la / de ltar na mi rung ba chen por 'gyur bas / rnam gzhag de dag ma 'chol bar khas blangs pas chog pa dang spyi gzhi mthun sogs dngos po'i de kho na nyid du grub pa khegs pa'i gnyis tshogs de ji lta yin snyam pa dang / khyad par du bum 'dzin rtog pa dang kun mkhyen nges pa'i rtog pa la sogs pa'i nges yul rang mtshan du grub na rtog pa de dag ma 'khrul bar 'gyur bas dgag sgrub thams cad cig car bya dgos pa dang nges yul rang mtshan du grub pa bkag na rang mtshan de dag nges pa'i yul du 'jog tshul de dag shin tu dka' zhing nges pa'i yul du ma gyur na yod nges su mi rung bas rnam gzhag thams cad byar mi rung bar 'gyur te /...*
>
> "The first [viz., the presentation of the points of doubt which arise amongst the knowledgable] is as follows: we see that universal *(spyi = sāmānya),* particular *(bye brag = viśeṣa),* logical reason *(rtags = liṅga),* what is to be proved *(bsgrub bya = sādhya),* example *(dpe = dṛṣṭānta),* negative phenomenon *(dgag pa = pratiṣedha),* positive phenomenon *(sgrub pa = vidhi),* one *(gcig = eka),* different *(tha dad = bhinna; nānā)* and so forth are explained to be superimpositions *(sgro btags pa = samāropa; samāropita)* due to thought *(rtog pa),* and yet if it is so that when something is a universal it is pervaded by being a superimposition and similarly that logical reasons and the like are so pervaded, then one can account for neither the secondary abilities to accomplish an aim *(don byed nus pa phal pa)* which are required if we are to seek [certain] fruits, nor

> the main points which we strive after, such as omniscience and so forth. So then there will be enormous inappropriate [consequences]. Therefore, one wonders how to combine both, viz., being able to accept these accounts [of omnisciences, karmic fruits, etc.] as not being muddled, and [yet] rule out that universal, common basis *(gzhi mthun = samānādhikaraṇa)*, and so forth are established as having the quiddity *(de kho na nyid)* of real entities *(dngos po)*. Specifically, if the ascertained objects *(nges yul)* of thought apprehending vases or thought ascertaining omniscience, etc. were to be established as particulars *(rang mtshan = svalakṣaṇa)*, then these thoughts would be non-erroneous *(ma 'khrul ba = abhrānta)*, and thus all [the object's] positive and negative [qualities] would have to be established simultaneously; if the ascertained objects are ruled out from being particulars, then it becomes extremely difficult to account for the particulars [in question] being objects which are ascertained *(nges pa'i yul du)*. And if they are not objects which are ascertained, then they cannot be ascertained to exist, so therefore all accounting [for Buddhist doctrines, like omniscience, etc.] would become absurd."[11]

Tsong kha pa then goes on to list a number of other wrong positions and confusions and concludes that the obstacle *(gegs)* to our understanding the logicians' version of conventional and ultimate truths, and hence all the other points, is as follows:

> *rtog pa'i yul rang mtshan ma yin pa dang rang mtshan rtog pa'i yul yin pa gnyis 'gal bar 'dzin pa nyid yin no* / "It is precisely to grasp as contradictory the pair [of propositions] that the object of thought *(rtog pa'i yul)* is not particular and that particulars are the objects of thought."[12]

The initial doubt expressed in the passage from *Tshad ma'i brjed byang* is naturally unfounded for Tsong kha pa himself—the passage begins with a *pūrvapakṣa*. Tsong kha pa himself maintains a classic "Tibetan" position, which (as we shall see below) is very widespread in *bsdus grwa* logic and must stem from the gSang phu *bsdus pa* tradition, that although universal, reason, *sādhya*, etc. are mentally created, it does not follow that if x is a universal, etc., x is mentally created. In Tibetan: *spyi sgro btags pa yin, spyi yin na sgro btags yin pas ma khyab,* literally translated as, "Universal is [a] superimposition, if [something] is [a] universal, it is not pervaded by being a superimposition." This notion and others like it, such as *sādhya,* logical reason, etc., behave in this way in keeping with a general principle, which is what Tsong kha pa refers to in the passage concerning the "obstacle" to understanding the two truths: although objects of thought, such as universal, *sādhya* etc., are themselves no more than mind-created appearances/representations *(snang ba = pratibhāsa)* or exclusions *(ldog pa = vyāvṛtti),* it does not follow that if *x* is such an object of thought, *x* is mind-created—real particulars can be said to be the ascertained objects *(nges yul),* or equally, to use the words of dGe 'dun grub pa and lCang skya rol pa'i rdo rje, they are the explicit objects *(dngos yul)* of thought; elsewhere in Tsong kha pa and virtually all other dGe lugs pa writers on the matter, it is routinely mentioned that they actually appear *(snang ba)* to thought.[13]

rGyal tshab rje, in *rNam 'grel thar lam gsal byed,* has a longer version involving several examples of apparent paradoxes or oppositions, including our thinking that there must be a contradiction in saying that appearance *(snang ba)* to thought is not a particular and that there are particulars which are appearances (or do appear) to thought. He then says that the difficult point is that we are reluctant to accept both poles in the apparent oppositions as being equally established—if we assent to one, we negate the other. The consequences of not understanding this compatibility are, according to rGyal tshab rje (who faithfully echoes Tsong kha pa), serious indeed. We will create a false dilemma: either, in order to preserve thought's ability to "contact" *(reg pa)* particulars, we will give up the *apoha*-principle that thought apprehends fictions, applies by exclusion *(sel 'jug)* and does not apply positively *(sgrub 'jug),* or we will end up saying that thought cannot "contact" *(reg pa)* particulars at all and applies just by its own inflated misconceptions *(rlom pa tsam = [abhi]mānamātra).*[14] The rest of the account in Tsong kha pa, rGyal tshab, dGe 'dun grub, lCang skya *et al.* speaks about particulars appearing as mixed up *('dres nas)* with the mind-created appearances/representations *(snang ba).* And the result of all this is that the dGe lugs pa will diagnose the unconscious error inherent in thought as being that a conceptually created fictional representation and the particulars *appear (snang ba)* to thought as being one *(gcig tu)* and *indistinguishable (so so dbyer med pa),* although they are, in themselves, very different, the former being unreal, the latter real (see n. 28 below).

In brief: following Tsong kha pa and rGyal tshab, there are two closely related key elements which we supposedly have to understand to correctly grasp the difficult point and hence avoid falling into a seductive dilemma:

I. The separation between unreal *A* itself and the various real *A*'s: Something like universal or *sādhya* itself is unreal, but not all universals, etc., are. In other words, universal, *sādhya,* etc. are not in opposition *('gal ba = viruddha)* with real entities, i.e., particulars, but have a common basis *(gzhi mthun = samānādhikaraṇa)* with particulars (see n. 6). Strange as it will probably seem to one used to Indian texts, in this Tibetan ontology, the various universals (e.g., sound, tree, etc.), *sādhyas* (e.g., impermanent things), *sādhanas* (e.g., products), and so forth are also particulars! The result is that the dGe lugs pa are obliged to make an extremely difficult to defend split between *sāmānya* (*spyi* "universal") and *sāmānyalakṣaṇa (spyi mtshan),* the latter being only fictional and completely in opposition with particulars, so that there are no *sāmānyalakṣaṇa* which are also real and particular. Whether we think all this is elegant or not, or philologically sound or not, is another matter, let us just stress for now that what we have described is an essential feature of the dGe lugs pa system.[15]

II. What we shall term the "appearance principle": real particulars must actually appear to thought, be apprehended *('dzin pa)* by it, and even be its explicit object *(dngos yul),* all be the appearance of particulars "mixed up" *('dres pa)* with that of fictions.

First of all, turning to point **I**, it seems quite clear that Tsong kha pa thought that the separation between unreal *A* and real *A*'s in the case of *sāmānya, sādhya,* etc. was to be *explained* by the general statement that "the object of thought is not a particular but particulars are the objects of thought." A very similar formulation is to be found in lCang skya, who first cites the cases of *sāmānya, sādhya* and the like, and then gives what he takes to be the *reason (rgyu mtshan)* why these terms admit a separation between unreal *A* itself and real *A*'s:

lCang skya grub mtha' p. 100 ed. Klein; p. 71 ed. rDo rje rgyal po: *de'i rgyu mtshan yang rtog pa'i dngos yul gyi rang ldog rang mtshan ma yin kyang rang mtshan rtog pa'i dngos yul du 'gyur ba mi 'gal bas /...* "The reason for this, moreover, is that there is no contradiction [in the fact] that the **svavyāvṛtti* (*rang ldog,* "own exclusion") of (an) explicit object of thought *(rtog pa'i dngos yul)* is not a particular, but that particulars are explicit objects of thought."

In fact I think that this quintessential formulation of the difficult point, in spite of using a phrase like *de'i rgyu mtshan,* does not actually *explain* why *sāmānya,* etc. are unreal but *sāmānyas,* etc. can be real. What it and other similar formulations do is much more like restating the problematic *A-A*'s separation in a different, more general form, but our puzzlement will probably remain. Thus, universal itself *(spyi kho rang)* is unreal but universals may not be; appearance to thought *(rtog pa la snang ba)* itself is unreal, but the various appearances (or alternatively those things which appear) may not be *(= rtog pa la snang ba yin na, de yin pas ma khyab),*[16] object of thought *(rtog pa'i yul)* itself is unreal, but objects of thought may not be *(rtog pa'i yul yin na, de yin pas ma khyab),* etc. etc. Whether we're dealing with universals, appearances or objects of thought, the logic is the same and turns on being able to speak of unreal *A* itself *(kho rang)* or mere *A (tsam),* or the "own exclusion" of *A (rang ldog)* in contrast to the various real and particular *A*'s.

Now, this differentiation between an *A* itself and the various *A*'s is extremely foreign to us and seems absent in Indian Buddhist logic. Moreover, for many Tibetans, too, it must have seemed a mysterious, paralogical or even completely sophistical move, as we see by Go rams pa's characterization of it as just "verbal obscurantism" *(tshig gi sgrib g.yogs)* (see n. 6). A tempting way to dismiss the strangeness, would be to say that we are dealing with *no more* than language-based problems. In keeping with Go rams pa, we too might think that all this is no more than wordplay, of about the same level of interest as the numerous *bsdus grwa* tricks turning on features of Tibetan-like ambiguities in the use of the genitive, etc.—in short, a bad joke which, as usual, does not translate very well. Or, more charitably, one might wonder, in a Whorfian vein, if the position in question were not somehow a reflection of metaphysical features internal to Tibetan itself. I think that both these explanations would be unsatisfactory. True, there are serious problems of clarity in that a sentence like "universal is mind-created" is plainly bad English—we cannot meaningfully say in a language like English, which has to use articles for count nouns, that "'universal' or 'logical reason' is mind-created." In Tibetan, which does not use articles, nor generally singular and plural, one can and does say these things—the result is that our translation problems become acute and we naturally feel a need to know whether a Tibetan is speaking about "a universal," "the universal(s)," "some universals," or "all universals." That said, I don't think we are dealing with mere sophisms or tricks, nor an incommensurable metaphysic inherent in the structure of Tibetan or Sanskrit, for in general we can and do manage to translate very satisfactorily the articleless nouns in ordinary Tibetan, in Sanskrit, in medieval logic in Latin or in Mohist logic in Chinese by ourselves supplying the "a," "the," "some," or the generic "the," where necessary.[17] The real sticking point is rather that the dGe lugs pa's *own* peculiar explanation of the use of nouns to designate *A* itself as different from *A*'s is very difficult for us to comprehend.[18] This, as we shall see, is not at all an explanation which every Tibetan school adopted, and as such, it does not seem to be due inevitably to the features of Tibetan itself. I think it is worth stressing that we are not faced with the "internal logic" of Tibetan, but rather a choice by one school as to how to formulate a semantic and metaphysical system on the basis of possibilities offered by the Tibetan language. In brief: although Tibetan makes a dGe lugs pa position possible—it would probably never be entertained in English—it does not make it inevitable. We are forced to adopt strange solecistic uses of English in our translations in order to be able to avoid distorting the dGe lugs pa's peculiar and dead serious theoretical views on *apoha* and the semantics of his own language.

Why then did the dGe lugs pa accept this theoretical view that one had to make distinctions between an unreal entity *A* itself and real *A*'s? I think that the most satisfactory explanation we can give is that the dGe lugs pa, and probably the gSang phu-based tradition in general, seem to have been genuinely unable to find any *other* way out of the dilemma described above, where one is supposedly caught between, on the one hand, contradicting Dignāga and Dharmakīrti by accepting real universals just like any non-Buddhist heretic, or, on the other hand, having to say that thought operates only on its own unreal things and cannot contact particulars at all. In short, it was primarily the inability to overcome this dilemma *in any other way* that launched the dGe lugs pa and their predecessors on the tortuous path of differentiating universal, *sādhya, vyāvṛtti,* reason, example and so forth from universals, *sādhyas, vyāvṛttis,* reasons and examples. What we see in the opposing arguments of the Sa skya pa Rigs gter ba is precisely that this type of separation between unreal *A* and real *A*'s is avoided by means of a very different exegesis of Indian texts, one which allows them to say that *all* universals, reasons, examples etc. are indeed unreal (there is no distinction here between *A* and *A*'s), but that we can nonetheless use them to contact real entities. The essential points of their explanation turn on Sa skya paṇḍita's distinction, in *Rigs gter* 5, between theoretical explanation *('chad pa)* and practical application *('jug pa)*—when we critically explain what it is, then a term in a reasoning or an object of thought is indeed *only* a mentally created universal, but from the practical point of view, we do, due to unconscious error, "speak about" *svalakṣaṇa.*[19] There is thus, according to the Sa skya pa Rigs gter ba, no need to subscribe to the fundamental dGe lugs pa idea of universals like *byas pa tsam, shing tsam* ("mere product," "mere tree") and so forth really existing in the full-fledged sense, but being "in" or "substantially identical with" particulars—this odd position is considered to be a just gross hypostatization, like saying that besides our two hands or two eyes, we also have a really existent "hand" *(lag pa)* or "eye" *(mig).*[20]

There is also, of course, a historical dimension to this *A-A*'s separation. Indeed, as we mentioned earlier, we can be confident that the dGe lugs pa did not invent the major features of their logic on their own; they were no doubt following some broad lines already developed by earlier gSang phu scholars. The *A-A*'s separation, and in fact much of the "dilemma" in the so-called difficult point, was already described by Sa skya paṇḍita in his critique of certain views on the conceptually created exclusions *(ldog pa = vyāvṛtti)* which Buddhist logic took to be the pseudo-universals directly expressed by words. Sa paṇ attacked the (absurd) views professed by "most Tibetans" *(bod rnams phal cher)* and "most of the [thinkers] of the land of the snows who pride themselves on being logicians" *(kha ba can gyi rtog ge bar rlom pa phal che ba rnams),* his polemical shorthand for gSang phu-inspired schools. There are a number of variations in the presentations of these views being attacked, but they have the same essential structure of *A* versus *A*'s: the *vyāvṛtti* itself is conceptually created, but the *x* which is the *vyāvṛtti* may not be. Glo bo'i mkhan chen speaks of one variant as being that of the later followers of the *bsdus pa* (of Phya pa), and not surprisingly, it does indeed correspond precisely to what we find in dGe lugs pa *bsdus grwa* texts.[21]

Second, how did the dGe lugs pa (and probably some earlier followers of the gSang phu traditions) come to hold that real particulars actually appear to thought?[22] This "appearance principle" was trenchantly criticized by the Sa skya pa opponents, and especially so by Śākya mchog ldan, who did not accept that real particulars appeared to thought, were apprehended by thought, or were explicit objects of thought at all. For him, *adhyavasāya* leads to knowledge of particulars by unconscious error; we call *(tha snyad byas pa)* the pseudo-sounds, etc. which appear to thought "substances," but when we critically explain *('chad pa'i tshe)* the process, it is only unreal *sāmānyalakṣaṇa* which actually appear or which are apprehended.[23] In this he was in keeping with the mainstream position of Buddhist logic, as found in Dignāga's *Pramāṇasamuccayavṛtti* (PSV) *ad* I.2:

> *svalakṣaṇaviṣayaṃ hi pratyakṣaṃ sāmānyalakṣaṇaviṣayam anumānam iti pratipādayiṣyāmaḥ* / "We will show that perception has [only] *svalakṣaṇa* as its object and inference has [only] *sāmānyalakṣaṇa* as object."

Note that word "only," which is very important here, is not just our doing: it figures in Jinendrabuddhi's commentary as well as in the versions of this passage found in the non-Buddhist writers, Mallavādin and Siṃhasūri. It does no doubt reflect the usual Indian understanding of the passage.[24]

Śākya mchog ldan was also in keeping with statements from Dharmakīrti (see PVin II.2, 8–10 above), Dharmottara (see above), and with those of later writers like Jñānaśrīmitra and Ratnakīrti.[25] Indeed, I think it's safe to say that the Sa skya pas have an overwhelmingly strong case, for it is almost impossible to defend an interpretation of Dignāga and Dharmakīrti which allows particulars actually to appear to thought, and what is perhaps worse, to be the explicit objects *(dngos yul)* of thought. Interestingly enough, the idea of thought applying by *rlom pa tsam* or *abhimānamātra,* an idea which the dGe lugs pa are criticizing as a disastrous consequence of misunderstanding the "difficult point," may well have Indian antecedents, as it seems to be alluded to by Durvekamiśra in his sub-commentary on the phrase *svalakṣaṇam avasitam* in the passage from the *Nyāyabinduṭīkā* which we cited above; Śākya mchog ldan's development of the distinction between *rlom tshod* as opposed to *song tshod* may also be related to this idea.[26] But, on the other side of the debate, the dGe lugs pa's idea of real particulars actually appearing to thought does not seem to be present in other Indian writers, although of course one cannot rule out that there may yet be some or another source to be discovered. At any rate, there were later thinkers, like Mokṣākaragupta who, following Jñānaśrīmitra and Ratnakīrti, had allowed that universals could appear to perception, but none that I know of that allowed that particulars could appear to thought or actually be apprehended by thought.[27]

Although the dGe lugs pa do, of course, have interpretations of Dignāga's and Dharmakīrti's key statements about only *sāmānyalakṣaṇa* being the objects of thought, in the end it is quite apparent that this textual exegesis is intertwined with the other key element of the so-called difficult point, viz., the separation between unreal *A* and real *A*'s. In brief: thought's appearing object *(rtog pa'i snang yul),* its apprehended object *(rtog pa'i gzung yul)* and the appearance or representation itself *(rtog pa'i snang ba)* are said to be indeed *sāmānyalakṣaṇas*, but not everything which appears or is apprehended by thought is: *rtog pa'i snang yul [or snang ba] spyi mtshan yin; rtog pa la snang na spyi mtshan yin pas ma khyab.* And we are more or less back to where we started, once again faced with the peculiar talk about an unreal *A* in itself, as opposed to real *A*'s, being used to save consistency with Indian texts.[28]

Part of the dGe lugs pa's motivation for insisting that real particulars must actually appear to thought was an aprioristic reasoning about what is needed to preserve a distinction between (partially!) right or valid thoughts, like inferences, and utterly wrong thoughts *(log shes),* like thinking that sound is permanent. As we saw in the initial passages quoted from Tsong kha pa, the idea that all thought just worked by "inflated misconceptions" *(rlom pa tsam = abhimānamātra)* was taken to be a catastrophe: this was so for him because if all thought were mere inflated misconceptions *(rlom pa tsam),* no distinction between right and wrong would be possible, and every thought would be simply wrong. Thus a hierarchy of error was deemed necessary, and the dGe lugs pa felt that there had to be some point which distinguished the two sorts of error, viz., valid *(tshad ma)* thought, which is only erroneous in a very specific way about what appears, and utterly wrong thought *(log shes),* where nothing real appears at all and error occurs on the level of determination.

Not surprisingly, perhaps, this idea of a twofold hierarchy of error has only a very strained grounding in Dharmakīrti, who repeatedly stresses the complete similarity of the psychological processes of valid and utterly wrong thoughts and just relies upon the criterion *arthakriyā* and upon indirect causal connections *(sambandha)* with particulars to make the necessary distinctions. (See e.g., PV I, k. 81.). Śākya mchog ldan does not bother with the hierarchy of error at all, and actually speaks of valid thought about *samānādhikaraṇa, viśeṣa,* etc. as being nothing other than wrong cognitions *(log shes kho na),* "because they apprehend them by superimposition" *(sgro btags nas 'dzin pa'i phyir)* (see n. 19 below).

The dGe lugs pa arguments are, I think, so strikingly weak on this score,[29] that one is tempted to look for other explanations. Do all these "solutions" of dilemmas come down to a case of the fascination which philosophers have notoriously had with rhetorical parallelisms and inversions, thinking that they somehow embody profundity?[30] Alas, this is probably part of what's going on when Tsong kha pa and rGyal tshab put forth a long series of inversions along the lines of "objects of thought are not particulars, but particulars are objects of thought." However, some remarks of Klein, which I have also frequently heard from Tibetans, lead me to think that we are not dealing so much with arguments couched in potent rhetorical figures, as with, above all, a certain fixed idea or dominant metaphor of how *sāmānyalakṣaṇa* operates in thought.[31] The dGe lugs model, as Klein very correctly states, is something like mirroring (a variant on the mirror metaphor which I have often heard is glass or crystal)—a vase actually appears to thought via a *sāmānyalakṣaṇa,* just like an object might actually appear via a mirror or crystal. Moreover, since thought must understand its object via this "medium," then if the vase did not appear in this mirror or crystal-like *sāmānyalakṣaṇa,* we would not know anything about it all—our ideas would be *just* inventions and misconceptions. Representations, appearances, etc. thus end up being taken as faithful duplications, rather than as *constructed proxies* which convey only an extremely limited and partial picture of the object and even involve various distortions. Undoubtedly, however, it is the latter idea of constructions, rather than that of *sāmānyalakṣaṇa*-as-mirrors or *sāmānyalakṣaṇa*-as-crystal, which better captures the sense of invention/creation and imagination in the term *kalpanā* and which squares with the fundamental idea of Dignāga's *apoha* theory that thought functions by exclusion *(sel 'jug)* to focus on a very limited number of the object's otherwise many qualities.

Sāmānyalakṣaṇa-as-mirrors, if we stick to this metaphor, looks more like a transformation of thought into a type of positive application *(sgrub 'jug),* like perception, where *everything* about the object must appear in an undifferentiated unity. In short, appearance of an object in a mirror would be a meaningful metaphor only if conceptual representations were also more or less directly caused by their objects and were not partial in the way all Buddhist logicians say they actually are.[32]

Finally, it remains to ask how important for dGe lugs pa philosophy was their "solution" to the dilemma-like difficult point? How much of a role did it actually play in their *apoha*-related doctrines? In other words, was it really the key point for them that they said it was? I think the answer to the latter question must be a strong "Yes." For better or for worse, they were right when they spoke about it being, for them, the supreme difficult point of the logicians' tradition, or the principal obstacle to understanding the logician's version of the two truths—*for them* it was very important, as is clear from even a quick perusal of the list of key concepts which Tsong kha pa mentioned in the passage from *Tshad ma'i brjed byang* which we cited earlier on. Indeed, this "difficult point" was not just important in usual *apoha*-related problems, such as questions of universals and semantics, but elements of this doctrine crop up in numerous other areas of dGe lugs pa philosophy. A few examples should suffice to show what I mean.

The quirky character of *bsdus grwa* logic

The differentiation between *A* and *A*'s is extremely widespread in this system of logic, and does not just involve logical terms like *sādhya, sādhana,* etc. One very frequently finds statements along the lines of *shes bya chos can rtag pa yin* ("knowable thing, the topic, is permanent, [i.e., unreal]") and *shes bya yin na rtag pa yin pas ma khyab, dper na gser bum bzhin* ("if something is a knowable thing, it need not be permanent [i.e., unreal], like a golden vase").[33] This and very many other statements like it turning on the *A*/*A*'s separation are at the core of many of the seemingly paradoxical examples which M. Goldberg (1985) gave in a list of "puzzles" found in *bsdus grwa.* What Goldberg also correctly noticed was that *A* itself is sometimes an *A* and sometimes not, and that it is very difficult to give anything other than *ad hoc* or merely intra-systemic explanations as to when one outcome is to be endorsed rather than the other.[34] The word "quirky," as I am using it here, doesn't mean "formally deviant" in the technical sense intended by W.V. Quine or Susan Haack, namely, a logic which would reject key classical theorems. Formally speaking, *bsdus grwa* is a coherent, functional and even quite a sophisticated system of logic, having analogues to variables, rather unusual quantifiers and a number of classically behaving formal structures of implication, contradiction and so forth.[35] But, in its semantic aspects, it is quirky or unpredictable, in that we simply have a hard time saying convincingly when and why a number of statements should be true and others false. And this quirkiness is very often due to the recurring problematical distinctions between *A* and *A*'s.[36]

Parallels between the difficult point in *apoha* and the two truths in Madhyamaka

In *rNam 'grel thar lam gsal byed*, vol. 1, p. 110, we find the following passage:

> *bsgrub bya sgrub byed sogs tha dad pa'i cha dang de dag gi rang ldog rtog pas btags (brtags?) par ston pa yin gyi / de dag yin na rtog pas brtags pas khyab par ston pa ni rnam pa kun tu mi rung ste / lugs gzhan du bden stong don dam pa'i bden pa yin yang bden stong yin na des ma khyab par bshad pa bzhin no //* "One teaches that the fact of there being a difference *(tha dad pa'i cha)* between *sādhya* and *sādhana,* as well as the 'own exclusions' *(rang ldog = *svavyāvṛtti)* of these [terms, *sādhya* and *sādhana*], are things imagined by thought. However, it is totally wrong to teach that if something is one of these [i.e., if it is the *sādhya* or *sādhana,* etc.] it must be imagined by thought *(rtog pas brtags pa)*. It is like in another tradition [i.e., the Madhyamaka] where it is said that 'void of truth' *(bden stong)* is the ultimate truth *(don dam bden pa),* but that if something is void of truth, it need not be the latter [i.e., it need not be ultimate truth]."

I think that the structure which we have discussed under the problem of the difficult point, namely *A* itself being unreal, but *A*'s being real, is so obvious here with regard to *sādhya,* etc. as to need few further remarks.[37] What is however noteworthy is that, following the dGe lugs pa, the Madhyamaka gets drawn into using a similar type of logical structure where one makes a general separation between *A* and *A*'s. In short, elements of the so-called difficult point in *apoha* also become key elements in the dGe lugs pa understanding of Madhyamaka.

Continua and gross objects

The fundamental separation between unreal *A* and real *A*'s is also largely present in the dGe lugs formulations of an ontology of real continua *(rgyun = saṃtāna)* and gross *(rags pa = sthūla)* objects extended in space. The dGe lugs pa came up with a peculiar interpretation of these two notions so that *saṃtāna* and *sthūla* themselves are unreal, but if something is either of these it need not be unreal. Dreyfus (1991: 173ff.) has explained these positions in mKhas grub rje. What is relevant for us here is that the passage of mKhas grub rje which Dreyfus cites makes a very clear connection between the *A* versus *A*'s structure as applied to universals and the same structure applied to continua and gross objects. In short, the argument is a pure case of the so-called difficult point.

> *sDe bdun yid kyi mun sel* f.34a1–2: *spyi dang rags pa dang rgyun zhes bya ba ni sgro btags rdzas su ma grub pa'i spyi mtshan yin kyang spyi dang rags pa dang rgyun yin na rdzas su grub pa dang rang mtshan la sogs pa yin par mi 'gal zhing / spyi mtshan yin pas ma khyab bo / de'i phyir bum pa lta bu spyi yang yin rags pa yang yin rgyun yang yin rang mtshan yang yin la spyi mtshan ma yin no zhes shes par gyis shig /* "When one speaks of universal, gross object and continuum, they are imagined *sāmānyalakṣaṇa* which are not established as substances. However, it is not contradictory for something which is a universal, a gross object or a continuum to be established as a substance and to be a particular; it does not have to be a *sāmānyalakṣaṇa.* Therefore, know that something like a vase is a universal and a gross object as well as a continuum and a particular, but is not a *sāmānyalakṣaṇa.*"

It is high time to draw some conclusions. The above discussion shows, if there is really still need to show such a thing, the necessity for a *critical* historico-philological approach to dGe lugs pa philosophy, an approach which takes seriously both the Indian and purely Tibetan aspects of this complex system. Equally, I think that Paul Williams (1994) is quite right in saying that this type of material cries out for sensitive and in-depth philosophical treatment. And that must also mean logical analysis. Notwithstanding the admirable work of Klein and others, the whys and wherefores of the logic of the dGe lugs pa system still remain very obscure—we cannot in future just translate or paraphrase dGe lugs pa texts and oral traditions on *apoha* and yet hope to navigate satisfactorily through the very complex, and often seemingly paralogical, Tibetan arguments. There is, in being "faithful" in this way, the real danger of an illusory understanding, one where we have essentially just learned to think adroitly in the same language as rGyal tshab *et al.*, viz., Tibetan *apoha*-ese. Lastly, as the dGe lugs pa's own major contribution to *apoha*-theory, the so-called difficult point, turns inextricably on two rather marginal positions probably having little to do with Indian thought, we should definitively lay to rest the seductive idea of the dGe lugs-gSang phu tradition being a kind of extremely subtle "magic key" *('phrul gyi lde'u mig)* for understanding this vital aspect of Dharmakīrtian epistemology.[38]

Notes to Chapter 10

1 Cf. Steinkellner (1979) pp. 26–27; see also PVin-*Ṭīkā* 7, 1–3 in Steinkellner and Krasser (1989).

2 Certain universals can be said to qualify particular entities due to an *indirect causal relation* between the particulars, on the one hand, and, on the other, the thoughts which have these universals as their apprehended objects. The particulars cause direct perceptions, which leave imprints on one's mind, and these imprints in turn cause the thought of a universal. The process was explained by Dharmakīrti in various places. See e.g., PV III *(pratyakṣa)*, k. 52–53. Here Dharmakīrti was faced with the problem as to how a universal *(sāmānya)* could be connected with real, particular entities

like form, given that cognitions of universals arise even when the real entity is absent.

> PV III, k. 53: *bhāvadharmatvahāniś ced bhāvagrahaṇapūrvakam / tajjñānam ity adoṣo 'yaṃ /.* "If it is said that [universals] will lose [their status of] being properties of entities, this is not a fault, for the cognition of the [universal] was preceded by an apprehension of the entity."

Devendrabuddhi, in commenting on k. 53, fleshes out the argument: a universal *U* is a quality of particulars p_1, p_2, p_3, etc., because the thought of *U* is causally conditioned by tendencies imprinted by direct perceptions of p_1, p_2, p_3, these perceptions being causally linked to p_1, p_2, p_3.

> PVP 167b8–168a1: *gzugs la sogs pa mthong bas bsgos pa'i bag chags la brten nas rnam par rtog pa skye ba na / rang nyid kyi gzung ba'i rnam pa la gzugs la sogs pa'i rnam pa nyid du zhen pas 'jug pa de ltar na gzugs la sogs pa mthong ba'i stobs kyis skye ba'i phyir dang / der zhen pa'i phyir dngos po'i chos yin no zhes tha snyad du byas pa yin pa yin no //* "When thought *(vikalpa)* arises in dependence upon tendencies *(vāsanā)* which were instilled due to one's having seen [particular] forms and so forth, it determines *(zhen pa = adhyavasāya)* apprehended aspects *(rnam pa = ākāra)* of its own as being the aspects of form and so forth and thus practically applies [to forms, etc.]. In this way, [thought of form, etc., i.e., thought of the universal] arises [indirectly] due to the influence of seeing [particular] forms and so forth, and determines [its own aspects] to be those [i.e., real aspects of form], and therefore [for these two reasons] one does call [the universal] a property of the entity."

Cf. Japanese trans. by H. Tosaki (1979), p. 123. See also, e.g.,

> PV I, k. 80–81: *sa ca sarvaḥ padārthānām anyonyābhāvasaṃśrayaḥ / tenānyāpohaviṣayo vastulābhasya cāśrayaḥ // yatrāsti vastusambandho yathoktānumitau yathā /.* "Now all this [i.e., thought] is based on things being separate the one from the other. Thus, it has as object an exclusion and is the ground for reaching the real entity when it is necessarily connected with the real entity, as in the case of the inference which was just explained."

See Steinkellner (1971) p. 189ff; Frauwallner (1932) pp. 269–70. For a dGe lugs pa version of the indirect causal relation with particulars and their explanation of *prāpakatva,* see n. 3 below.

3 It is telling that in *Tshad ma'i brjed byang chen mo* 16a6–21b3 (= pp.

182–93), which is the source for most of the original developments in the dGe lugs pa theory of *apoha,* Tsong kha pa devotes about ten pages to the discussion centered around the "obstacle" (i.e., the "difficult point"), and then devotes about one line and a half to a perfectly ordinary version of the causal link between particulars and thought and the way in which we are "made to reach/obtain" particulars. His version is (21b3–5; p. 193):

> *rtog pa la brten nas rang mtshan thob pa'i rgyu mtshan don rang mtshan 'dzin pa'i mngon sum gyis don du zhen pa'i bag chags 'jog pa'i rgyu byas / bag chags la brten nas don du zhen pa'i rtog pa skye zhing des rang mtshan la 'jug par byed cing zhugs pa las don thob nus pa yin no //* "The reason for us obtaining particulars *(svalakṣaṇa)* in reliance on thought is as follows: the perception *(mngon sum = pratyakṣa)* which apprehends the *svalakṣaṇa* object constitutes the cause for instilling a tendency *(bag chags = vāsanā)* for determining *(zhen pa = adhyavasāya)* [an appearance] to be the object. In dependence upon the *vāsanā,* a thought arises which determines [the appearance] as the object and this makes one practically apply oneself to the *svalakṣaṇa*—due to this practical application the object can be obtained."

dGe 'dun grub pa, in *Tshad ma rigs rgyan* p. 354, also shows the same minimal interest in the causal account, dealing with it in even less space: *gal te rtog pa'i snang ba dngos por med na rtog pas rang mtshan ji ltar thob ce na / dang por rang mtshan 'dzin pa'i mngon sum gyis bag chags pa bzhag pa las skyes pa'i rtog pas rang mtshan la zhen nas zhugs pas rang mtshan thob pa yin no /.*

4 On this point, see L. van der Kuijp (1985: 33–34).

5 See Dreyfus (1992), (1994), as well as the chapters on universals and *apoha* in Dreyfus (1991). The latter work, to which I am heavily indebted, goes into considerable detail on the debates between the Sa skya pa and dGe lugs pa thinkers on some of these major issues of epistemology.

6 Thus, Go rams pa, in his *Rigs gter dka' gnas* 55a1–5, criticizes some "Tibetans" *(bod dag)* who reject real universals *(spyi dngos po ba),* but accept that there can be a common basis *(gzhi mthun = samānādhikaraṇa),* between "universal" *(spyi)* and "real entity" *(dngos po).* This position, which is *exactly* like the dGe lugs pa account of universals in their *bsdus grwa* texts, comes down to saying that "universal itself" is unreal, but that there are universals which are real entities. In short, this is the ubiquitous dGe lugs pa-gSang phu move of making a separation between an unreal *A* itself and real *A*'s which we discuss in detail below. Go rams pa dismisses the move as verbal

obscurantism *(tshig gi sgrib g.yogs),* and cites a passage from Śākyabuddhi's commentary on PV, "There is no real entity at all which is said to be a universal," concluding with the caustic admonition, "Think about whether or not they are in contradiction with this proposition!" *(śākya blos / spyi zhes bya ba'i dngos por gyur ba ni cung zad kyang yod pa ma yin no zhes gsungs pa'i don dang 'gal mi 'gal soms shig).* Surprisingly enough, however, Sa skya paṇḍita's disciple, 'U yug pa rigs pa'i seng ge, was on the realist side of the debate, and seems to have played a significant role in developing the Tibetan "moderate realist" view that there are "universals which exist in the [real] objects" *(don la yod pa'i spyi)*—see Dreyfus (1992: 39–40). Note that there was also a *Rigs gter* commentary by rGyal tshab, the *Rigs gter rnam bshad,* which attempted, with rather unconvincing arguments, to explain the *Rigs gter* from the realist standpoint of the gSang phu tradition. See Dreyfus (1994). See also Jackson (1987: 157, n. 68), who mentions that according to Śākya mchog ldan "many of the major seminaries maintained the study or class of the 'Summaries' [Phya pa's *bsdus pa*] in accordance with the *Rigs gter.*" There were therefore also *syntheses* of the Rigs gter ba and Phya pa traditions.

7 The *bsdus pa* tradition of Phya pa enjoyed considerable prestige for its sophistication and subtleties even up until around the fifteenth century, whereas the interest in *Rigs gter* had comparatively faded in the thirteenth and fourteenth centuries, only to be revived by gYag ston sangs rgyas dpal and Śākya mchog ldan—see Jackson (1987: 137–38). On gSang phu sne'u thog, Phya pa and the complex influence of this tradition on the dGe lugs pa and Sa skya pa, the research is developing rapidly and the references are becoming numerous: besides the pioneering publications of van der Kuijp (1978), (1983), see Onoda (1992a), especially chapter 2 (1992b), Dreyfus (1991), (1994) and Jackson (1987). [Editor's note: see also Dreyfus (1997).]

8 See Tillemans (1984a: 64–65, n. 5).

9 See van der Kuijp (1983: 46 and 286, n. 173). On Bhavyarāja, see also Naudou (1968: 183ff.).

10 Paṇ chen bsod nams grags pa, *rNam 'grel bka' 'grel* 70b (= p. 192): *gnyis pa* [i.e., *dogs pa skye ba'i rgyu mtshan rtogs dka' ba'i gnas kyi gtso bo*] *yod de / rtog pa la bum pa ma yin pa las log par snang ba rang gi mtshan nyid kyis grub pa bkag na / rang gi mtshan nyid kyis grub pa'i bum pa ma yin pa las log pa yang 'jog mi shes la / bum pa ma yin pa las log pa rang gi mtshan nyid kyis grub pas / rtog pa la bum pa ma yin pa las log par snang ba yang rang gi mtshan nyid kyis grub par khas len dogs snyam pa ni dogs pa skye ba'i rgyu mtshan yin pa'i phyir /.* Note that, if one compares this passage with rGyal tshab's text (see

n. 14), then it is clear that bSod nams grags pa on occasion speaks of *bum pa ma yin pa las log pa* where he should have spoken of *bum pa ma yin pa las log par snang ba.* For Se ra chos kyi rgyal mtshan, see *rNam 'grel spyi don* 105a *et seq.* He cites rGyal tshab, but with the spelling *dka' gnad* rather than *dka' gnas.*

11 Cf. *Tshad ma rigs rgyan,* p. 350, which is very close to this passage.

12 *Tshad ma'i brjed byang chen mo* 19a (= p. 188):

> *yang rtog pa'i nges yul rang mtshan du grub pa 'gog pa skad byas pa dang rang mtshan rtog pa'i nges yul du bsgrub ma bde nas rtog pas rlom pa tsam mam sel ngor yod ces khas len pa ma gtogs don dam bzhag sa med pas don dam pa'i phyogs la skur pa btab par 'gyur bas kun rdzob mtha' dag rtog btags tsam du rang lugs la tshad mas legs par grub pa dang dngos po thams cad rang gi mtshan nyid kyis grub par 'jog shes pa'i bden gnyis kyi rnam dbye 'jog shes pa'i gegs ni rtog pa'i yul rang mtshan ma yin pa dang rang mtshan rtog pa'i yul yin pa gnyis 'gal bar 'dzin pa nyid yin no //* "Also once one has said that it is ruled out that the ascertained object *(nges yul)* of thought *(rtog pa)* is a particular, and when one has difficulties establishing that particulars are ascertained objects of thought, then one can only accept that [*sādhya, sādhana,* etc.] are just mere inflated misconceptions *(rlom pa tsam = (abhi)mānamātra)* due to thought or that they exist qua exclusions *(sel ngor yod),* but there is no way to account for them as ultimate, and so one denigrates the side of the ultimate. Therefore, the obstacle to understanding how to account for the division of the two truths, where one knows how to account for [the facts] that all conventional things are established correctly by a *pramāṇa* in this tradition as merely imagined by thought *(rtog btags tsam)* and that all real entities are established by their own characters *(rang gi mtshan nyid = svalakṣaṇa),* is as follows: it is precisely to grasp as contradictory the pair [of propositions] that the object of thought *(rtog pa'i yul)* is not particular and that particulars are the objects of thought."

13 See *Tshad ma rigs rgyan,* p. 357, *rang mtshan rtog pa'i dngos yul yin yang...*; for *lCang skya grub mtha'* see our quotation in the next section of this article. "Explicit" *(dngos)* is to be understood in the context of the Tibetan opposition between *dngos su rtogs pa* and *shugs la rtogs pa* ("explicit and implicit knowledge/realization"), which figures so frequently in dGe lugs epistemology. Klein (1986: 135) gives 'Jam dbyangs bzhad pa's definition of *dngos rtogs:*

"[an awareness] realizing [its object] from the viewpoint of the aspect of that object appearing to the awareness." To say that a *svalakṣaṇa* is the explicit object of thought means that it is the object whose aspect appears. For additional quotations showing the important dGe lugs idea that *svalakṣaṇa* appear to thought, see n. 28 and n. 14: "When one has [correctly!] established that there is a *svalakṣaṇa* which appears as excluded from non-vase *(bum pa ma yin pa las log par snang ba'i rang mtshan yod par bsgrub pa na).*" See also *Tshad ma'i brjed byang* 19b3 (= p. 189): *gser bum bum par 'dzin pa'i rtog pa la gser bum bum par snang zhing* ... Finally, see also the discussion in Klein (1991: 29–36) for bsTan dar lha ram pa's additional scholastic distinctions between explicit objects of expression *(dngos gyi brjod bya)* and explicit expressions *(dngos su brjod pa),* as well as between explicit apprehensions *(dngos su 'dzin)* and explicit realizations *(dngos su rtogs pa).* I think, however, that it will become clear that that these are rather sterile distinctions, made to preserve an extremely difficult dialectical situation.

14 Here is the passage from rGyal tshab in full (*rNam 'grel thar lam gsal byed,* I, p. 76):

> *gnyis pa* [see *ibid,* p. 74.7: *dogs pa skye ba'i rgyu mtshan rtogs dka' ba'i gnas kyi gtso bo ngos bzung ba*] *ni / dper brjod na / rtog pa la bum pa ma yin pa las log par snang ba rang gi mtshan nyid kyis grub pa bkag pa na rang gi mtshan nyid kyis grub pa'i bum pa ma yin pa las log par snang ba yang khegs nas 'jog mi shes par 'gyur la / bum pa ma yin pa las log par snang ba'i rang mtshan yod par bsgrub pa na rtog pa la bum pa ma yin par snang ba yang rang gi mtshan nyid kyis grub pa mi khegs shing rang gi* [text: *gis*] *mtshan nyid kyis grub par khas len dgos la rtog pas btags pa tsam du 'jog mi shes par 'gyur / spyi mtshan dngos po yin pa bkag na / dngos po nyid kyang khegs nas tshad mas sgrub mi shes par 'gyur zhing / dngos po khas blangs na spyi mtshan yang dngos por khas len dgos pa kun rdzob tsam du yod pa dang don dam du yod pa'i chos gnyis / gcig tshad mar bzung nas ci shos sun 'byin pa'i 'gal 'du 'ba' zhig tu 'gyur ba 'di / gzhung lugs 'di'i rtogs dka' ba'i gnas kyi gtso bo dam pa yin no // 'di ma rtogs par rang mtshan rtog pa'i yul du khas blangs na sgrub 'jug tu song nas tshad ma gzhan don med par 'gyur ba dang sgra dang rtags la sogs pa sel 'jug tu khas blangs na / de dag rang mtshan la ye ma reg par 'jug tshul rnams rlom pa tsam 'ba' zhig go snyam pa'i log rtog rnams 'byung bar 'gyur ro // mdor na rtog pas btags tsam gyi chos la tshad ma'i gzhal bya skyon med rang mtshan dang mtshungs par 'jog mi shes na / spyir lugs dam pa 'di'i gnad legs par rtogs pa mi srid cing / khyad par tha snyad tsam du yod pa'i kun rdzob kyi don ma rtogs par 'gyur la / de nyid dang don byed nus pa'i*

gzhi mthun khas blangs na lugs 'di'i thun mong ma yin pa'i don dam gyi tshul mi rtogs par 'gyur // "Secondly [the recognition of the main point which is difficult to understand and is the reason for doubts arising] is as follows. Let's take some examples. When one has ruled out 'appearance to thought as excluded from non-vase, [where this appearance is] established by its own characteristics' *(rtog pa la bum pa ma yin pa las log par snang ba rang gi mtshan nyid kyis grub pa),* one would also rule out and then be unable to account for 'appearance to thought as excluded from non-vase [where the vase is] established by its own characteristics' *(rang gi mtshan nyid kyis grub pa'i bum pa ma yin pa las log par snang ba).* When one has established that there is a *svalakṣaṇa* which appears as excluded from non-vase *(bum pa ma yin pa las log par snang ba'i rang mtshan yod par bsgrub pa na),* one would then also not rule out 'appearance to thought as excluded from non-vase, [where this appearance is] established by its own characteristics,' and one would [feel he] was obliged to accept that it [i.e., this appearance] was established by its own characteristics *(rang gi mtshan nyid kyis grub par),* so that one would be unable to account for it being merely imagined by thought *(rtog pas btags pa tsam du).* When one has ruled out '*sāmānyalakṣaṇa* which is a real entity' *(spyi mtshan dngos po yin pa),* one would thereby rule out real entityness *(dngos po nyid)* too and be unable to establish it by means of a *pramāṇa,* and when one has accepted 'real entity' *(dngos po)* one would [feel he] was obliged to accept that the *sāmānyalakṣaṇa* was also a real entity. The two [sorts of] *dharma*s which exist ultimately and those which exist merely conventionally would become just a collection of contradictions so that when one was established by a *pramāṇa* the other would be refuted—this constitutes the supreme main point which is difficult to understand in this tradition *(gzhung lugs 'di'i rtogs dka' ba'i gnas kyi gtso bo dam pa yin).* When one doesn't understand it, then wrong views will arise, such as thinking that if one accepted that a *svalakṣaṇa* was an object of thought, then [thought] would apply positively *(sgrub 'jug)* and then other *pramāṇa*s would be useless, or if one accepted that words, logical reasons, and so forth applied by exclusion *(sel 'jug),* they could not contact *svalakṣaṇa* at all and the way they applied would just be by mere inflated misconceptions *(rlom pa tsam).* In short, if one is unable to account for dharmas which are just imagined by thought being similar to the *svalakṣaṇa* which are faultless objects of *pramāṇa*s, then in general one cannot understand well the points of this supreme tradition and, in particular, one will not understand conventional states of affairs which exist simply by *vyavahāra.* But if one accepts [that there is] a common basis *(gzhi mthun = samānādhikaraṇa)* between that [i.e., the conventional] and what is able to accomplish an aim, one will not understand the special way of the ultimate in this tradition."

15 The "fictions" *(brtags pa / btags pa)* of which we are speaking are *sāmānya-lakṣaṇa,* and are generally termed object-universals *(don spyi = arthasāmānya).* The term figures prominently in Tibetan texts stemming from the gSang phu tradition: its use by "Tibetans" *(bod rnams* = the followers of Phya pa) is discussed polemically in *Rigs gter* I and *Rigs gter rang 'grel,* where Sa skya Paṇḍita argues extensively against the Phya pa tradition's position that *don spyi* is an object of thought; Sa paṇ considered this *don spyi* not to be an object *(yul)* at all, just like nonexistent things. See Fukuda *et al.* (1989: 10ff.) Sa paṇ was also very aware of Indian uses of the terms *śabdasāmānya* and *arthasāmānya* in the Sāmmitīya tradition; this Śrāvaka school (contrary to Phya pa and his followers) took the two *sāmānya* to be established as substances *(rdzas su grub pa).* See *Rigs gter rang 'grel ad* I.1; Fukuda *et al.* (1989: 34). The pair *śabdasāmānya (sgra spyi)* and *arthasāmānya (don spyi)* also has definite antecedents in Dignāga's *apoha* theory; see the very lucid article by Pind (1991) in which he examines passages from PS V and from Dignāga's lost text, the *Sāmānyaparīkṣā,* to show how Dignāga construed the *vācyavācaka* ("signified-signifier") relation as holding between two types of universals, *śabdasāmānya* and *arthasāmānya,* rather than between particular words and objects (*śabdaviśeṣa* and *arthaviśeṣa*). As Pind points out, Dignāga's views are similar on this score with those of Bhartṛhari—only the word-type or *jāti* signifies—and go back to Kātyāyana. Dharmakīrti, however, adopted a somewhat different position in which *śabdasāmānya* had a lesser role. Pind (1991: 277) argues that although the terms do figure every once in a while in subsequent Indian texts (e.g., Vinītadeva's *Nyāyabinduṭīkā* on NB I.5's definition of *kalpanā,* ed. Louis de la Vallée Poussin, p. 41), "the concepts of *arthasāmānya* and *śabdasāmānya* no longer play any role in post-Dharmakīrti Buddhist epistemology." I think it is important to note that this is true, but only for the major Indian authors: *somehow or another, the Phya pa tradition resurrected these terms—possibly from Dignāgean sources or from a minor figure like Vinītadeva—and used them constantly to interpret Dharmakīrti.* It is ironic that this comparatively minor technical term *arthasāmānya (don spyi),* which seems to have largely fallen out of favor in India after Dignāga, came to be used virtually everywhere in dGe lugs pa philosophy in the sense of a "mental image" or "conceptual representation."

16 *rtog pa la snang ba yin na* (or *snang na*) *rang mtshan yin pas ma khyab* admits of two translations which are quite different for us: *a.* "If something

is an appearance to thought, it is not pervaded by being particular"; *b.* "If something appears to thought, …." There is often an ambiguity in Tibetan between nouns and verbs, and this is the case here with *snang ba* ("something which appears"; "appearance"). The result is that this specific example presents an *additional* problem of imprecision, one which does not occur in the case of "object of thought" *(rtog pa'i yul),* "universal" *(spyi),* "reason" *(gtan tshigs),* etc. which do not have the possibility of being taken as verbal forms.

17 I don't want to rule out the possibility of someone doing a study on how fundamental Tibetan notions of being, existence, instantiation, predication, etc. are conditioned by features inherent in the Tibetan logical language. Here one would have to take account of the blurring in the count noun versus mass noun distinction. It would indeed be valuable to do a study along the philologically rigorous lines of A.C. Graham's *Disputers of the Tao* (1989), *Later Mohist Logic, Ethics and Science* (1978) and his earlier "Being in Western Philosophy Compared with *Shih/Fei* and *Yu/Wu* in Chinese Philosophy" (*Asia Major* 7, 1959), or one in the same vein as Chad Hansen's work on Chinese in *Language and Logic in Ancient China,* 1983. Moreover, such a study would have to take very seriously the Quinean ideas of ontological relativity and indeterminacy of translation. That said, however, the specific feature we are speaking of now, i.e., the *A-A*'s separation, is probably too theoretical and philosophically inspired to be good material for this sort of approach.

18 An overly facile way out would be to say that Tibetan locutions along the lines of "*A* itself" are actually expressing *A*-ness or "being an *A*." Thus, on this scenario, there would be little difficulty in saying that *A*-ness or "being an *A*" is mind-created, but that the individual *A*'s are not. Unfortunately, this move would only work in a very limited number of cases. If we applied the same interpretation to *bum pa kho rang* ("vase itself") and most other such banal cases, we would go against what the dGe lugs pa themselves accept: for them, *bum pa kho rang* is *not* to be taken as mind-created, nor is it to be taken as the same as vaseness or "being a vase," two notions which figure regularly in Tibetan and which would be better expressed by *bum pa nyid* and *bum pa yin pa* respectively.

19 *Rigs gter* 8b6 (ed. Nor bu, p. 120):

> *'chad dang 'jug pa'i gang zag gi // dbye bas gnyis gnyis rnam pa bzhi // 'chad tshe rnam par phye bas mkhas // 'jug tshe gcig tu 'khrul bas thob //* "There are two [types of significata *(brjod bya = vācya)*] and two [types of signifiers *(brjod byed = vācaka)*], in other words, four sorts,

according to whether one classifies a person as explaining critically *('chad pa)* or as practically applying *('jug pa = pravṛtti)*. When explaining critically, one is an expert [on modes of being *(gnas lugs)*] due to making distinctions. When practically applying, one erroneously takes [the *svalakṣaṇa* and *sāmānyalakṣaṇa*] to be identical and thus [by using agreed-upon symbols *(brda = saṃketa)*] one obtains [the *svalakṣaṇa* object]."

Additions follow the *Rigs gter rang 'grel* 43b4–6 (ed. Nor bu, p. 120). See e.g., *Tshad ma rigs gter dgongs rgyan smad cha* 56a (= p. 111):

> *des na grub pa'i don ni / 'chad tshe'i rnam gzhag la brjod byed sgra'i brjod bya dang / rtog pas bzung ba dang 'dzin pa dang rtogs pa yin na rang mtshan min dgos la / 'jug pa'i tshe na sgra'i dngos kyi brjod bya dang rtog pas dngos su bzung ba sogs yin na rang mtshan min mi dgos zhes zhib cha sbyar bar bya'o //* "Thus the point which is proven is as follows: In an account where one explains things critically, then the significata *(brjod bya = vācya)* of signifying words, or the things which are apprehended by thought and which thought apprehends or knows, must not be particulars, but in the context of practical application, the explicit significata of words and the things explicitly apprehended by thought need not be non-particulars. One should be careful about this."

An equally very important distinction, found extensively developed in Śākya mchog ldan's account of terms in reasonings, is that between an *x* in terms of what it is *(song tshod)* and in terms of the inflated misconceptions about it *(rlom tshod)*, the former being a mind-created *apoha* and the latter being a *svalakṣaṇa*. Thus e.g., *Tshad ma rigs gter dgongs rgyan smad cha* f.79a, p. 149 on *samānādhikaraṇa, viśeṣa*, etc.:

> *yang song tshod kyi gzhi 'thun dang bye brag ni shing dang tsan dan gyi ldog pa gnyis tshogs pa'i gzhan sel de nyid yin la / rlom tshod ni tsan dan rang mtshan pa de nyid do / de ltar rlom pa rtog pa de yang tsan dan gcig nyid du mar med bzhin du sgro btags nas 'dzin pa'i phyir log pa'i shes pa kho na'o / de lta na yang shing la ltos pa'i spyi dang gzhi 'thun 'dzin pa'i rtog pa chos can / shing gsal rang mtshan la mi bslu ba yin te / de la rgyud nas 'brel zhing de yul du byed pa'i phyir / nor bu'i 'od la nor bur zhen pa'i blo bzhin no //.*

See Dreyfus (1991: 246, 248 *et passim*).

20 See *Tshad ma rigs gter dgongs rgyan smad cha* 76b–77a (= pp. 152–53).

21 See *Rigs gter* IV (in bold letters below) and the *Rigs gter rang 'grel* 7b4–5 and 38b3–5 (ed. Nor bu, p. 11 and 109):

> ***gal te khyed kyi ldog pa de // dngos po yin na spyi dang mtshungs // dngos med yin na dgos nus med // des na ldog pa mi dgos lo //*** *ldog pa'ang gzhan sel de dngos po yin na spyi dngos por 'dod pa la brjod pa'i skyon mtshungs la / dngos med yin na ci'ang med pas dgos nus med do zhe na / 'di'i lan la gnyis las gzhan gyi lan dgag na /* ***'di la bod nams phal cher ni // dngos po'i ldog pa dngos por 'dod //*** *kha ba can gyi rtog ge bar rlom pa phal che ba rnams dngos med kyi ldog pa dngos med yin yang dngos po'i ldog pa dngos po yin te dngos po dang ngo bo dbyer med pa'i phyir ro zhes zer ro //* "[Objection:] **If *vyāvṛttis* are real entities *(dngos po = bhāva; vastu)* for you then they will be like universals. If they are unreal, then they won't be of any use. Thus, it would follow that *vyāvṛttis* would be unnecessary.** Suppose it is said that if a *vyāvṛtti* or an *anyāpoha* is a real entity, then the faults will be like those which were stated when it was accepted that universals were real entities, but if they are unreal, then they won't be of any use whatsoever. To this there are two replies. First, let us refute the reply of some adversaries. **In this vein, most Tibetans accept the *vyāvṛtti* of real entity to be (a) real entity.** Most of the [thinkers] of the land of the snows who pride themselves on being logicians say that although *vyāvṛtti* of non-entity *(abhāva)* is non-entity, the *vyāvṛtti* of real entity *(bhāva)* is real entity, because the former is essentially indistinguishable from real entity."

Śākya mchog ldan sums up these views (*Rigs gter dgongs rgyan smad cha,* p. 152):

> *bod snga phyi thams cad na re / shing tsam de shing gi ldog pa yin zhing / rdzas su grub pa yang yin no zhes zer ro /* "All earlier and later Tibetans say that mere tree is the *vyāvṛtti* of tree and that [mere tree] is established substantially *(rdzas su grub pa).*"

Note too that Glo bo'i mkhan chen distinguishes between two variants of the "Tibetan" view: 1. that the *vyāvṛtti* of *bhāva* is *bhāva,* and 2. that only *bhāva (dngos po nyid)* is the *vyāvṛtti* of *bhāva.* He attributes the latter view to latter exponents of the *bsdus pa* (i.e., the *Tshad ma'i bsdus pa* of Phya pa). Indeed this second variant is precisely the view which we find in the dGe lugs pa's *bsdus grwa* texts. See Glo bo'i mkhan chen (*Tshad ma rigs gter gyi 'grel pa,* p. 118):

> *di'i lan la / kha ba can gyi rtog ge par rlom pa snga phyi phal mo che rnams na re / dngos med kyi ldog pa dngos med yin yang / dngos po'i*

ldog pa dngos po yin te / dngos po dang dngos po'i ldog pa dbyer med pa yin pa'i phyir ro zhes zer ro // yang phyi rabs kyi bsdus pa smra ba rnams ni dngos po nyid kyang dngos po'i ldog pa yin no zhes zer ro //.

22 Cf. Klein (1991: 29–36). What is at stake in the dGe lugs pa theory is not just the (banal) idea of one thing *seeming* to be another, but the idea of both things actually appearing, but mixed up—this idea looks un-Indian. A possible factor in the dGe lugs-gSang phu tradition adopting the idea of particulars actually appearing indistinguishably mixed up with fictions may have been their very confused understanding of Dharmakīrti's definition of thought. Their version of this definition and an indigenous *bsdus pa* or *bsdus grwa*-style adaptation of it may have led them to think that Dharmakīrti himself regularly had recourse to the notion of "mixed or indistinguishable appearances" or of "two things which appear mixed up as one and which are indistinguishable from the point of view of appearance" *(de gnyis gcig tu 'dres nas snang zhing snang ngor so so dbyer med pa).* See *Tshad ma'i brjed byang chen mo,* p. 189. See also *Tshad ma rigs rgyan,* p. 353 and *lCang skya grub mtha',* p. 100, where virtually the exact same passage from Tsong kha pa is cited. (It is noteworthy that someone like lCang skya discusses the "difficult point" with its use of the idea of *'dres nas snang* and then proceeds directly to a discussion of the definition of thought which uses *'drer rung tu 'dzin pa* and *'drer rung tu snang ba*). The definition of thought given in Dharmakīrti's *Pramāṇaviniścaya* and *Nyāyabindu* I.5 reads: *rtog pa ni brjod pa dang 'drer rung ba snang ba'i shes pa.* The Sanskrit admits of two versions depending upon whether we read the *tatpuruṣa* compound °*pratibhāsapratītiḥ* or a *bahuvrīhi,* °*pratibhāsā,* qualifying *pratītiḥ: abhilāpasaṃsargayogyapratibhāsapratītiḥ kalpanā* or *abhilāpasaṃsargayogyapratibhāsā pratītiḥ kalpanā.* Choosing the *tatpuruṣa* version, we should have a translation like that of Hattori (1968: 85): "a cognition of [a] representation which is capable of being associated with a verbal designation" (Kajiyama [1966: 41] is identical apart from translating *abhilāpa* as "words"). If, however, we follow Dharmottara's *Nyāyabinduṭīkā* and read °*pratibhāsā,* as seems preferable, we would have something like "*kalpanā* is a cognition in which a representation is capable of being associated with a verbal designation."

First of all, we should note that *'drer rung ba snang ba'i shes pa* corresponds to the *tatpuruṣa saṃsargayogyapratibhāsapratītiḥ,* and that *'dre = saṃsarga* does not have the sense here of being "indistinguishably mixed up," nor is it at all commented upon in that way by Dharmottara: rather it simply means "being associated." Secondly, the natural tendency in Tibetan is to read *snang ba (= pratibhāsa)* as a verb beginning a relative clause, i.e., "to which appears ...," rather than the correct way, which is as the noun "representation"/"image." Thirdly, Tibetan texts often, but not always, read *rung bar,* rather than *rung ba,* and thus further change the sense radically. The result of all this is that the frequent Tibetan misinterpretation of this definition becomes something like "thought is a cognition to which [something] appears as capable of being mixed up with an expression." Apart from a perhaps somewhat doubtful rendering of *snang ba'i* by "perceives," Klein (1991: 138) is quite faithful to this misunderstanding when she translates: "a thought consciousness is a consciousness which perceives [a meaning-of-a-term] as suitable to be mixed with an expression."

To conclude: My argument is admittedly speculative, but I think it is worthwhile to consider if the Tibetans may have started on a wrong track due to some fairly rudimentary philological errors. They may well have come up with a notion of *'dres nas snang ba,* based on a misinterpretation of *Pramāṇaviniścaya* and *Nyāyabindu's* term *saṃsargayogyapratibhāsapratīti (= 'drer rung ba[r] snang ba'i shes pa)* as "a cognition to which [something] appears as capable of being mixed up with..." The misconstrual of *snang ba'i* coupled with *'drer* in *Nyāyabindu* and *Pramāṇaviniścaya* might well, therefore, have created (already in the earlier gSang phu schools?) a kind of pseudo-precedent for an Indian source which spoke of two things actually appearing to thought, or *x* actually appearing to thought as indistinguishably mixed up with *y*.

Finally, note that the dGe lugs-gSang phu tradition came up with their own definition of thought, *sgra don 'dres rung tu 'dzin pa'i blo* "a cognition which apprehends a *śabdasāmānya* and an *arthasāmānya* as fitting to be mixed up," as a reworking of Dharmakīrti's definition in PVin. See n. 15 on the bona fide Indian terms *śabdasāmānya* and *arthasāmānya.* While rGyal tshab and dGe dun grub pa took *sgra don* as *sgra spyi* and *don spyi,* mKhas grub rje protested that this was impossible, and he, as well as lCang skya, came up with a different definition *(sgra don 'dzin pa'i blo)* in order to be able to take *sgra don* as the equivalent of Dharmakīrti's use of *śabdārtha* ("object of a word") in PV III, k. 287. See *Tshad ma rigs rgyan,* p. 36ff. (definition of *rtog pa*); *sDe bdun yid kyi mun sel* 56b–57b (= pp. 114–16); *lCang skya grub mtha',* p. 100ff; Klein (1991: 129–40). mKhas grub, for example, argued, *inter alia,* that rGyal tshab's version of *sgra don 'dres rung tu 'dzin pa'i blo* was absurd because "it is contradictory to accept that the meaning of 'mixed up' would be that name and object would appear as identical; if we did, then one would have to accept that the meaning of 'being fitting to be mixed up' was also that the name and object were fitting to appear as identical" (57a: *'dres pa'i don ming don gcig lta bur snang ba la 'dod pa'ang 'gal ba yin te / de lta na / 'drer rung ba'i don kyang ming don gcig lta bur snang du rung ba la 'dod dgos /).* This turns on the misunderstanding of *saṃsargayogya / 'drer rung ba* as "fit to be indistinguishably mixed up," the misreading *rung tu* and the reading of *snang ba* as a verb rather than as the noun *pratibhāsa,* "representation." In conclusion, I think that we can safely say that this discussion (and especially the "refutations" in mKhas grub and lCang skya) was a confused debate, where a misreading of PVin's definition and its equally doubtful transformation into an indigenous Tibetan version, led to a long, but woolly and useless controversy.

23 Cf. e.g., *Tshad ma rigs gter dgongs rgyan (smad cha)* 51b–52a (= pp. 102–3): *'di dag la* [i.e., *rdzas, log pa, gsal ba, dngos po la sogs pa la*] *gnyis gnyis te / don la gnas pa'i rdzas sogs dang / sel ngo'i rdzas la sogs pa'o / dang po ni / don la gnas pa'i sgra rang mtshan pa lta bu'o / gnyis pa ni / rtog pa la snang ba'i sgra la sogs pa'o // 'di ni gzhan sel kho na yin gyi / rdzas la sogs pa mtshan nyid pa min kyang rtog pa la snang ba'i sgra sogs la / don rang mtshan gyi sgra sogs su zhen nas zhugs pas / mthar de rang mtshan la mi bslu ba'i phyir / rdzas la sogs pa'i tha snyad byas pa yin no //.* Ibid. 55b–56a (= pp. 110–11): *sgra mi rtag rtogs kyi rjes dpag tshad mas sgra mi rtag pa rang mtshan rtogs so zhes tha snyad byas pa de ni 'jug tshe gcig tu 'khrul pa'i rnam gzhag la yin gyi / 'chad tshe rnam par phye ba'i rnam gzhag la min te / 'chad pa'i tshe rtog pas rang mtshan 'dzin na ji skad bshad pa'i rigs pas gnod pa'i phyir / 'di la bod phyi ma rnams rtog pas rang mtshan dngos su 'dzin na zhes pa'i zhib cha sbyor mod / gzhung gi don ma yin te / rang mtshan 'dzin na dngos su 'dzin dgos te / rang mtshan gyi gzhan sel 'dzin pa'i blo yin na rang mtshan 'dzin par 'gal ba'i phyir /.*

24 For Dignāga's PSV, see Hattori (1968: 24 and n. 1.14). Significantly, Hattori takes *svalakṣaṇaviṣayaṃ pratyakṣam* and *sāmānyalakṣaṇaviṣayam anumānam* as "perception has *only* the particular for its object and inference *only* the universal" (my italics). Mallavādin and Siṃhasūri speak of *svalakṣaṇaviṣayaniyatam* and *sāmānyalakṣaṇaviṣayaniyatam* and Jinendrabuddhi's *Pramāṇasamuccayaṭīkā* adds *kho na = eva.*

25 Jñānaśrīmitra, *Apohaprakaraṇa,* 226.2: *adhyavasāyas tv agṛhīte 'pi pravartanayogyatānimittaḥ.* See the discussion of Jñānaśrī's position in Katsura (1986b). Katsura (1986b: 176) sums up the usual Indian position: "Thus, roughly speaking, an external particular object *(svalakṣaṇa)* is the indirect object to be determined and acted upon by conceptual knowledge, and a mental image (which is *sāmānya-lakṣaṇa)* is the direct object to be grasped by conceptual knowledge."

26 *Dharmottarapradīpa,* p. 72.20–21: *svalakṣaṇam avasitam ity etad apy abhimānād abhidhīyate / na punaḥ svalakṣaṇaṃ avasāyasya gocaraḥ /* "When [Dharmottara] speaks of the "determined particular," this too is said because of inflated misconception: the particular is not, however, the object of the determination." For Śākya mchog ldan's terms *song tshod* and *rlom tshod,* see n. 19 above.

27 See *Tarkabhāṣā* §7.1 and also Kajiyama (1973: 166).

28 Cf. the debate in *Yongs 'dzin blo rigs* 4b: *kho na re / bum pa chos can / rang 'dzin rtog pa'i 'dzin stangs kyi yul yin par thal / bdag med yin pa'i phyir / khyab pa khas / 'dod mi nus te / rang 'dzin rtog pa'i snang yul yin pa'i phyir te / de la snang ba'i phyir na ma khyab /.* In the last line of this argument the opponent says that the vase must be the appearing object *(snang yul)* of the thought of vases because it appears to that thought. The reply is short and swift: "That does not follow" *(ma khyab).* rGyal tshab gives the usual explanation in all its details in *rNam 'grel thar lam gsal byed,* vol. 1, 104–6:

> *shing ma yin las log par snang ba de phyi rol gyi gsal ba rnams la rjes su 'gro ba'i spyi yin nam / blo'i snang ba kho na la rjes su 'gro / dang po ltar na / shing gsal rang mtshan pa rnams rtog pa la shing ma yin las log par snang ba de yin dgos pas / rang mtshan rtog pa'i snang yul du mi rung bar khyod kyis khas blangs pa dang 'gal la / gnyis pa ltar na yang khyed kyis shing gsal rnams 'bras bu mtshungs shing / shing ma yin las log par yang mtshungs pas shing ma yin las log pa dang / shing ma yin las log par snang ba gnyis de dag gi spyir khyed kyis bzhag pa dang 'gal lo // mi rtag pa dang bdag med la sogs pa de dag kyang rtog pa'i snang ba tsam kho nar zad pas / blo'i snang ba tsam las tha dad pa'i mi rtag pa dang bdag med sogs dngos po'i gnas tshod kyi chos ma yin zhing de dag mi rtogs par 'gyur la / de lta na khyed kyis bstan bcos su spyi dang gzhi mthun dang bsgrub bya sgrub byed la sogs pa'i rnam gzhag du ma zhig byas pa dgos pa cung zad kyang med par 'gyur ro zhe na zhes pa'o //*
>
> *lan ni / shing ma yin las log par snang ba rtog pas btags shing don byed mi nus kyang shing gsal rang mtshan pa rtog pa la shing ma yin las log par snang ba yin pa la 'gal ba cung zad kyang med pas de dag spyi gsal du 'thad la / de lta na yang rang mtshan rtog pa'i gzung yul du thal bar mi 'gyur te / rtog pa la shing gsal rang mtshan yang shing ma yin las log par snang / rang la rgyangs chad du snang ba'i shing 'dzin rtog pa'i gzung bya de yang rtog pa la shing ma yin las log par snang bas shing ma yin las log pa yin pa dang ma yin pa gnyis / rtog pa la shing ma yin las log par 'dres nas snang zhing so sor mi snang bas de ma yin bzhin du der snang ba des bsgribs nas shing ma yin las log pa'i thun mong ma yin pa'i ngo bo de / gzhan dang ma 'dres par mthong mi nus pas shing rang mtshan gzung yul du thal bar ga la 'gyur / spyi gzhi mthun dang / bsgrub bya sgrub byed sogs kyi rang ldog rnam par rtog pa'i snang ba kho nas zad kyang de dag gi gzhir dngos po'i chos rnams kyang 'gyur bas / spyi chos la 'jus nas lkog gyur gyi rang mtshan rnams go bar byed pas / de dag ni gnas skabs dang mthar thug gi don rtogs pa'i*

thabs su byas pas dgos pa med par mi 'gyur ro //

"Objection: This 'appearance as excluded from non-tree' *(shing ma yin las log par snang ba de),* is it a universal *(spyi = sāmānya)* which is co-present in the external instances, or is it co-present only in mental appearances *(blo'i snang ba kho na)*. In the first case, the particular tree-instances would have to appear to thought as excluded from non-trees, and thus, granted that [according to your position] a *svalakṣaṇa* cannot be thought's appearing object *(rtog pa'i snang yul),* there would be a contradiction with what you accept. In the second case, too, for you the tree-instances would have similar effects and would also be similar in being excluded from non-tree, and thus there would a contradiction with your having posited 'excluded from non-tree' *(shing ma yin las log pa)* and 'appearance as excluded from non-tree' *(shing ma yin las log par snang ba)* as both being universals of those instances. Since impermanence, selflessness and the like would also be nothing more than mere appearances to thought, then impermanence, selflessness, etc. different from these mere mental appearances would not be qualities belonging to the real being of entities and the latter [qualities] would not be understood. In that case, there would no point whatsoever for you to formulate, in treatises, numerous accounts concerning *sāmānya, samānā-dhikaraṇa, sādhya, sādhana,* etc.

The reply is as follows. Although 'appearance as excluded from non-tree' *(shing ma yin las log par snang ba)* is imagined by thought and is not capable of accomplishing an aim *(don byed mi nus),* still there is absolutely no contradiction for the particular tree-instances to appear to thought as excluded from non-trees *(shing gsal rang mtshan pa rtog pa la shing ma yin las log par snang ba yin pa)*. Therefore, it is logically correct for these to be [respectively] universals and instances. And in that case, there would not be the absurd consequence that a *svalakṣaṇa* would be thought's apprehended object *(rtog pa'i gzung yul = grāhyaviṣaya)*. The particular tree-instances appear to thought as excluded from non-tree; what is apprehended *(gzung bya)* by thought grasping trees and appears to it to be something separate also appears to thought as excluded from non-tree; so, both what is and is not excluded from non-tree are mixed up and then appear *('dres nas snang)* to thought as being excluded from non-tree, and do not appear separately; and therefore due to this appearance as such [i.e., as excluded from non-tree] all the while not being so [i.e., excluded from non-tree], it [i.e., thought] is obscured and cannot therefore see the special nature of 'exclusion from non-tree' in a way which is not mixed up with anything else. Thus, how could there be the absurd consequence that the particular tree would be the apprehended object *(gzung yul = grāhyaviṣaya)*? Although the **svavyāvṛtti (rang ldog)* of *sāmānya, samānādhikaraṇa, sādhya, sādhana* and so forth are nothing more than just appearances to thought *(rtog pa'i snang ba), dharmas* which are real entities *(dngos po)* are also the bases *(gzhi)* of these [notions, i.e., of *sāmānya*, etc.], and so by grasping *dharmas* which are universals *(spyi'i chos),* one makes understood imperceptible *(lkog gyur = parokṣa)* particulars, and for this reason because these [*sāmānya, sādhya,* etc.] are therefore means for understanding states of affairs which are real conditions and are ultimate, they will not be pointless."

29 See Tsong kha pa, *Tshad ma'i brjed byang chen mo* 20a–b (= pp. 190–1) on the way in which some thought is in error concerning its appearing object *(snang yul),* but is *not* utterly wrong: *gser bum bum par snang ba de nyid phyi rol gyi don dang bum ma yin las log pa ma yin bzhin du de gnyis gcig lta bur snang bas snang yul la 'khrul ba yin no // yul la 'jug pa'i tshe gser bum bum par snang ba phyi rol gyi don du med pa la phyi rol don du zhen nas 'jug pa yin yang / blo'i 'dzin stangs la gser bum bum pa'o snyam du 'dzin gyi sgra don bum pa'o snyam pa dang gser bum gyi snang ba 'di nyid bum pa'o snyam du zhen pa sogs med pas zhen yul la 'khrul ba'i skyon med do //. lCang skya grub mtha'* (p. 100 ed. Klein; p. 71 ed. rDo rje rgyal po) is a condensed version of the same and is translated in Klein (1991: 129). See also *ibid.* p. 129 for the standard dGe lugs pa view, which is summarized by a Tibetan informant:

> *1)* appearance (the actual object) and imputation (the mental image) appear undifferentiably mixed, and *2)* the image of pot appears to *be* a pot but is not. Although an image and a pot *appear* to be one, thought does not actively *conceive* them to be one. Thus, it is not a wrong consciousness *(log shes)* even though it is a mistaken consciousness *('khrul shes).* [The italics are those of Klein.]

Similar explanations by Tibetan informants are found in Napper (1986; 132ff); see also Klein (1986: 15–6).

The central idea of Tsong kha pa *et al.* can be paraphrased as follows: *1.* Thought practically applies by determining a fictional representation to be the external object. *2.* However, in its way of apprehension *(blo'i 'dzin stangs la)* it does not consciously entertain the proposition: "a fiction is a particular." Thus one is not deceived with regard to the *adhyavaseya,* in that one does not explicitly or consciously hold that the fictional representation is the particular. (Indeed, if in thinking, one constantly had before one's mind absurd propositions like "the *sāmānyalakṣaṇa* is the particular," it would be impossible to distinguish valid thought, like inferences, from utterly wrong conceptions *(log shes)*. It's hard to see that anyone would want to contest this idea of Tsong kha pa, as it looks like little more than a restatement of the central idea of thought proceeding by *unconscious* error. On the other hand, it's also extremely difficult to see that this truism about not consciously and explicitly thinking "the *sāmānyalakṣaṇa* is the particular," would prove that the error in thought had to be on the level of appearances and not determinations.)

30 Cf. William James' pronouncement that the rational statement is that we feel sorry because we cry, not that we cry because we are sorry, cited in Kripke (1982: 93, n. 76). Kripke gives a list of these surprisingly frequent inversions and parallelisms in philosophy, including examples from James, Hume and Wittgenstein. The statement "the object of thought is not a particular, but particulars are objects of thought" is, however, in all fairness, not quite the same thing as what Kripke is describing, in that Kripke's examples all involve a "because"-clause and work their effect by reversing philosophical priorities. Nonetheless, the phenomenon of an inversion seeming to be "subtle" and to undo a conceptual knot is there too.

31 See Klein (1986: 136): "In other words, just like looking in a mirror can cause one to realize something about the reflected image, so through the image of an object thought can correctly realize something about the actual object."

32 The general question of the Buddhist use or rejection of a mirror theory of cognition is of interest to comparative philosophy, especially in the light of R. Rorty's theses in his *Philosophy and the Mirror of Nature*. Now, it is well-known that the Sautrāntika Sākāravādins hold that perceptual knowledge *(pratyakṣa)* of external objects comes about because the objects leave an image or likeness *(ākāra)* on the mirror of consciousness. See Kajiyama (1965: 429f.), Mookerjee (1935: 77f.) and Mimaki (1976: 72). Glass/crystal *(sphaṭika)* is often used as a metaphor for *perceptual knowledge* in non-Buddhist schools, like the Sāṃkhya, who take *buddhi* or the "inner organ" *(antaḥkaraṇa)* as being like glass which is "colored" by the substances underneath it. See *Nyāyabhāṣya ad Nyāyasūtra* 3.2.9 *(sphaṭikānyatvābhimānavat tadanyatvābhimānaḥ)* and also *Bai lun* T. 1569 *shang* 171c 22–25; see Tillemans (1990, endnote 344). Depictions of conceptual thought *(vikalpa)* in terms of mirroring or glass, however, seem rarer, although they do seem to have some limited support in Indian texts. Dharmakīrti in PV III, k.164 and 165 does speak of *vikalpapratibimba* "the representations/reflections belonging to thought" and "the representation/reflection of the object" *(arthaprati-*

bimbaka). (Note that *pratibimbaka = pratibimba,* see Böhtlingk *Sanskrit-Wörterbuch* s.v. *pratibimbaka.*) Moreover k. 165 specifies that *arthapratibimbaka* appears in a cognition which arises due to words—the most we can say is that the cognition with this representation is very indirectly caused by *svalakṣaṇa.* Accordingly, the *pratibimba* is still better taken as a purely fictional *constructed* representation, rather than as a reflection in a stricter causal sense where a *svalakṣaṇa* would actually appear in thought via mirroring. The representation involved in thought, thus, is not at all of the same type of "mirroring" as that in a Sautrāntika theory of perception where external objects are said to be mirrored as *ākāra.* Finally, we should note that there are Indian Buddhist contexts in which glass/crystal and mica *(abhraka)* are used as similes to explain the degrees of vividness of the representation in thought. This is notably the case in NBT *ad* NB 1.11 *(bhūtārthabhāvanāprakarṣaparyantajaṃ yogijñānam),* where Dharmottara discusses "yogic perception" *(yogipratyakṣa)* of reality as arising right after the utmost vivid stage of conceptualisation of this reality, namely, after the very last moment before conceptual meditation becomes non-conceptual yogic perception, the *bhūtārthabhāvanāprakarṣaparyanta* "limit of the superior stage of meditation on the truth." The superior stage *(prakarṣa)* is when the object begins to become clear; at the limit, it is as if one sees via mica, and finally in perception, it is as if via crystal *(amalaka).* I think, however, that here we are just dealing with illustrations of *degrees of clarity (sphuṭābhatva)* in a rather special case, the transition to yogic perception: the NBT passage is not, as far as I can see, citing the example of crystal and mica in the context of a general cognitive model for all mundane conceptualisation, thus supplanting the model of construction and imagination.

33 Cf. *Rwa stod bsdus grwa* 4a2 (= p. 7) *shes bya chos can / dngos po ma yin par thal / dngos med yin pa'i phyir / ma grub na / de chos can / der thal / rtag pa yin pa'i phyir /.* Ibid. 4a3: *gzhi grub na rtag pa yin pas khyab zer na / gser bum chos can / der thal / de'i phyir /. gzhi grub* and *shes bya* are coextensive. See Tillemans (1989: 277–82).

34 For some of the *ad hoc* decisions, see Goldberg (1985: 178–80). See also e.g., *ibid,* p. 171: "In the absence of a contradictory condition an entity is considered to be an instance of itself."

35 See Tillemans (1989) and (1992a) [reprinted in the present volume as chapters 6 and 9, respectively].

36 I should stress here that this diagnosis is not a dismissal of *bsdus grwa* as being irrational or incoherent, or as *only* being a kind of word-game, as some

Tibetan adversaries would depict it—far from it. Interestingly enough, *bsdus grwa,* in its quirkiness but formal orthodoxy, reminds one significantly of the complicated but largely *ad hoc* schemata for classifying Chinese discourse which A.C. Graham and others have investigated in the Mohist canon. (My point is a logical one, and not one of historical relations.) This *ad hoc* character is not very prominent in the Indian logic to which *bsdus grwa* is (very uneasily) related. A comparison with structures in Mohist logic is well beyond the scope of our present paper, but suffice it to say here that such comparisons have yet to be made and they will, I'm confident, contribute to demystifying some of the peculiar logical features at stake. An interesting first attempt at comparing Buddhist *hetuvidyā,* Aristotelian and Later Mohist logic is found in Paul (1994).

37 The Indian doctrine being explained here is generalizable to span not just *sādhya* and *sādhana,* but also *dharma* and *dharmin,* and has its source in one of the earliest works attributable to Dignāga, the mysterious *Hetumukha* which is cited in *Pramāṇavārttikasvavṛtti* (PVSV ed. Gnoli, p. 2.22) and elsewhere:

> *sarva evāyam anumānānumeyavyavahāro buddhyārūḍhenaiva dharmadharmibhedena na bahiḥ sadasattvam apekṣate /.* "Absolutely all this convention concerning *anumāna* [i.e., the reason *(liṅga)**] and *anumeya* [i.e., the *sādhyadharmin* and *sādhyadharma**] is due to the distinction between *dharma* and *dharmin,* which [in turn] is just dependent upon our thought *(buddhyārūḍhenaiva);* [the convention] does not depend upon [this difference in fact] existing or not outside [of the mind]."

*These additions follow Karṇakagomin's *Ṭīkā* on PVSV. There is, however, absolutely no reason to believe that Dignāga himself wished to distinguish here between unreal *anumeya/anumāna* itself, and possibly real *anumāna*s/*anumeya*s. See Frauwallner (1959: 104); Steinkellner (1971: 199–200) on this passage from the *Hetumukha.*

38 Of course, much of the dGe lugs pa explanation of the various *apoha* sections in the texts of Dharmakīrti *et al.* is indeed very valuable in understanding Indian Buddhism, and in other areas of *pramāṇa* these commentaries are also very useful. But that's not my point. I'm speaking about the dGe lugs pa's *own* coloring of the *apoha* theory (not their paraphrases of Dharmakīrtian *kārikā*s or other aspects of their commentarial duties) stemming from the ensemble of doctrines called "the difficult point."

11: What Can One Reasonably Say about Nonexistence?

With Donald S. Lopez, Jr., University of Michigan

THE FALLACY of *āśrayāsiddhahetu*, or a "logical reason whose basis is unestablished" arises when the subject of an argument is nonexistent; in usual cases, this subject failure implies that the proposition to be proved *(sādhya)* cannot be established—Buddhists such as Dharmakīrti repeatedly stress that when the subject fails, a debate about its properties ceases. To take an invented example, if one says that "Pegasus flies around the Aegean," it suffices to show that there is no Pegasus and one will have, *ipso facto,* short-circuited the question of "his" flight, or even proved the contrary, i.e., that he does not fly. Similarly, if someone shows that the Primordial Matter *(pradhāna)* accepted in Sāṃkhya philosophy, does not actually exist, then the Sāṃkhya's own thesis that *pradhāna* has such and such properties will thereby be refuted.[1] The problem however becomes thorny when one is proving simple nonexistence of some pseudo-entity, for then the case should be different from that of Pegasus's supposed flight. The height of absurdity would be if all proofs of nonexistence became self-refuting because the subject failed to exist.

The problem of *āśrayāsiddha* is taken up in various Buddhist contexts—typically in connection with proofs of momentariness *(kṣaṇabhaṅgasiddhi)*[2] and in connection with later Madhyamaka proofs of the absence of intrinsic nature *(niḥsvabhāvatā).* Although it is certainly not our intention to inventory all the considerable Indian and Tibetan Buddhist literature on this problem of *āśrayāsiddha,* or even the majority of texts in which the problem figures, certain seminal works do stand out and are repeatedly cited. Besides passages from Dignāga, we should mention the substantial and influential sections in Dharmakīrti's PV IV, k. 136–48 and PVin III, as well as those in the works of Kamalaśīla, in particular his *Madhyamakāloka* (MĀ). The Tibetan treatment is largely centered around

Tsong kha pa's *dBu ma rgyan gyi zin bris*, his commentary on Śāntarakṣita's *Madhyamakālaṃkāra* (MA), in which he integrates and elaborates upon the key passages in Dignāga, Dharmakīrti and Kamalaśīla. Although there are some relatively brief passages in the Sa skya pa *Rigs gter* and *Pramāṇavārttika* commentaries (e.g., gSer mdog paṇ chen śākya mchog ldan sketches out some significant differences from the treatment in *dBu ma rgyan gyi zin bris*[3]), it does seem that the problem of *āśrayāsiddha* was not treated nearly as thoroughly in the other schools as in the dGe lugs, where it became a recurring topos figuring markedly in numerous works. The present article consists primarily in a translation of the section on *āśrayāsiddha* in a text by A lag sha ngag dbang bstan dar (1759–1840), a dGe lugs pa scholar who was from the A la shan region of Inner Mongolia but wrote in Tibetan and who was, in our opinion, remarkable for his clear and often quite innovative thinking. His *gCig du bral gyi rnam bzhag* is a Madhyamaka work, one that treats of various problems centered around the Svātantrika Madhyamaka's use of the *ekānekaviyogahetu* (= *gcig du bral gyi gtan tshigs* "neither one nor many reason [for *śūnyatā*]"). For Ngag dbang bstan dar the problem of *āśrayāsiddha* arises when the Madhyamaka uses logical reasons like the *ekānekaviyogahetu* to prove ultimate voidness of things; it also occurs when he uses logical reasoning to prove that pseudo-entities do not exist at all. Ngag dbang bstan dar, thus, like his Indian and Tibetan Svātantrika predecessors, zig-zags between the Madhyamaka and logicians' positions, using the latter to buttress the former.

A striking aspect of the later Indian and Tibetan explanations of *āśrayāsiddha* is that certain earlier texts are almost invariably cited in later ones, giving a kind of "unfolding telescope" effect where each subsequent text includes its predecessors but seems to enlarge upon them and carry the ideas a few steps further, all the while seeking to remain faithful to the original intentions of Dignāga. This impression is, however, potentially misleading. In fact, be it the position of Kamalaśīla, that of Tsong kha pa or Ngag dbang bstan dar, what is at stake is a complex synthesis of disparate doctrine that has been elaborated over time; it would thus be a mistake if the seeming elegance of the unfolding telescope presentations lulled us into thinking that the later presentation was also ahistorically present *ab initio*. Lopez, in his *Study of Svātantrika*, has described the Tibetan theory on *āśrayāsiddha* as it is found in Tsong kha pa, rGyal tshab and lCang skya rol pa'i rdo rje and others: this constitutes the received position for Ngag dbang bstan dar. The section in *dBu ma rgyan gyis zin bris* treating of *āśrayāsiddha* has been translated in Tillemans (1984c). As we shall try to show in the rather extensive explanatory notes to our translation, the positions that we find in Tsong kha pa, Ngag dbang bstan dar and others had an intricate history that certainly did not just consist in bringing out what Dignāga, Dharmakīrti and Kamalaśīla had already understood.

Various works of bsTan dar have been studied by now, and it is becoming clear that this later dGe lugs pa thinker did make significant contributions, especially in the domain of ideas and arguments where he often shows originality in building upon and reinterpreting earlier writers.[4] The *gCig du bral gyi rnam bzhag*, and in particular the section on *āśrayāsiddha*, is a good case in point. On certain topics, such as avoidance of *āśrayāsiddha* in cases of simple, non-implicative, negation *(prasajyapratiṣedha)*, bsTan dar makes a radical break with his Indian and Tibetan predecessors, and arguably he is right to do so. The rapprochement with the Madhyamaka debate on "concordantly appearing subjects" *(chos can mthun snang ba)* is also noteworthy for its philosophical interest, turning as it does on the general problem of the incommensurability of rival theories.

Readers will probably recognize that the problem of talking about non-being has a long history, not only in the East, but in the West, including its twentieth century technical treatment in formal logic's theory of descriptions and in the theory of presuppositions. We add this later Tibetan position on what is one of the most recurrent and interesting problems of philosophy.

Translation of the Excerpt from the gCig du bral gyi rnam bzhag *of A lag sha ngag dbang bstan dar*

§1. Second, the doubt that the subject *(chos can; dharmin)* might be unestablished when one presents the formal argument *(sbyor ngag; prayogavākya)*. [Objection:] If we follow what is literally stated in the *Madhyamakālaṃkāra*, it is evident that one also presents partless consciousness, Primordial Matter *(spyi gtso bo; pradhāna)* and so forth[5] as subjects of enquiry *(shes 'dod chos can)* for a valid logical reason.[6] Thus this [reason] would have an unestablished basis *(gzhi ma grub pa; āśrayāsiddha)*. Would it not then result that the reason would be one which is unestablished *(ma grub pa; asiddha)* because the entity of the subject does not exist?[7]

§2. By way of a reply to this [objection], many scholars have said that there is no [such] fault so long as one presents simple negations *(med dgag; prasajyapratiṣedha)* as both the reason and the property to be proved *(bsgrub bya'i chos; sādhyadharma)*, but that should one present a positive phenomenon *(sgrub pa; vidhi)* or an implicative negation *(ma yin dgag; paryudāsapratiṣedha)*, it will then be an unestablished reason.[8] This does indeed seem to be based on certain statements in [the works] of Tsong kha pa and his disciples, such as [the passage] in [Tsong kha pa's] *dBu ma dgongs pa rab gsal* that reads:

> The fact that there is no fault, even though the subject stated for that reason might be negated, is due to the essential feature that both the reason and the property [to be proved] are mere exclusions *(rnam bcad tsam; vyavacchedamātra)*.

However, this alone can not eliminate all doubt. Thus it is necessary to explain things as follows. There are cases where [the reason] would not be a reason that is unestablished, in spite of the fact that one might present either an implicative negation or a positive phenomenon for both the reason and the property to be proved. For example, an argument such as "Take as the subject, a rabbit's horn; it is fitting to be designated by the word 'moon,' because it exists as an object of conceptual thought"—this [argument] is the idea of 'Jam dbyangs bzhad pa'i rdo rje.[9] Alternatively [there could be the argument], "Take as the subject, being gored by a rabbit's horn; this is a fallacious reason for proving that a person is in pain, because it is reason that does not have the triple character [needed] for proving that a person is in pain"—this [argument] is the idea in [dGe 'dun grub pa's] *Tshad ma rigs rgyan*.[10]

§3. The reason why these [arguments] are not reasons that are unestablished because the entity of the subject does not exist devolves from the essential feature that when something is [qualified by] either the reasons or properties to be proved in the proof of these [propositions], it need not be existent. So, even when simple negations are presented as both the reason and property [to be proved], there can also be the fault of the subject being unestablished provided that either the reason or property to be proved in the proof in question is pervaded by being existent, as for example when one proves that [something nonexistent like a rabbit's horn] is the subtle selflessness of the elements *(chos kyi bdag med; dharmanairātmya)* by means of the reason, "being the consummate [nature]" *(yongs grub; pariniṣpanna).*[11] Consequently, when one presents an unestablished basis as the subject, then all cases where a thing's being held to be [qualified by] the reason necessitates its being existent will [incur the fault of] being fallacious reasons unestablished because of the nonexistence of the entity of the subject, but when being held to be [qualified by] the reason does not necessitate being existent, then the [reason] will not be fallacious. The details of this way [of distinguishing between faulty reasons and valid ones] should be correctly brought out.

§4. In general, the subject of an argument is of two sorts, the subject that is the [proponent's] own [intended] locus *(rang rten chos can)*[12] and a nominal subject *(chos can 'ba' zhig pa; kevaladharmin).*[13] Between these two, the subject that is the [proponent's] own [intended] locus is, e.g., when one proves to a Sāṃkhya that sound is impermanent by means of the reason that it is produced, for at that time one proves impermanence based upon the simple [commonly recognized entity] sound. A nominal subject is, e.g., when one proves to a Vaiśeṣika that the space, which is [taken by the Vaiśeṣika to be] a real entity *(dngos por gyur pa'i nam mkha'; vastubhūtākāśa),* is not [in fact] a permanent substance [as they maintain it is] by means of the reason that it does not serve as the locus for other qualities. [This is called a "nominal subject"] because, at that time, one is not proving that being a permanent substance is located in a real entity, space, and thus this type of space is just merely presented as the subject, but is not the locus or subject.[14] Now, something's being a "nominal subject" means that although it might be stated as the subject, it is not the locus of the property to be proved *(sādhyadharma),* and is thus an unrelated subject. Consequently, although the nominal subject, i.e., the stated subject [as Tsong kha pa refers to it in §2 above], in the argument in question [against the Vaiśeṣika] is an unestablished basis, the subject that is the [proponent's] own [intended] locus does exist, because at that time it is what appears to the conceptual thought grasping the real entity space *(vastubhūtākāśa)* as excluded from the contrary of real space that is the [actual] subject or locus for the proof in question. It follows that this is so, because [this appearance] is like that [i.e., is the actual locus], due to the fact that the desire to know *(shes 'dod; jijñāsā)* occurs once the opponent has mistakenly taken this type of space and the [conceptual] appearance as such [a space] to be identical.[15] Therefore, in order that we understand this difference between the fact that in the argument in question the subject that is the [proponent's] own locus is an established basis, while the nominal subject that is presented in the actual words is not an established basis, [Dignāga] stated in the *Pramāṇasamuccaya:*

> With regard to the [proponent's] own locus *(rang rten la),* [a thesis is not opposed] by perceptible states of affairs, by inference, by authorities or by what is commonly recognized.[16]

The purpose behind [Dignāga's] not saying "the [proponent's] own subject" *(rang gi chos can; svadharmin)* here but rather "the [proponent's] own locus" *(rang gi rten),* was explained *in extenso* in thirteen verses from the *Pratyakṣapariccheda* in *Pramāṇvārttika,* verses that begin *"sarvatra vādino ...sva°..."*.[17]

§5. [Objection:] Then, it would follow [absurdly] that the appearance as something excluded from not-sound *(sgra ma yin pa las log par snang ba)* would also be the subject that is the [proponent's] own locus when proving that sound is impermanent by means of the reason that it is produced, because that is what you asserted [about space].

§6. [Reply:] This is not the same, because of the following: if something is a valid reason it must be established on the basis of the subject of enquiry in accordance with its mode of presentation *('god tshul),*[18] and so, because the appearance to conceptual thought as something excluded from not-sound is an imagined entity *(kun brtags; parikalpita),* it does not concord at all with being a product.[19] This follows, for it was stated in [Tsong kha pa's] *dBu ma rgyan gyi zin bris:*

> If one is proving that sound is impermanent because it is produced, then as the exclusion *qua* appearance *(snang ldog),* which appears to conceptual thought as excluded from not sound, is not a real entity *(dngos po),* the reason, i.e., being produced, does not qualify it. Rather, [being produced] must qualify the basis of the appearance *(snang gzhi),* i.e., sound. This is due to the essential feature that real entities *(dngos po)* are taken as the reason and property to be proved.

The [latter] necessary implication *(khyab pa; vyāpti)* holds, because (a) it is obvious that a conceptual appearance will not be established as the subject of enquiry of an argument where real entities are presented as the reason and property to be proved, and (b) it was stated in the *rNam nges dar ṭīk* [of rGyal tshab rje]:

> The [two cases] are not the same, because the conceptual appearance of space is the subject that is the basis ascertained as [qualified by] the previous reason [in the argument against the Vaiśeṣika], but what appears to conceptual thought as sound cannot be the basis that is ascertained as produced.

§7. To summarize, although we present space as the subject to the Vaiśeṣika, it is not the subject, but the appearance of this [space] is the subject. And when we prove that sound is impermanent by means of the reason, being produced, what appears as sound to conceptual thought does not serve as the subject, rather it is mere sound itself that serves as the subject that is the [proponent's] own [intended] locus. The reason for this, if one carries it as far as possible, comes down to whether there is or is not a subject that appears concordantly *(chos can mthun snang ba)* to both the Buddhist and the Vaiśeṣika, for the Buddhist accepts space as being a simple negation *(med dgag)* consisting in the mere denial of obstruction and contact, whereas the Vaiśeṣika accepts that it is a real entity *(dngos po)* that is independent *(rang dbang ba)* and is a positive phenomenon *(sgrub pa)*.[20]

§8. [Objection:] Then it would follow that even sound would not appear concordantly to both [parties], because the Buddhist asserts that sound is derived from the elements *('byung 'gyur; bhautika)*, whereas the Vaiśeṣika asserts that sound is a quality of space *(nam mkha'i yon tan; ākāśaguṇa)*.

§9. [Reply:] This is completely different on account of the essential feature that, to both these [parties], a mere object grasped by the auditive consciousness is established as appearing concordantly as an object found by non-erroneous means of valid cognition *(tshad ma; pramāṇa)*,[21] whereas in the case of case of space, if [the parties] were to search for the designated object *(btags don)*, they would find no object established as appearing concordantly apart from the mere verbal designation.

§10. Moreover, the omniscient lCang skya [rol pa'i rdo rje] has said that rGyal tshab rje maintained that the conceptual appearance *(rtog pa'i snang ba)* was the subject, but that mKhas grub rje did not accept that verbal objects *(sgra don; śabdārtha)* [i.e., conceptual entities] were the subject.[22] And the omniscient 'Jam dbyangs bzhad pa has said that taking Primordial Matter as the subject was Dignāga's idea, and that Dharmakīrti's idea was to take the conceptual appearance as the subject. However, suppose we examine their ideas carefully. Then whosoever's position we might take, be it that of Dignāga and his disciple [Dharmakīrti] or that of Tsong kha pa and his disciples [rGyal tshab rje and mKhas grub rje], if we presented an argument like "Take as the subject, Primordial Matter; it is not the substratum *(nyer len; upādāna)* for its various manifestations *(rnam 'gyur; vikṛti),* because it is not perceived to be the substratum of its various manifestations,"[23] none would deny that it is correct to take what appears as excluded from not-Primordial Matter to the conceptual thought grasping Primordial Matter *(gtso bo 'dzin pa'i rtog pa la gtso bo ma yin pa las log par snang ba)* as being the subject of this argument. For it was stated in the *Madhyamakāloka* [of Kamalaśīla]:

> It is just what exists as an aspect of mind, but is metaphorically designated by the infantile as external and real, that is the subject. Therefore, one negates Primordial Matter and the like in dependence upon that.[24]

§11. There is a necessary implication *(khyab pa; vyāpti)* here [between what the passage from the *Madhyamakāloka* says and the fact that the subject is a conceptual appearance], because [Kamalaśīla's] words "It is just what exists as an aspect of mind that is the subject" make it clear that he holds the conceptual appearance to be the subject.[25] This is also the case because of the following quotations. It is said in the *Svārthānumānapariccheda* [of Dharmakīrti's *Pramāṇavārttika*]:

> A verbal object [can] be a *dharma* of three types [a basis for existence, for nonexistence or for both].

[To which] [Dharmakīrti's] *Svavṛtti* states:

> Thus, those who depend upon this subject [deliberate about existence and nonexistence, asking whether] this object that is represented by the word "Primordial Matter" [does or does not have a real substratum].[26]

In the commentary on this [passage] Śākyabuddhi says:

> What is expressed by the word "Primordial Matter," that alone is the subject.

And in [mKhas grub rje's] *rNam 'grel ṭīk chen rigs pa'i rgya mtsho* it is said:

> This means that because it is generally taught that all conceptual appearances are verbal objects *(sgra don; śabdārtha)*,[27] what appears as Primordial Matter to the conceptual thought grasping Primordial Matter is also established as being a verbal object. And in this way it is the exclusion *qua* basis *(gzhi ldog)* of the verbal object for Primordial Matter, or [in other words] it is just what appears as Primordial Matter to conceptual thought, that is the subject of this argument.[28]

§12. Here an opponent might say: Take as the subject the verbal object for Primordial Matter *(gtso bo'i sgra don)*; it would follow that this would be the subject of that argument [mentioned earlier], because the appearance as Primordial Matter to the conceptual thought grasping Primordial Matter *(gtso bo 'dzin pa'i rtog pa la gtso bor snang ba)* is the subject of that argument.

§13. [We would reply:] There is no necessary implication *(ma khyab)*.

§14. [The opponent:] It would follow that there is a necessary implication, because the appearance as Primordial Matter to conceptual thought is the verbal object for Primordial Matter.

§15. [We would reply:] Again there is no necessary implication, because there is a difference between an exclusion *qua* thing itself *(rang ldog)* and an exclusion *qua* basis [of the thing] *(gzhi ldog)*.[29] For it was stated in the same *[rNam 'grel] ṭīk chen* [of mKhas grub rje]:

> Therefore, the subject when one says "Primordial Matter is not existent, because it is not perceived" is neither a real *(dngos po ba)* Primordial Matter, nor is it the exclusion *qua* thing itself of the verbal object for Primordial Matter *(gtso bo'i sgra don gyi rang ldog)*. Why? This very appearance as Primordial Matter to conceptual thought is asserted by the Sāṃkhyas to be the [actual] Primordial Matter endowed with the five qualities, but in our own system we assert that it is a verbal object. Thus, the conceptual appearance as Primordial Matter is considered to be the subject, because it is the basis of the debate about whether [something] is or is not the Primordial Matter endowed with the five qualities.

A differentiation between the exclusion *qua* thing itself *(rang ldog)* and the exclusion *qua* basis [for the thing] *(gzhi ldog)* is extremely valuable in this context.[30]

§16. This [point] is related to the essential feature that although the Sāṃkhya believes in this type of conceptual appearance, he does not believe that this appearance is a verbal object, for in [mKhas grub rje's] *Tshad ma yid kyi mun sel* it is said:

> Also for the foolish opponent to say that the verbal object for this type of [autonomous and substantially existent *(rang rkya thub pa'i rdzas yod)*] self is the subject would be a proclamation of his own faults since he accepts that the verbal object of this type of self *(de lta bu bdag gi sgra don)* does not [really] exist.

§17. Thus, it is indeed correct that the conceptual appearance is the subject, but when one is refuting an opponent's position, one does not have to present literally the conceptual appearance as being the subject. Why? It is because the very Primordial Matter, permanent Īśvara, autonomous persons and so forth in which the opponent believes must be explictly presented as the subjects in just the same way [as the opponent believes in them]. Otherwise there would be the fault that Primordial Matter and so forth would not be negated in themselves *(rang ldog nas)*.[31] For in [rGyal tshab rje's] *rNam 'grel thar lam gsal byed* it was said:

> Their thought according to the Lord of scholars, Kamalaśīla, was that Primordial Matter had to be refuted by [explicitly] taking it as the subject. Otherwise, although [the property of] being the substratum of various manifestations might be negated, Primordial Matter would not be negated in itself *(rang ldog nas)*. The basis for ascertaining the reason with a *pramāṇa* is maintained to be just the appearance as Primordial Matter *(gtso bor snang ba nyid)*.[32]

§18. [Objection:] In that case, it follows that the conceptual appearance cannot correctly be held to be the subject, because it is void of ability to perform a function *(don byed nus pa; arthakriyāsāmarthya)*. There is a necessary implication, because whatever is void of ability to perform a funtion cannot properly be a basis of deliberation for the perspicacious *(rtog ldan; prekṣāvat)*. In this vein, the *Pramāṇavārttika* stated:

> What point is there, for those who have such an aim, in deliberations about a thing that has no ability to perform a function? Why should a woman filled with desire wonder whether a eunuch was handsome or not?

§19. [We reply:] There is no necessary implication *(ma khyab)*. This is for the following reasons. The meaning of this quotation is that when someone hopes his desired effect will ensue from some basis, then the basis about which he deliberates must have the ability to perform the function. Thus, [Dharmakīrti] illustrates [his point about the uselessness of deliberation about inefficient things] saying that it is inappropriate, because it would be like, for example, a woman, intent upon sexual pleasure, who took as the subject [of her thought] a eunuch, and after [mistakenly] hearing that he could perform the acts that would give [her pleasure], wondered whether he was handsome or not. Nonetheless, in general, things that are void of ability to perform a function can properly be bases for [positive] proofs and negations. Indeed, the direct basis *(dngos rten)* for proofs and negations must inevitably be a verbal object. This follows, because:

(a) the reason why the direct basis must be a verbal object when one is denying that sound is permanent or proving that it is impermanent by the reason of its being produced is also grounded in the fact[33] that the conceptual thought that proves or negates relies upon verbal objects;

(b) it was said in the *Parārthānumānapariccheda* [of *Pramāṇavārttika*],

> ...We accept that all [positive] proof and negation *(vidhiniṣedhana)* here [in practical activity (*vyavahāra*)] is in reliance upon a verbal object..., which has no external basis;[34]

(c) when it is said that permanence is negated and impermanence is proved with regard to sound, what is meant [here] is the performance of the function of conceptual thought *(rtog pa'i don byed)*, and thus, on such an occasion, particular *(rang mtshan pa; svalakṣaṇa)* sounds, impermanent things or products and so forth do not directly *(dngos su)* appear to the conceptual thought that proves or negates.

In this vein, it was stated in [Tsong kha pa's] *dBu ma rgyan gyi zin bris:*

> The *[Pramāṇa]vārttika,* the sense of Dignāga's statements, states:

> However, this condition of practical designations in terms of what infers *(anumāna)* [i.e., the logical reason] and the proposition to be inferrred *(anumeyārtha)* is constructed in dependence upon a difference established by means of [conceptual] thought.[35]
>
> Following this explanation, in cases where the basis must be a real entity *(dngos po),* [such as when one is] proving that sound is impermanent because it is produced or that there is fire on the smoky hill, the direct basis *(dngos rten)* for these proofs and negations is just the object that is the appearance of sound or hill to conceptual thought as things excluded from what they are not. Sound and hill are not, however, themselves direct bases, because they do not directly appear to the conceptual thought that proves or negates.

As for the meaning of conceptual thought performing the function of negation and proof, it is as follows. When, for example, the quality of the subject *(phyogs chos; pakṣadharma)* is established for proving sound to be impermanent by the reason that it is a product, then from the perspective of the opponent, it is as if sound is initially established and after that producthood newly depends upon sound. There is such an appearance *(snang tshul),* but in reality *(gnas tshod la)* there is no such progression.

Tibetan Text of the Excerpt from the gCig du bral gyi rnam bzhag

§1. [**453.2; f. 16b**] gnyis pa sbyor ngag tu bkod na chos can ma grub pa'i dogs pa ni / *dBu ma rgyan* gyi tshig zin ltar na / shes pa cha med dang spyi gtso bo sogs kyang rtags sbyor yang dag gi shes 'dod chos can du bkod par mngon pas / de gzhi ma grub pa yin pas rtags de chos can gyi ngo bo med nas ma grub pa'i gtan tshigs su mi 'gyur ram zhe na /

§2. de'i lan la mkhas pa mang pos / rtags dang bsgrub bya'i chos gnyis char med dgag yin pa bkod na skyon med kyang sgrub pa dang ma yin dgag bkod na ma grub pa'i rtags su 'gyur zhes smras so // de ni *rNam bshad dgongs pa rab gsal* las /

> rtags des[36] smras pa'i chos can bkag kyang skyon med pa ni rtags dang chos gnyis ka rnam bcad tsam[37] yin pa'i gnad kyis so //[38]

zhes pa lta bu **rJe yab sras** kyi gsung 'ga' zhig la brten par snang mod / de tsam gyis dogs pa'i mtha' sel mi nus pas 'di ltar bshad dgos te / rtags dang bsgrub bya'i chos gnyis char ma yin dgag dang sgrub pa gang rung bkod kyang ma grub pa'i rtags su mi 'gyur ba yang yod de / ri bong rwa chos [454; f. 17a] can zla ba zhes pa'i sgras brjod rung yin te / rtog yul na yod pa'i phyir zhes pa'i sbyor ba lta bu'o // 'di **'Jam dbyangs bzhad pa'i rdo rje**'i dgongs pa'o // yang ri bong rwas phug pa chos can / skyes bu sdug bsngal bar sgrub pa'i rtags ltar snang yin te / skyes bu sdug bsngal bar sgrub pa'i tshul gsum ma yin pa'i gtan tshigs yin pa'i phyir zhes pa'i sbyor ba lta bu ste / 'di *Tshad ma rigs rgyan* gyi dgongs pa'o //

§3. de dag chos can gyi ngo bo med nas ma grub pa'i gtan tshigs su mi 'gyur ba'i rgyu mtshan de sgrub kyi rtags dang bsgrub bya'i chos gang rung yin na yod pa yin mi dgos pa'i gnad kyis yin pas / des na rtags chos gnyis kar med dgag bkod na yang de sgrub kyi rtags dang bsgrub bya'i chos gang rung yin na yod pas khyab pa can yin na chos can ma grub pa'i skyon du 'gyur ba yang yod de / dper na yongs grub kyi rtags kyis chos kyi bdag med phra mo sgrub pa lta bu'o // de'i phyir gzhi ma grub pa chos can du bkod pa'i tshe rtags su bzung ba de yin na yod pa yin dgos phyin chos can gyi ngo bo med nas ma grub pa'i gtan tshigs ltar snang du 'gyur la / rtags su bzung ba de yin na yod pa yin mi dgos na gtan tshigs ltar snang du mi 'gyur ba'i tshul la zhib cha legs par thon dgos so //

§4. spyir sbyor ba'i chos can la rang rten gyi chos can dang chos can 'ba' zhig pa gnyis las / rang rten gyi chos can ni / **Grangs can pa**'i ngor[39] byas pa'i rtags kyis sgra mi rtag par sgrub pa lta bu yin te / de'i tshe sgra nyid la mi rtag pa brten [455; f. 17b] par sgrub pa yin pa'i phyir ro // chos can 'ba' zhig pa ni / **Bye brag pa**'i ngor yon tan gzhan gyi rten mi byed pa'i rtags kyis dngos por gyur pa'i nam mkha' rtag rdzas ma yin par sgrub pa lta bu yin te / de'i tshe dngos por gyur ba'i nam mkha' la rtag rdzas brten par sgrub pa ma yin pas / de 'dra'i nam mkha' de rten gzhi chos can du ma song bar chos can du bkod pa 'ba' zhig pa yin pa'i phyir / chos can 'ba' zhig pa zhes pa'i don yang chos can du smras kyang bsgrub bya'i chos kyi rten du ma song bar chos can yan gar bar song ba'i don yin pas / de'i phyir sbyor ba de sgrub kyi chos can 'ba' zhig pa ste smras pa'i chos can gzhi ma grub kyang rang rten gyi chos can yod pa yin te / de'i tshe dngos gyur gyi nam mkha' 'dzin pa'i rtog pa la dngos gyur gyi nam mkha' ma yin pa las log par snang ba de sgrub kyi rten gzhi'i chos can du song ba yin pa'i phyir / der thal / phyi rgol gyis de 'dra ba'i nam mkha' dang der snang ba gnyis gcig tu 'khrul nas shes 'dod zhugs pa'i rgyu mtshan gyis de ltar yin pa'i phyir / des na sbyor ba de sgrub kyi rang rten gyi chos can gzhi grub cing tshig yin la bkod pa'i chos can 'ba' zhig pa gzhi ma grub pa'i khyad par 'di 'dra shes pa'i ched du / *Tshad ma kun btus* las /

> mngon sum don dang rjes dpag dang yid ches grags pas rang rten la'o //[40]

zhes rang gi chos can ma smos par rang gi rten smos pa'i dgos pa / *rNam 'grel mngon sum le'u* las /

> kun tu[41] rgol ba bdag nyid kyi /[42]

zhes sogs kyi tshigs bcad bcu gsum gyis rgyas par **[456; f. 18a]** 'chad pa yin no //

§5. 'o na sgra ma yin pa las log par snang ba'ang byas pa'i rtags kyis sgra mi rtag par sgrub pa'i rang rten gyi chos can yin par thal / 'dod pa'i phyir zer na

§6. mi mtshungs te / rtags yang dag yin na shes 'dod chos can gyi steng du 'god tshul dang mthun par grub dgos pas / rtog pa la sgra ma yin pa las log par snang ba kun btags yin pas byas pa dang mthun lugs med pa'i phyir / der thal / *dBu ma rgyan gyi zin bris* las /

> byas pas sgra mi rtag par sgrub pa na / rtog pa la sgra ma yin pa las log par snang ba'i snang ldog[43] dngos por med pas byas pa'i rtags de la 'grub pa[44] min[45] gyi / snang gzhi sgra la grub[46] dgos te / dngos po[47] rtags dang bsgrub bya'i chos su byed pa'i gnad kyis so //[48]

zhes gsungs pa'i phyir / khyab ste / dngos po rtags dang bsgrub bya'i chos su bkod pa'i rtags sbyor gyi shes 'dod chos can la rtog pa'i snang ba mi 'jog par shin tu gsal zhing / *rNam nges dar ṭīk* las kyang /

> rtog pa la nam mkha' snang ba sngar gyi rtags de nges pa'i gzhi chos can yin la / rtog pa la sgrar snang ba byas par nges pa'i gzhir mi rung ba'i phyir mi mtshungs so //[49]

zhes gsungs pa'i phyir /

§7. mdor na **Bye brag pa**'i ngor nam mkha' chos can du bkod kyang de chos can du ma song bar de'i snang ba chos can du song zhing / byas pa'i rtags kyis sgra mi rtag par sgrub pa'i tshe rtog pa la sgrar snang ba chos can du mi 'gro bar sgra nyid rang rten gyi chos can du 'gro ba'i rgyu mtshan mthar gtugs na / **Sangs rgyas pa** dang **Bye brag pa** gnyis ka'i ngor chos [457; **f. 18b**] can mthun snang ba yod med la gtugs pa yin te / **Sangs rgyas pa**s nam mkha' thogs reg bkag tsam gyi med dgag tu 'dod pa gang zhig / **Bye brag pa**s sgrub pa rang dbang ba'i dngos por 'dod pa'i phyir /

§8. 'o na sgra yang de gnyis ka'i ngor mthun snang du grub pa med par thal / **Sangs rgyas pa**s sgra 'byung 'gyur du 'dod pa gang zhig / **Bye brag pa**s sgra nam mkha'i yon tan du 'dod pa'i phyir zhe na /

§9. shin tu mi mtshungs te / de gnyis ka'i ngor nyan shes kyi gzung byar gyur pa'i don tsam zhig ma 'khrul ba'i tshad mas rnyed don du mthun snang du grub pa yod la / nam mkha' la ming tsam ma gtogs mthun snang du grub pa'i don btags don btsal na mi rnyed pa'i gnad kyis so //

§10. gzhan yang **lCang skya** thams cad mkhyen pas / **rGyal tshab rje**s rtog pa'i snang ba chos can du bzhed kyang / **mKhas grub rje**s sgra don chos can du mi bzhed par gsungs la / kun mkhyen **'Jam dbyangs bzhad pas** / gtso bo chos can du bzung ba **Phyogs glang** gi dgongs pa dang / rtog pa'i snang ba chos can du bzung ba **Chos grags** kyi dgongs pa yin gsungs kyang / dgongs pa zhib tu brtag na **Phyogs glang yab sras** dang **rJe yab sras** su'i lugs byas kyang / gtso bo chos can / rnam 'gyur sna tshogs kyi nyer len du med de / rnam 'gyur sna tshogs kyi nyer len du ma dmigs pa'i phyir / zhes pa'i sbyor ba 'di la mtshon na / gtso bo 'dzin pa'i rtog pa la gtso bo ma yin pa las log par snang ba rtags sbyor de'i chos can du 'dzin rigs pa la sus kyang bsnyon du med de / *dBu ma snang ba* las /

> byis pa rnams kyis phyi rol dang dngos po nyid du nye bar btags pa blo la rnam pa[50] yod [458; **f. 19a**] pa nyid chos can yin te / de'i phyir de la brten nas gtso bo la sogs pa 'gog par byed do //[51]

zhes gsungs pa'i phyir /

§11. khyab ste / blo la rnam pa yod pa nyid chos can yin zhes pas rtog pa'i snang ba chos can du 'dzin par gsal zhing / *Rang don le'u*r /

> sgra don chos ni rnam pa gsum //[52]

zhes dang / *Rang 'grel* las /

> de bas na chos can de la brten nas ci[53] gtso bo'i sgra las snang ba'i don 'di ni / [dngos po nye bar len pa can nam ma yin zhes yod pa dang med pa nyid dpyod par byed do][54]

zhes dang / de'i 'grel bshad du / **Śākya blo**s kyang /

> gtso bo la sogs pa'i sgras brjod par bya ba de nyid ni chos can yin la /[55]

zhes dang / *rNam 'grel ṭīk chen rigs pa'i rgya mtsho* las /

> de ltar rtog pa'i snang ba thams cad sgra don yin no zhes spyir bstan pas gtso bo 'dzin pa'i rtog pa[56] la gtso bor snang ba'ang sgra don du grub la / de ltar gtso bo'i sgra don gyi gzhi ldog rtog pa la gtso bor snang ba de nyid rtags sbyor de'i chos can yin zhes bya ba'i don no //[57]

zhes gsungs pa'i phyir /

§12. de la kho na re / gtso bo'i sgra don chos can / rtags sbyor de'i chos can yin par thal / gtso bo 'dzin pa'i rtog pa la gtso bor snang ba rtags sbyor de'i chos can yin pa'i phyir na /

§13. ma khyab /

§14. khyab par thal / rtog pa la gtso bor snang ba gtso bo'i sgra don yin pa'i phyir na /

§15. yang ma khyab / rang ldog dang gzhi ldog gi khyad par yod pa'i phyir te / *Ṭīk chen* de nyid las /

> des na gtso bo ni yod pa ma yin te ma dmigs pa'i phyir zhes pa'i rtags kyi shes 'dod chos can ni / gtso bo dngos po ba yang ma yin la / gtso bo'i sgra don gyi rang ldog kyang ma yin gyi / 'o na ci zhe na / rtog pa la gtso bor snang ba de nyid **Grangs can [459; f. 19b] pa**[58] dag gtso bo khyad par lnga ldan du 'dod la / rang lugs la sgra don du 'dod pas / khyad par lnga ldan gyi gtso bo yin min rtsod pa'i gzhi yin pa'i phyir rtog pa la gtso bor snang ba chos can du gzung bar byas pa yin no //[59]

zhes gsungs pa'i phyir / rang ldog dang gzhi ldog gi khyad par phye ba skabs 'dir shin tu gces so //

§16. de yang **Grang can pas** de lta bu'i rtog pa'i snang ba khas len kyang snang ba de sgra don du khas mi len pa'i gnad la thug pa yang yin te / *Tshad ma yid kyi mun sel* /

> yang blun po kha cig gis de lta bu bdag gi sgra don chos can yin no zhes zer ba ni / de lta bu bdag gi sgra don med par khas blangs pa yin pas rang gi mtshang bsgrags pa yin no //[60]

zhes gsungs pa'i phyir /

§17. de ltar rtog pa'i snang ba chos can du rigs mod / 'on kyang pha rol po'i 'dod pa 'gog pa na rtog pa'i snang ba tshig zin la chos can du 'god dgos pa yang ma yin no // 'o na ci zhe na / spyi gtso bo dang rtag pa'i dbang phyug dang gang zag rang rkya ba sogs pha rol pos gang khas blangs pa de nyid ji lta ba bzhin chos can du dngos su 'god dgos te / de lta ma yin na gtso bo la sogs pa rang ldog nas mi khegs pa'i skyon yod pa'i phyir te / *rNam 'grel thar lam gsal byed* las /

> de dag gi dgongs pa mkhas pa'i dbang po **Ka ma la śī las** / gtso bo nyid chos can du bzung nas dgag dgos kyi / de min na rnam 'gyur sna tshogs kyi nyer len yin pa khegs kyang / gtso bo rang ldog nas mi khegs par 'gyur la / rtags tshad mas nges pa'i gzhi ni gtso bor snang ba nyid la bzhed do //[61]

zhes gsungs pa'i phyir /

§18. de la gal te rtog pa'i snang ba [**460; f. 20a**] chos can du 'dzin mi rigs par thal / de don byed nus stong yin pa'i phyir / khyab te / don byed nus pa ma yin na rgol ba rtog ldan gyi dpyad gzhir mi rung bas khyab pa'i phyir / de skad du *rNam 'grel* las /

> don byed nus pa ma yin la //
>
> don gnyer brtag pas ci zhig bya //
>
> ma ning gzugs bzang mi bzang zhes //
>
> 'dod ldan[62] rnams kyis brtag ci phan //[63]

zhes gsungs pa'i phyir na /

§19. ma khyab ste / lung de'i don ni rang 'dod pa'i 'bras bu gzhi de las 'grub tu re nas dpyod pa'i gzhi la don byed nus pa dgos zhes pa yin pas / de ni dper na 'khrig pa'i bde ba don du gnyer ba'i bud med kyis / ma ning khyad gzhir bzung nas des skyes pa'i bya ba byed par go nas de'i gzugs mdzes mi mdzes la dpyod pa dang 'dra bas mi 'thad ces ston pa yin gyi / spyir dgag sgrub kyi gzhi la don byed nus stong rung bar ma zad / dgag sgrub byed pa'i dngos kyi rten la sgra don nges can du dgos pa'i phyir / der thal / byas pa'i rtags kyis sgra la rtag[64] dgag pa dang mi rtag pa sgrub pa'i dngos kyi rten sgra don yin dgos pa'i rgyu mtshan yang / dgag sgrub byed pa'i rtog pa rnams sgra don la brten pa'i rgyu mtshan gyis yin pa'i phyir / *gZhan don le'u* las /

> phyi rol rten min sgra don la //
>
> brten nas 'dir ni sgrub pa dang //
>
> dgag pa thams cad 'dod pa yin //[65]

zhes gsungs pa'i phyir dang / sgra'i steng du rtag pa dgag pa dang mi rtag pa sgrub ces pa'i don yang rtog pa'i don byed pa yin pas / de'i tshe dgag sgrub byed pa'i rtog pa de dag la sgra dang byas mi rtag sogs rang mtshan pa dngos su mi [**461; f. 20b**] snang ba'i phyir / de skad du *dBu ma rgyan gyi zin bris* las /

> **Phyogs glang** gis gsungs pa'i don *rNam 'grel* las /
>
> dpag bya dpog par byed pa yi[66] //
>
> don gyi tha snyad gnas pa 'di //
>
> shes pa la grub tha dad la //
>
> brten nas rnam par brtags pa[67] yin //[68]
>
> zhes gsungs pa ltar / gzhi dngos po dgos pa byas pas sgra mi rtag pa dang du ba la la[69] me yod du sgrub pa la yang / rtog pa la sgra dang la gnyis de gnyis ma yin pa las log par snang ba'i don nyid dgag sgrub kyi dngos rten yin gyi / sgra dang la

nyid dngos kyi rten ma yin te / dgag sgrub byed pa'i rtog pa la dngos su mi snang ba'i phyir dang /[70]

zhes gsungs pa'i phyir / dgag sgrub rtog pa'i don byed ces pa'i don yang dper na byas pa'i rtags kyis sgra mi rtag par sgrub pa'i phyogs chos grub pa na / phyi rgol de'i rtog ngo na / sgra dang por grub nas de'i rjes su sgra la byas pa gsar du brten pa lta bu'i snang tshul yod cing / gnas tshod la rim pa de 'dra med pa'i don no //.

Notes to Chapter 11

The original publication contains the following statement: "This article is a result of a collaboration that took place between the authors in seminars at Lausanne in May 1996 and at Ann Arbor in September 1997 as part of the exchange agreement between the University of Lausanne and the University of Michigan. The authors would like to gratefully acknowledge financial support from the two universities and from the Elisabet de Boer Foundation."

1 See n. 17 and 7.

2 See Mimaki (1976: 60–61).

3 See, e.g., his *Tshad ma rigs gter dgongs rgyan smad cha* 76a1–7 (= p. 151). Śākya mchog ldan's position turns on the Rigs gter ba *apoha* theory's contrast between theoretical explanation *('chad pa)* and pratical application *('jug pa)* and especially the contrast between an object of conceptual thought as it really is *(song tshod)* (i.e., a mental representation) and what we mistakenly assume it to be *(rlom tshod)*. See Tillemans (1995a: 869 and n. 19) and Dreyfus (1997: 161, 163, 167 *et passim*). Note that this latter schema, i.e., *song tshod kyi chos can* and *rlom tshod kyi chos can*, is applied to the problem of *āśrayāsiddha* in a way that does not seem to coincide fully with the *svadharmin* and *kevaladharmin* contrast. See n. 13 on *svadharmin* vs. *kevaladharmin*.

4 Selections from his work on particulars and universals, i.e., his *Rang mtshan spyi mtshan gyi rnam bzhag rtsom 'phro*, have been translated in Klein (1991). A translation of his commentary on the *Heart Sūtra* appears in Lopez (1988:

137–59). His work on the proof of the Buddha's authority in Dharmakīrti's PV, i.e., the *sTon pa tshad ma'i skyes bur sgrub pa'i gtam*, has been translated and studied in Tillemans (1993a). Lopez (1987) refers to many parts of bsTan dar's *gCig du bral gyi rnam bzhag*. Finally, elements of bsTan dar's grammatical work, the *Sum cu pa dang rtags 'jug gi don go sla bar bsdus pa'i bshad pa skal ldan yid kyi pad ma 'byed pa'i snang ba'i mdzod*, have been studied in T. Tillemans and D. Herforth (1989).

5 Cf. MA, k. 1: *niḥsvabhāvā amī bhāvās tattvataḥ svaparoditāḥ / ekānekasvabhāvena viyogāt pratibimbavat //*. Śāntarakṣita proposes to show that entities accepted by Buddhists as well as those advocated by non-Buddhist adversaries are without any intrinsic nature *(svabhāva)* because of being neither one nor many different things. Skt. in *Bodhicaryāvatārapañjikā* 173, 17–18; translation Ichigō (1985: cxxxv). Note that following rGyal tshab's *dBu ma rgyan gyi brjed byang* (Sarnath ed. p. 80), the refutation of partless consciousness is in the context of the refutation of the Sautrāntika view that the "manifold is non-dual" *(sna tshogs gnyis med pa)*. The Madhyamaka argues that the aspects/images *(rnam pa; ākāra)* cannot be substantially distinct *(rdzas tha dad)* from each other, because they are not substantially distinct from a partless unitary consciousness *(shes pa cha med gcig): mDo sde pa'i lugs dgag pa la / sna tshogs gnyis med pa / sgo nga phyad tshal ba / rnam shes grangs mnyam pa'i lugs dgag pa'o // dang po ni / shes sogs bzhi la / shes pa gcig la sngo ser dkar dmar sogs rnam pa du ma shar ba'i tshe rnam pa de rnams rdzas tha dad min par thal / de rnams shes pa cha med gcig dang tha dad min pa'i phyir /*. Cf. MA, k. 34 *et sq.*; cf. also Tsong kha pa's *dBu ma rgyan gyi zin bris* 8a (Sarnath ed. p. 41; trans. Tillemans [1984c: 365]): *gal te sbyor ba 'di rang rgyud du byed na / gzhan gyis smras pa'i bdag dang dbang phyug la sogs pa dang / rang sdes smras pa'i sdug bsngal dang / shes pa cha med kyi chos can ma grub pas / phyogs chos ma grub par 'gyur bas mi 'thad do zhe na /*. The entities accepted by others include the *ātman* and Īśvara, while those accepted by the Buddhists include suffering, partless consciousnesses and so forth.

6 The term is an adaptation of the Indian Buddhist requirement that debate is about what the opponent desires to know *(jijñāsā, jijñāsita)*, i.e., whether a certain property qualifies a certain subject. Cf., e.g., NBT *ad* NB III, 92: *prativādino hi yaj jijñāsitaṃ tat prakaraṇāpannam /*. On the term *shes 'dod chos can (*jijñāsitadharmin)*, see the definition in *Yongs 'dzin rtags rigs* (ed. Onoda: 17).

7 For the varieties of *asiddhahetu*, see NB III, 57 *et sq.* (trans. Stcherbatsky: 172ff.) and in particular NB III, 65 on *dharmyasiddha;* for the dGe lugs pa classification see *Yongs 'dzin rtags rigs*, p. 57, which speaks of a triple classification

of *asiddhahetu,* those which are due to objective facts *(don la ltos pa),* due to attitudes *(blo la ltos pa)* such as doubt, and those which are due to the debaters *(rgol ba la ltos pa)* having incompatible views on the nature of the subject. The "reason that is unestablished *(asiddha)* because of the nonexistence of the entity of the subject" *(chos can gyi ngo bo med nas ma grub pa'i gtan tshigs)* is a subdivision of the first category.

8 On these two types of negation, see Kajiyama (1973: 167f.) and the references in his n. 1. Indian Buddhist logicians had the important insight that proving a mere negation of existence is, in its logical structure, quite different from proving positive qualities, and that in the former case (i.e., simple denial along the lines of "it is not so that *S* is existent") subject failure is not a problem at all whereas in the latter case it is. Cf. Matilal (1970). Tibetan explanations of *āśrayāsiddha,* such as those found in *dBu ma rgyan gyi zin bris* and *lCang skya grub mtha',* generally cite a passage from Kamalaśīla's MĀ as being the source for this idea. The quotation in question is found in MĀ, D. 172a6–b1, P. 188a3–6: *gang la dngos po'i chos yod pa'i ngo bor sgrub par mi 'dod kyi don kyang sgro btags pa'i chos rnam par gcad pa sgrub pa tsam zhig brjod par 'dod pa de la ni ma grub pa nyid la sogs pa'i nyes pa brjod pa tha snyad du yang dngos por gyur pa'i chos can mi dgos te / de ni de'i chos ma yin pa'i phyir ro // de la ltos nas kyang de'i chos can nyid du mi 'thad pa'i phyir ro // de ma grub tu zin kyang bsgrub par bya ba med na de mi 'byung ba'i gtan tshigs mngon par 'dod pa'i don grub pa la gegs byed pa med pa'i phyir ro //;* translated in Lopez (1987: 358). On Kamalaśīla's different treatment of *āśrayāsiddha* in his earlier *Madhyamakālaṃkārapañjikā* and in the later MĀ, see Kobayashi (1989). The Tibetan dGe lugs pa treatment of the problem has been developed in detail in Lopez (1987: 168–80), Klein (1991: 118–19, 173–81, *et passim*).

In fact the central idea in the MĀ that one avoided *āśrayāsiddha* when the property being proved was a simple negation was already clearly formulated well before Kamalaśīla. What we find in the Indian Buddhist literature is that Dharmakīrtian commentators, like Devendrabuddhi and Śākyabuddhi, in their explanations of PV IV, k. 136–48, emphasize the idea that subjects, like space, taken as real *(dngos por gyur pa = vastubhūta)* by the opponents, are *kevala* in nonexistence proofs where the property to be proved and the reason are "mere exclusions" *(rnam par gcod pa tsam = vyavacchedamātra);* in these special cases, the subjects can be negated with impunity. Although Devendrabuddhi himself does not gloss these "mere exclusions" by the notion of non-implicative negations *(prasajyapratiṣedha)* so often invoked in Buddhist philosophy, the transition is very natural and is, indeed, explicitly made by Śākyabuddhi: mere exclusion means that no entity or positive property is stated, implied or presupposed. See PVP D. 296b4 *et seq.* and PVT D. 269a4–5:

gtan tshigs rnam par gcod pa'i ngo bo ma grub pa nyid ma yin no zhes bya ba ni / cig car sgra sogs rgyu min phyir / zhes bya ba'i gtan tshigs rnam par gcod pa tsam gyi ngo bo med par dgag pa *tsam gyi mtshan nyid ma grub pa nyid ma yin te / dngos por gyur pa'i chos can med na yang tha snyad pa'i chos can rnam par gcod pa tsam la gnod pa med pa'i phyir ro //* "When [Devendrabuddhi] says 'a logical reason that is of the nature of an exclusion is not unestablished,' he means that a logical reason like 'because it is not the cause for [producing its various effects like] sound etc. all at once,' which is of the nature of a mere exclusion, i.e., which has the character of a simple *prasajyapratiṣedha,* is not unestablished. This is because in spite of there being no subject that would be a real entity, there is no invalidation of the mere exclusion of the conventionally designated subject."

Our thanks to Mr. Ryusei Keira for making us aware of this passage from Śākyabuddhi.

This position concerning "mere exclusion" was adopted by later Indian writers such as Prajñākaragupta, Kamalaśīla and by Tibetans such as Tsong kha pa, *et al.*, with the *further* development that it was argued that when a Buddhist logician was proving a mere exclusion, or non-implicative negation (e.g., that such and such a pseudo-entity did not exist), the Buddhist proponent's intended subject, the *svadharmin,* was just the conceptual image. (In the case of Dharmakīrti and Devendrabuddhi it is not at all clear that this last additional development is also attributable to them. See n. 13. [Editor's note: see also chapter 8 in the present volume.]) Ngag dbang bstan dar shows the rough edges and pitfalls of this Indo-Tibetan attempt to use the distinction between the two types of negation as a watertight way to delineate between harmless subject failures and genuine *āśrayāsiddha.*

9 Unidentified in 'Jam dbyangs bzhad pa. The example purports to show that the property being predicated of a nonexistent subject (like a rabbit's horn) can be a positive entity *(vidhi)* or an implicative negation: it need not necessarily be a *prasajyapratiṣedha* if we are to avoid *āśrayāsiddha.* The property being proved here, viz., "being fit *(rung ba = yogya)* to be designated by the word 'moon,'" is itself a positive entity. Ngag dbang bstan dar, supposedly following 'Jams dbyangs bzhad pa, has hearkened back to the argumentation found in the *pratītibādhā* section in PV IV, k. 109–30, NB III, PVin III, etc., where Dharmakīrti develops the idea that any word is fit (*yogya*) to designate any object, the use and correctness of words depending only upon the speaker's linguistic intention *(vivakṣā).* Cf. PV IV, k.109:

> *arthesv apratisiddhatvāt puruṣecchānurodhinaḥ / iṣṭaśabdābhidheya-tvasyāpto 'trākṣatavāg janaḥ //* "An intended word's designatum *(abhidheya),* which is in keeping with people's wishes, is unrestricted with regard to objects. Therefore, the person [i.e., the user of language], whose speech is unopposed, is an authority here [i.e., with regard to the designatum of the word]."

This doctrine of unrestricted *yogyatā* is being alluded to in the present argument. Thus, a rabbit's horn is indeed fit to be the designatum *(abhidheya)* of the word "moon," in that there is no objective or intrinsic nature found in words or objects that would preclude such a use.

Ngag bdang bstan dar is obviously playing with a frequently found reasoning *(prayoga)* called *grags pa'i rtags* ("reason based on what is commonly accepted" *[grags pa = prasiddha, pratīti]*). This reasoning is given in Indian and Tibetan texts to establish the fact that *śaśin* (*ri bong can,* "that which has a rabbit," "that which is hare-marked") is fit to be the designatum of the word *candra* ("moon"). The trick is to change *ri bong can* to *ri bong rwa* ("the rabbit's horn"). On the Indian reasoning, see Durvekamiśra's *Dharmottara-pradīpa* 184.16–17:

> *evaṃ tu prayoga draṣṭavyaḥ yo 'rtho vikalpavijñānaviṣayaḥ sa sāṃketikena śabdena vaktuṃ śakyaḥ / yathā śākhādimānartho vṛkṣaśabdena / vikalpavijñānaviṣayaś ca śaśīti /* "The formal argument *(prayoga)* should be regarded as follows: 'Whatever entity is the object of a conceptual cognition, can be designated by an agreed upon word, just like the entity having branches and so forth [can be designated] by the word 'tree'. Now, *śaśin* is the object of a conceptual cognition.'" (The conclusion is that *śaśin* can be designated by the agreed upon word *candra.*)

The usual Tibetan formulation of the *prayoga* is: *ri bong can la zla ba zhes pa'i sgras brjod rung ba yin te / rtog yul na yod pa'i phyir /* "That which is hare-marked is fitting to be designated by the word 'moon' because it exists as an object of conceptualization"; see *Yongs 'dzin rtags rigs,* p. 46.

10 See *Tshad ma rigs rgyan* 117a.

11 See Lopez (1987: 173–74). Just as it was shown that avoidance of *āśrayāsiddha* is possible even where the property is a positive entity, so now Ngag bdang bstan dar shows that the reason and property being non-implicative negations will not guarantee that *āśrayāsiddha* is avoided. To say that the rabbit's horn is the subtle seflessness of the elements because it is their consummate nature *is* a case of *āśrayāsiddha,* even though both the

reason and the property are simple negations. In short, it is not so that *āśrayāsiddha* is avoided *if and only if* the reason and property are *vyavacchedamātra*. Ngag dbang bstan dar, to his credit, proposes a stricter criterion than had his Indo-Tibetan predecessors: *āśrayāsiddha* will be avoided if and only if the reason and property do not imply existence. The innovation here is discrete, but it represents a radically different, and even in some ways better, approach: it turns on the sound logical insight that certain properties (like being blue, etc.) imply existence, while others (like "being thought of") do not, and that subject failure will lead to refutation in all and only the former types of cases.

12 The term *rang rten chos can* is most likely a Tibetan invention, based on Tibetan writers' choice of a rather misleading Tibetan translation of the PSV, a translation which was also reflected in the sDe dge and Co ne editions of PS III, k. 2. See Tillemans (1984c: 42) for the details. In brief, PSV(a) *ad* PS III, k. 2cd reads *de yang ma bsal ba'o // mngon sum don dang rjes dpag dang // yid ches grags pas rang rten la'o,* whereas the Peking version of PS III, k. 2cd and of PSV(b) have: *rang gi chos can la mngon sum don dang rjes dpag dang // yid ches grags pas ma bsal ba'o //.* See Kitagawa (1973: 471–72). What happened is that major dGe lugs and Sa skya writers cited PSV(a)'s text *mngon sum … rang rten la'o* without the initial *de yang ma bsal ba'o,* which they probably considered to be an independent sentence due to its final particle. Now, we do have Sanskrit fragments of PS III, k. 2:

> *svarūpeṇaiva nirdeśyaḥ svayam iṣṭo 'nirākṛtaḥ / pratyakṣārthānumānāptaprasiddhena svadharmiṇi //* "[A valid thesis] is one which is intended *(iṣṭa)* by [the proponent] himself *(svayam)* as something to be stated *(nirdeśya)* according to its proper form alone *(svarūpeṇaiva)* [i.e., as a *sādhya*]; [and] with regard to [the proponent's] own subject *(svadharmin),* it is not opposed *(anirākṛta)* by perceptible objects *(pratyakṣārtha),* by inference *(anumāna),* by authorities *(āpta)* or by what is commonly recognized *(prasiddha).*"

It can be seen that *anirākṛta = ma bsal ba,* and that placing this before *mngon sum…rten la'o* is an attempt to follow the Sanskrit word order, but is virtually incomprehensible in Tibetan: hence PSV(b) and the Peking version of PS III, k. 2 is preferrable, also because it reads *rang gi chos can (=svadharmin).* Nonetheless, most Tibetan writers seem to have chosen PSV(a)'s reading; such is the case for Tsong kha pa, Go rams pa bsod nams seng ge, Śākya mchog ldan, but also for the earlier writer bTsun pa ston gzhon (thirteenth century), who in his *rNam 'grel gyi rnam bshad gangs can gyi rgyan,* p. 438 clearly gives credence to PSV(a): *rang rten la'o zhes rang gi chos can smos pa la dgos pa ci yod …* Finally not just Tsong kha pa, but rGyal tshab in his *rNam 'grel thar lam gsal byed* to PV IV, k. 136–48 repeatedly phrased his explanations in terms of *rang rten chos can*. In what is an ironic, but understandable blunder, Ngag dbang bstan dar will subsequently on p. 455 argue that Dignāga himself did not speak of *rang gi chos can (svadharmin)*, but rather *rang gyi rten*.

13 Ngag dbang bstan dar has introduced one of the key themes in the Indo-Tibetan explanations of *āśrayāsiddha*, viz., the contrast between *svadharmin* and *kevaladharmin*. Amongst Indian authors, the starting point in their discussion of *āśrayāsiddha* consists in Dignāga's definition of the thesis *(pakṣalakṣaṇa)* in PS III, k. 2, in particular, the specification that the thesis should not be opposed *(anirākṛta)* by perception and other means of valid cognition *with regard to the proponent's own intended subject* (*svadharmiṇi* "with regard to his own subject"). See n. 12. While Dignāga only spoke of *svadharmin*, Dharmakīrti in PV IV, k. 136–48 introduced the idea of a contrast between *svadharmin* and *kevaladharmin*, the latter being a nominal or unrelated subject, one which may be merely stated but which is not actually what is qualified by the property to be proved. This contrast comes up again and again in Ngag dbang bstan dar, and indeed he mentions the twelve *kārikās* in PV IV (not III!) as being the Indian source.

Important in the philosophical background to this discussion of *svadharmin* and *kevaladharmin* (although not so often explicitly cited in Tibetan texts) is Dignāga's treatment in the *Nyāyamukha* of the Sāṃkhya's arguments concerning Primordial Matter *(pradhāna)* and other such postulates in the Sāṃkhya system. Dignāga had argued "*pradhāna* and so forth do not exist because they are not perceived" *(na santi pradhānādayo 'nupalabdheḥ)* and spoke of "non-perception being a property of an imagined object" *(kalpitasyānupalabdhir dharmaḥ)*. See Katsura (1992: 230–31); Tucci (1930: 16–17); Sanskrit fragments in *Svavṛtti* (ed. Gnoli: 105 and 107). This idea of an imagined subject was then generalized by Dharmakīrti to form a key part of his *apoha* theory. In particular, he took the anti-Sāṃkhya argument in Dignāga's NM proving the nonexistence of *pradhāna* as well as the NM's phrase *kalpitasyānupalabdhir dharmaḥ* to lead to the general principle in PV I, k. 205–12, the *Svavṛtti* and PVin III that the directly designated objects of words were always conceptual representations *(kalpanā);* he then maintained that although *pradhāna* did not exist as something real and external, its conceptual representation, or in other words, the verbal object *(śabdārtha)* existed, so that the charge of *āśrayāsiddha* did not apply.

In later developments, including what we find in the dGe lugs pa positions and clearly in Ngag dbang bstan dar, the Dharmakīrtian general principle of designata being only concepts will be combined with the *svadharmin* versus *kevaladharmin* contrast to explain when *āśrayāsiddha* is avoidable and when it is not. *Grosso modo*, in nonexistence proofs the *svadharmin* is the concept and no more; the *kevaladharmin* is the pseudo-entity. Ngag bdang bstan dar here (following Tsong kha pa and others) applies this point of view to PV IV, k. 141–42's discussion where the Buddhist refutes the Vaiśeṣika's version of space. Thus the Vaiśeṣika's space becomes the *kevaladharmin,* whereas the conceptual representation of space is the *svadharmin,* i.e., the subject accepted by the Buddhist himself. Although the *kevaladharmin* is obviously refuted, the *svadharmin* is not and hence *āśrayāsiddha* is avoided. However, this synthesis is arguably a later invention. Tillemans is of the opinion that while for a writer like Kamalaśīla (who figures so prominently in the Tibetan theories) this move to combine the notions of *svadharmin* and conceptual subjects is present in his MĀ, in the case of Dharmakīrti this combination is not very likely. The *kārikās* in PV IV (viz., k. 141–42) that are often interpreted as supporting this combination are probably better interpreted differently. First of all, Prajñākaragupta's PVBh *ad* PV IV, k. 141–42 clearly specifies two interpretations of the *kārikās* at stake. One advocates proving nonexistence with regard to a subject that is "completely derived from conceptual thought" *(vikalpapariniṣṭhite dharmiṇi)* and thus that the conceptual subject is the *svadharmin.* The other paraphrases the controversial reasoning about space in such a way that the *svadharmin* becomes a real entity acceptable to the Buddhist, namely, the impermanent space that Buddhists themselves accept. See PVBh 550.18: *tathāpy anityam ākāśaṃ dharmī bhaviṣyati.* Secondly, this latter interpretation in PVBh fits noticeably better into the rest of the argumentation in PV IV, k. 136–48, where a completely parallel reasoning against the Sāṃkhya *sukhādi* ("pleasure, etc." = the three *guṇas*) is introduced by *tathaiva* ("in precisely this way") in k. 144–45. This time the *svadharmin* is clearly taken by Dharmakīrti as *not* being the conceptual representation of *sukhādi,* but as being the ordinary, impermanent sensations of pleasure that the Buddhist himself acknowledges. The impression is that reading an advocacy of the *combination* of *svadharmin* with conceptual subjects into Dharmakīrti is a later position that may well change Dharmakīrti's own stance. The *svadharmin* may well have been no more than an entity acceptable as real (and not conceptual) to the Buddhist himself. And determining what this actual subject was seems to have involved paraphrasing of the explicitly stated arguments, but had little to do with postulating conceptual subjects. [Editor's note: see chapter 8 in the present volume.]

14 Ngag dbang bstan dar is (correctly) simplifying the argument. As it stands in Dharmakīrti, the reasoning at stake seeks to prove that space does not have "a novel nature unproduced by other conditions," in other words, a permanent but real intrinsic nature. Cf. PV IV, k. 141–42:

yathā parair anutpādyāpūrvarūpaṃ [1] na khādikam / sakṛcchabdā-

dyahetutvād ity ukte prāha dūṣakaḥ // tadvad vastusvabhāvo 'san dharmī vyomādir ity api / naivam iṣṭasya sādhyasya bādhā kācana [2] vidyate // "When [the Buddhist] states that space, etc. do not have a novel nature unproduced by other [conditions] because they are not causes for [producing their qualities such as] sound, etc. all at once, then the [Vaiśeṣika] adversary might say that like that the subject, space, etc., would also not have the nature of a real entity. [Dharmakīrti's position:] In this fashion [even though the subject is invalidated (3)], there is in fact no invalidation of the intended [proposition] to be proved *(sādhya)* at all."

[1] Miyasaka's *anutpādyā pūrvarūpan* is wrong; [2] Miyasaka: *kvacana*—cf. Tib. *'ga' yang;* [3] PVV *evaṃ dharmibādhane 'pi.*

15 The argument presupposes some fundamental positions in the dGe lugs pa understanding of *apoha.* In brief, the dGe lugs pa explain the conceptual representation of real space *(dngos gyur gyi nam mkha' = vastubhūtākāśa)* as being "what appears as excluded from the contrary of real space" *(dngos gyur gyi nam mkha' ma yin pa las log par snang ba).* They then add the additional step that not only does the conceptual appearance/representation (*snang ba*) itself appear in this way but real space itself (albeit nonexistent) also appears *(snang)* as excluded from the contrary of real space. The result is that the dGe lugs can argue that the *svadharmin,* the actual *dharmin* that is being argued about, i.e., the conceptual representation, appears concordantly *(mthun snang)* to both parties in the debate. However, the Vaiśeṣika, who believes in *vastubhūtākāśa,* does not know that it is only a mentally invented concept being argued about rather than *vastubhūtākāśa* itself. The opponent thus has the impression that he is arguing about actual space, while the Buddhist proponent knows that they are both only arguing about the concept. This is said to be possible because both real space itself and the representation/appearance *(snang ba)* appear erroneously mixed together *('dres nas)* to conceptual thought. An analysis of this type of argumentation is to be found in Tillemans (1995a); see Lopez (1987: 178–79) for rGyal tshab's use of the same type of argument; see Klein (1991: 35–36) on lCang skya's and bsTan dar's position that "the actual object appears, mixed with its image, to thought"; see also Yoshimizu (1997: 1107–8); Dreyfus (1992: 36 *et sq.*). Tillemans stresses that the position that *X* itself appears *(snang ba)* to the conceptual thought about *X* is by and large a dGe lugs pa-gSang phu ba development, with problematic or no antecedents at all in India. It seems to be equally rejected by Sa skya pas like Śākya mchog ldan; see Tillemans (1995a: 872 *et sq.*). In part, the position was facilitated by the syntactical ambiguities in the Tibetan term *snang ba,* which can mean "appears," "what appears" and "ap-

pearance." [Editor's note: Tillemans (1995a) is reprinted as chapter 10 in the present volume.]

16 See n. 12 for PS III, k. 2cd.

17 These verses are not from the *Pratyakṣa* (PV III) chapter; they are from the *Parārthānumāna* chapter, i.e., PV IV, k. 136–48. Nor did Dignāga use *rang rten* instead of *rang gi chos can (= svadharmin);* see n. 12. Here are some of the principal verses amongst the twelve. Additions generally follow Manorathanandin's PVV:

> 136: *sarvatra vādino dharmo yaḥ svasādhyatayepsitaḥ / taddharmavati*[1] *bādhā syān nānyadharmeṇa dharmiṇi //* "Always, invalidation *(bādhā)* [of the thesis] would occur in a case of [invalidation of] the possessor of that property *(dharma)* that the proponent himself intends to prove *(sādhya),* but not in the case of a subject *(dharmin)* [that is qualified] by some other property."
>
> 143: *dvayasyāpi hi sādhyatve sādhyadharmoparodhi yat / bādhanaṃ dharmiṇas tatra bādhety etena varṇitam //* "Indeed, given that both are to be proved *(sādhyatva),* then when invalidating the subject negates the property to be proved, in that case there will be an invalidation [of the thesis]. Such is what is expressed by the [words 'his own subject' *(svadharmin)*]."
>
> 147: *svayam iṣṭo yato dharmaḥ sādhyas tasmāt tadāśrayaḥ / bādhyo na kevalo nānyasaṃśrayo veti sūcitam //* "It was asserted [by Dignāga] that as the property that [the proponent] intends himself is what is to be proved (*sādhya*), therefore, the basis of this [property] is what is to be invalidated, and not something nominal or the basis for a [property] other [than the one being proved]."
>
> [1] Read *taddharmavati* instead of Miyasaka's *tad dharmavati.*

18 Ngag dbang bstan dar refers here to one of the three characteristics *(rūpa)* of valid reasons: the *pakṣadharmatva* ("[the reason's] being a quality of the subject"). Cf. the definition of the *pakṣadharma(tva)* in *Yongs 'dzin rtags rigs,* p. 23:

> *de sgrub kyi shes 'dod chos can skyon med kyi steng du 'god tshul dang mthun par yod pa nyid du tshad mas nges pa /* "It [i.e., the reason] is ascertained by a *pramāṇa* to exist relative to the faultless subject of enquiry in accordance with the mode of presentation."

The *'god tshul,* or "mode of presentation," in Ngag dbang bstan dar (as in

Yongs 'dzin rtags rigs) refers to the type of verb stated in the reason, i.e., the copula *yin* as in e.g., *byas pa yin pa'i phyir* or *byas pa'i phyir* "because...is a product" or the existential *yod* as in *du ba yod pa'i phyir* "because there is smoke." We thus have the possibility of *yin 'god* or *yod 'god*. The point of including *'god tshul dang mthun par* in the definition of the *pakṣadharma(tva)* is a rather cumbersome way to guarantee that the subject possesses the property of the reason in the very same way as the proponent has stated, i.e., *yin* or *yod*.

19 Ngag dbang bstan dar's reply here and in what follows turns on the principle that the reason must be a property of the subject, i.e., of the *svadharmin*: in other words, the reason must be a *pakṣadharma* (see n. 18). Now, when we prove that space is not a permanent substance, the conceptual representation of space is indeed not a substance, and will also be qualified by the reason. Thus the *pakṣadharmatva* will hold. On the other hand, if we are validly proving that sound is impermanent because it is produced, then sound itself (and not the concept of sound) must be the *svadharmin*. This is because sound is both impermanent and something causally produced—hence the *pakṣadharmatva* holds with regard to that subject, i.e., sound *qua* particular, rather than the concept of sound. See Lopez (1987: 175–76).

20 On the Tibetan development of the problem of *chos can mthun snang ba* ("concordantly appearing subjects") see D. Lopez (1987: 78 *et passim*); Hopkins (1989); Yotsuya (1995); Tillemans (1990: 42f.); Tillemans and Tomabechi (1995: n. 25). The term *chos can mthun snang ba* is a Tibetan invention with no Sanskrit equivalent. The notion is developed by Tsong kha pa in *Lam rim chen mo, Drangs nges legs bshad snying po* and other works as a philosophical elaboration upon a section in the Bhāvaviveka-Candrakīrti debate in PrP I (ed. L. de la Vallée Poussin, reprint ed.: 26. *et seq*.), where Realist and Śūnyavādin conceptions are argued to be radically incommensurable so that there are no commonly acknowledged *(ubhayaprasiddha)* subjects when the two parties are debating about ultimate truth—see Tillemans (1992c: n. 5) for a translation of the passage from PrP. The issue is also taken up by non-dGe lugs pa writers (such as Go rams pa bsod nams seng ge in his *lTa ba'i ngan sel* 41af.), but plays a particularly important, and undeniably complex, role in the dGe lugs pa Svātantrika Madhyamaka system.

Ngag bdang bstan dar is presupposing an understanding of Tsong kha pa's position on Svātantrika. The point in the argument is delicate. Judging by the previous discussion, bsTan dar seems to accept that the *svadharmin* in the Buddhist-Vaiśeṣika argument, viz., the concept of space, is what both parties are actually arguing about—nonetheless this conceptual *svadharmin*, as he had said earlier, could not be *explicitly* acknowledged by the Vaiśeṣika opponent, who thinks he is arguing about real space *(vastubhūtākāśa)*. bsTan dar then argues that space itself is incommensurable for both parties, i.e., given the parties' differing respective views on what space is, a concordantly appearing and commonly acknowledged *(ubhayaprasiddha)* space cannot be what they are arguing about: space is thus the *kevaladharmin* and cannot be the *svadharmin.* (Here one could reasonably ask if the *svadharmin,* i.e., the concept, appears concordantly to both, given their respective positions.) In what follows, Ngag dbang bstan dar alludes to an objection in PrP that if the Realist and Śūnyavādin have no commonly recognized subject, then nor do Buddhists and Vaiśeṣikas when they argue about sound being impermanent or not, given that both have different conceptions of what sound is; see PrP (reprint ed.: 29). The dGe lugs pa reply, based on Candrakīrti, is that sound, irrespective of one's philosophical theories, is *heard* commonly by both parties, whereas space is just a purely theoretical notion without any perceptual content in common for both parties.

21 Ngag bstan dar is arguing from a Svātantrika position where concordantly appearing subjects and especially non-erroneous valid cognitions must be possible for both parties, as this is a condition for the logical reasons being "autonomous" *(rang rgyud = svatantra)*. The phrase *ma 'khrul ba'i tshad ma'i rnyed don du mthun snang du grub pa* ("established as appearing concordantly as an object found by non-erroneous means of valid cognition") alludes to the dGe lugs pa view that for a Svātantrika, who holds a type of limited realism, a *pramāṇa* is non-erroneous in apprehending its objects as being established by their own intrinsic natures *(rang gi mtshan nyid kyis grub pa)*. Note that for a Prāsaṅgika, by contrast, a *pramāṇa* can supposedly never be correct in this way, because these intrinsic natures do not exist at all, and thus for him all *pramāṇa*s without exception would be erroneous. The incommensurability between Realist and Śūnyavādin then lies in the fact that the way the subject is established by a *pramāṇa (tshad mas grub tshul)* will differ for the two parties, the realist taking the *pramāṇa* as non-erroneous and the Śūnyavādin holding it to be erroneous. Cf. *sTong thun chen mo*, p. 496 (f.157b3–6):

> *des na mdor bsdus te go bde bar brjod na / rang gi mtshan nyid kyis grub pa'i gzhal bya la ma 'khrul pa'i tshad mas rnyed don yin par snga rgol phyi* rgol gnyi ga'i lugs la mthun snang du grub pa'i chos can gyi steng du / snga rgol gang la dpag 'dod zhugs pa'i bsgrub bya'i chos sgrub byed kyi gtan tshigs su bkod pa / zhes pa rang rgyud kyi rtags kyi don yin la / chos can de nyid tshad mas 'grub tshul snga rgol phyi rgol gnyi ga'i mthun snang du grub pa med kyang spyir chos can de nyid snga rgol gyi lugs la'ang tshad mas grub phyi rgol gyi lugs la'ang tshad mas*

grub cing chos can dang phyogs chos sogs phyi rgol lugs la tshad mas grub pa'i khas blangs la 'khrid nas bkod pa'i gtan tshigs ni gzhan la grags kyi rjes dpag ces bya'o //. *Text has *gyi.* "So let us summarize and explain [things] in an easily comprehensible manner *(sic!).* The meaning of 'autonomous logical reason' *(rang rgyud kyi rtags = svatantra-liṅga)* is: what is presented as a logical reason establishing the *sādhyadharma* that the proponent wishes to infer on the basis of a *dharmin* established as appearing concordantly *(mthun snang du grub pa)* for both the proponent's and the opponent's traditions, namely, [appearing concordantly] as being an entity found by a *pramāṇa* that is unmistaken with regard to *prameyas* established by their own characters *(rang gi mtshan nyid = svalakṣaṇa).* [As for 'opponent-acknowledged' inferences:] Although the way in which this *dharmin* is established by *pramāṇas* does not appear concordantly for both the proponent and opponent, nonetheless in general *(spyir)* this *dharmin* is established by a *pramāṇa* in the proponent's tradition and is also established by a *pramāṇa* in the opponent's tradition; when the logical reason is presented after we have 'guided' *('khrid nas)* the *dharmin, pakṣadharma* and so forth in terms of positions established by a *pramāṇa* in the opponent's tradition, this is said to be an 'opponent-acknowledged inference' *(gzhan la grags kyi rjes dpag).*"

22 See Lopez (1987: 178–79).

23 Cf. n. 13 for Dignāga's arguments against the Sāṃkhya.

24 bsTan dar cites MĀ somewhat out of context, as if the quote was unproblematically Kamalaśīla's own position. In fact, it is to be found in a very long *pūrvapakṣa* where a logician's position is presented, one which Kamalaśīla replied to by drawing partial parallels with his own philosophical project of proving ultimate lack of intrinsic nature *(niḥsvabhāvatā).* The logician's position, which looks to be a type of *Alīkākāravāda* ("false images"), held that: (a) the *dharmin* is said a mental entity, but in reality is not mind and has no real existence at all, being only an imagined and unreal mental image *(ākāra);* (b) the ordinary person erroneously conflates the image with the objects themselves; (c) mind really exists although the images are unreal. (Note that Śāntarakṣita and Kamalaśīla are usually represented in texts on philosophical tenets *[grub mtha' = siddhānta]* as leaning towards *Satyākāravāda [rnam bden dang mthun pa];* see Mimaki [1982: 29–31, 35].) See MĀ, D. 174a4–175a1:

ji ste thog ma med pa'i rang gi sa bon yongs su smin pa las yang dag par byung ba'i rnam par rtog pas yongs su bsgrubs pa / byis pa rnams kyis phyi rol dang dngos po nyid du nye bar brtags pa blo la yod pa nyid chos can yin te / de'i phyir de la brten nas gtso bo la sogs pa 'gog par byed do // de ni don dam par ngo bo nyid med kyang rnam par 'khrul pa'i dbang gis phyi rol lta bu dang / gtso bo la sogs pa dang / tha mi dad pa lta bu dang / nus pas stong pa la sogs pa'i chos mtha' dag dang ldan pa lta bur rtog go // de la gtso bo la sogs pa'i ngo bo nyid dgag pa sgrub pa la gtso bo la sogs pa dgag pa bsgrub par bya ba dang / sgrub pa dag gzhi gcig pa nyid kyang grub pa kho na yin te / 'di ltar de nyid byis pa rnams kyis phyi rol dang / gtso bo la sogs pa nyid du nye bar gzung ba rgol ba dang phyir rgol ba dag kyang rab rib can gyis zla ba gnyis su mthong ba bzhin du de dang tha mi dad par sems pa kho nas tha snyad 'dogs pa'i phyir // de ni blos kun brtags pa yin yang de'i rnam pa nyid kyis blo zhes nye bar 'dogs te / 'di dngos su ni blo'i ngo bo yang ma yin te / de ni de dang mtshan nyid mi mthun pa'i ngo bo nyid du snang ba'i phyir ro // de'i phyir de ngo bo med pa nyid du rab tu bsgrubs kyang blo ngo bo nyid med pa nyid du thal ba ni ma yin te / de la phyi rol dang gtso bo la sogs pa'i ngo nyid dgag pa tshad mas sgrub par byed kyi / de nyid dgag pa'i phyir gtan tshigs sbyor ba ma yin no / … de'i phyir rjes su dpag par bya ba dang / rjes su dpag pa la sogs pa'i tha snyad 'di thams cad ni blo la yod pa'i chos can kho na brten nas 'jug pa nyid de / rnam pa gzhan mi srid pa'i phyir ro zhes bya bar 'dod na /

gal te de lta yin na / 'o na don dam par ngo bo nyid med kyang kun brtags pa'i chos can la brten nas dgag pa la sogs pa rab tu sgrub par byed pa la yang gzhi ma grub pa nyid la sogs pa'i nyes pa mi 'jug na ci ste nan gyis kho bo cag la klan ka tshol bar byed / ji ltar khyed don dam pa la 'jug par bya ba'i phyir gtso bo la sogs pa dgag par kun brtags pa'i chos can kho na la bsgrub par bya ba dang / sgrub pa'i sems pa rgyas par byed pa de bzhin du kho cag kyang gzugs dang sgra la sogs pa grags pa dag la / yod pa dang med pa la sogs pa'i ngo bo nyid du sgro btags pa dgag par byis pa rnams la de dag sgyu ma dang / smig rgyu dang / rmi lam dang / gzugs brnyan dang mtshungs pa nyid du ston par byed do // de la ji ltar brtags pa'i chos can la dngos po'i ngo bo nyid du sgro btags pa la sogs pa bkag tu zin kyang rgol ba dang phyir rgol ba dag la snang ba'i phyir ma grub pa nyid la sogs pa'i nyes pa mi 'jug pa de bzhin du gzugs la sogs pa yang gnag rdzi'i chung ma yan chad kyi skye bo la snang ba'i phyir ji ltar ma grub pa nyid du 'gyur //.

"[Objection:] It is just something existing in the mind that is the subject, [something] established by conceptualisations stemming from the ripening of their own beginningless [karmic] tendencies [and] which is metaphorically designated by the infantile as being external and real. Thus it is with reference to that [fictional mental existent] that one negates *pradhāna* and so forth. Although that [mental existent] does not ultimately have any nature, still, due to error, it is conceived of as if it were external, as if it were not different from *pradhāna* and the like, and as if it had all the various properties like being void of efficacy and so forth. In that case, when we negate the natures of *pradhāna* and so forth, the *sādhya* consisting of negations of *pradhāna,* etc. and the *sādhana* [for these negations] not only have the same locus but are in fact established. This is because the infantile grasp this [mental existent] alone as being external and as being *pradhāna,* etc. and the proponent and opponent both apply conventional designations simply because they think that this [mental existent] is not different from [the pseudo-entities themselves], just as when a person suffering from [the eye-disease] *timira* sees the moon as two. Although this [mental existent] is something [merely] imagined by the mind, it is metaphorically designated as the mind due to its being an image. In reality, however, it is not of the nature of the mind, in that it appears as something different in character from the [mind]. Hence even though it is acknowledged that this [mental existent] is without any nature, it does not follow that the mind is without nature. In that case, the negations of natures such as the external and *pradhāna,* etc. are proven by means of a *pramāṇa.* But one does not apply the logical reasons in order to negate the [mind] itself.... Consequently, all these conventions, like inferable objects *(anumeya),* inferring [reasons] *(anumāna)* and so forth, operate only in reliance upon subjects existing in the mind. Any other way is impossible.

[Reply:] Suppose this were so. Now, even when one proved negations and so forth in reliance upon imagined subjects, though they be ultimately without any nature, no fault like *āśrayāsiddha,* etc. would be committed. So then why direct your criticisms so vociferously against us! Just as you develop ideas of *sādhya* and *sādhana* in reliance upon imagined subjects in order to negate *pradhāna* etc. so that you may have access to the ultimate, in the same fashion we too, in order to negate superimpositions of natures like existence and nonexistence, etc. upon commonly recognized things like form and sound, demonstrate to the infantile that these [commonly recognized things like form, etc.] are like illusions, mirages, dreams and reflections. In that case, just as [for you], even though [you] do negate the superimposed nature of being a real entity with reference to imagined subjects [like *pradhāna,* etc.], there are no faults like *[āśraya-]asiddha[hetu]* because these [subjects] appear to both the proponent and the opponent, so too, since form and so forth also appear to everyone from cowherds' wives on up, how is it that they would be unestablished *(asiddha)*?"

25 See n. 24.

26 Ngag dbang bstan dar has truncated the passage from the *Svavṛtti.* The additions to our translation follow the missing portions of the Sanskrit and Tibetan of the *Svavṛtti.* Note that it is clear from the Sanskrit that Ngag dbang bstan dar is wrong in reading *spyi gtso bo'i sgra,* and that the reading *ci (= kim) gtso bo'i sgra* in the *bsTan 'gyur* is the correct one. Ngag dbang bstan dar seems to have been seduced by the homonymity of *spyi* and *ci,* plus the fact that *pradhāna* is usually rendered as *spyi gtso bo* by indigenous Tibetan authors of the dGe lugs school. Our translation of the quotation follows the *Svavṛtti's* Sanskrit and the Tibetan in the *bsTan 'gyur,* which must yield a different understanding from that of Ngag dbang bstan dar himself. Unfortunately, it is difficult to guess how the latter would have understood the passage. But a natural reading of bsTan dar's version of the *Svavṛtti* passage would be something like: "Thus, in dependence upon this subject, this object that appears due to the word *pradhāna...*"

27 "Verbal object" *(sgra don; śabdārtha)* is, for a logician, always a conceptually created entity, one having no real existence. Cf. PV III, k. 287ab: *śabdārthagrāhi yad yatra taj jñānaṃ tatra kalpanā //.* "Wherever consciousness apprehends a verbal object, it is conceptual."

28 On *gzhi ldog* and the argument at issue, see n. 30.

29 See n. 30.

30 The term *ldog pa (=vyāvṛtti)* is a pivotal term in the Indian and Tibetan *apoha* theories of meaning; see Tillemans (1993a: 69–70, n. 6) for explanations and references to PV I. The fundamental idea is that the object directly designated by a word for *X* is a conceptual construction proceeding by exclusion of all which is non-*X.* As for *rang ldog* and *gzhi ldog,* these are terms whose Indian origins, if indeed they have any, seem quite obscure. The terms figure preeminently in the *bsdus grwa* literature (and hence in dGe lugs pa *pramāṇa* commentaries) as part of a scholastic category of different sub-types of the Indian logician's notion of *vyāvṛtti,* including also *don ldog* ("exclusion *qua* object") and *spyi ldog* ("exclusion *qua* universal"). Given their place in a

literature heavily influenced by the *Tshad ma bsdus pa* texts of gSang phu traditions, it is not unlikely that the interpretation of these four subvarieties of *vyāvṛtti*, and possibly even their origin, is due to the gSang phu traditions stemming from Phya pa chos kyi seng ge. See, e.g., the third chapter of *Yongs 'dzin bsdus grwa chung*, the chapter concerning *ldog pa ngos 'dzin* "recognizing exclusions" (in T. Kelzang and S. Onoda, eds., 1985). The argumentation in Ngag dbang bstan dar turns essentially on the distinction between knowing an object *X* as being simply an *X* itself *(rang)*, and knowing an instance, or basis *(gzhi)*, of *X* but under some other name or description—the first case is that of *rang ldog* and the second *gzhi ldog*. Thus, for example, the *rang ldog* pertaining to a vase *(bum pa'i rang ldog)*, is just the vase and not, e.g., some particular bulbous golden object that is able to carry water—the latter would be a *gzhi ldog* of vase. In the context at hand, a Buddhist and a Sāṃkhya, when arguing about Primordial Matter, are both arguing about a mere concept of Primordial Matter, i.e., a verbal object *(sgra don)*. Nonetheless they cannot be arguing about the *rang ldog* of the verbal object *(sgra don gyi rang ldog)* of Primordial Matter because this would mean that both know the verbal object to be just a verbal object, i.e., a conceptually and verbally created fiction; clearly, the Sāṃkhya does not know this, but thinks that Primordial Matter is more than just a verbal object, because it is for him fully real. Thus they are both thinking and arguing about a type of verbal object, but one that both parties don't consciously recognize as such—hence the insistence on the subject of their deliberations being the *gzhi ldog* of a verbal object. See also n. 15 on the dGe lugs pa idea of an object (like Primordial Matter, etc.) and its conceptual representation appearing "mixed" *('dres nas snang ba)* and hence indistinguishable to the opponent.

31 Literally, "from their exclusions *qua* the things themselves." On *rang ldog*, see n. 30. On the argument at stake, see n. 32.

32 The point is that if we *explicitly* presented the subject as being something along the lines of the concept of Primordial Matter, and not Primordial Matter itself, we would not actually succeed in refuting Primordial Matter. The argument would not tell against the Sāṃkhya opponent, who is convinced that there really is such an entity and that it is *a fortiori* not a mere concept. On the other hand, when we establish by means of a *pramāṇa* that the reason is a property of the subject *(pakṣadharma)*, then the subject can only be the conceptual construct, i.e., only the appearance as Primordial Matter *(gtso bor snang ba nyid)*. The argument at stake is, in effect, that both the *kevaladharmin* and *svadharmin* have their purpose: the former assures that the refutation presents the subject as the opponent conceives it, while the latter is the proponent's actual subject that will serve as the basis upon which will be

assessed the three characteristics of the logical reason. Finally, note that we cannot say with any certainty which exact passage(s) from the MĀ rGyal tshab rje had in mind.

33 Literally: "the reason…*(…rgyu mtshan yang)*…is also due to the reason *(rgyu mtshan gyis yin)*."

34 PV IV, k. 228bcd. The whole *kārikā* reads:

> *tasmād āśritya śabdārthaṃ bhāvābhāvasamāśrayam / abāhyāśrayam atreṣṭaṃ sarvaṃ vidhiniṣedhanam // Tib.: de phyir dngos dngos med rten can // phyi rol rten min sgra don la // brten nas 'dir ni sgrub pa dang // dgag pa thams cad 'dod pa yin //* "Therefore, we accept that [positive] proof and negation here [in practical activity *(vyavahāre)*] in reliance upon a verbal object, which is the basis for being and non-being [and] which has no external basis."

For the interpretation of the compounds *samāśrayam* and *abāhyāśrayam*, see PVV: ***tasmāc chabda****syā****rtham*** *aropitabahīrūpam anyavyavacchedam* ***abāhyāśrayaṃ*** *bāhyaviṣayarahitaṃ ya eva* ***bhāvābhāvayor*** *vidhipratiṣedhavikalpapratipādyayor* ***samāśraya****s tam* ***āśritya*** *vyavahāre* ***sarvaṃ vidhiniṣedhanam iṣṭam*** *//.*

35 The *kārikā* is closely related to the well-known fragment attributed to Dignāga's *Hetumukha* and cited in PVSV (Gnoli: 2–3): *sarva evāyam anumānānumeyavyavahāro buddhyārūḍhena dharmadharmibhedena.* Note that the Tibetan of k. 183c reads *shes pa la grub* "established in/for thought," whereas the *Pramāṇavārttikavṛtti* (PVV) reads ***pratyayena*** *vikalpakenaikavyāvṛttimātraviṣayena* ***saṃsiddham****…*"established by means of conceptual thought, which has as object only an exclusion of unity." Finally, note that Manorathanandin in PVV takes *artha* as going only with *anumeya,* i.e., *anumeyārtha,* which is also in keeping with PV Tib. Cf. PVV *ad* k. 183: *ato 'numānahetutvād* ***anumānasya*** *liṅgasyā****numeyārthasyā****nayor upalakṣaṇatvāt (!) dharmiṇaś ca* ***vyavahārasthitis tv iyam****…*

36 *dGongs pa rab gsal: des.* bsTan dar: *de'i.*

37 bsTan dar omits *tsam.*

38 *dBu ma dgongs pa rab gsal* 200a.

39 bsTan dar: *bor.*

40 PSV(a) *ad* PS III, k. 2cd. See n. 12.

41 PV Tib.: *tu.* bsTan dar: *du.*

42 PV IV, k.136. See n. 17.

43 *dBu ma rgyan gyi zin bris* 10a and other editions in Tillemans (1984c: 385): *snang ldog.* bsTan dar: *snang ldog dang.*

44 *Zin bris: 'grub.* bsTan dar: *sgrub.*

45 *Zin bris: min.* bsTan dar: *ma yin.*

46 *Zin bris: grub.* bsTan dar: *sgrub.*

47 *Zin bris* 10a and other editions: *dngos po.* bsTan dar: *dngos pos.*

48 *dBu ma rgyan gyi zin bris* 9b-10a. See Tillemans (1984c: 385).

49 *rNam nges dar ṭīk,* f. unidentified.

50 *rnam pa* not in Peking and sDe dge editions of MĀ. See n. 24.

51 P. 190a, D. 174a. See n. 24.

52 PV I, k.205cd: *śabdārthas trividho dharmo bhāvābhāvobhayāśrayaḥ //.*

53 *Svavṛtti* Tib.: *ci.* bsTan dar: *spyi.* See n. 26.

54 PVSV *ad* PV I, k.206 (P. 477a3-4; D. 321a2): *de bas na chos can 'di la brten nas ci gtso bo'i sgra las snang ba'i don 'di ni [dngos po nye bar len pa can nam* ma yin zhes yod pa dang med pa nyid dpyod** par byed do] /.* (*P. omits *nam.***P.D. *spyod*) Skt. ed. Gnoli p. 106: *tad atra dharmiṇi vyavasthitāḥ [sadasattvaṃ cintayanti] (/) kim ayaṃ pradhānaśabdapratibhāsy artho [bhāvopādāno na veti]/.* See n. 26.

55 PVT P. 279b7, D. 238a3.

56 *rNam 'grel ṭīk chen: gtso 'dzin rtog pa.*

57 Vol. *tha* 149a.

58 *rNam 'grel ṭīk chen* reads *gangs can pa*, which is surely wrong.

59 *rNam 'grel ṭīk chen* vol. *tha* 149a-b.

60 151b.

61 95b-96a.

62 PV Tib.: *'dod ldan (= kāminyāḥ).* bsTan dar: *rtog ldan.*

63 PV I, k. 211: *arthakriyāsamarthasya vicāraiḥ kiṃ tadarthinām / ṣaṇḍhasya rūpavairūpye kāminyāḥ kiṃ parīkṣayā //.*

64 bsTan dar: *rtags.*

65 PV IV, k. 228bcd: *[tasmād] āśritya śabdārthaṃ [bhāvābhāvasamāśrayam] / abāhyāśrayam atreṣṭaṃ sarvaṃ vidhiniṣedhanam /.* See n. 34.

66 PV Tib., *Zin bris*: *yi.* bsTan dar: *dag.*

67 PV Tib, *Zin bris*: *brtags pa.* bsTan dar: *dag pa.*

68 PV IV, k. 183: *anumānānumeyārthavyavahārasthitis tv iyam / bhedaṃ pratyayasaṃsiddham avalambya prakalpyate //.* The text of PV Tib. cited in *dBu ma rgyan gyi zin bris* shows none of bsTan dar's "variants."

69 See Tillemans (1984c: 385, n. 12) on *du ba la la.* bsTan dar: *du bas la. Zin bris* 9b: *du ba la.*

70 9a-b. Tillemans (1984c: 384).

Bibliography

A lag sha ngag dbang bstan dar [1759–1840]. *gCig du bral gyi rnam bzhag = gCig du bral gyi rnam bzhag legs bshad rgya mtsho las btus pa'i 'khrul spong bdud rtsi'i gzegs ma.* In vol. 1 of the *Collected gSung 'bum of bsTan-dar lha-ram of A-lag-sha.* New Delhi: Lama Guru Deva, 1971.

———. *Phyogs glang gis mdzad pa'i phyogs chos 'khor lo nyes pa'i bstan bcos gsal bar byed pa'i rin chen sgron me.* Included in the *Collected gSung 'bum of bsTan-dar lha-ram of A-lag-sha.* Vol. *ka:* 135–55. New Delhi: Lama Guru Deva, 1971.

———. *Rang mtshan spyi mtshan gyi rnam bzhag rtsom 'phro.* Included in the *Collected gSung 'bum of bsTan-dar lha-ram of A-lag-sha.* Vol. *ka:* 156–208. New Delhi: Lama Guru Deva, 1971.

———. *sTon pa tshad ma'i skyes bur sgrub pa'i gtam bde chen khang bzang 'dzegs pa'i rin chen them skas.* Included in the *Collected gSung 'bum of bsTan-dar lha-ram of A-lag-sha.* Vol. *ka:* 32–62. New Delhi: Lama Guru Deva, 1971. [Edited and translated in Tillemans (1993a).]

Āryadeva 廣百論. *Catuḥśataka.* Skt. fragments ed. by Haraprasad Shāstrī (1914). Skt. and Tib. (chap. 8–16) ed. by V. Bhattacharya (1931). Skt. and Tib. ed. and trans. in K. Lang (1986). Chinese trans. by Xuanzang: T. XXX 1570. Tib. trans. P. 5246, 5266.

Austin, J.L. (1950) "Truth," in *Proceedings of the Aristotelian Society.* Supplementary vol. 24: 111–28.

Barth, E.M. and J.L. Martens, eds. (1982) *Argumentation: Approaches to Theory Formation.* Studies in Language Companion Series vol. 8. Amsterdam: John Benjamins B.V.

Belnap, Nuel D. and J. Michael Dunn. (1968) "The Substitution Interpretation of the Quantifiers." *Noûs* 2/2: 179–85.

Beth, Evert Willem. (1970) *Aspects of Modern Logic.* Dordrecht: D. Reidel Publishing Company.

Bhartṛhari. *Vākyapadīya.* Ed. by Wilhalm Rau. Wiesbaden: Franz Steiner Verlag, 1977.

Bhattacharya, K. (1986) "Some Thoughts on *antarvyāpti, bahirvyāpti,* and *trairūpya*" in B.K. Matilal and R. Evans, eds. (1986): 89–105.

Bhattacharya, V. (1931) *The Catuḥśataka of Āryadeva: Sanskrit and Tibetan Texts with Copious Extracts from the Commentary of Candrakīrti.* Chaps. 8–16. Calcutta: Viśvabhāratī Bookshop.

Bocheński, I.M. (1956) *A History of Formal Logic.* First published as *Formale Logik,* Freiburg/Munich: Karl Alber Verlag, 1956. References are to the second edition of the English translation, Notre Dame, Indiana: Notre Dame University Press, 1970.

Bronkhorst, Johannes. (1992) "L'absolu dans le Vākyapadīya et son lien avec le Madhyamaka." AS/EA 46/1: 56–80.

———. (1996) "The Correspondence Principle and its Impact on Indian Philosophy." *Studies in the History of Indian Thought (Indo-shisōshi kenkyū)* 8: 1–19.

bSe ngag dbang bkra shis [1678–1738]. *bSe bsdus grwa = Tshad ma'i dgongs 'grel gyi bstan bcos chen po rnam 'grel gyi don gcig tu dril ba blo rab 'bring tha gsum du ston pa legs bshad chen po mkhas pa'i mgul rgyan skal bzang re ba kun skong.* Included in *Tshad ma'i dgongs don rtsa 'grel mkhas pa'i mgul rgyan = Yinmingxue gaiyao ji qi zhushi.* Beijing: Minzu chubanshe, 1985.

bSod nams rgya mtsho, ed. (1969) *Sa skya pa'i bka' 'bum* (= SKB): *The Complete Works of the Great Masters of the Sa skya sect of the Tibetan Buddhism.* sDe dge edition (plus supplementary texts of the Sa skya pa tradition). Tokyo: The Toyo Bunko.

bTsun pa ston gzhon [thirteenth century]. *rNam 'grel gyi rnam bshad gangs can gyi rgyan.* Quinghai: Zhongguo zangxue chubanshe, 1993.

Bu ston rin chen grub [1290–1364]. *rNam nges ṭīkā = Tshad ma rnam par nges pa'i ṭīkā tshig don rab gsal.* Included in *Collected Works of Bu ston*, vol. 24, New Delhi, 1971.

Bugault, Guy. (1983) "Logic and Dialectics in the *Madhyamakakārikās.*" JIP 11: 7–76.

———. (1989) "Les paradoxes de la *Vajracchedikā:* une connexion qui opère une coupure" in *Cahiers d'études chinoises* 8 (Hommage à N. Vandier-Nicolas): 45–63.

Candrakīrti. *Catuḥśatakaṭīkā* or *Catuḥśatakavṛtti* (= CSV). Skt. fragments contained in H. Shāstrī (1914).

———. *Madhyamakāvatāra.* Ed. by L. de la Vallée Poussin, *Bibliotheca Buddhica*, Vol. 9, St. Petersburg: 1907–12. Trans. by L. de la Vallée Poussin, *le Muséon* 8 (1907): 249–317; 11 (1910): 271–358; 12 (1911): 235–327.

———. *Prasannapadā* (= PrP). *See* ed. in L. de la Vallée Poussin (1903–13).

Carroll, Lewis. (1885) *Through the Looking Glass.* Reprint edition, Penguin, 1974.

Chos kyi rgyal mtshan. *See* Se ra rje btsun chos kyi rgyal mtshan.

Copi, Irving. (1971) *The Theory of Logical Types.* Monographs in Modern Logic Series. London: Routledge and Kegan Paul.

de la Vallée Poussin, Louis, ed. (1903–13) *Les Mūlamadhyamakakārikā de Nāgārjuna, éditées avec la Prasannapadā de Candrakīrti.* Reprint edition Osnabrück: Biblio Verlag, 1970.

———, ed. (1913) *The Tibetan Translation of the Nyāyabindu of Dharmakīrti with the Commentary of Vinītadeva.* Bibliotheca Indica No. 171. Calcutta: The Asiatic Society. Reprinted 1984.

de la Vallée Poussin, Louis. (1933) "Réflexions sur le Madhyamaka." *Mélanges chinois et bouddhiques* 2: 1–59.

Devendrabuddhi. *Pramāṇavārttikapañjikā* (= PVP). Tib. trans. by Subhutiśrī and dGe ba'i blo gros. P. 5717, D. 4217.

dGe 'dun grub pa [1391–1474]. *dBu ma la 'jug pa'i bstan bcos kyi dgongs pa rab tu gsal ba'i me long*. Recent Indian blockprint [this ed. used in chap. 6]. Also included in *The Collected Works of the First Dalai Lama*, vol. 3.

———. *The Collected Works of the First Dalai Lama Dge 'dun grub pa*. Reproduced from prints from 'Bras spungs dga' ldan pho brang carved about 1894; from the library of the Ven. Dar mdo Rin po che of Kalimpong. Gangtok: 1981.

———. *Tshad ma rigs rgyan = Tshad ma'i bstan bcos chen po rigs pa'i rgyan*. Mundgod, Karnataka: Drepung Loseling Press, 1984. Also included in *The Collected Works of the First Dalai Lama*, vol. 4, 1981 [this edition used in chap. 11].

———. *Tshad ma rnam 'grel legs par bshad pa zhes bya ba thams cad mkhyen pa dge 'dun grub kyis mdzad pa las rang don rjes su dpag pa'i le'u'i rnam bshad*. Included in *Collected Works of the First Dalai Lama*, vol. 5, 1–85.

dGe bshes ngag dbang nyi ma. [contemporary]. *bsDus grwa brjed tho*. Leiden: 1970s. This handwritten text records a large number of orally passed-on debates, sophisms, definitions, etc., many of these not appearing in other *bsdus grwa* texts.

Dharmakīrti. *Hetubindu*. Ed. and trans. in Steinkellner (1967).

———. *Nyāyabindu*. Skt. ed. in D. Malvania (1955).

———. *Pramāṇavārttika*. Skt. and Tib. ed. by Y. Miyasaka (1972).

———. *Pramāṇavārttikasvavṛtti* (= PVSV or *Svavṛtti*). Skt. ed. by R. Gnoli (1960).

———. *Pramāṇaviniścaya* (= PVin). P. 5710, D. 4211. PVin I ed. and trans. in Vetter (1966). PVin II ed. and trans. in Steinkellner (1973, 1979).

———. *Vādanyāya*. Ed. and trans. in Much (1991). Skt. ed. in Swāmī Dvārikādāsa Śāstrī, ed., *Vādanyāyaḥ Saṃbandhaparīkṣā ca*. Bauddha Bharati Series 8. Varanasi: 1972.

Dharmapāla 大乘廣百論釋論. T. XXX 1571. [Commentary on CS extant only in Chinese.]

Dharmottara. *Nyāyabinduṭīkā* (= NBT). *See* Malvania (1955).

Dignāga. *Nyāyamukha*. T. XXXII 1628. *See* S. Katsura (1977, 1978, 1979, 1981, 1982, 1984, 1987). *See also* G. Tucci (1930).

———. *Pramāṇasamuccaya*. P. 5700, D.4203.

———. *Pramāṇasamuccayavṛtti*. P. 5701, D. 4204 (= PSVa) and P. 5702 (= PSVb).

Dreyfus, Georges. (1991) "Ontology, Philosophy of Language and Epistemology in Buddhist Tradition. A study of Dharmakīrti's philosophy in the light of its reception in the later Indo-Tibetan tradition." Ph.D. dissertation, University of Virginia. University Microfilms, Ann Arbor, Michigan.

———. (1992) "Universals in Indo-Tibetan Buddhism," in S. Ihara and Z. Yamaguchi, eds., (1992): 29–46.

———. (1994) Introduction to *A Recent Rediscovery: Rgyal-tshab's Rigs gter rnam bshad: A Facsimile Reproduction of a Rare Blockprint Edition*, ed. by G.B.J. Dreyfus in collaboration with Shunzō Onoda. Biblia Tibetica 2. Kyoto: Nagata Bunshodo.

———. (1995) "Is Dharmakīrti a Pragmatist?" AS/EA 49/4: 671–91.

———. (1997) *Recognizing Reality: Dharmakīrti's Philosophy and Its Tibetan Interpretations*. Albany: State University of New York Press.

Dunne, John D. (1999) "Foundations of Dharmakīrti's Philosophy: A Study of the Central Issues in his Ontology, Logic and Epistemology with Special Attention to the *Svopajñavṛtti*." Unpublished Ph.D. dissertation, Harvard University.

Durvekamiśra. *Dharmottarapradīpa*. *See* Malvania (1955).

Faris, John A. (1968) *Quantification Theory*. Monographs in Modern Logic Series. London: Routledge and Kegan Paul.

Flew, Anthony. (1971) *An Introduction to Western Philosophy*. London: Thames and Hudson.

Frauwallner, Erich. (1932) "Beiträge zur Apohalehre I." WZKM 39: 247–85 [*Kleine Schriften*, 367–405].

———. (1957) Review of R. Sāṅkṛtyāyana's edition of the *Pramāṇavārttikabhāṣya*. *Journal of the American Oriental Society* 77: 58–60 [= *Kleine Schriften*, 883–85].

———. (1959) "Dignāga, sein Werk und seine Entwicklung." WZKSO 3: 83–164 [*Kleine Schriften*, 759–841].

———. (1961) "Landmarks in the History of Indian Logic." WZKSO 5: 125–48 [=*Kleine Schriften*, 847–70].

———. (1982) *Kleine Schriften / Erich Frauwallner*. Ed. by G. Oberhammer and E. Steinkellner. Wiesbaden: Franz Steiner Verlag.

Fukuda, Y. *et al.* (1989) *Chibetto ronrigaku kenkyū* 1. Studia Tibetica 17, Tokyo: The Toyo Bunko. [Ed. and Japanese trans. of the *Tshad ma rigs gter*.]

Gautama. *Nyāyasūtra* (= NS). Ed. with the *Bhāṣya* of Vātsyāyana by P. Shāstrī and H. Shukla. Kashi Sanskrit Series. Varanasi: 1970.

Gillon, Brendan S. (1991) "Dharmakīrti and the Problem of Induction" in E. Steinkellner, ed., *Studies in the Buddhist Epistemological Tradition*. Vienna: 53–58.

Gillon, Brendan S. and Richard P. Hayes. (1982) "The Role of the Particle *eva* in (Logical) Quantification in Sanskrit." WZKS 26: 195–203.

———. (1991) "Introduction to Dharmakīrti's Theory of Inference as Presented in *Pramāṇavārttika svopajñavṛtti* 1–10." JIP 19: 1–73.

Gillon, Brendan S. and M. L. Love. (1980) "Indian Logic Revisited: *Nyāyapraveśa* reviewed." JIP 8: 349–84.

Glo bo mkhan chen bsod nams lhun grub = Glo bo mkhan chen [1456–1532]. *rTags rigs = rTags kyi rnam gzhag rigs lam gsal ba'i sgron me*. Ed. in S. Onoda (1992).

———. *Tshad ma rigs pa'i gter gyi 'grel pa = Tshad ma rigs gter gyi 'grel pa'i rnam bshad rigs lam gsal ba'i nyi ma*. Ed. rDo rje rgyal po. Qinghai: Zhongguo zangxue chubanshe, 1988.

Gnoli, Raniero. (1960) *The Pramāṇavārttikam of Dharmakīrti: The First Chapter with the Autocommentary*. Serie Orientale Roma 23. Rome: Istituto Italiano per il Medio ed Estremo Oriente.

Go rams pa bsod nams seng ge [1429–89]. *Kun tu bzang po'i 'od zer = rGyas pa'i bstan bcos tshad ma rnam 'grel gyi rnam par bshad pa kun tu bzang po'i 'od zer*. SKB vol. 11.

———. *Kun tu bzang po'i nyi ma = rGyas pa'i bstan bcos tshad ma rnam 'grel gyi ngag don kun tu bzang po'i nyi ma*. SKB vol. 11.

———. *lTa ba ngan sel = dBu ma la 'jug pa'i dkyus kyi sa bcad pa dang gzhung so so'i dka' ba'i gnas la dpyad pa lta ba ngan sel.* SKB vol. 13.

———. *Rigs gter gyi dka' gnas = Tshad ma rigs pa'i gter gyi dka' ba'i gnas rnam par bshad pa sde bdun rab gsal.* SKB vol. 12.

———. *Tshad ma rigs gter gyi don gsal byed = sDe bdun mdo dang bcas pa'i dgongs pa phyin ci ma log par 'grel pa tshad ma rigs pa'i gter gyi don gsal bar byed pa.* SKB vol. 11.

Goldberg, Margaret. (1985a) "Entity and Antinomy in Tibetan Bsdus grwa Logic (Part I)," JIP 13: 153–99.

———. (1985b) "Entity and Antinomy in Tibetan Bsdus grwa Logic (Part II)," JIP 13: 273–304.

Goodman, Russell B. (1995) *Pragmatism: A Contemporary Reader.* New York, London: Routledge.

Griffiths, Paul J. (1981) "Buddhist Hybrid English: Some Notes on Philology and Hermeneutics for Buddhologists." JIABS 4: 17–32.

Grzegorczyk, A. (1975) *An Outline of Mathematical Logic.* Dordrecht: D. Reidel Publishing Company.

gSer mdog paṇ chen śākya mchog ldan [1428–1507]. *Kun bzang chos kyi rol mtsho = rGyas pa'i bstan bcos tshad ma rnam 'grel gyi rnam bshad kun bzang chos kyi rol mtsho.* In volume 18 of *The Complete Works (gsung 'bum) of gSer-mdog Paṇ-chen Śākya-mchog-ldan.* Thimphu: 1975. Reprinted by Ngag dbang stobs rgyal. Delhi: 1988.

———. *Tshad ma rigs gter dgongs rgyan smad cha = Tshad ma rigs gter gyi dgongs rgyan rigs pa'i 'khor los lugs ngan pham byed.* In vol. 10 of *The Complete Works.* Reprinted by Ngag dbang stobs rgyal. Delhi: 1988.

———. *Tshad ma rigs gter gyi rnam bshad = Tshad ma rigs pa'i gter gyi rnam par bshad pa sde bdun ngag gi rol mtsho.* In vol. 19 of *The Complete Works.* Reprinted by Ngag dbang stobs rgyal. Delhi: 1988.

gTsang nag pa brtson 'grus seng ge [?–1171]. *Tshad ma rnam par nges pa'i ṭīkā legs bshad bsdus pa.* Otani University Tibetan Works Series II, 1989. Introduction by L.W.J. van der Kuijp.

Haack, Susan. (1974) *Deviant Logic: Some Philosophical Issues.* Cambridge: Cambridge University Press.

Hattori, Masaaki. (1968) *Dignāga on Perception: Being the Pratyakṣapariccheda of Dignāga's Pramāṇasamuccaya.* Harvard Oriental Series 47. Cambridge, MA: Harvard University Press.

Hayes, Richard. (1984) "The Question of Doctrinalism in the Buddhist Epistemologists." *Journal of the American Academy of Religion* 52.4: 645–70.

———. (1988) *Dignāga on the Interpretation of Signs.* Studies of Classical India 9. Dordrecht: D. Reidel.

Herzberger, Hans. (1975) "Double Negation in Buddhist Logic." JIP 3: 3–16.

Herzberger, Radhika. (1986) *Bhartṛhari and the Buddhists: An Essay in the Development of Fifth and Sixth Century Indian Thought.* Studies of Classical India 8. Dordrecht: D. Reidel.

Hopkins, Jeffrey P. (1989) "A Tibetan Delineation of Different Views of Emptiness in the Indian Middle Way School." *Tibet Journal* 1: 10–43.

Ichigō, Masamichi. (1985) *Madhyamakālaṃkāra of Śāntarakṣita with his own commentary or Vṛtti and with the subcommentary or Pañjikā of Kamalaśīla.* Kyoto: Buneidō.

Ihara, Shōren and Zuihō Yamaguchi, eds. (1992) *Tibetan Studies: Proceedings of the 5th Seminar of the International Association for Tibetan Studies.* Narita: Naritasan Shinshoji.

Inami, Masahiro. (1991) "On *Pakṣābhāsa*" in E. Steinkellner, ed., *Studies in the Buddhist Epistemological Tradition: Proceedings of the Second International Dharmakīrti Conference.* Vienna: Verlag der Österreichischen Akademie der Wissenschaften.

Inami, Masahiro, K. Matsuda and T. Tani. (1992) *A Study of the Pramāṇavārttikaṭīkā by Śākyabuddhi from the National Archives Collection, Kathmandu.* Part I: Sanskrit Fragments Transcribed. Studia Tibetica 23. Tokyo: The Toyo Bunko.

Inami, Masahiro and Tom J.F. Tillemans. (1986) "Another Look at the Framework of the *Pramāṇasiddhi* Chapter of *Pramāṇavarttika.*" WZKS 30: 123–42.

Jackson, David P. (1987) *The Entrance Gate for the Wise (Section III): Sa skya Paṇḍita on Indian and Tibetan Traditions of Pramāṇa and Philosophical Debate.* WSTB 17.1 and 17.2. Vienna: Arbeitskreis für Tibetische und Buddhistische Studien Universität Wien.

Jackson, Roger. (1993) *Is Enlightenment Possible? Dharmakīrti and rGyal tshab rje on Knowledge, Rebirth, No-Self and Liberation.* Ithaca, NY: Snow Lion Publications.

'Jam dbyangs bzhad pa'i rdo rje ngag dbang brtson 'grus = 'Jam dbyangs bzhad pa [1648–1722]. *bsDus sbyor gyi snying po kun bsdus rig pa'i mdzod.* Included in vol. *ba* (15) of *The Collected Works of 'Jam dbyangs bzhad pa'i rdo rje.* Published by Ngag dbang dge legs de mo. Delhi: Geden sungrab minyam gyunphel series, 1973.

———. *rTags rigs* = *rTags rigs kyi rnam bzhag nyung gsal legs bshad gser gyi phreng mdzes.* Included in vol. *ba* (15): 177–301 of *The Collected Works of 'Jam-dbyangs-bzhad-pa'i-rdo-rje.*

'Jam dbyangs phyogs (mchog?) lha 'od zer [1429–1500]. *Rwa stod bsdus grwa* = *Tshad ma rnam 'grel gyi bsdus gzhung shes bya'i sgo 'byed rgol ngan glang po 'joms pa gdong lnga'i gad rgyangs rgyu rig lde mig.* Published by Dam chos bzang po. Dharamsala, India: 1980.

James, William. (1907) *Pragmatism, A New Name for Some Old Ways of Thinking.* New York: Longmans, Green and Co.

Jinendrabuddhi. *Pramāṇasamuccayaṭīkā (Viśālāmalavatī).* P.5766, D. 4268.

Kajiyama, Yūichi. (1958) "On the Theory of Intrinsic Determination of Universal Concomitance in Buddhist Logic." IBK 7/1: 364–60. Reprinted in K. Mimaki *et al.*, eds. (1989).

———. (1963) "*Tripañcakacintā*, Development of the Buddhist Theory on the Determination of Causality." *Miscellanea Indologica Kiotiensia*, 4–5. Kyoto: 1–15. Reprinted in K. Mimaki *et al.*, eds. (1989).

———. (1965) "Controversy between the Sākāra- and Nirākāra-vādins of the Yogācāra school—some Materials." IBK 14/1: 429–18. Reprinted in K. Mimaki *et al.*, eds. (1989).

———. (1966) *An Introduction to Buddhist Philosophy.* An Annotated Translation of the *Tarkabhāṣā* of Mokṣākaragupta. Kyoto: Memoirs of the Faculty of Letters 10. Reprinted in K. Mimaki *et al.,* eds. (1989).

———. (1973) "Three Kinds of Affirmation and Two Kinds of Negation in Buddhist Philosophy," WZKS 17: 161–75. Reprinted in K. Mimaki *et al.*, eds. (1989).

———. (1999) *The Antarvyāptisamarthana of Ratnākaraśānti.* Bibliotheca Buddhica II. Tokyo: Soka University.

Kalff, M. (1983) "Rgyal tshab rje's Interpretation of the *astināstivyatikrama* in Nāgārjuna's Ratnāvalī" in E. Steinkellner and H. Tauscher, eds. (1983): 73–88.

Kamalaśīla. *Madhyamakāloka* (= MĀ). P. 5287, D. 3887.

Karṇakagomin. *Pramāṇavārttikasvavṛttiṭīkā* (= PVSVT). Skt. ed. by R. Sāṅkṛtyāyana *Pramāṇavārttikasvavṛttiṭīkā: Ācāryadharmakirteḥ Pramāṇavārttikam (svārthānumānaparicchedaḥ) svopajñavṛttyā Karṇakagomiviracitayā ṭaṭṭīkayā ca sahitam.* Allahabad: 1943. Reprinted by Rinsen Books, Kyoto: 1982.

Katsura, Shōryū. (1977, 1978, 1979, 1981, 1982, 1984, 1987) "Inmyō shōrimonron kenkyū." *Bulletin of the Faculty of Letters of Hiroshima University* 37 (1977): 106–27; 38 (1978): 110–30; 39 (1979): 63–82; 41 (1981): 62–82; 42 (1982): 82–99; 44 (1984): 43–74; 46 (1987): 46–85.

———. (1983) "Dignāga on Trairūpya." IBK 32/1: 544–38.

———. (1984) "Dharmakīrti's Theory of Truth." JIP 12: 215–35.

———. (1986a) *Indo Ronrigaku ni okeru Henjū Gainen no Seisei to Hatten—Carakasaṃhitā kara Dharmakīrti made.* Hiroshima: Hiroshima Daigaku Bungakubu Kiyō (Hiroshima University Studies, Faculty of Letters), vol. 45, Special supplement no. 1.

———. (1986b) "Jñānaśrīmitra on *Apoha,*" in B.K. Matilal and R.D. Evans, eds. (1986): 171–83.

———. (1986c) "On the Origin and Development of the Concept of *vyāpti* in Indian Logic." *Tetsugaku* 38, Hiroshima: 1–16.

———. (1992) "Dignāga and Dharmakīrti on *adarśanamātra* and *anupalabdhi.*" AS/EA 46/1: 222–31.

Kelsang, Tshulkrim and Shunzō Onoda. (1985) *Textbooks of Se-ra Monastery for the Primary Course of Studies.* Biblia Tibetica 1. Kyoto: Nagata Bunshodo.

Kirkham, Richard L. (1995) *Theories of Truth: A Critical Introduction.* Cambridge, MA: MIT Press.

Kitagawa, H. (1973) *Indo koten ronrigaku no kenkyū. Jinna no taikei.* Revised edition. Tokyo: 1973. Includes a partial edition and translation of PS and PSV.

Klein, Anne C. (1986) *Knowledge and Liberation: Tibetan Buddhist Epistemology in Support of Transformative Religious Experience.* Ithaca, N.Y.: Snow Lion Publications.

———. (1991) *Knowing, Naming and Negation: A Sourcebook on Tibetan Sautrāntika.* Ithaca, NY: Snow Lion Publications.

Kneale, William and Martha. (1962) *The Development of Logic.* Oxford: Clarendon Press. Revised edition, 1975.

Kobayashi, M. (1989) "The Mādhyamika Argument for *niḥsvabhāvatā* and the Fallacy of *āśrayāsiddha:* Kamalaśīla's View in the *Madhyamakāloka. Bunka* 50/3: 218–199 [in Japanese with comprehensive English summary].

Krabbe, Erik C.W. (1982) "Theory of Argumentation and the Dialectical Garb of Formal Logic," in Barth and Martens (1982): 123–32.

Kripke, Saul A. (1982) *Wittgenstein on Rules and Private Language.* Oxford: Basil Blackwell. Reprinted 1989.

Lang, Karen. (1986) *Āryadeva's Catuḥśataka: On the Bodhisattva's Cultivation of Merit and Knowledge.* Copenhagen: Akademisk Forlag.

lCang skya rol pa'i rdo rje [1717–86]. *lCang skya grub mtha' = Grub pa'i mtha' rnam par bzhag pa gsal bar bshad pa thub bstan lhun po'i mdzes rgyan.* Sarnath: Pleasure of Elegant Sayings Press, 1970. *See also* Klein (1991).

Linsky, Leonard, ed. (1971) *Reference and Modality.* Oxford: Oxford University Press.

Lopez, Donald. (1987) *A Study of Svātantrika.* Ithaca, NY: Snow Lion Publications.

———. (1988) *The Heart Sūtra Explained: Indian and Tibetan Commentaries.* Albany: State University of New York Press.

Łukasiewicz, Jan. (1935) "Zur Geschichte der Aussagenlogik." *Erkenntnis* 5: 111–31.

———. (1957) *Aristotle's Syllogistic from the Standpoint of Modern Formal Logic.* Second edition, Oxford.

Maitreya (attributed). *Madhyāntavibhāga.* Ed. with Vasubandhu's *Bhāṣya* and Sthiramati's *Ṭīkā* by G. M. Nagao. Tokyo: 1964.

Malvania, Dalsukh. (1955) *Nyāyabindu of Dharmakīrti with Nyāyabinduṭīkā of Dharmottara and Paṇḍita Durvekamiśra's Dharmottarapradīpa.* Tibetan Sanskrit Works Series 2. Patna: Kashi Prasad Jayaswal Research Institute. Second edition, 1971.

Manorathanandin. *Pramāṇavārttikavṛtti* (= PVV). Ed. by R. Sāṅkṛtyāyana with the notes of Vibhūticandra in the appendices to the *Journal of the Bihar and Orissa Research Society* 24 (1938) part III [ed. used in ch.1]. Also ed. by D. Shāstrī, Varanasi: Bauddha Bharati 3, 1968.

Marcus, Ruth Barcan. (1962) "Interpreting Quantification." *Inquiry* 5/3: 252–59.

———. (1972) "Quantification and Ontology." *Noûs* 6/3. Reprinted in R.B. Marcus, *Modalities: Philosophical Essays.* Oxford University Press, 1993: 75–87.

———. (1978) "Nominalism and the Substitutional Quantifier." *The Monist* 61/3. Reprinted in R. B. Marcus, *Modalities,* 1993: 111–24.

Mates, Benson. (1972) *Elementary Logic.* Oxford: Clarendon Press.

Matilal, Bimal K. (1970) "Reference and Existence in Nyāya and Buddhist Logic." JIP 1: 83–110.

———. (1971) *Epistemology, Logic, and Grammar in Indian Philosophical Analysis.* The Hague: Mouton.

———. (1986) *Perception: An Essay on Classical Indian Theories of Knowledge.* Oxford: Clarendon Press.

———. (1998) *The Character of Logic in India.* Ed. by Jonardon Ganeri and Heeraman Tiwari. Albany: State University of New York Press.

Matilal, Bimal K. and R.D. Evans, eds. (1986) *Buddhist Logic and Epistemology.* Studies in the Buddhist Analysis of Inference and Language. Studies of Classical India 7. Dordrecht: D. Reidel Publishing Company.

McCall, R.J. (1961) *Basic Logic.* New York: Barnes and Noble. Reprint ed.

McDermott, A.C.S. (1969) *An Eleventh Century Buddhist Logic of "Exists," Ratnakīrti's Kṣaṇabhaṅgasiddhiḥ Vyatirekātmikā, edited with translation, introduction and notes.* Dordrecht: D. Reidel Publishing Company.

———. (1970) "Empty Subject Terms in Late Buddhist Logic." JIP 1: 22–29.

McTaggart, J.M.E. (1921, 1927). *The Nature of Existence.* 2 vols. Cambridge: Cambridge University Press. Vol. 1, 1921, vol. 2 (ed. C.D. Broad), 1927. Reprinted by Scholarly Press, Grosse Pointe, Michigan, 1968.

Miller, William Ian. (1997) *The Anatomy of Disgust.* Cambridge, MA: Harvard University Press.

Mimaki, Katsumi. (1976) *La Réfutation bouddhique de la permanence des choses (sthirasiddhidūṣaṇa) et la preuve de la momentanéité des choses (kṣaṇabhaṅgasiddhi).* Paris: Publications de l'institut de civilisation indienne, fascicule 41.

———. (1982) *Blo gsal grub mtha'.* Kyoto: Zinbun Kagaku Kenkyusyo.

———. (1992) "The Intellectual Sequence of Ratnākaraśānti, Jñānaśrīmitra and Ratnakīrti." AS/EA 46/1: 297–306.

Mimaki, Katsumi *et al.*, eds. (1989) *Y. Kajiyama: Studies in Buddhist Philosophy.* Kyoto: Rinsen.

Miyasaka, Yūshō, ed. (1972) *Pramāṇavārttika-kārikā: Sanskrit and Tibetan.* Acta Indologica 2. Naritsan Shinshoji: 1–206.

mKhas grub dge legs dpal bzang po = mKhas grub rje [1385–1438]. *rNam 'grel ṭīk chen = rGyas pa'i bstan bcos tshad ma rnam 'grel gyi rgya cher bshad pa rigs pa'i rgya mtsho.* Included in the *Collected Works* (*mKhas grub rje'i gsung 'bum*). dGa' ldan phun tshogs gling edition. Vol. *tha, da.* Nepal, 1980's.

———. *sTong thun chen mo = Zab mo stong pa nyid kyi de kho na nyid rab tu gsal bar byed pa'i bstan bcos skal bzang mig 'byed. Collected Works,* vol. *ka.*

———. *Tshad ma yid kyi mun sel = sDe bdun yid kyi mun sel = Tshad ma sde bdun gyi rgyan yid kyi mun sel. Collected Works,* vol. *tha.*

Mokṣākaragupta. *Tarkabhāṣā.* (1952) Ed. R. Iyengar, *Tarkabhāṣā and Vādasthāna.* Mysore: 1952. *See also* Kajiyama (1966).

Mookerjee, Satkari. (1935) *The Buddhist Philosophy of Universal Flux.* University of Calcutta. Reprinted Delhi: Motilal Banarsidass, 1980.

Mookerjee, Satkari and Hojun Nagasaki, trans. (1964) *The Pramāṇavārttika of Dharmakīrti.* Patna: Nava Nālandā Mahāvihāra.

Much, Michael T. (1986) "Dharmakīrti's Definition of 'Points of Defeat' (*nigrahasthāna*)," in B.K. Matilal and R.D. Evans, eds. (1986): 133–42.

———. (1991) *Dharmakīrti Vādanyāyaḥ.* 2 vols. Vienna: Verlag der Österreichischen Akademie der Wissenschaften.

Nāgārjuna. *Mūlamadhyamakakārikā.* See ed. in L. de la Vallée Poussin (1903–13).

Nakamura, H. (1983) *Bukkyō-go dai jiten.* Reprint edition. Tokyo: Shoseki.

Napper, Elizabeth and Lati Rinbochay. (1986) *Mind in Tibetan Buddhism.* Ithaca, NY: Snow Lion Publications, 1986 [third printing].

Naudou, Jean. (1968) *Les Bouddhistes kaśmīriens au moyen âge.* Annales du Musée Guimet 67. Paris: Presses Universitaires de France.

Ngag dbang bstan dar. *See* A lag sha ngag dbang bstan dar.

Ngag dbang nyi ma. *See* dGe bshes ngag dbang nyi ma.

Oetke, Claus. (1991) "Remarks on the Interpretation of Nāgārjuna's Philosophy." JIP 19: 315–23.

———. (1994) *Studies on the Doctrine of Trairūpya.* WSTB 33. Vienna: Arbeitskreis für Tibetische und Buddhistische Studien, Universität Wien.

Ono, Motoi. (1986) "Dharmakīrti ni okeru shuchōmeidai no teigi ni tsuite." IBK 35/2: 850–47.

Onoda, Shunzō. (1979a) "Chibetto no sōin ni okeru mondō no ruikei (Patterns of the Tibetan Monachal Debate)." *Bukkyō Shigaku Kenkyū* (The Journal of the History of Buddhism) 22/1: 1–16.

———. (1979b) "Mondō ni okeru *khyod* no kinō ni tsuite." *Nihon Chibetto Gakkai Kaihō* (Report of the Japanese Association for Tibetan Studies) 25.

———. (1980) "ldog-chos ni tsuite." IBK 29/1: 385–82.

———. (1982a) "spyi to bye-brag ni tsuite." IBK 30/2: 915–12.

———. (1982b) "Chibetto ni okeru ronrigaku kenkyū no mondai." *Tōyō Gakujutsu Kenkyū* (The Journal of Oriental Studies) 21/2: 193–205.

———. (1982c) " 'brel-ba to 'gal-ba ni tsuite." IBK 31/1: 395–92.

———. (1983) "rjes-'gro ldog-khyab ni tsuite." IBK 32/1: 437–34.

———. (1992a) *Monastic Debate in Tibet: A Study of the History and Structures of bsdus grwa Logic.* WSTB 27. Vienna: Arbeitskreis für Tibetische und Buddhistische Studien Universität Wien.

———. (1992b) "Phya pa Chos kyi Seng ge's Theory of *'gal ba*" in S. Ihara and Z. Yamaguchi, eds., (1992): 197–202.

Paṇ chen bsod nams grags pa [1478–1554]. *rNam 'grel bka' 'grel = rGyas pa'i bstan bcos tshad ma rnam 'grel gyi bka' 'grel dgongs pa rab gsal zhes bya ba mkhas pa'i dbang po bSod nams grags pas mdzad pa blo gsal mkhas pa'i mgrin rgyan.* In vol. 1 of *The Collected Works (gsung 'bum) of Paṇ-chen bsod-nams-grags-pa.* Drepung Loseling Library Society, Mundgod, Karnataka, 1989.

Patzig, Günther. (1969) *Die Aristotelische Syllogistik.* Third and revised edition, Göttingen.

Paul, G. (1994) "Argumente für die Universalität der Logik. Mit einer Darstellung äquivalenter Axiome aristotelischer Syllogistik, spätmohistischer Logik und buddhistischer Begründungstheorie," in *Hōrin,* Vergleichende Studien zur japanischen Kultur. Düsseldorf: 57–86.

Peirce, Charles S. (1931–58) *Collected Papers of Charles Sanders Peirce.* Cambridge, MA: Harvard University Press.

Perdue, Daniel. (1976) "Debate in Tibetan Buddhist Education." M.A. Thesis for

University of Virginia, 1976. Reprint, Library of Tibetan Works and Archives, Dharamsala.

Phur bu lcog. *See* Yongs 'dzin phur bu lcog byams pa tshul khrims rgya mtsho.

Pind, Ole. (1991) "Dignāga on *śabdasāmānya* and *śabdaviśeṣa*," in E. Steinkellner, ed., *Studies in the Buddhist Epistemological Tradition.* Vienna: Verlag der Österreichischen Akademie der Wissenschaften: 269–280.

Prajñākaragupta. *Pramāṇavārttikabhāṣya* or *Vārttikālaṃkāra* (= PVBh). Skt. ed. by R. Sāṅkṛtyāyana. Tibetan Sanskrit Works Series 1. Patna: 1953.

Priest, G. (1979) "The Logic of Paradox." *Journal of Philosophical Logic* 8: 219–41.

Quine, Willard V. (1953) "On What There Is" in *From a Logical Point of View.* Cambridge, MA: Harvard University Press.

———. (1954) "Quantification and the Empty Domain." *Journal of Symbolic Logic* 19: 177–79.

———. (1970) *The Philosophy of Logic.* Englewood Cliffs, NJ: Prentice Hall.

Ratnākaraśānti. *Antarvyāptisamarthana.* Ed. by H. Shāstrī, *Six Buddhist Nyāya Tracts in Sanskrit.* Bibliotheca Indica, New Series no. 1226. Calcutta: 1910. See Kajiyama (1999).

Red mda' ba gzhon nu blo gros [1349–1412]. *dBu ma bzhi brgya pa'i 'grel pa.* Sarnath: Sakya Students' Union, 1974.

Rescher, Nicholas. (1995) "Pragmatism" in Ted Honderich, ed., *The Oxford Companion to Philosophy.* Oxford University Press.

Rescher, Nicholas and R. Brandom. (1980) *The Logic of Inconsistency.* Oxford: Basil Blackwell.

rGyal tshab dar ma rin chen = rGyal tshab rje [1364–1432]. *bZhi brgya pa'i rnam bshad legs bshad snying po.* Sarnath: Pleasure of Elegant Sayings Press, 1971.

———. *dBu ma rgyan gyi brjed byang.* Sarnath: Pleasure of Elegant Sayings Press, 1976.

———. *rNam 'grel thar lam gsal byed = Tshad ma rnam 'grel gyi tshig le'ur byas pa'i rnam bshad thar lam phyin ci ma log par gsal bar byed pa.* 2 vols. Sarnath: Pleasure of Elegant Sayings Press, 1974 [this ed. used in chaps. 1 and 7]. Also included in the *Collected Works* (Lhasa edition), vol. *cha* [this ed. used in chap. 11].

———. *rNam nges dar ṭīk = bsTan bcos tshad ma rnam nges kyi ṭīk chen dgongs pa rab gsal.* Included in the *Collected Works* (Lhasa edition), vol. *ja* and *nya* [used in chap. 11].

Robinson, Richard. (1967) *Early Mādhyamika in India and China.* Madison: University of Wisconsin Press. Reprint edition, Delhi: 1970.

Rorty, Richard. (1980) *Philosophy and the Mirror of Nature.* Princeton.

Routley, R. (1966) "Some Things Do Not Exist." *Notre Dame Journal of Formal Logic* 7/3: 251–76.

Ruegg, David Seyfort. (1977) "The Uses of the Four Positions of the *catuṣkoṭi* and the Problem of the Description of Reality in Mahāyāna Buddhism." JIP 5: 1–71.

———. (1983) "On the Thesis and Assertion in the Madhyamaka/Dbu ma," in E. Steinkellner and H. Tauscher, eds. (1983): 205–41.

———. (1985) "Purport, Implicature and Presupposition: Sanskrit *abhiprāya* and Tibetan *dgongs pa / dgongs gzhi* as hermeneutical concepts." JIP 13: 309–25.

———. (1986) "Does the Madhyamaka Have a Position?" in B.K. Matilal and R. Evans, eds. (1986): 229–37.

Sa skya paṇḍita kun dga' rgyal mtshan = Sa paṇ [1182–1251]. *Rigs gter = Tshad ma rigs pa'i gter.* SKB vol. 5. Ed. along with the *Rigs gter rang 'grel* by Nor brang o rgyan in *Tshad ma rigs pa'i gter gyi rtsa ba dang 'grel pa.* Xizang renmin chubanshe, 1989. Cf. also Fukuda, *et al.* (1989).

———. *Rigs gter rang 'grel = Tshad ma rigs pa'i gter gyi rang gi 'grel pa.* SKB vol. 5.

Śākya mchog ldan. *See* gSer mdog paṇ chen śākya mchog ldan.

Śākyabuddhi. *Pramāṇavārttikaṭīkā* (= PVT). P. 5718, D. 4220. For Skt. fragments, *see* Inami, *et al.*, (1992).

Śaṅkarasvāmin. *Nyāyapraveśa. See* Tachikawa (1971).

Śāntarakṣita. *Madhyamākaṃkāra. See* Ichigō (1985).

———. *Vādanyāyavṛtti Vipañcitārthā.* Skt. ed. in Swāmī Dvārikādāsa Śāstrī, ed., *Vādanyāyaḥ Saṃbandhaparīkṣā ca.* Bauddha Bharati Series 8. Varanasi: 1972

Se ra rje btsun chos kyi rgyal mtshan = Chos kyi rgyal mtshan [1469–1546]. *rNam 'grel spyi don = rGyas pa'i bstan bcos tshad ma rnam 'grel gyi don 'grel rgyal tshab dgongs pa rab gsal shes bya ba le'u dang po'i dka' ba'i gnas la dogs pa gcod pa.* Blockprint, textbook *(yig cha)* of Se ra byes monastic college, Byllakuppe, Mysore, India 1970s.

———. *sKabs dang po'i spyi don = bsTan bcos mngon par rtogs pa'i rgyan 'grel pa dang bcas pa'i rnam bshad rnam pa gnyis kyi dka' ba'i gnad gsal bar byed pa legs bshad skal bzang klu dbang gyi rol mtsho zhes bya ba las skabs dang po'i spyi don.* Blockprint, textbook *(yig cha)* of Se ra byes monastery. Byllakuppe, Mysore district, Karnataka, India, 1970s.

Shāstrī, Haraprasad. (1914) "The *Catuḥśatikā* of Ārya Deva." *Memoirs of the Asiatic Society of Bengal* 3/8: 449–514.

Sierksma, F. (1964) "Rtsod-Pa: The Monachal Disputations in Tibet." *Indo-Iranian Journal* 8: 130–52.

Staal, J. Frits. (1973) "The Concept of Pakṣa in Indian Logic." JIP 2: 156–66.

———. (1975) *Exploring Mysticism.* Berkeley: University of California Press.

Stcherbatsky, Theodore. (1930/32). *Buddhist Logic.* 2 vols. Leningrad: Bibliotheca Buddhica 26. Reprinted by Mouton and Co.: The Hague, 1958.

Steinkellner, Ernst. (1966) "Bemerkungen zu Īśvarasenas Lehre vom Grund." WZKSO 10: 73–85.

———. (1967) *Dharmakīrti's Hetubinduḥ.* Teil I: Tibetische Text und rekonstruierter Sanskrit-Text. Teil II: Übersetzung und Anmerkungen. Vienna: Österreichische Akademie der Wissenschaften.

———. (1971) "Wirklichkeit und Begriff bei Dharmakīrti." WZKS 15: 179–211.

———. (1973, 1979) *Dharmakīrti's Pramāṇaviniścayaḥ, Zweites Kapitel: svārthānumānam.* Teil I, 1973. Teil II, 1979. Vienna: Österreichische Akademie der Wissenschaften.

———. (1983) "*Tshad ma'i skyes bu*: Meaning and Historical Significance of the Term," in Steinkellner, E. and H. Tauscher, eds. (1983): 275–84.

———. (1984) "Svabhāvapratibandha again" in *Studies of Mysticism in Honor of the 1150th Anniversary of Kōbō-Daishi's Nirvāṇam*. Acta Indologica 6: 457–76.

———. (1988) "Remarks on *niścitagrahaṇa*" in G. Gnoli and L. Lanciotti, eds., *Orientalia Iosephi Tucci Memoriae Dicata*. Serie Orientale Roma 56/3. Rome: 1427–44.

Steinkellner, Ernst and Helmut Krasser. (1989) *Dharmottaras Exkurs zur Definition gültiger Erkenntnis im Pramāṇaviniścaya*. Vienna: Österreichische Akademie der Wissenschaften.

Steinkellner, Ernst and Helmut Tauscher, eds. (1983) *Contributions on Tibetan and Buddhist Religion and Philosophy, Proceedings of the Csoma de Körös Symposium*. WSTB 10, 11. Vienna: Arbeitskreis für Tibetische und Buddhistische Studien, Universität Wien.

Strawson, P.F. (1952) *Introduction to Logical Theory*. London: Methuen. [References are to the reprint ed. from 1966.]

Tachikawa, Musashi. (1971) "A Sixth-Century Manual of Indian Logic (A Translation of the *Nyāyapraveśa*)." JIP 1: 111–29.

Tibetan Tripiṭaka, Derge edition. Reproduced in A. W. Barber, ed., *The Tibetan Tripitaka: Taipei Edition*. Taipei: SMC Publishing Inc., 1991.

Tibetan Tripiṭaka, Peking edition. Tokyo-Kyoto: Tibetan Tripiṭaka Research Institute, 1955–1961.

Tillemans, Tom J.F. (1982) "The 'Neither One nor Many' Argument for *Śūnyatā* and its Tibetan Interpretations: Background Information and Source Materials." *Études de Lettres*, University of Lausanne, 3, July–September, 103–28.

———. (1983) "The 'Neither One nor Many' Argument for *Śūnyatā* and its Tibetan Interpretations" in E. Steinkellner and H. Tauscher, eds. (1983): 305–20.

———. (1984a) "On a Recent Work on Tibetan Buddhist Epistemology," AS/EA 38/1: 59–66.

———. (1984b) "Sur le *parārthānumāna* en logique bouddhique." AS/EA 38/2: 73–99.

———. (1984c) "Two Tibetan Texts on the 'Neither One Nor Many' Argument for *Śūnyatā*." JIP 12: 357–88.

———. (1986a) "Dharmakīrti, Āryadeva and Dharmapāla on Scriptural Authority." *Tetsugaku* 38, Hiroshima: 31–47. Reprinted in present volume, chap. 1.

———. (1986b) "Identity and Referential Opacity in Tibetan Buddhist *Apoha* Theory," in B.K. Matilal and R.D. Evans, eds. (1986): 207–27.

———. (1986c) "Pramāṇavārttika IV (1)." WZKS 30: 143–62.

———. (1987) "Pramāṇavārttika IV (2)." WZKS 31: 141–61.

———. (1988) "Some Reflections on R.S.Y. Chi's *Buddhist Formal Logic*." JIABS 11/1: 155–71.

———. (1989) "Formal and Semantic Aspects of Tibetan Buddhist Debate Logic," JIP 17: 265–97. Reprinted in present volume, chap. 6.

———. (1990) *Materials for the Study of Āryadeva, Dharmapāla and Candrakīrti.* The *Catuḥśataka* of Āryadeva, chapters XII and XIII, with the commentaries of Dharmapāla and Candrakīrti: Introduction, translation, Sanskrit, Tibetan, and Chinese texts, notes. 2 vols. WSTB 24.1 and 24.2. Vienna: Arbeitskreis für Tibetische und Buddhistische Studien Universität Wien.

———. (1991a) "Dharmakīrti on Some Sophisms" in E. Steinkellner, ed., *Studies in the Buddhist Epistemological Tradition: Proceedings of the Second International Dharmakīrti Conference.* Vienna: Verlag der Österreichischen Akademie der Wissenschaften: 403–18.

———. (1991b) "More on *parārthānumāna*, theses and syllogisms." AS/EA 45/1: 133–48. Reprinted in the present volume, chap. 4.

———. (1992a) "La logique bouddhique est-elle une logique non-classique ou déviante? Remarques sur le tétralemme (*catuṣkoṭi*)" in J.-L. Solère, ed., *Les Cahiers de Philosophie* 14. L'Orient de la pensée: philosophies en Inde: 183–98. English trans. by J. Dunne printed in present volume, chap. 9.

———. (1992b) "Pramāṇavārttika IV (3)." AS/EA 46: 437–67.

———. (1992c) "Tsong kha pa *et al.* on the Bhāvaviveka-Candrakīrti Debate" in S. Ihara and Z. Yamaguchi (1992): 315–26.

———. (1993a) *Persons of Authority. The sTon pa tshad ma'i skyes bur sgrub pa'i gtam of A lag sha Ngag dbang bstan dar.* A Tibetan text on the central religious questions of Buddhist epistemology. Tibetan and Indo-Tibetan Studies 5. Stuttgart: Franz Steiner Verlag.

———. (1993b) "Pramāṇavārttika IV (4)." WZKS 37: 135–64.

———. (1994) "Pre-Dharmakīrti Commentators on Dignāga's Definition of a Thesis (*pakṣalakṣaṇa*)" in T. Skorupski and U. Pagel, eds., *The Buddhist Forum, Volume III.* Papers in Honour and Appreciation of Professor David Seyfort Ruegg's Contribution to Indological, Buddhist and Tibetan Studies. London: School of Oriental and African Studies, University of London: 295–305. Reprinted in present volume, chap. 3.

———. (1995a) "On the So-called Difficult Point of the *Apoha* Theory" in AS/EA 49/4: 853–89. Reprinted in present volume, chap. 10.

———. (1995b) "Pramāṇavārttika IV (5)." WZKS 34: 103–50.

———. (1995c) "Remarks on Philology." JIABS 18/2: 269–77.

———. (1998) "A Note on *Pramāṇavārttika, Pramāṇasamuccaya,* and *Nyāyamukha.* What is the *svadharmin* in Buddhist Logic?" JIABS 21/1: 111–24. Reprinted in present volume, chap. 8.

Tillemans, Tom J.F. and Derek Herforth. (1989) *Agents and Actions in Classical Tibetan.* WSTB 21. Vienna: Arbeitskreis für Tibetische und Buddhistische Studien Universität Wien.

Tillemans, Tom J.F. and Donald Lopez. (1998) "What Can One Reasonably Say about Nonexistence? A Tibetan Work on the Problem of *āśrayāsiddha.*" JIP 26: 99–129. Reprinted in present volume, chap. 11.

Tillemans, Tom J.F. and Toru Tomabechi. (1995) "Le *dBu ma'i byung tshul* de Śākya mchog ldan." AS/EA 49/4: 853–89.

Tosaki, Hiromasa. (1979, 1985) *Bukkyō Ninshikiron no Kenkyū.* (Jōkan = 1979; Gekan = 1985). Skt. ed. and Jap. trans. of PV III. Tokyo: Daitōshuppansha.

Tsong kha pa blo bzang grags pa [1357–1419]. *Collected Works of Tsong kha pa* or *Khams gsum chos kyi rgyal po Tsong kha pa chen po'i gsung 'bum.* Tashi lhunpo edition. Ge den sung rab mi nyam gyun phel series 79–105. Published by Ngag dbang dge legs de mo. Delhi: 1975–79.

———. *dBu ma dgongs pa rab gsal = bsTan bcos chen po dbu ma la 'jug pa'i rnam bshad dgongs pa rab gsal.* In vol. *ma* of the *Collected Works.*

———. *dBu ma rgyan gyi zin bris. Collected Works,* vol. *ba.* [this ed. used in chap. 2]. Also published in Sarnath: Pleasure of Elegant Sayings Press, 1976.

———. *mNgon sum le'u'i ṭīkā rje'i gsung bzhin mkhas grub chos rjes mdzad pa.* [A record of Tsong kha pa's explanations on the *pratyakṣa* chapter of the *Pramāṇavārttika* written by mKhas grub dge legs dpal bzang po]. Included in the *Collected Works,* vol. *ma,* pp. 446–649.

———. *rTsa shes ṭīk chen = dBu ma rtsa ba'i tshig le'ur byas pa shes rab ces bya ba'i rnam bshad rigs pa'i rgya mtsho. Collected Works,* vol. *ba,* pp. 1–566. Also Sarnath: Pleasure of Elegant Sayings Press, 1973.

———. *sDe bdun la 'jug pa'i sgo don gnyer yid kyi mun sel. Collected Works,* vol. *tsha,* pp. 494–542. Also Sarnath: Pleasure of Elegant Sayings Press, 1972.

———. *Tshad ma'i brjed byang chen mo = rGyal tshab chos rjes rje'i drung du gsan pa'i tshad ma'i brjed byang chen mo. Collected Works,* vol. *pha,* pp. 152–245.

Tucci, Guiseppe. (1930). *The Nyāyamukha of Dignāga.* Materialen zur Kunde des Buddhismus 15. Heidelberg. Reprint, Chinese Materials Center, Taiwan: 1976.

'U yug pa rigs pa'i seng ge [?–1253]. *Tshad ma rnam 'grel gyi 'grel pa rigs pa'i mdzod.* Published by bSod nams rgyal mtshan, Delhi, 1982.

Uddyotakara. *Nyāyavārttika* (= NV). Ed. in *Nyāyadarśanam with Vātsyāyana's Bhāṣya, Uddyotakara's Vārttika, Vācaspatimiśra's Tātparyaṭīkā, and Viśvanātha's Vṛtti.* Rinsen Sanskrit Text Series I.1 and I.2. Kyoto: 1982.

van Bijlert, Vittorio A. (1989) *Epistemology and Spiritual Authority.* The development of epistemology and logic in the old Nyāya and the Buddhist school of epistemology with an annotated translation of Dharmakīrti's *Pramaṇavārttika* II *(Pramāṇasiddhi)* vv. 1–7. WSTB 20. Vienna: Arbeitskreis für Tibetische und Buddhistische Studien Universität Wien.

van der Kuijp, Leonard W.J. (1978) "Phya-pa Chos-kyi seng-ge's Impact on Tibetan Epistemological Theory." JIP 5: 355–69.

———. (1983) *Contributions to the Development of Tibetan Buddhist Epistemology. From the Eleventh to the Thirteenth Century.* Alt- und Neu-Indische Studien 26. Wiesbaden: Franz Steiner Verlag.

———. (1985) "Miscellanea à propos of the Philosophy of Mind in Tibet: Mind in Tibetan Buddhism," *The Tibet Journal* 10/1: 32–43.

———. (1987) "The Monastery of Gsang-phu ne'u-thog and Its Abbatial Succession from ca. 1073 to 1250," *Berliner Indologische Studien* 3: 103–27.

———. (1989) *An Introduction to Gtsang-nag-pa's Tshad ma rnam-par nges-pa'i ṭīkā legs-bshad bsdus pa.* Otani University Tibetan Works Series, vol. 2. Kyoto: Rinsen.

Vernant, Denis. (1986) "Quantification substitutionnelle, contextes intensionnels et question d'existence." *Dialectica* 40/4: 273–96.

Vetter, Tilmann. (1966) *Dharmakīrti's Pramāṇaviniścayaḥ. 1. Kapitel: Pratyakṣam.* Vienna: Österreichische Academie der Wissenschaften.

Vidyabhusana, Satis Chandra. (1920) *A History of Indian Logic.* Reprint ed. Delhi: Motilal Banarsidass, 1988.

Vinītadeva. *Nyāyabinduṭīkā* (= NBT). Ed. in L. de la Vallée Poussin (1913).

Watanabe, C. (1998) "A Translation of *Madhyamakahṛdayakārikā* with the *Tarkajvālā* III. 137–46." JIABS 21/1: 125–55.

Watanabe, S. (1976) "Shōrimonron chūshakusha PV 4, 27 shiron" in *Okuda Jiō Sensei Kiju Kinen Bukkyōshisō ronshū.* Tokyo: 973–85.

Yaita, Hideomi. (1987) "Dharmakīrti on the Authority of Buddhist Scriptures (*āgama*)—An Annotated Translation of the *Pramāṇavārttika-svasvṛtti ad* v. 213–17" in *Nanto Bukkyō:* 1–17.

Yanagida, Seizan, ed. (1959) *Lin Ji Lu* (*Rinzai Roku*). Kyoto: Kichūdo.

Yongs 'dzin phur bu lcog byams pa tshul khrims rgya mtsho [1825–1901]. *Yongs 'dzin blo rigs = Tshad ma'i gzhung don 'byed pa'i bsdus grwa'i rnam bzhag rigs lam 'phrul gyi lde mig ces bya ba las rigs lam che ba yul yul can dang blo rigs gi rnam par bshad pa.* In T. Kelsang and S. Onoda (1985).

———. *Yongs 'dzin bsdus grwa = Tshad ma'i gzhung don 'byed pa'i bsdus grwa'i rnam bzhag rigs lam 'phrul gyi lde'u mig* (3 vols: *chung, 'bring, che ba*). Included in Kelsang, T. and S. Onoda (1985).

———. *Yongs 'dzin rtags rigs = Tshad ma'i gzhung don 'byed pa'i bsdus grwa'i rnam par bshad pa rigs lam 'phrul gyi lde'u mig las rigs lam che ba rtags rigs kyi skor.* Ed. by Shunzō Onoda, *The Yoṅs 'dzin rtags rigs.* Nagoya University: Studia Asiatica 5, 1981. Also included in T. Kelsang and S. Onoda, eds., (1985).

Yotsuya, K. (1995) "An Introduction to 'Svatantra-reasoning.'" *Sōtōshu Kenkyūin Kenkyū Kiyō* 22: 1–28.

Yoshimuzu, Ch. (1997) "Tsong kha pa on *don byed nus pa*" in H. Krasser, *et al.*, eds. *Tibetan Studies,* vol. 2: 1103–20. Vienna: Verlag der Österreichischen Akademie der Wissenschaften.

Index

A few clarifications. (a) When pages from the main body of the text are indicated, corresponding notes are not mentioned if they only provide bibliographical references. Notes are generally mentioned when the information given is more substantial. (b) Some terms have multiple translations of more or less equal accuracy. This inelegance came about because the reprinted essays were written over a longish time span. It seemed best to leave translations of technical terms as they were. (c) Page references with an asterisk provide the most complete or important treatment of the term in question.

A

A lag sha ngag dbang bstan dar, 89, 114 n. 39, 145 n. 41
  on *āśrayāsiddha*, 173, 180, *chap. 11 *passim*
  on the Buddha's authority, 31, 35 n. 17
  on explicit objects of expression and explicit expressions, 232 n. 13
  on the mode of presentation *('god tshul)*, 274–75 n. 18,
  research on his works, 249, 265–66 n. 4
abhimānamātra (mere inflated misconception), 216, 221, 222, 231 n. 12, 233 n. 14
abhrānta (non-erroneous), 8, 10–11, 50 n. 9, 215, 253
  in Yogācāra perspective, 21 n. 16
  in Svātantrika position, 276 n. 21
  see also *bhrānti/bhrānta*
abhūtaparikalpa (unreal conceptual construction), 196
abhyupagama (acceptance)
  of a scripture, 34 n. 14, 37, 44, 45
  of a treatise as indicating that all within the treatise is the *sādhya*, 57, 59
  of a thesis as not relying on a treatise, see *śāsatrānapekṣa*
  see also *āgama*
abstract entities, 3–4
adarśanamātra (merely not seeing [a counterexample]), 54, 61 n. 5, 105, 126, 127
  see also counterexample
  see also *ma khyab pa'i mu*
adhyavasāya (determination), 209–11, 221, 222, 228 n. 2, 229 n. 3, 240 n. 25, 243–44 n. 29
adṛśyānupalabdhihetu (reason that consists in the nonperception of an imperceptible thing), chap. 7 *passim*
  in Dharmakīrti's PVin, PV and PVSV, 156–57, 159, 160, 167 n. 9, 168 n. 13
  and inaccessible things *(viprakṛṣṭārtha)*, 155–56
  invalid use of, 153
  E. Steinkellner's views on, 153, 158–60, 164 n. 6, 167–68 n. 11, 168 n. 12
  major Tibetan developments of, 153–55, 161–63, 164–66 n. 7, 167 n. 8
  valid use of, 153–55
āgama (scripture), 27, 30, 33 n. 1, 42–43, 152
  acceptance *(abhyupagama)* of, 34 n. 14, 37, 44, 45
  and the goals of man, see *puruṣārtha*
  judged immaculate, 35 n.15, 38, 48 n. 4
  and perception and inference, 2–3, 27
  and supersensible matters, 11
  see also threefold analysis of scripture
  see also *śāstra*
  see also *śāstrāṇapekṣa*
  see also *āgamāśritānumāna*

About the Author

Tom Tillemans studied analytic philosophy in Canada, and then continued with philosophy, Sanskrit and Chinese in Lausanne and Geneva. During his somewhat younger years, he lived in India, where he worked with Tibetan lamas (and had a Tibetan cook). He held a research scholarship at Hiroshima and has taught as a visiting professor in a number of universities. He currently co-edits (with Cristina Scherrer-Schaub) the *Journal of the International Association of Buddhist Studies.*

ABOUT WISDOM

WISDOM PUBLICATIONS, a not-for-profit publisher, is dedicated to making available authentic Buddhist works. We publish translations of the sutras and tantras, commentaries and teachings of past and contemporary Buddhist masters, and original works by the world's leading Buddhist scholars. We publish our titles with the appreciation of Buddhism as a living philosophy and with the special commitment to preserve and transmit important works from all the major Buddhist traditions.

If you would like more information or a copy of our mail-order catalog, please contact us at:

Wisdom Publications
199 Elm Street
Somerville, Massachusetts 02144 USA
Telephone: (617) 776-7416 • Fax: (617) 776-7841
Email: info@wisdompubs.org • www.wisdompubs.org

Wisdom Publications is a non-profit, charitable 501(c)(3) organization and a part of the Foundation for the Preservation of the Mahayana Tradition (FPMT).

STUDIES IN INDIAN AND TIBETAN BUDDHISM

THIS SERIES WAS CONCEIVED to provide a forum for publishing outstanding new contributions to scholarship on Indian and Tibetan Buddhism and also to make accessible seminal research not widely known outside a narrow specialist audience, including translations of appropriate monographs and collections of articles from other languages. The series strives to shed light on the Indic Buddhist traditions by exposing them to historical-critical inquiry, illuminating through contextualization and analysis these traditions' unique heritage and the significance of their contribution to the world's religious and philosophical achievements. We are pleased to make available in these volumes some of the best contemporary research on the Indian and Tibetan traditions.